THE EU REGULATIONS ON MATRIMONIAL PROPERTY AND
PROPERTY OF REGISTERED PARTNERSHIPS

An open access online version of this book is available,
thanks to financing by the European Union's Justice
Programme (2014–2020).
Visit www.intersentiaonline.com for more information.

E-training on EU Family Property regimes — EU-FamPro -
N. 101008404 — JUST-AG-2020 /JUST-JTRA-EJTR-AG-2020

Deliverable No D5 EU-FamPro Book

 This publication was funded by the European Union's Justice Programme (2014–2020)

The content of this publication represents only the views of the authors and is their sole responsibility. The European Commission does not accept any responsibility for use that may be made of the information it contains.

THE EU REGULATIONS ON MATRIMONIAL PROPERTY AND PROPERTY OF REGISTERED PARTNERSHIPS

Edited by
Lucia RUGGERI
Agnė LIMANTĖ
Neža POGORELČNIK VOGRINC

Cambridge – Antwerp – Chicago

Intersentia Ltd
8 Wellington Mews
Wellington Street | Cambridge
CB1 1HW | United Kingdom
Tel: +44 1223 736 170
Email: mail@intersentia.co.uk
www.intersentia.com | www.intersentia.co.uk

Distribution for the UK and
Rest of the World (incl. Eastern Europe)
NBN International
1 Deltic Avenue, Rooksley
Milton Keynes MK13 8LD
United Kingdom
Tel: +44 1752 202 301 | Fax: +44 1752 202 331
Email: orders@nbninternational.com

Distribution for Europe
Lefebvre Sarrut Belgium NV
Hoogstraat 139/6
1000 Brussels
Belgium
Tel: +32 (0)800 39 067
Email: mail@intersentia.be

Distribution for the USA and Canada
Independent Publishers Group
Order Department
814 North Franklin Street
Chicago, IL 60610
USA
Tel: +1 800 888 4741 (toll free) | Fax: +1 312 337 5985
Email: orders@ipgbook.com

The EU Regulations on Matrimonial Property and Property of Registered Partnerships
© The editors and contributors severally 2022

The editors and contributors have asserted the right under the Copyright, Designs and Patents Act 1988, to be identified as authors of this work.

An online version of this work is published under a Creative Commons Open Access license CC-BY-NC-ND 4.0 which permits re-use, distribution and reproduction in any medium for non-commercial purposes providing appropriate credit to the original work is given. You may not distribute derivative works without permission. To view a copy of this license, visit https://creativecommons.org/licenses/by-nc-nd/4.0.

Intersentia was given an exclusive commercial license to print and distribute the printed version of the book.

Enquiries concerning reproduction which may not be covered by the Creative Commons Open Access license above should be addressed to Intersentia.

All versions of this work may contain content reproduced under license from third parties. Permission to reproduce this third-party content must be obtained from these third parties directly.

Artwork on cover: Avgust Avgustus / Alamy Stock Photo

ISBN 978-1-83970-199-3
D/2022/7849/2
NUR 822

British Library Cataloguing in Publication Data. A catalogue record for this book is available from the British Library.

FOREWORDS

IRMANTAS JARUKAITIS

Back in 1950, Robert Schuman stated in his famous declaration that 'Europe will not be made all at once, or according to a single plan. It will be built through concrete achievements which first create a *de facto* solidarity.' The history of European integration has witnessed a lot of steps forward, big and small (and, in fact, some steps backwards as well). Thus, from a broader, macro perspective of the EU integration process, adoption of Council Regulations 2016/1103 and 2016/1104, of 24 June 2016, implementing enhanced cooperation in the area of jurisdiction, applicable law and the recognition and enforcement of decisions in matters of matrimonial property regimes and in matters of property consequences of registered partnerships could be treated as one of those small steps contributing to the growth of *de facto* solidarity. However, there is no doubt that for those who are the intended 'recipients' of the benefits of these regulations, they represent a huge step forward in securing their rights and providing for legal certainty in their everyday lives. This is so because, both in the daily management of their property, and, for example, in its division if the couple separates, those transnational couples within the EU face many practical and legal difficulties. Besides, problems faced by couples in a registered partnership are frequently predetermined by disparities between the applicable rules governing the property effects of such unions, both in terms of substantive law and private international law. With the continuing increase in the number of transnational families and couples, the importance of these regulations will certainly increase over time.

Needless to say, rules in the field of private international law tend to be complicated and an ever-growing body of jurisprudence from the Court of Justice of the European Union in this area is a true reflection of this statement. This is one of the reasons to congratulate an international team of scientists for their commitment to undertaking a complex research project and delivering its results in the form of this collection, *The EU Regulations on Matrimonial Property and Property of Registered Partnerships*. This book is striking in terms of its depth and scope of the performed analysis, it accurately covers not only every single aspect of the Twin Regulations but also explores them in a broader context with other EU and national rules and the practice of their application.

I have no doubt that both scholars and practitioners will find this volume an invaluable resource for their further research or daily legal practice. Undoubtedly, such legal practice will lead to disputes regarding different aspects of interpretation of the Twin Regulations allowing the Court of Justice of the European Union to play its part in the development of the common European legal space.

Irmantas Jarukaitis
Judge, Court of Justice of the European Union
September 2021

Forewords

PAOLO PASQUALIS

I have great pleasure, as a law practitioner, to take the opportunity to congratulate those who worked on the drafting of this volume and, even before, who worked with a great passion for the organisation and the conduct of numerous and successful seminars – in which I have had the honour of participating – on the topics concerning the two EU Regulations on Matrimonial Property and Property of Registered Partnerships. The passion and quality of the in-depth analysis carried out by those who participated in the project can be clearly recognised in the contributions that form this volume. The open access, online publication of this book also testifies to the desire to give maximum dissemination to the reflections and studies carried out.

The European legislator, in years of preparation, has provided us with texts full of interesting solutions, options and ideas, which jurists are now called upon to enrich even more with the contributions that will certainly arise from practical experience. To do this in the best possible way, the only solution we have is not to close ourselves within the confines of national interpretations but to operate in constant dialogue with scholars and practitioners from different countries, and not only within the European Union.

Perhaps, however, the hardest challenge will be to make the new European rules known to citizens, who are, in the end, the main recipients of the rights therein and interested parties. As a notary in my country, I can easily testify to a phenomenon that is well known to us all, namely the continuous, progressive, increase of the number of transnational couples and families. Couples and families that may differ in their structure and in their legal recognition. Situations in which legal professionals must be particularly prepared to suggest the best options and solutions when advising their clients. The new regulations offer a wide scope for private autonomy, which deserves to be exploited to the fullest by the parties concerned.

In this regard, I would like to recall how all of us notaries of the European Union feel it is an urgent duty to deepen our training on the issues concerning the patrimonial aspects of couples and families in order to provide – as 'proximity lawyers' (*juristes de proximité*, as the French say) – the best possible contribution to our fellow citizens.

As such, thanks once again to the 'EU-FamPro' team for their work and for asking for our participation in their activities.

Paolo Pasqualis
Civil Law Notary, former President of the Council of the Notariats of the
European Union (CNUE)
September 2021

ALBERTO PEREZ CEDILLO

It is a pleasure for me to write a foreword for *The EU Regulations on Matrimonial Property and Property of Registered Partnerships*, a scientific book developed within the EU co-funded project EU-FamPro on behalf of the International Academy of Family Lawyers (IAFL), an international association which recognises the need for international couples to be better informed of the legal consequences of relationships with a cross-border element. The association has as one of its main objectives to help its members as legal advisors to be fully equipped to inform couples of the implications that lie ahead and therefore the project was at the core of the objectives the association pursues. It is true that spouses who want to choose a court to settle their divorce may not be able to do so. They are, however, able to coordinate the different family proceedings through the existing possibilities given in EU Regulations, and the adoption of the Twin Regulations is a giant step towards this aim. We are also happy that in accordance with the trend that, over recent years, has characterised judicial cooperation in civil matters, the Regulations provide ample space for party autonomy, encouraging liberalisation within European private international law. This is important in an area where party autonomy was traditionally excluded or extremely limited.

Some Member States have signalled their difficulty in accepting any proposal which would impact, even indirectly, on the definition of marriage under national law, and matrimonial matters are a highly sensitive political issue on which it is difficult to reach a broad agreement. I am dually qualified as a Spanish and English lawyer and, therefore, I often work at the intersection between Common Law and Civil Law systems and hope that the Regulations will also achieve an approximation of substantive laws between Member States, such as the Common Franco-German Matrimonial Regime (applicable since 1 May 2013) providing an optional matrimonial regime for couples with a habitual residence in France or Germany. The instrument thereby overcomes legal differences in matrimonial matters between both Member States. Other countries are explicitly invited to join this instrument. Bilateral agreements such as this may be potential solutions even between Members States and non-Member States.

Training and awareness-raising efforts for legal practitioners and citizens are always a main objective for the IAFL, with a view to achieving fully effective functioning of the Regulations. This is the reason why we welcome initiatives such as this aim to provide for a better understanding of national differences, mutual trust and enabling the smooth resolution of potential conflicts of law.

Alberto Perez Cedillo
President Elect, IAFL European Chapter
September 2021

FERNANDO RODRIGUEZ PRIETO

There is a universal tendency to extend the scope of the autonomy of will in the regulation of family relations, with a progressive relaxing of the earlier mandatory rules. Perhaps a growing number of family forms, that are not based on marriage, has contributed to this. Indeed, for many years in the Western world the social pressure on couples to formally marry has been decreasing. At the same time, legal consequences for couples living 'more *uxorio*', whose legal bond is created when the partners wish to give stability to their relationship and to this end agree to formal acts such as registration of their partnership in public registers, gains recognition with a wide range of possible agreements for the regulation of such unions. When couples may choose marriage or registered partnership, and in the latter case have broad freedom to regulate their property relations, the preservation of marriage as a legal institution requires it to be made more flexible and to strengthen the freedom of agreement in marital relations. In this way, the tendency of increasing party autonomy in private law affects family and inheritance law, reflecting the socially-demanded changes.

The Twin Regulations 2016/1103 and 2016/1104 follow this trend and use the need to establish common conflict of laws rules for marriages and partnerships with international elements as an opportunity to also extend the autonomy of will of cross-border couples. For example, even if the spouses share the same nationality, it is sufficient for them to live in another country in order for them to be subject to that country's rules for their property regime and to be able to take advantage of the possibilities for property agreement that this national law allows.

A real challenge arises for legal practitioners that need to adapt to these new possibilities and be able to give appropriate advice tailored to the couples' needs. The choice of applicable law will very often be made by entering into formal agreements. In these agreements, it will be more and more common to include clauses providing for the legal consequences in case of the break-up of a partnership or a marriage, or the liquidation of common property due to the death of one of the spouses (partners) – agreements which in many countries have been rare so far.

Any one of the provisions that may be included in the matrimonial (partnership) property agreement, or in the mere agreement on the choice of law, can result in a considerable social and personal benefit for the parties concerned. I am referring to agreements to submit to mediation in the event of the break-up of a partnership or a marriage. Taking into account that family break-ups are quite common and complex problems arise from them, in particular where the couple has minor children, family courts in many countries have become overloaded as a consequence. The complexity of the situation is amplified in the case of international couples, in particular when the ex-spouses or ex-partners reside in different countries. In such situations, a peaceful agreement will almost always offer a better solution than a hostile, and sometimes lengthy, court dispute with an uncertain outcome. In this regard, it is clear that mediation, which opens up opportunities for a mutually beneficial solution, understanding and cooperation, should be encouraged and that legal professionals should take this into account when offering their advice.

Fernando Rodríguez Prieto
Notary, mediator, and trustee of the Signum Foundation
August 2021

JUAN IGNACIO SIGNES DE MESA

The adoption of any legislative instrument by the European Union is a reason for congratulation. Not only because of the technical and consensus efforts that they require within the European institutions, mostly because they respond to crucial needs for European citizens. This is the case of Council Regulations 2016/1103 and 2016/1104, of 24 June 2016, implementing enhanced cooperation in the area of jurisdiction, applicable law and the recognition and enforcement of decisions in matters of matrimonial property regimes and in matters of property consequences of registered partnerships. Both regulations represent a major step in the efforts of maintaining and developing an area of freedom, security and justice in which the free movement of persons is ensured and where judicial cooperation in civil matters having cross-border implications is also guaranteed.

The present book, which I have the honour to preface, is the result of a collective scientific initiative, under the recognised leadership of Professor Lucia Ruggeri, in which a consecrated group of scholars, researchers and specialists, from the University of Camerino, the Law Institute of the Lithuanian Centre for Social Sciences, the University of Almeria, the University of Ljubliana and the Rijeka University, examine in detail the most relevant legal issues raised by the application across Europe of the so-called 'Twin Regulations'. It deserves praise not only from an academic perspective, but also for its indisputable significance for all legal practitioners who have to apply Regulations 2016/1103 and 2016/1104, and for national judges before which legal questions of interpretation and application frequently arise since the adoption of both legal instruments. With this volume, we now have at our disposal an in-depth analysis shedding light on the development and adoption of both regulations, on their objectives and purposes, on their scope and meaning, and on the intersection with other EU and national instruments in this same area.

I must personally celebrate the publication of this *ouvrage* as a tool for the jurists devoted to the interpretation of EU law within the Court of Justice of the European Union, which will have the task to give an answer to the preliminary rulings that regularly reach the European jurisdiction concerning private law issues related to matrimonial regimes and property consequences of registered partnerships. This specific field of European family law is certainly more approachable and intelligible now that Regulations 2016/1103 and 2016/1104 have been scrutinised with rigour and excellence by such an exquisite group of experts.

Juan Ignacio Signes de Mesa
Legal Secretary, Court of Justice of the EU
September 2021

PREFACE

On 1 January 2020, 13.5 million people were living in one of the EU Member States with the citizenship of another EU Member State, representing 3 per cent of the EU population. In addition, around 5 per cent of the population EU-wide were third country nationals residing in EU states.[1] Naturally, many of them formed cross-border couples where the spouses or partners were of different nationalities or where the spouses or partners with the same nationality lived in another country than that of their origin.

Being a cross-border couple, however, is not always easy. Besides practical and emotional difficulties often faced by cross-border couples, this is also true from the legal perspective. The set of legal rules regulating different aspects of a cross-border relationship is much more extensive and complicated than that regulating the situation of a single nationality couple living in its home country. Often, in the family law field, national laws of several countries might come into play, raising many questions for the couples.

To address this and bring more legal certainty and predictability to couples in cross-border situations, the EU has adopted several instruments, often referred to as EU private international family law. The two most recent EU instruments in the family law field are the Matrimonial Property Regulation (Regulation (EU) 2016/1103)[2] and the Regulation on the Property Consequences of Registered Partnerships (Regulation (EU) 2016/1104),[3] together called the Twin Regulations. Covering the property law aspects of cross-border couples, in the few years since their adoption, they proved to be a crucial piece of the European family law puzzle – a piece that is of quintessential importance for European cross-border families on an everyday basis.

This volume explores many different aspects of the Twin Regulations. It seeks not only to reveal the substance of the provisions of the regulations but also to take a broader look and to discuss the questions that are closely related to matrimonial and partnership property regimes. The authors also cover the

---

[1] Eurostat, <https://ec.europa.eu/eurostat/en/web/products-eurostat-news/-/ddn-20210325-2>.
[2] Council Regulation (EU) 2016/1103 of 24 June 2016 implementing enhanced cooperation in the area of jurisdiction, applicable law and the recognition and enforcement of decisions in matters of matrimonial property regimes [2016] OJ L 183.
[3] Council Regulation (EU) 2016/1104 of 24 June 2016 implementing enhanced cooperation in the area of jurisdiction, applicable law and the recognition and enforcement of decisions in matters of the property consequences of registered partnerships [2016] OJ L 183.

relevant CJEU case law and, where available, the national case law of the partner countries.

Part I, Setting the Scene: Towards the EU Rules on Property of International Couples, opens by presenting the interconnected system of EU legal sources in family law (Chapter 1 by Dr. Agnė Limantė) and describing the path that led to the adoption of the Twin Regulations (Chapter 2 by Dr. Eglė Kavoliūnaitė-Ragauskienė). This part introduces the readers to the topic by analysing how EU instruments regulate different aspects of family law and locates the EU property regulations in this complicated system. It also uncovers the reasons behind the adoption of the Twin Regulations.

Part II, Anatomy of the Twin Regulations, systemically scrutinises the EU Regulation on Matrimonial Property and the EU Regulation on the Property Consequences of Registered Partnerships. It seeks to cover all the essential aspects of the regulations and to provide guidance to challenges that arise when applying them in practice. Firstly, the substantive, territorial and temporal scope of the regulations are examined. Chapter 3, written by Prof. Dr. María Jose Cazorla González and Prof. Dr. Mercedes Soto Moya explains the main concepts used in the instruments and defines in which situations the Twin Regulations need to be consulted and when they need to be applied. Then, two fundamental chapters follow. These are the chapters examining the rules regarding the jurisdiction (Chapter 4 by Prof. Dr. Ivana Kunda and Dr. Agnė Limantė) and the applicable law (Chapter 5 by Assist. Prof. Dr. Neža Pogorelčnik Vogrinc) of the Twin Regulations. They analyse meticulously the rules that need to be applied whenever the judge needs to establish jurisdiction or applicable law under the Twin Regulations. Chapter 6, by Prof. Dr. Jerca Kramberger Škerl, focuses on the second part of the 'life' of a court decision – its recognition and enforcement in another EU Member State. The chapter, therefore, deals with the question, which decisions can circulate under the rules of the Twin Regulations, explains the procedure of recognition, the declaration of enforceability, and the grounds for refusal of recognition and enforcement. Part II concludes with Chapter 7, by Prof. Dr. Ivana Kunda and Assist. Martina Tičić, on authentic instruments and court settlements, which have a significant role in the frame of the Twin Regulations.

Part III, The Intersection between the Twin Regulations and Other EU and National Instruments, discloses links between the Twin Regulations and other EU instruments and national rules. It focuses on specific and cross-cutting issues related to applying the relevant EU regulations and touches upon some specific questions that surface when applying them. Chapter 8, by Prof. Dr. Francesco Giacomo Viterbo and Dr. Roberto Garetto, stresses some of the risks that arise in exercising party autonomy and choosing the jurisdiction and the applicable law for the regimes of matrimonial property and property of registered partnerships. The two chapters that follow exhaustively study legal aspects of the property relations of cross-border same-sex couples (Chapter 9 by Assist. Filip Dougan) and property relations of cross-border *de facto* couples (Chapter 10 by Assist. Prof. Dr. Sandra Winkler). Chapter 11, by Prof. Dr. Lucia Ruggeri and Dr. Manuela Giobbi, is dedicated to another important question that arises in practice – the use of the national land registers, especially the problems that occur when registering the property legal facts of the cross-border couples. Chapter 12, by Dr. Stefano Deplano, emphasises an important interplay between the Twin Regulations and the Succession Regulation. It focuses mainly on the agreements under the Succession Regulation and their impact on the property regimes of spouses and registered partners. The volume concludes with the chapter by Prof. Dr. Nenad Hlača (Chapter 13), discussing philosophical and factual aspects of migration in the EU and its legal consequences in the national and European legal context. It emphasises how migration shapes private international family law.

It should be noted that this volume was written implementing the EU co-funded project 'E-training on EU Family Property regimes' (EU-FamPro). This project and, as a result, this volume, unites researchers from the University of Camerino (Italy), the University of Rijeka (Croatia), the University of Ljubljana (Slovenia), the University of Almeria (Spain), and the Law Institute of the Lithuanian Centre for Social Sciences (Lithuania). The EU-FamPro project builds on the well-known European motto 'united in diversity', with its purpose to recognise and implement common solutions at the European level whilst taking into account domestic specifics and legal realities. The main focus of the project is the continuous research of the Twin Regulations and increased knowledge of practitioners from all over Europe on these two important legal documents. One of the key deliverables of the EU-FamPro project is this scientific monograph, which – we sincerely hope – will become a significant contribution to the literature on private international family law in general and on EU property regimes of cross-border couples in particular.

Lucia Ruggeri, Agnė Limantė
and Neža Pogorelčnik Vogrinc

CONTENTS

Forewords v
   Irmantas Jarukaitis. v
   Paolo Pasqualis. vii
   Alberto Perez Cedillo viii
   Fernando Rodríguez Prieto ix
   Juan Ignacio Signes de Mesa xi
Preface xiii
List of Cases xxi
List of Abbreviations xxv
List of Contributors xxvii

PART I. SETTING THE SCENE: TOWARDS THE EU RULES ON PROPERTY OF INTERNATIONAL COUPLES

The System of EU Private International Family Law Instruments
   Agnė LIMANTĖ 3

1. Introduction 4
2. The Set of European Private International Family Law Instruments. 5
3. EU Instruments Applicable to Dissolution of Matrimonial Ties 8
4. Instruments Applicable to Parental Responsibility Matters 12
5. Regulation of Private International Law Aspects of Maintenance
   Obligations. 15
6. Instruments Covering Matrimonial Property and Property
   of Registered Partners 18
7. Case Study: Interaction of the Instruments. 20
8. Concluding Remarks 22

The Twin Regulations: Development and Adoption
   Eglė KAVOLIŪNAITĖ-RAGAUSKIENĖ 25

1. Introduction 25
2. A Need for the EU Legislative Intervention 26
3. Harmonisation of Couples' Property Regimes in a Historical
   Perspective. 30
4. Procedure of Adoption of the Twin Regulations 32
5. Concluding Remarks 37

PART II. ANATOMY OF THE TWIN REGULATIONS

Main Concepts and Scope of Application of the Twin Regulations
María José Cazorla González and Mercedes Soto Moya............ 41

1. Introduction 41
2. Defining the Main Concepts................................... 42
3. Scope of Application of the Twin Regulations 48
4. Concluding Remarks 70

Jurisdictional Provisions in the Twin Regulations
Ivana Kunda and Agnė Limantė..................................... 71

1. Introduction 71
2. Concentration of Jurisdiction as the Key Principle 73
3. Jurisdiction in 'Other Cases' 82
4. Remaining Jurisdiction Rules 88
5. Coordination Among Concurrent Proceedings in Different
   Member States.. 95
6. Concluding Remarks 99

Applicable Law in the Twin Regulations
Neža Pogorelčnik Vogrinc... 101

1. Introduction 102
2. Connecting Factors in the Absence of an Agreement on the
   Choice of Law 102
3. Rules Supporting and Supplementing the Application of Connecting
   Factors 110
4. Agreement on the Choice of Law............................... 118
5. Case Study 126

Recognition, Enforceability and Enforcement of Decisions under the Twin Regulations
Jerca Kramberger Škerl.. 129

1. Introduction 130
2. Recognition 136
3. The Declaration of Enforceability (*Exequatur*)............... 138
4. Grounds for Refusal of Recognition and Enforcement........... 146
5. Concluding Remarks 153

Authentic Instruments and Court Settlements under the Twin Regulations
Ivana Kunda and Martina Tičić 157

1. Introduction 158

2. The Notions of 'Authentic Instrument' and 'Court Settlement' 161
3. Extending the Effects of Authentic Instruments and Court Settlements.... 175
4. Concluding Remarks 187

PART III. THE INTERSECTION BETWEEN THE TWIN REGULATIONS
AND OTHER EU AND NATIONAL INSTRUMENTS

Choosing Law and Jurisdiction for Matrimonial Property and Property
Consequences of Registered Partnerships: Associated Risks
    Francesco Giacomo Viterbo and Roberto Garetto 191

1. Introduction 192
2. Risks Associated With Timing and Context of Choice of Law
   and Jurisdiction: Preliminary Remarks............................. 193
3. Risks Associated with Choice Made before or at Time of Conclusion
   of Marriage or Registered Partnership............................. 195
4. Risks of a Delayed Choice Made During Marriage or Registered
   Partnership... 199
5. Implicit or Tacit Choice of Applicable Law Admitted................ 202
6. The Context Surrounding the Choice of Law: Psychological
   Approach to Legal Issues.. 205
7. Risks Associated with Inadequate Legal Advice Prior to Agreement
   and Safeguards to Protect Weaker Party 212
8. Concluding Remarks 217

Property Relations of Cross-Border Same-Sex Couples in the EU
    Filip Dougan 219

1. Introduction 219
2. The Issue of Same-Sex Couples – One of the Major Reasons for a
   Lengthy Path to the Adoption of the Twin Regulations 221
3. Material and Personal Scope of Application........................ 223
4. Alternative Jurisdiction 232
5. Party Autonomy – A Possible Solution to Uncertainty?.............. 234
6. Recognition and Enforcement 240
7. Concluding Remarks 243

De Facto Couples: Between National Solutions and European Trends
    Sandra Winkler... 245

1. Introduction 245
2. *De Facto* Couples: European Legal Systems in Comparison............ 248
3. *De Facto* Couples in European Family Law......................... 260
4. Concluding Remarks 267

Property Regimes and Land Registers for Cross-Border Couples
Lucia RUGGERI and Manuela GIOBBI 269
1. Land Registers in Europe: A Fragmented Regulatory Framework 269
2. Autonomy of the will and Protection of Third Parties: A Difficult Combination 273
3. The Arduous, but Necessary, Dialogue between *Lex Causae* and *Lex Registri* 276
4. The Principle of Unity and the Protection of the Third Party 279
5. Law Applicable to the Property Regime and Knowledge Held by Third Parties 282
6. Recording of Rights *in Rem* and the Scope of the Twin Regulations 285
7. Disclosure of Assets and Effects in Respect of Third Parties 287
8. Adaptability of Rights *in Rem*. 289
9. Concluding Remarks 291

Succession Regulation, Matrimonial Property Agreements and Inconsistencies Among European Private International Law Rules
Stefano DEPLANO 293

1. Introduction 293
2. Understanding of 'Agreement as to Succession' and its Relation to National Instruments 297
3. Problems Linked to Agreements on Succession of Several Persons 300
4. Limitations on Party Autonomy under Article 25 Succession Regulation 304
5. Challenges in Applying Succession Regulation and Twin Regulations in Parallel 307
6. Concluding Remarks 311

Miscellaneous Thoughts on Europe, its People and Migration
Nenad HLAČA 313

1. European History of Migration 313
2. Current Migration Challenges for the European Union 314
3. Conceptualising European Identity against the Background of Migration. 319
4. Migration and Cross-Border Families 321

Index. 323

LIST OF CASES

CASE-LAW OF THE COURT OF JUSTICE OF THE EUROPEAN UNION

Case C-43/77, *Industrial Diamond Supplies v Luigi Riva*, ECLI:EU:C:1977:188 138
Case C-125/79, *Bernard Denilauler v SNC Couchet Frères*, ECLI:EU:C:1980:130 132
Case C-144/86, *Gubisch Maschinenfabrik KG v Giulio Palumbo*,
   EU:C:1987:528 .... 97–98, 123
Case C-145/86, *Horst Ludwig Martin Hoffmann v Adelheid Krieg*,
   ECLI:EU:C:1988:61 .... 138, 181, 242
Case C-351/89, *Overseas Union Insurance Ltd and Deutsche Ruck*,
   EU:C:1991:279 98
Case C-261/90, *Mario Reichert, Hans-Heinz Reichert and Ingeborg
   Kockler v Dresdner Bank AG.*, EU:C:1992:149 95
Case C-406/92, *The owners of the cargo lately laden on board the ship
   'Tatry' v the owners of the ship 'Maciej Rataj'*, EU:C:1994:400 .... 97, 99
Case C-414/92, *Solo Kleinmotoren GmbH v Emilio Boch*,
   ECLI:EU:C:1994:221 .... 171–172, 242
Case C-279/93, *Finanzamt Köln-Altstadt v Schumacker*,
   ECLI:EU:C:1995:31 196
Case C-341/93, *Danværn Production A/S v Schuhfabriken
   Otterbeck GmbH & Co.*, EU:C:1995:239 94
Case C-336/94, *Eftalia Dafeki* [1997] EU:C:1997:579 .... 176, 178
Case C-391/95, *Van Uden Maritime BV, trading as Van Uden Africa Line v
   Kommanditgesellschaft in Firma Deco-Line and Another*, ECLI:EU:C:1998:543 132
Case C-99/96, *Hans-Hermann Mietz v Intership Yachting Sneek BV*,
   ECLI:EU:C:1999:202 132
Case C-351/96, *Drouot assurances SA v Consolidated metallurgical industries (CMI)
   industrial sites), Protea assurance and Groupement d' intérêté conomique (GIE)
   Réunion européenne*, EU:C:1998:242 98
Case C-260/97, *Unibank A/S v Flemming G. Christensen*, EU:C:1999:312 162–163
Case C-391/97, *Gschwind v Finanzamt Aachen-Außenstadt*, EU:C:1999:409 196
Case C-7/98, *Dieter Krombach v André Bamberski*, EU:C:2000:164. .... 148, 180, 242
Case C-38/98, *Régie nationale des usines Renault SA v Maxicar SpA
   and Orazio Formento*, EU:C:2000:225 .... 148, 180
Case C-387/98, *Coreck Maritime GmbH c. Handelsveem BV and others*,
   EU:C:2000:606, point 13 205
Case C-87/99, *Patrik Zurstrassen v Administration des contributions directes*,
   EU:C:2000:251 196

List of Cases

Case C-148/02, *Carlos Garcia Avello v Belgian State*, EU:C:2003:539 107
Case C-283/05, *ASML Netherlands BV v Semiconductor Industry
  Services GmbH (SEMIS)*, EU:C:2006:787 151
Case C-435/06, *C*, EU:C:2007:714 13
Case C-68/07, *Sundelind Lopez*, EU:C:2007:740 9
Case C-420/07, *Meletis Apostolides v David Charles Orams, Linda Elizabeth
  Orams*, EU:C:2009:271 138
Case C-523/07, *A*, EU:C:2009:225 .... 10, 69, 87, 104, 105
Case C-168/08, *Laszlo Hadadi v Csilla Marta Mesko*, EU:C:2009:474 .... 88, 107
Joined Cases C-509/09 and C-161/10, *eDate Advertising GmbH v X and
  Olivier Martinez, Robert Martinez v MGN Limited*, EU:C:2011:685 104
Case C-296/10, *Bianca Purrucker v Guillermo Vallés Pérez (Purrucker II)*,
  EU:C:2010:665 97
Case C-497/10 PPU, *B. Mercredi v R. Chaffe*, EU:C:2010:829 .... 10, 87
Case C-543/10, *Refcomp SpA c. Axa Corporate Solutions Assurance SA*,
  EU:C:2013:62 205
Case C-619/10, *Trade Agency Ltd v Seramico Investments Ltd.* EU:C:2012:531 140
Case C-456/11, *Gothaer Allgemeine Versicherung AG and Others v
  Samskip GmbH*, EU:C:2012:719 98
Case C-156/12, *GREP GmbH v Freitstaat Bayern*, EU:C:2012:342 146
Case C-157/12, *Salzgitter Mannesmann Handel GmbH v SC Laminorul SA*,
  EU:C:2013:597 139
Case C-255/13, *I c. Health Service Executive*, EU:C:2014:1291. 196
Case C-302/13, *flyLAL-Lithuanian Airlines*, EU:C:2014:2319 180
Case C-184/14, *A v B*, EU:C:2015:479 .... 22, 217
Case C-376/14, PPU, *C.*, EU:C:2014:2268 .... 10, 87
Case C-185/15, *Marjan Kostanjevec v F&S Leasing, GmbH.*, EU:C:2016:763 94
Case C-484/15, *Ibrica Zulfikarpašić v Slaven Gajer*, EU:C:2017:199 164
Case C-499/15, *W and V v X*, EU:C:2017:118 .... 10, 87, 104
Case C-507/15, *Agro Foreign Trade & Agency Ltd v Petersime NV*,
  EU:C:2017:129 242
Case C-551/15, *Pula parking d.o.o. v Sven Klaus Tederahn*, EU:C:2017:193 164
Case C-218/16, *Aleksandra Kubicka v Przemysława Bac*, EU:C:2017:755 ...... 52, 290, 296
Case C-558/16, *Doris Margret Lisette Mahnkopf v Sven Mahnkopf*,
  EU:C:2018:138 .... 49, 296, 310
Case C-673/16, *Relu Adrian Coman and Others* v *Inspectoratul General
  pentru Imigrări and Ministerul Afacerilor Interne*, EU:C:2018:385 .... 56–57, 263
Case C-20/17 *Oberle*, EU:C:2018:485 296
Case C-111/17, PPU, *O.L. v P.Q.*, EU:C:2017:436 .... 10, 87
Case C-214/17, *Alexander Mölk v Valentina Mölk*, EU:C:2018:744 .... 201, 217
Case C-386/17, *Stefano Liberato v Luminita Luisa Grigorescu*, EU:C:2019:24 ..... 147, 153
Case C-512/17, *H.R.*, EU:C:2018:513 .... 10, 87
Case C-658/17, *WB v Notariusz Przemysława Bac*, EU:C:2019:444 ...... 163, 165–166, 296
Case C-85/18, *CV v DU*, EU:C:2018:220 14
Case C-102/18 *Brisch*, EU:C:2019:34 296
Case C-393/18, PPU, *UD v XB*, EU:C:2018:835 .... 10, 87, 104
Case C-468/18, *R v P*, EU:C:2019:666 22

Case C-80/19, *E.E.*, EU:C:2020:569 .... 76, 77, 296
Case C-249/19, *JE v KF*, EU:C:2020:570 .... 11, 198
Case C-253/19, *MH, NI v OJ, Novo Banco SA*, ECLI:EU:C:2020:585 104
Case C-501/20, *M.P.A.* (currently pending) 87

EUROPEAN COURT OF HUMAN RIGHTS

C-*Hämäläinen v Finland*, no. 37359/09. ECHR 2014\50 43

LIST OF ABBREVIATIONS

TFEU	Treaty on the Functioning of the European Union [2012].
CJEU	Court of Justice of the European Union.
ECHR	Convention for the Protection of Human Rights and Fundamental Freedoms (commonly known as European Convention on Human Rights).
Matrimonial Property Regulation	Council Regulation (EU) 2016/1103 of 24 June 2016 implementing enhanced cooperation in the area of jurisdiction, applicable law and the recognition and enforcement of decisions in matters of matrimonial property regimes.
Regulation on the Property Consequences of Registered Partnerships	Council Regulation (EU) 2016/1104 of 24 June 2016 implementing enhanced cooperation in the area of jurisdiction, applicable law and the recognition and enforcement of decisions in matters of the property consequences of registered partnerships.
Twin Regulations	The Matrimonial Property Regulation and the Regulation on the Property Consequences of Registered Partnerships together.
Brussels II bis Regulation	Council Regulation (EC) No 2201/2003 of 27 November 2003 concerning jurisdiction and the recognition and enforcement of judgments in matrimonial matters and the matters of parental responsibility, repealing Regulation (EC) No 1347/2000 [2003] OJ L 338. As of August 2022, it will be replaced by the Council Regulation (EU) 2019/1111 of 25 June 2019 on jurisdiction, the recognition and enforcement of decisions in matrimonial matters and the matters of parental responsibility, and on international child abduction.

List of Abbreviations

Rome I Regulation	Regulation (EC) No 593/2008 of the European Parliament and of the Council of 17 June 2008 on the law applicable to contractual obligations (Rome I).
Rome II Regulation	Regulation (EC) No 864/2007 of the European Parliament and of the Council of 11 July 2007 on the law applicable to non-contractual obligations (Rome II).
Rome III Regulation	Council Regulation (EU) No 1259/2010 of 20 December 2010 implementing enhanced cooperation in the area of the law applicable to divorce and legal separation.
Maintenance Regulation	Council Regulation (EC) No 4/2009 of 18 December 2008 on jurisdiction, applicable law, recognition and enforcement of decisions and cooperation in matters relating to maintenance obligations.
Succession Regulation	Regulation (EU) No 650/2012 of the European Parliament and of the Council of 4 July 2012 on jurisdiction, applicable law, recognition and enforcement of decisions and acceptance and enforcement of authentic instruments in matters of succession and on the creation of a European Certificate of Succession.
1978 Hague Convention on the Law Applicable to Matrimonial Property Regimes	Hague Convention of 14 March 1978 on the Law Applicable to Matrimonial Property Regimes.
1980 Hague Child Abduction Convention	Hague Convention of 25 October 1980 on the Civil Aspects of International Child Abduction.
1996 Hague Convention	Hague Convention of 19 October 1996 on Jurisdiction, Applicable Law, Recognition, Enforcement and Co-operation in Respect of Parental Responsibility and Measures for the Protection of Children.
2007 Hague Child Support Convention	Hague Convention of 23 November 2007 on the International Recovery of Child Support and Other Forms of Family Maintenance.
2007 Hague Protocol on the Law Applicable to Maintenance Obligations	Hague Protocol of 23 November 2007 on the Law Applicable to Maintenance Obligations.

LIST OF CONTRIBUTORS

Editors

Lucia Ruggeri is Full Professor of Private Law at the School of Law of the University of Camerino. She coordinates the PhD curriculum Civil law and Constitutional Legality at the School of Advanced Studies of the University of Camerino. Moreover, she is the director of the School of Specialization in Civil Law at the University of Camerino. She has been a speaker at various conferences and seminars. She is an author and a curator of numerous publications focused on Contract and Property Family Law. She was the coordinator of the EU Consortium PSEFS 'Personalized Solution in European Family and Succession Law PSEFS'. Currently, she is the coordinator of the EU Consortium EU-FamPro 'EU-FamPro: E-Training on EU Family Property Regimes'.

Agnė Limantė is a chief researcher at the Law Institute of the Lithuanian Centre for Social Sciences. She has received an MA in EU law from King's College London (awarded with the Prize for Best Dissertation on the MA in EU Law) and a PhD from Vilnius University, Lithuania.

Dr. Limantė is an expert in private international family law and has a number of publications in the area. After defending her PhD thesis, Agnė Limantė published over 30 scientific papers. Dr. Limantė also has extensive experience working in international teams and conducting comparative research. Recently, she took part in two EU co-funded projects that were designed to train judges, lawyers and social services on private international family law instruments ('4 EU training sessions on family law regulations for Cross-border Lawyers and Social Services' (C.L.A.S.S.4EU) and 'EU Judiciary Training on Brussels IIa Regulation: From South to East'). Moreover, Dr. Limantė has extensive teaching experience and for a number of years has been teaching at Vilnius University and the European Humanities University in Lithuania.

Neža Pogorelčnik Vogrinc is an Assistant Professor of civil and commercial law at the Faculty of Law, University of Ljubljana, and a researcher at the Institute for Comparative Law at the Faculty of Law in Ljubljana, Slovenia. Her main fields of interests are civil procedural law, European civil procedural law and mediation. After internship at the Ljubljana Court of Appeals, she passed the Slovenian Bar Exam in 2012. She defended her doctoral thesis with the title 'Provisional measures in civil court procedures' in 2014 at the University of Ljubljana (*cum laude*). She is a member of the national projects 'Pravna in ekonomska analiza vpliva staranja prebivalstva na zakonodajo', 'Vključevanje pravnega izrazja evropskega prava v slovenski pravni sistem' and 'Pravo dolžnikov in upnikov – normativna in pravno empirična analiza'. She is also a team member of the European projects 'En4S' (JUST-AG-2018), 'PAX – Private international law in motion (JUST-JCOO-AG-2019) and 'EU-FamPro' (JUST-AG-2020). She has published papers in several national and foreign journals, is an author of the individual chapters of ten books and a sole author of the book *Začasne odredbe v civilnih sodnih postopkih* (Provisional measures in civil court procedures).

Contributors

María José Cazorla González has been a Full Professor of civil law at the University of Almería, Spain, since 2000. Her leadership skills and ability to work in research teams are reflected in her work as a coordinator of master and PhD studies and in her research work in different national and international research projects. She has published papers in Italian, Spanish and English. She has been recognised by the Spanish Ministry of Universities for her active research and knowledge transfer capacity, because she passes the evaluation by the National Agency for Quality Assessment and Accreditation (ANECA) every six years.

She is a lecturer at the Institute of International and Comparative Agrarian Studies of Firenze, Italy, Faculty of Law of Montevideo, Uruguay and at the University Eduardo Mondlane. She is a visiting professor at the universities of Rosario and Azul, Faculty of Law in Montevideo, Peruggia, Rome Tre, and Camerino, Nitra, Bucharest, and Poznan. She is an author of publications such as: 'Ley aplicable al régimen económico matrimonial después de la disolución del matrimonio tras la entrada en vigor del Reglamento UE. 2016/1104'; and 'How to resolve transnational conflicts in marriages, registered partnerships and successions' (in easy reading). She is a co-author of the research works 'Matrimonial property regimes with cross-border implications: Regulation (EU) 2016/1103' and 'Guidelines for practitioners in cross-border family property and succession law'.

Stefano Deplano was awarded a PhD degree for his thesis 'I problemi civilistici della persona' at University of Sannio, Italy in 2013. He was a research fellow at the Università degli Studi di Cagliari (2013–2015) and at the Università Politecnica delle Marche (2016–2018).

He is an Associate Professor in civil law at the University of Campania 'Luigi Vanvitelli' in Caserta, Italy. His research areas are contractual law, succession and family law. He has participated in numerous research projects and conferences and published a number of academic papers. He was part of the research team for the project 'Personalized Solution in European Family and Succession Law PSEFS'. In addition, he is a member of the editorial boards of several legal journals.

List of Contributors

Filip Dougan obtained his bachelor's and master's degree at the University of Ljubljana, Slovenia (Faculty of Law), where he now works as a Teaching and Research Assistant at the Department of Civil Law. His work mainly focuses on Private International Law and Civil Procedural Law. In both fields, he actively participates in several national and EU funded research project. Currently, he is also enrolled in a doctoral degree programme at the University of Ljubljana (Faculty of Law), where he researches property regimes of cross-border couples. He speaks and works in Slovenian, English, German and French. In 2021 he passed the Slovenian Bar Exam.

Roberto Garetto graduated in Law (JD) at the University of Camerino, Italy, and in Spain (*Prueba de Conjunto*). He obtained a Bachelor of Philosophy degree at the University Tor Vergata of Rome, Italy. He achieved a Teaching Certificate degree at the University of Murcia, Spain. He earned his PhD in 'Civil Law in Constitutional Legality' at the University of Camerino, Italy. He was visiting scholar at the University UNNE of Corrientes, Argentina, and at the University of Pittsburgh, USA. He has several years' experience teaching in secondary schools and in adult education programs, as well as at university level, as teaching fellow and adjunct professor. He has published legal articles in English, Spanish and Italian, mainly dealing with personal and fundamental rights, marriage and family law, and environmental law. He has been invited to speak at several conferences. He was a team member of the project 'Personalized Solution in European Family and Succession Law – PSEFS'. Roberto Garetto is a research fellow in private law at the Law School of the University of Camerino.

Manuela Giobbi, former research fellow at the University of Perugia, is now a research fellow in Private Law at University of Camerino. She graduated from the School of Specialization in Civil Law at the University of Camerino and later received PhD in Law and Economics (2010). She is a member of the Foundation Scuola di Alta Formazione Giuridica.

Her main areas of interest are consumer protection, property regimes and market regulation. She has been a speaker at national and international conferences and she is author of several scientific articles. She was research member in the EU Project PSEFS – 'Personalized Solution in European Family and Succession Law'.

Nenad Hlača graduated from the Faculty of Law, University of Rijeka, Croatia in 1980. Before he started working in academia in 1982, he was a clerk at the Municipal Court in Rijeka. In 1984, he received a master's degree in civil law from the Faculty of Law, University of Belgrade. In 1990, he received the title of Doctor of Laws from the Faculty of Law, University of Zagreb by defending a doctorate dissertation with the title 'Family Law Aspects of Transgender persons'. In 1991, he was nominated an assistant professor, and in 1998 he became Professor of Family law at the Faculty of Law, University of Rijeka. He was elected as a Vice-Dean twice: from 1990–1994 and from 1999–2001. From 1991–1994 and 2009–2011, he acted as editor-in-chief of the Collected Papers of the Law Faculty of the University of Rijeka. He is a member of the international advisory board of the review FamRZ (*Zeitschrift für das gesamte Familienrecht mit Betreuungsrecht, Erbrecht, Verfahrensrecht, Öffentlichem Recht*). From 1999–2015, prof. Hlača was a Vice-President of the Croatian Section of the *Commission Internationale de l'Etat Civil* in Strasbourg. While being a member of the working group (1994–1998), formed by the Ministry of Work and Social Welfare of the Republic of Croatia, he worked on the draft proposal on the Family Act. Prof. Hlača actively participates at international and national seminars and conferences, and has published a number of scientific papers and articles.

Eglė Kavoliūnaitė-Ragauskienė is an experienced researcher and trainer. Two of her main research areas are family law and private international family law. She has written several publications and conducted numerous trainings for professionals in the area of EU private international family law, including trainings organised by ERA (Academy of European Law) on EU legislation on property effects of marriage and registered partnership. She was a team member of an EU co-funded project 'EU Judiciary Training on Brussels IIa Regulation: From South to East'. At the national level, she wrote PhD thesis on family law and family policy and delivered a number of trainings on family law to national experts and family-related service providers.

Jerca Kramberger Škerl is an Associate Professor of private international law, civil procedure and French legal language, and the Vice-Dean of the Law Faculty of the University of Ljubljana, Slovenia. She has published extensively in the field of private international law, including European family law. Recently, her article on recognition and enforcement of foreign judgments in Slovenia was published in the renowned *Yearbook of Private International Law*. She has been active in national and EU co-founded research projects in her areas of expertise.

Ivana Kunda is a Full Professor and the Head of the International and European Private Law Department at the Faculty of Law of the University of Rijeka, Croatia and a Vice-Dean for Research. She was awarded the University of Rijeka Foundation Award for the Year 2008. She received grants including the Fulbright Research Fellow scholarship in 2010 for research at the Columbia University, the GRUR scholarship in 2007, 2008 and 2014 for research at the MPI for Innovation and Competition and the IRZ scholarship in 2002 for research at the MPI on comparative and international private law and the University of Hamburg.

She authored papers and book chapters published in Croatia and abroad and a monograph on overriding mandatory provisions. Ivana was or currently is involved in research under a dozen EU, international and national projects, in particular on the European private international law including two EU-funded projects on property and succession regulations and four EU-funded projects on cross-border civil procedure. She is a co-editor of the Balkan *Yearbook of European and International Law* (BYEIL, Springer), member of the Editorial Board of the *Santander Art and Culture Law Review* (SACLR) and an editor of the global blog www.conflictoflaws.net. She is also a member of the international team at the UNESCO Chair on Cultural Property Law of the University of Opole in Poland. She was visiting professor at the University of Navarra, the IULM, the University of Antwerp, the University of Ljubljana, WIPO Summer School and the MSU Croatia Summer Institute. Ivana is regularly called upon by domestic and foreign institutions to provide training to judges and legal professionals in the area of EU private international law. Among her professional memberships are ILA and ATRIP, while she also acts as deputy-president of the Croatian Comparative Law Association. She passed the Croatian Bar Exam in 2004.

Mercedes Soto Moya is a Full Professor of private international law at the University of Granada, Spain. She received her PhD from the University of Granada with the thesis 'Marital situations in intra-community traffic: a model of relationship between private international law and immigration law'. She is a member of the research project BJU2002-01180 (European private law), funded by the Ministry of Science and Technology 'Los retos de la regulación jurídico-patrimonial del matrimonio y de otras realidades familiares (uniones de hecho) en los planos supraestatal y estatal', and a member of the research group SEJ175 (European Community and Private International Law), financed by the Regional Government of Andalusia.

She is an author of various publications, including 'Las situaciones conyugales en el tráfico intracomunitario: un modelo de relación entre el Derecho internacional privado y el Derecho de extranjería'; 'La aplicación del Derecho español a la determinación del régimen patrimonial de las parejas registradas: cuna cuestión controvertida', and 'Ámbito de aplicación personal del Reglamento 2016/1104 sobre régimen patrimonial de la pareja registrada'.

Martina Tičić is a doctoral candidate at the University of Rijeka, Faculty of Law, funded by the Croatian Science Foundation. She is a research assistant in conducting research on the topic of the cross-border enforcement in the European Union, in particular for the project 'Train to Enforce' co-funded from the EU Justice Programme. She received an award from the Dean of the Faculty of Law in Rijeka for her achievements as a member of the Price Moot Court 2020 team for second place in the regional oral part of the competition and second place for the written memorandum in the worldwide competition.

Francesco Giacomo Viterbo is Associate Professor of Private Law at the University of Salento, Italy. He has obtained the national scientific qualification to work as a Full Professor. He is a member of the national study commission on "Family Law" at the "Società Italiana degli Studiosi del Diritto Civile" (SISDiC). His research interests relate to Italian and European Union civil law and mainly include family law, contract law, legal drafting, the protection of personal rights and, in particular, privacy and personal data protection, rights relating to the removal of architectural barriers, gender identity He was a team member of the project 'Personalized Solution in European Family and Succession Law – PSEFS'. He is a member of 'Scuola di Alta Formazione Giuridica' Foundation; 'Società Italiana degli Studiosi del Diritto Civile (SISDiC); and 'Associazione Dottorati di Diritto Privato' (ADP).

Sandra Winkler is an Assistant Professor at the Chair of Family Law of the Faculty of Law, University of Rijeka, Croatia. Before she joined the Faculty of Law University of Rijeka in 2006, she worked in a law firm in Italy. From 2001–2006, she collaborated as an external researcher with the Chair of Private Law and the Chair of Civil Law at the Faculty of Law University of Trieste, Italy. In 2009, she received her PhD degree in Law from the Faculty of Law, University of Verona, Italy. She was awarded a research grant at the *Max Planck Institut für ausländisches und internationales Privatrecht* in Hamburg, Germany on several occasions. She was a Visiting Professor at the Faculties of Law in Verona, Trieste, Camerino and Trento.

Since November 2019, she has been the Vice-Dean for International Affairs at the Faculty of Law in Rijeka. Her research interests include family law and European family law. She is a member of the European Law Institute (ELI) and of the Croatian Comparative Law Association (HUPP). She actively participates in international and national seminars and conferences and has published scientific papers and articles in the field of family law and European family law. She led the PRAVRI team in the project 'Personalized Solution in European Family and Succession Law – PSEFS'. Currently she leads the PRAVRI team in the project "EU-FamPro: E-Training on EU Family Property Regimes".

PART I
SETTING THE SCENE
Towards the EU Rules on Property of International Couples

THE SYSTEM OF EU PRIVATE INTERNATIONAL FAMILY LAW INSTRUMENTS

Agnė Limantė*

1. Introduction 4
2. The Set of European Private International Family Law Instruments 5
3. EU Instruments Applicable to Dissolution of Matrimonial Ties 8
   3.1. Brussels II bis Regulation 9
   3.2. Rome III Regulation 11
4. Instruments Applicable to Parental Responsibility Matters 12
   4.1. Brussels II bis Regulation 13
   4.2. 1996 Hague Convention on Parental Responsibility and
        Protection of Children 14
   4.3. 1980 Hague Child Abduction Convention 15
5. Regulation of Private International Law Aspects of Maintenance
   Obligations 15
   5.1. Maintenance Regulation 16
   5.2. 2007 Hague Child Support Convention 17
   5.3. 2007 Hague Maintenance Protocol 17
6. Instruments Covering Matrimonial Property and Property
   of Registered Partners 18
   6.1. Matrimonial Property Regulation 19
   6.2. Regulation on the Property Consequences of Registered
        Partnerships 19
7. Case Study: Interaction of the Instruments 20
8. Concluding Remarks 22

---

* Agnė Limantė, MA, PhD, is Chief Researcher at the Law Institute of the Lithuanian Centre for Social Sciences.

1. INTRODUCTION

Traditionally, private international law had been an issue of national law wherein each European state had its own rules to deal with jurisdiction, applicable law and recognition and enforcement of foreign judgments. However, in the EU, characterised by the area of freedom, security and justice, in which free movement of goods, persons, services and capital is ensured, it soon became clear that a common solution was needed in order to deal with intra-EU cases, leaving national private international rules to regulate situations concerning third countries or to supplement the EU laws.

As a result of the Treaty of Amsterdam,[1] which entered into force on 1 May 1999, the EU acquired its own legislative competence in the field of private international law. This was the starting date for the development of European rules in this area. Since the adoption of the Treaty of Lisbon[2] (1 December 2009), the rules for the harmonisation of conflict were therein governed by Title V (Articles 67–89) of Part III of the Treaty on the Functioning of the European Union (TFEU).[3]

Of particular relevance with regard to this chapter are Articles 67 and 81 of the TFEU. Article 67(4) of the TFEU declares that the EU has to facilitate access to justice, in particular through the principle of mutual recognition of judicial and extrajudicial decisions in civil matters. Article 81 requires the EU to develop judicial cooperation in civil matters having cross-border implications, based on the principle of mutual recognition of judgments and of decisions in extrajudicial cases. It also specifies that such cooperation may include the adoption of measures for the approximation of the laws and regulations of the Member States.

Article 81(3) of the TFEU, which serves as a legal basis for the EU instruments in the area of family law, specifies that measures concerning family law with cross-border implications are to be established by the Council, acting in accordance with a special legislative procedure, under which the Council will act unanimously after consulting with the European Parliament. Moreover, a measure will not be adopted when it is opposed by national Parliaments. Such a procedure allows Member States to retain control over the measures being adopted by the EU and allows them to oppose the instrument if it deals with sensitive matters.

---

[1] Treaty of Amsterdam amending the Treaty on European Union, the Treaties establishing the European Communities and certain related acts [1997] OJ C 340.
[2] Treaty of Lisbon amending the Treaty on European Union and the Treaty establishing the European Community, signed at Lisbon [2007] OJ C 306.
[3] Consolidated version of the Treaty on the Functioning of the European Union [2012] OJ C 326.

Having been granted competence to act, during the last two decades, the EU has since adopted a number of private international law instruments that are designed to address the issues arising out of cross-border movements of families. In addition, several instruments adopted by The Hague Conference on Private International Law are directly applicable in the EU.[4] These instruments together are often referred to as the European private international family law. They cover three types of questions traditionally distinguished in private international law: (i) which court has jurisdiction to deal with a case with an international element ('jurisdiction'); (ii) which law has to be applied to the case ('applicable law'); and (iii) under which conditions a judgment can be recognised and enforced in another state ('recognition and enforcement').

There are several advantages of having unified EU regulation instead of relying solely on national systems. 'Europeanising' the choice-of-law rules in family law increases legal certainty and predictability; without analysing national rules it is clear which instrument (EU regulation) applies and such instrument is easily accessible. Moreover, unification grants better protection to the legitimate expectations; at least to some extent it limits forum shopping and saves costs for the parties. Finally, European rules guarantee the simple cross-border movement of court decisions as recognition and enforcement are either automatic or simplified.[5]

This chapter analyses the system of EU private international family law, seeking to draw a map of the applicable instruments and to clarify the links between them. The chapter will define the scope of each instrument and its place within the interconnected network. This analysis will thus serve as a basis for a better understanding of the location of the Matrimonial Property Regulation and the Regulation on the Property Consequences of Registered Partnerships within the overall system of the European private international family law and the connection of these regulations to other instruments.

2. THE SET OF EUROPEAN PRIVATE INTERNATIONAL FAMILY LAW INSTRUMENTS

Out of all of the EU instruments, the most important ones pertaining to the area of family law are Brussels II bis Regulation defining jurisdiction in

---

[4] The Hague Conference is the World Organisation for Cross-border Co-operation in Civil and Commercial Matters. The European Union became a member of the Hague Conference on Private International Law on 3 April 2007.

[5] On aims and objectives of European international family law see N.A. BAARSMA, *The Europeanisation of International Family Law*, T.M.C. Asser Press, The Hague 2011, pp. 270–273.

matrimonial and parental responsibility matters[6] (recast version will be applied as of August 2022[7]), the Rome III Regulation[8] setting out the rules on the choice of law applicable to divorce, the Maintenance Regulation,[9] the Matrimonial Property Regulation[10] and the Regulation on the Property Consequences of Registered Partnerships.[11,12] This list is further extended by the instruments adopted in the framework of The Hague Conference on Private International Law, in particular by the 1980 Hague Child Abduction Convention,[13] the 1996 Hague Convention,[14] the 2007 Hague Child Support Convention[15] and the 2007 Hague Protocol on the Law Applicable to Maintenance Obligations.[16]

It should be noted that the EU instruments adopted in the private international family law area vary not only on the topics that they cover but also by the scope of rules which they include. Some instruments are 'complete' instruments, and as such, they include rules on jurisdiction, applicable law and recognition and enforcement. Such are the Maintenance Regulation, the Succession Regulation, the Matrimonial Property Regulation and Regulation on the Property Consequences of Registered Partnerships. The other instruments cover only

---

[6] Council Regulation (EC) No 2201/2003 of 27 November 2003 concerning jurisdiction and the recognition and enforcement of judgments in matrimonial matters and the matters of parental responsibility, repealing Regulation (EC) No 1347/2000 [2003] OJ L 338.

[7] Council Regulation (EU) 2019/1111 of 25 June 2019 on jurisdiction, the recognition and enforcement of decisions in matrimonial matters and the matters of parental responsibility, and on international child abduction [2019] OJ L 178.

[8] Council Regulation (EU) No 1259/2010 of 20 December 2010 implementing enhanced cooperation in the area of the law applicable to divorce and legal separation, OJ L 343, pp. 10–16.

[9] Council Regulation (EC) No 4/2009 of 18 December 2008 on jurisdiction, applicable law, recognition and enforcement of decisions and cooperation in matters relating to maintenance obligations [2009] OJ L 7.

[10] Council Regulation (EU) 2016/1103 of 24 June 2016 implementing enhanced cooperation in the area of jurisdiction, applicable law and the recognition and enforcement of decisions in matters of matrimonial property regimes [2016] OJ L 183.

[11] Council Regulation (EU) 2016/1104 of 24 June 2016 implementing enhanced cooperation in the area of jurisdiction, applicable law and the recognition and enforcement of decisions in matters of the property consequences of registered partnerships [2016] OJ L 183.

[12] The Succession Regulation is strictly speaking not part of EU private international family law, although is strongly related to it. It will not be analysed in more detail in this chapter. Regulation (EU) No 650/2012 of the European Parliament and of the Council of 4 July 2012 on jurisdiction, applicable law, recognition and enforcement of decisions and acceptance and enforcement of authentic instruments in matters of succession and on the creation of a European Certificate of Succession [2012] OJ L 201.

[13] Hague Convention of 25 October 1980 on the Civil Aspects of International Child Abduction.

[14] Hague Convention of 19 October 1996 on Jurisdiction, Applicable Law, Recognition, Enforcement and Co-operation in Respect of Parental Responsibility and Measures for the Protection of Children.

[15] Hague Convention of 23 November 2007 on the International Recovery of Child Support and Other Forms of Family Maintenance.

[16] Hague Protocol of 23 November 2007 on the Law Applicable to Maintenance Obligations.

part of the conflict of law rules (jurisdiction, recognition and enforcement or applicable law). Such are, for instance, the Brussels II bis Regulation and the Rome III Regulation which respectively focus on jurisdiction, recognition and enforcement (Brussels II bis Regulation) and applicable law (Rome III Regulation) in matrimonial cases.

There are, naturally, certain common features between all of the above instruments. First, be it jurisdictional rules or the applicable law rules, connecting factors will seek to refer to the forum/law of the state with which the case is most closely connected. Therefore, in the case of applicable law, *lex fori* will rarely be the option. In case such a possibility will be foreseen, it will be linked to the fact that jurisdictional rules were set to establish the forum of a closely connected state.[17] Secondly, in all the instruments, habitual residence is the main connecting factor. Nationality is given due regard; however, habitual residence is usually granted a stronger position. This, together with the principle of universality, means that, for example, the Brussels II bis Regulation applies not only to EU citizens but also to third-country nationals who are habitually resident in the EU. Furthermore, the European choice-of-law rules in the field of family law preclude the application of *renvoi*, i.e. choice-of-law rules refer solely to the substantive rules of the applicable law. Foreign choice-of-law rules are not referred to, thereby excluding 'bouncing' between jurisdictions. This strengthens predictability and simplifies the planning of the procedure. Lastly, to a greater or lesser extent, EU private international family law instruments increasingly incorporate rules on party autonomy.[18]

All the EU family law instruments are strongly interrelated and in many cases are applied together as their areas of regulation supplement each other. This is not an easy task, since the list of instruments is long indeed and several of them might need to be consulted in a family case.

To further complicate the application of the instruments listed above, it should be mentioned that not all EU Member States take part in the private international family law rules. First, Denmark has opted out of EU regulations

---

[17] As notes Baarsma, in addition to general objectives of predictability and legal certainty, the principle of the closest connection ensures that the legal systems involved are equally and evenly eligible for application. This aspect is of great importance in the European Union, in which the principle of mutual recognition presumes an equivalence of the legal norms of the Member States. N.A. BAARSMA, *The Europeanisation of International Family Law*, T.M.C. Asser Press, The Hague, 2011, p. 292.

[18] See A. LIMANTE, N. POGORELČNIK VOGRINC, 'Party Autonomy in the Context of Jurisdictional and Choice of Law Rules of Matrimonial Property Regulation' (2020) 13(2) *Baltic Journal of Law & Politics* 135–158; L. WALKER, 'Party Autonomy, Inconsistency and the Specific Characteristics of Family Law in the EU' (2018) 14(2) *Journal of Private International Law* 225–261; F. MAULTZSCH, 'Party Autonomy in European Private International Law: Uniform Principle or Context-Dependent Instrument?' (2016) 12(3) *Journal of Private International Law* 466–491; I. VIARENGO, 'Choice of Law Agreements in Property Regimes, Divorce, and Succession: Stress-testing the New EU Regulations'(2016) 17 *ERA Forum*.

in family law matters.[19] Secondly, an important consideration is that, as noted above, the adoption of EU legislation on a private international law matters concerning family law requires unanimous action of the Council (Article 81(3), TFEU). Such unanimity, however, is often hard to achieve. With this in mind, the Lisbon Treaty enabled the creation of a 'multi-speed Europe' by establishing the enhanced cooperation procedure. When the requirement of unanimity in the Council resulted in several regulations being dropped from the regular procedure, a number of EU Member States decided to proceed via enhanced cooperation. As a result of Regulation Rome III, the Matrimonial Property Regulation and the Regulation on the Property Consequences of Registered Partnerships are applied only to the Member States participating in enhanced cooperation. This all results in an intertwined regulation that is well elaborated and highly developed but often not so easy to understand and apply.

The sections below discuss the main private international family law instruments applied in the EU by classifying them into the area of family law which they cover. The chapter does not seek to discuss the content of the instruments in detail. Instead, it focuses on their main features and links between different EU private international family law instruments.

3. EU INSTRUMENTS APPLICABLE TO DISSOLUTION OF MATRIMONIAL TIES

If a case on the dissolution of matrimonial ties reaches a court in an EU Member State and the situation has a cross-border element (the spouses are of different nationalities or live within jurisdictions other than that of their nationality), two EU regulations will need to be applied: the Brussels II bis Regulation and the Rome III Regulation. This is because the Brussels II bis Regulation only provides for rules concerning jurisdiction, recognition and the enforcement of decisions in matrimonial matters, but it contains no rules as to the applicable law. Applicable law rules to divorce are thus established in the Rome III Regulation, which was adopted via enhanced cooperation procedure.

It should be noted that EU law provides no definition of 'marriage' as there is no common agreement regarding this institution between the EU countries (in particular due to the different approach of Member States with respect to same-sex marriages).[20] Therefore, each Member State applies the Brussels II bis

---

[19] Protocol (No 21) On the Position of The United Kingdom and Ireland in Respect of the Area of Freedom, Security And Justice [2016] OJ C 202; Protocol (No 22) on the position of Denmark. [2012] OJ C 326.

[20] On the understanding of marriage in Europe see C. SÖRGJERD, 'Marriage in a European perspective' in J. M. SCHERPE, *European Family Law Volume III*, Edward Elgar, Cheltenham 2016, pp. 3–40.

Regulation, the Rome III Regulation and other instruments employing the notion of marriage provided in its own legal order.

Divorce/Legal separation			
Private international family law instrument	**Issues covered**	**Temporal scope of application**	**Geographical scope of application**
Brussels II bis Regulation /EU instrument	Jurisdiction Recognition and enforcement Cooperation	Applicable as of 1 March 2005 (recast version to be applied as of August 2022)	All Member States of the EU, except Denmark
Rome III Regulation /EU instrument	Applicable law	Applicable as of 21 June 2012	Enhanced cooperation 17 Member States

3.1. BRUSSELS II BIS REGULATION

Brussels II bis Regulation sets out the rules governing the jurisdiction, recognition and enforcement in matrimonial cases in the EU. It relates only to the dissolution of matrimonial ties (divorce, annulment and legal separation) but does not include ancillary issues, such as maintenance or the property consequences of marriage. However, parental responsibility matters that typically arise in connection to divorce (custody, access, visitation rights) are covered by this instrument (discussed in Section 4.1. below).

The Regulation establishes rules of jurisdiction that determine the Member State in which proceedings on dissolution of matrimonial ties can be initiated. It is important to note, however, that the Regulation refers only to international jurisdiction, i.e. identification of a concrete EU Member State, and not to a concrete court within the state. The latter question is left for the national rules of the state in question.

In general, the Brussels II bis Regulation covers all divorce cases with a cross-border element. The only situation where the regulation will not be applicable and national choice-of-law rules apply instead, is where the case concerns spouses both of whom are third-country nationals with a habitual residence in a third state. If at least one spouse is an EU national or has his or her habitual residence in an EU state, the regulation will come into play. This means that the connecting criteria expressly set in the regulation will be used to establish jurisdiction. In certain cases, however, where no court in the EU has jurisdiction in accordance with rules of the Brussels II bis Regulation, the regulation allows jurisdiction to be established under national rules (residual jurisdiction).[21]

---

[21] If no court of EU Member State has jurisdiction under Articles 3–5, Article 7 of the Brussels II bis Regulation (residual jurisdiction) is applicable. In such case, the regulation refers to national laws. This was confirmed by the CJEU in *Sundelind Lopez* case. Case C-68/07, *Sundelind Lopez*, ECLI:EU:C:2007:740.

The grounds for determining the jurisdiction are based on the principle of an objective connection between one or both spouses and the state of the forum. Two main criteria for the establishment of such a connection are habitual residence[22] of one or both spouses and common nationality, which should be evaluated at the moment of the commencement of the proceedings. In total, Article 3(1) provides for seven jurisdictional grounds: six grounds based on habitual residence and one on common nationality of the spouses. All seven grounds are of equal value and it is for the claimant to choose which of the available jurisdictions is best to start a marriage dissolution case.[23] As there are several available grounds of jurisdiction, it may result that the courts of more than one Member State will have jurisdiction over the same case. The issue of possible parallel proceedings is dealt with by the *lis pendens* rule established in Article 19(1) of the Brussels II bis Regulation.

In which EU state the divorce case will be started is important for several reasons, such as a more 'comfortable' location for the applicant or a state in which the applicant's mother tongue is spoken, for example. However, it is also important because the establishment of jurisdiction for divorce in a certain state might result in the attraction of the jurisdiction for linked questions. For instance, the general rule on jurisdiction set out in Article 5 of the Matrimonial Property Regulation links jurisdiction in divorce proceedings and jurisdiction in matrimonial property (in some cases, consent of spouses is required to limit the benefits of a rush to court (see Chapter 4 of this volume in this regard)). Moreover, the forum for a divorce case also influences applicable law, especially in the EU Member States where the Rome III Regulation does not apply.[24]

---

[22] On the understanding of habitual residence, see Case C-523/07, *A*, EU:C:2009:225; Case C-497/10, *Mercredi*, EU:C:2010:829; Case C-376/14, *C*, EU:C:2014:2268; Case C-499/15, *W and V*, EU:C:2017:118; Case C-111/17, *OL v PQ*, EU:C:2017:436; Case C-512/17, *HR*, EU:C:2018:513; Case C-393/18, *UD v XB*, EU:C:2018:835. See also T. KRUGER, 'Finding a Habitual Residence' in I. VIARENGO, F.C. VILLATA (eds.), *Planning the Future of Cross Border Families: A Path Through Coordination*, Hart Publishing, Oxford 2020; A. LIMANTE, 'Establishing Habitual Residence of Adults under the Brussels IIa Regulation: Best Practices from National Case-law' (2018) 14(1) *Journal of Private International Law* 160–181; M-Ph. WELLER, B. RENTSCH, '"Habitual Residence": A Plea for "Settled Intention"' in S. LEIBLE (ed.), *General Principles of European Private International Law*, Wolters Kluwer, 2016.

[23] See further C. RICCI, 'Jurisdiction in Matrimonial Matters' in C. HONORATI (ed.), *Jurisdiction in Matrimonial Matters, Parental Responsibility and International Abduction. A Handbook on the Application of Brussels IIa Regulation in National Courts*, Peter Lang, 2017.

[24] As notes Kruger, having possibility to choose jurisdiction means that parties have the option of submitting their divorce petitions to various legal systems, and they select their preferred one either because the court would apply the *lex fori*, or because they know which connecting factors the court would use to determine the applicable law. Th. KRUGER, 'Rome III and Parties' Choice', *Familie & Recht*, January 2014, DOI: 10.5553/FenR/.000013.

3.2. ROME III REGULATION

The Rome III Regulation was the first European private international family law instrument adopted via an enhanced cooperation procedure. Its initial proposal was submitted in 2006, but in 2008, the EU Council noted that unanimity had not been obtained and that insurmountable difficulties precluded unanimity then and also in the foreseeable future. As some of EU Member States were still willing to cooperate on the issue, in July 2010 the Council authorised enhanced cooperation in the area of the law applicable to divorce and legal separation. This resulted in the Rome III regulation being adopted on 20 December 2010. As identified in the Table above, 17 Member States[25] are now participating in the enhanced cooperation.

The scope of the Rome III Regulation is clearly limited – it applies only to the dissolution or loosening of marriage ties. Therefore, the law determined by the conflict-of-laws rules of this regulation applies to the grounds for divorce and legal separation. It does not cover such preliminary questions as legal capacity and the validity of the marriage, and matters such as the effects of divorce or legal separation on property, name, parental responsibility, maintenance obligations or any other ancillary measures (Recital 10 of the Rome III Regulation). Other EU regulations or national laws should be consulted for these questions.

The main connecting factor for establishing applicable law under the Rome III Regulation is the parties' choice. Under Article 5 of the Rome III Regulation, parties drafting an agreement regarding the law applicable to their divorce or legal separation may choose the applicable law from four possible options (three options include the laws of the states with which the parties have a special connection via habitual residence or nationality; the fourth option is the law of the forum). If no choice of law is made, Article 8 provides for a cascade of connecting factors. Be it the law chosen by the parties or the law applicable under Article 8, due to the principle of universal application (Article 4 of the Rome III Regulation), the law of any country in the world, not only those Member States that participate in the Rome III Regulation, might be applicable under the regulation. Application of *lex fori* is only possible where the law established under the regulation does not grant one of the spouses equal access to divorce or legal separation (Article 10 of the Rome III Regulation[26]).

By covering the law applicable to the dissolution or loosening of marriage ties, the Rome III Regulation supplements the Brussels II bis Regulation's rules on jurisdiction. Therefore, these instruments go together in marriage dissolution cases.

---

[25] Austria, Belgium, Bulgaria, Estonia, France, Germany, Greece, Hungary, Italy, Latvia, Lithuania, Luxembourg, Malta, Portugal, Slovenia, Spain and Romania.
[26] On interpretation of Article 10 of the Rome III Regulation see Case C-249/19, *JE v KF*, ECLI:EU:C:2020:570.

In fact, one of the arguments for the adoption of the Rome III Regulation was the need to limit possible forum shopping.[27] As discussed in Section 3.1. of this chapter, Article 3 of the Brussels II bis Regulation provides for numerous alternative grounds of jurisdiction. The applicant thus has the possibility to choose the court according to substantive considerations based on the desired outcome with regard to merit. Combined with the *lis pendens* rule of Article 19 of the Brussels II bis Regulation, which gives priority to the court first seized, the legal framework has provoked a rush to the courts. After the adoption of Rome III Regulation, rushing to court to choose one of the jurisdictions available under Article 3 of the Brussels II bis Regulation gives little advantage with respect to the law applicable to divorce, since the applicable law will be established on the basis of Rome III Regulation in every country participating in the enhanced cooperation.[28]

4. INSTRUMENTS APPLICABLE TO PARENTAL RESPONSIBILITY MATTERS

In addition to matrimonial matters discussed in Section 3 of this chapter, the Brussels II bis Regulation also deals with jurisdiction and judgments with regard to parental responsibility for children. However, similar to divorce cases, the Brussels II bis Regulation only provides for rules concerning jurisdiction, recognition and enforcement of decisions in parental responsibility matters. It contains no rules with regard to the applicable law. Conversely from the area of divorce, the applicable law is regulated not by another EU instrument, but by an international legal instrument – the 1996 Hague Convention on Parental Responsibility and Protection of Children (all EU Member States are the Contracting States). In cases where child abduction is alleged, the 1980 Hague Child Abduction Convention is applied together with the Brussels II bis Regulation.

---

[27] As stated in the Rome III Regulation, this regulation should create a clear, comprehensive legal framework in the area of the law applicable to divorce and legal separation in the participating Member States, provide citizens with appropriate outcomes in terms of legal certainty, predictability and flexibility, and prevent a situation from arising where one of the spouses applies for divorce before the other one does in order to ensure that the proceeding is governed by a given law which he or she considers more favourable to his or her own interests (Recital 9).

[28] S. CORNELOUP, 'Introduction' in S. CORNELOUP (ed), *The Rome III Regulation. A Commentary on the Law Applicable to Divorce and Legal Separation*, Edward Elgar, Cheltenham 2020, p. 8.

Parental responsibility matters			
Private international family law instrument	Issues covered	Temporal scope of application	Geographical scope of application
Brussels II bis Regulation /EU instrument	Jurisdiction Recognition and enforcement Co-operation between central authorities Specific rules on child abduction and access rights	Applicable as of 1 March 2005 (recast version will be applied as of 1 August 2022)	All Member States of the EU, except Denmark
1996 Hague Convention on parental responsibility and protection of children /adopted by the Hague Conference on Private International Law	Applicable law	The EU has authorised the Member States to accede to the Convention in 2002.[29] They ratified the Convention at different moments	All Member States of the EU
1980 Hague Child Abduction Convention /adopted by the Hague Conference on Private International Law	Specific rules on child abduction and access rights	All EU Member States ratified the Convention at different moments	All Member States of the EU

4.1. BRUSSELS II BIS REGULATION

As previously noted, the Brussels II bis Regulation, inter alia, establishes jurisdictional rules in parental responsibility cases. 'Parental responsibility' is defined broadly and includes all rights and duties relating to the person or the property of a child which are given to a natural or legal person by judgment, by operation of law or by an agreement having legal effect.[30]

Under the rules of the Brussels II bis Regulation, the jurisdiction in parental responsibility cases lies with courts of the state of the child's habitual

---

[29] Council Decision 2003/93/EC of 19 December 2002 authorising the Member States, in the interest of the Community, to sign the 1996 Hague Convention on jurisdiction, applicable law, recognition, enforcement and cooperation in respect of parental responsibility and measures for the protection of children [2003] OJ L 48.

[30] Case C-435/06, C, ECLI:EU:C:2007:714. On contents of parental responsibility see also D. DANIELI, 'Parental Responsibility' in I. VIARENGO, F.C. VILLATA, *Planning the Future of Cross Border Families: a path through coordination*, Hart Publishing, Oxford 2020.

residence (Article 8).³¹ Exceptions to this rule are noted in Articles 9, 10,³² 12 and 13 of the Brussels II bis Regulation.

More importantly, as the jurisdiction for divorce and the jurisdiction for parental responsibility are both analysed separately, this could mean that courts of different Member States have jurisdiction pertaining to both matters. Child maintenance (see Section 5.1. below) is, however, in many cases assessed together with the parental responsibilities case as the Maintenance Regulation link such cases.

4.2. 1996 HAGUE CONVENTION ON PARENTAL RESPONSIBILITY AND PROTECTION OF CHILDREN

The 1996 Hague Convention seeks to give international protection to children up to 18 years old. It regulates jurisdiction, applicable law, recognition, enforcement and cooperation with regard to parental responsibility and measures for the protection of children. It can be noted that part of the convention overlaps with the subjects covered by the Brussels II bis Regulation, and therefore, between the EU Member States this regulation takes precedence over the 1996 Hague Convention in intra-EU cases (Article 61 of the Brussels II bis Regulation). The Convention, however, remains applicable on the issues, which the regulation is silent about.

One issue wherein the 1996 Hague Convention supplements the provisions of the Brussels II bis Regulation is with the applicable law. In this regard, under Article 15 of the 1996 Hague Convention, the application of *lex fori* is the general rule, which clearly links the jurisdiction and applicable law.

---

[31] For extensive analysis of jurisdictional rules, see A. LIMANTE, I. KUNDA, 'Jurisdiction in Parental Responsibility Matters' in C. HONORATI (ed.), *Jurisdiction in Matrimonial Matters, Parental Responsibility and International Abduction. A Handbook on the Application of Brussels IIa Regulation in National Courts*, Peter Lang, 2017.

[32] A brief note should be made about Article 10 which concerns jurisdiction in cases of child abduction and which in general provides that any unilateral act of abduction of a child does not affect jurisdiction in parental responsibility cases. Only on very strict conditions, set in Article 10(a) and (b) jurisdiction may be attributed to the courts of the Member State to which the child was abducted. Recently the CJEU has ruled on the effect of this provision with regard to child maintenance, thus revealing cross-linkages between the EU instruments. The CJEU ruled that Article 10 of the Brussels II bis Regulation and Article 3 of the Maintenance Regulation, must be interpreted as meaning that in a case a child who was habitually resident in a Member State was wrongfully removed by one of the parents to another Member State, the courts of that other Member State do not have jurisdiction to rule on an application relating to custody or the determination of a maintenance allowance with respect to that child, in the absence of any indication that the other parent consented to his removal or did not bring an application for the return of that child. Case C-85/18, *CV v DU*, ECLI:EU:C:2018:220.

Establishing jurisdiction for parental responsibilities in a certain state under the Brussels II bis Regulation ultimately means that the law of the same state will be applicable.

4.3. 1980 HAGUE CHILD ABDUCTION CONVENTION

As is clear from its name, the 1980 Hague Convention focuses entirely on parental child abduction. The overall aim of the 1980 Hague Convention on Child Abduction is to restore the status quo by means of the prompt return of wrongfully removed or retained children through a system of cooperation among central authorities appointed by its Contracting Parties.

Similar to the 1996 Hague Convention, the 1980 Hague Convention supplements the Brussels II bis Regulation. The rules of the Brussels II bis Regulation take priority over the rules of the 1980 Hague Convention in relations between the Member States in all matters covered by the regulation (see Article 60 of the Brussels II bis Regulation). However, for questions not covered in the regulation, it refers directly to the 1980 Hague Convention. In particular, the 1980 Hague Convention is applied together with Article 11 of the Brussels II bis Regulation.[33] As parental child abduction will not be discussed in this volume, this instrument will not be analysed further.

5. REGULATION OF PRIVATE INTERNATIONAL LAW ASPECTS OF MAINTENANCE OBLIGATIONS

Similar to the areas discussed above, jurisdiction in maintenance cases and applicable law are regulated in separate instruments. Jurisdictional rules are established in the Maintenance Regulation while the law applicable to maintenance cases is regulated by the 2007 Hague Maintenance Protocol, which was approved by the EU[34] and is directly referred to in Article 15 of the Maintenance Regulation.

In addition, the 2007 Hague Child Support Convention covers certain issues not covered by the Maintenance Regulation. The Maintenance Regulation includes links to this instrument in several cases.

---

[33] On regulation of parental child abduction in the EU see C. HONORATI, A. LIMANTE, 'Jurisdiction in cases of child abduction. Proceedings for the return of the child' in C. HONORATI (ed.), *Jurisdiction in Matrimonial Matters, Parental Responsibility and International Abduction. A Handbook on the Application of Brussels IIa Regulation in National Courts*, Peter Lang, 2017.

[34] 2009/941/EC: Council Decision of 30 November 2009 on the conclusion by the European Community of the Hague Protocol of 23 November 2007 on the Law Applicable to Maintenance Obligations [2009] OJ L 331.

Maintenance obligations			
Private international family law instrument	Issues covered	Temporal scope of application	Geographical scope of application
Maintenance Regulation /EU instrument	Jurisdiction Applicable law (only reference to 2007 Hague Maintenance Protocol) Recognition and enforcement Cooperation	As of 18 June 2011	All Member States of the EU, except Denmark[35]
2007 Hague Child Support Convention /adopted by the Hague Conference on Private International Law	Central authority cooperation Recognition and enforcement	Applied in the EU as of 1 August 2014	All Member States of the EU, except Denmark
2007 Hague Maintenance Protocol /adopted by the Hague Conference on Private International Law	Applicable law	Applied in the EU as of 18 June 2011	All Member States of the EU, except Denmark

5.1. MAINTENANCE REGULATION

The Maintenance Regulation sets out the rules governing the jurisdiction, recognition and enforcement of maintenance orders within the EU Member States. It also includes a chapter regarding the applicable law, although, that chapter solely consists of one article (Article 15) which establishes that the law applicable to maintenance obligations shall be determined in accordance with the 2007 Hague Maintenance Protocol in the Member States bound by that instrument. The Maintenance Regulation covers both child support and spousal support, as well as other maintenance obligations from family relationship, parentage, marriage or affinity (Article 1).

In general, the jurisdictional rules (Article 3) are designed to preserve the interests of the maintenance creditor, who is considered to be a weaker party. Therefore, the regulation foresees a number of different jurisdictional bases for maintenance claims and offers the creditor the possibility to choose the forum from all possible options. For adult maintenance, the possibility to choose the forum is also foreseen; however, it is not an entirely free choice, as,

---

[35] Just part of provisions of the Maintenance Regulation are applied between EU countries and Denmark. See Agreement between the European Community and the Kingdom of Denmark on jurisdiction and the recognition and enforcement of judgments in civil and commercial matters [2009] OJ L 149.

similar to other EU instruments, the regulations list requires connecting factors (Article 4).

The Maintenance Regulation also links maintenance claims to parental responsibility claims. The creditor may choose the court which, according to its own law, has jurisdiction to entertain proceedings concerning the status of a person (for example: establishment of parentage) or parental responsibility where such a maintenance claim is ancillary to proceedings concerning the personal status or parental responsibility (an exception can be made where jurisdiction is based solely on the nationality of one of the parties).[36]

5.2. 2007 HAGUE CHILD SUPPORT CONVENTION

The 2007 Hague Child Support Convention and the Maintenance Regulation were negotiated simultaneously, and the EU sought coherence between both instruments. The 2007 Hague Convention was approved by the EU.[37] It applies to cross-border cases involving an EU Member State and a third-party country which is a Contracting State to the convention. Moreover, it covers certain issues that were not elaborated in the Maintenance Regulation (i.e. free legal aid in all child support cases or extensive duties for Central Authorities). In comparison to the Maintenance Regulation, the material scope of the 2007 Hague Child Support Convention is narrower, as it applies to child and spousal maintenance and only in exceptional cases covers the other forms of maintenance.

5.3. 2007 HAGUE MAINTENANCE PROTOCOL

The law applicable to maintenance cases is regulated by the 2007 Hague Maintenance Protocol[38] which was approved by the EU.[39] Similarly to the Maintenance Regulation, the 2007 Hague Maintenance Protocol has a wide material scope as it applies to maintenance obligations arising from a family relationship, parentage, marriage or affinity, including a maintenance obligation

---

[36] In accordance with Article 3(d) of the Maintenance Regulation, the court which has jurisdiction for parental responsibility will, in principle, also have jurisdiction to hear an application for maintenance which is ancillary to the parental responsibility proceedings pending before it.

[37] Council Decision of 9 June 2011 on the approval, on behalf of the European Union, of the Hague Convention of 23 November 2007 on the International Recovery of Child Support and Other Forms of Family Maintenance [2011] OJ L 192.

[38] Hague Protocol of 23 November 2007 on the Law Applicable to Maintenance Obligations.

[39] Council Decision 2009/941/EC of 30 November 2009 on the conclusion by the European Community of the Hague Protocol of 23 November 2007 on the Law Applicable to Maintenance Obligations [2009] OJ L 331.

in respect to a child regardless of the marital status of the parents (Article 1). The protocol focuses entirely on applicable law issues. The general rule on applicable law provides that maintenance obligations are governed by the law of the state of the habitual residence of the creditor (Article 3). In addition, certain rules favouring the situation of the creditor are also established (Article 4).

The applicable law rules of the 2007 Hague Maintenance Protocol are of universal application. In particular, the protocol applies even if the applicable law is that of a non-contracting state (Article 2).[40]

6. INSTRUMENTS COVERING MATRIMONIAL PROPERTY AND PROPERTY OF REGISTERED PARTNERS

The Matrimonial Property Regulation and its twin Regulation on the Property Consequences of Registered Partnerships are relatively new instruments, as they have been in effect only as of 29 January 2019. They are the most recent puzzle pieces of the EU private international family law. Similarly to the Rome III Regulation, the Twin Regulations were adopted through the enhanced cooperation mechanism and, therefore, apply only in the EU Member States that have joined these instruments.[41]

Matrimonial property and property of registered partners			
Private international family law instrument	Issues covered	Temporal scope of application	Geographical scope of application
Matrimonial Property Regulation /EU instrument	Jurisdiction Applicable law Recognition Enforceability Enforcement Cooperation	Applicable as of 29 January 2019	Enhanced cooperation 18 Member States
Regulation on the Property Consequences of Registered Partnerships /EU instrument	Jurisdiction Applicable law Recognition Enforceability Enforcement Cooperation	Applicable as of 29 January 2019	Enhanced cooperation 18 Member States

---

[40] See further M. ŽUPAN, M. DRVENTIĆ, 'Maintenance' in I. VIARENGO, F.C. VILLATA, *Planning the Future of Cross Border Families: a path through coordination*, Hart Publishing, Oxford 2020.

[41] Austria, Belgium, Bulgaria, Croatia, Cyprus, the Czech Republic, Finland, France, Germany, Greece, Italy, Luxembourg, Malta, the Netherlands, Portugal, Slovenia, Spain and Sweden.

6.1. MATRIMONIAL PROPERTY REGULATION

The Matrimonial Property Regulation together with the Regulation on the Property Consequences of Registered Partnerships, which are extensively discussed in this book were long-awaited building blocks in the EU system of instruments regulating cross-border couples. As the matrimonial property regime is of major relevance in the case of the separation of a couple, there was a clear demand for European rules regarding this issue.

The Matrimonial Property Regulation establishes rules on which a court should have jurisdiction to deal with matrimonial property issues, which law should apply and provides a mechanism for the recognition and enforcement of court judgments throughout the EU. It should be noted, that similar to other EU instruments, the regulation does not define 'marriage'. Recital 21 of the Matrimonial Property Regulation states that this regulation should not apply to other preliminary questions such as the existence, validity or recognition of a marriage, which continue to be covered by the national law of the Member States, including their rules of private international law. The preservation of domestic concepts of 'marriage' is further secured in Article 9 of the Matrimonial Property Regulation which allows the court to decline jurisdiction for matrimonial property if the country of the court does not recognise certain marriages for the purposes of matrimonial property regime proceedings.

The Matrimonial Property Regulation is strongly interlinked with the Brussels II bis Regulation and the Succession Regulation with regard to jurisdictional rules (the Matrimonial Property Regulation seeks to concentrate jurisdiction on the matrimonial property regime in the Member State whose courts are handling the succession of a spouse or the divorce, legal separation or marriage annulment[42]). With regard to the applicable law, the Regulation sets very clear rules that are designed to guarantee clarity and legal predictability.

6.2. REGULATION ON THE PROPERTY CONSEQUENCES OF REGISTERED PARTNERSHIPS

While the Matrimonial Property Regulation aims to clarify the property rights for international married couples, the Regulation on the Property Consequences of Registered Partnerships focuses solely on registered partnerships. However, regarding their content, both regulations are very close. The Regulation on the Property Consequences of Registered Partnerships substantially mirrors its twin Matrimonial Property Regulation. Most of the rules are identical or with some small changes needed due to a different type of relationship. Therefore, in most

---

[42] See Chapter 4 of this volume in this regard.

cases, these two regulations are discussed together in academic literature. The same approach will be taken in this volume, except within the cases where it will be necessary to underline the differences between the two instruments.

7. CASE STUDY: INTERACTION OF THE INSTRUMENTS

As noted earlier, in a cross-border case a set of instruments discussed above might need to be applied. To exemplify this, let us consider the following case study:

> In 2015, Romeo (Italian national) met Julija (Slovenian national) in Verona, Italy, where they were both studying Business Administration. They were married in 2017 in Paris, France and soon moved to live in Spain, where Julija was offered a decent position at a financial institution. Romeo was seeking employment in Spain, but with no success. He later began working online translating documents for an Italian company. In 2019, their son William was born. As Julija went on maternity leave, the couple moved to Brussels to try their luck there. At the time, Romeo went to the office and Julija stayed home with the baby. After a year, Julija was offered a promising post in Slovenia and decided to relocate, taking William with her. She hoped Romeo would join, however, Romeo made it very clear that he was not willing to move and remained in Brussels. In 2021, after more than half a year of living separately, the couple decided to divorce.

In such a situation, a lawyer approached by one of the spouses, or a court having received the claim where a spouse asks to settle the issues of divorce, parental responsibilities, maintenance and matrimonial property, would need to analyse a number of rules on jurisdiction and applicable law. In particular, it would first need to specify which legal instruments would be applicable for establishing the jurisdiction for dissolution of matrimonial ties, parental responsibilities, maintenance and division of matrimonial property. Then, the same exercise would be needed to define the applicable law. The main considerations of such analysis are summarised in the table below:

Possible step-by-step order or analysis	
Is there a cross-border element that would require the use of EU instruments?	Yes, both spouses are of different nationalities; they lived in several countries throughout their marriage.
Legal instrument establishing jurisdictional rules for dissolution of matrimonial ties	Regulation Brussels II bis. It is for the claimant to choose which of the available jurisdictions listed in Article 3(1) of the Brussels II bis Regulation is preferable in order to start a marriage dissolution case.
Legal instrument establishing the applicable law for the dissolution of matrimonial ties	Rome III Regulation. Under Article 5 of the Rome III Regulation, the parties may choose the law applicable to their divorce from four possible options. In the absence of the parties' choice, Article 8 applies.

(continued)

(continued)

Possible step-by-step order or analysis	
Legal instrument establishing jurisdictional rules for parental responsibilities	Brussels II bis Regulation. Article 8 sets the general jurisdictional rule. In addition, Articles 9, 13, 14 may be relevant in more specific cases. Article 12 of the Brussels II bis Regulation also permits (though limited) choice of court. In case of child abduction, Article 10 comes into play and is applied together with the 1980 Hague Child Abduction Convention.
Legal instrument establishing the applicable law for parental responsibilities	1996 Hague Convention. Under Article 15 the application of *lex fori* is the general rule.
Legal instrument establishing jurisdictional rules for maintenance claims (child maintenance and spousal maintenance)	Maintenance Regulation lists possible jurisdictions. In addition, the choice of court is possible for adult maintenance.
Legal instrument establishing the applicable law for maintenance	2007 Hague Maintenance Protocol. Article 3 and Article 4 are relevant.
Legal instrument establishing jurisdictional rules for matrimonial property	Matrimonial Property Regulation. Article 4–6 set the main rules. Article 7 provides for a limited choice of court rules.
Legal instrument establishing the applicable law for matrimonial property	Matrimonial Property Regulation. Article 22 foresees parties' choice as the main connecting factor. If the parties have not selected the applicable law, Article 26 applies.

It should be noted that all the Member States mentioned in the case study (Italy, Slovenia, Belgium and Spain) participate in the enhanced cooperation instruments (the Rome III Regulation and the Matrimonial Property Regulation). Thus, they are bound by all of the mentioned regulations.

Supposing that Julija begins the divorce process in Slovenia, the court would first have to confirm its jurisdiction referring to Article 3(1)(a) ident 6 of the Brussels II bis Regulation (the applicant is habitually resident in Slovenia for at least six months and she is a national of this country). Law applicable to the dissolution of matrimonial ties needs to be established under Article 8 of the Rome III Regulation (if no agreement on the choice of law is made). If the application for divorce is submitted less than a year after Julija returns to Slovenia, Belgian law will most likely be established as the applicable law (Article 8(b)). If the application is submitted later, *lex fori* applies (Article 8(d)).

To establish whether or not it has jurisdiction for parental responsibilities, the court must again consult the Brussels II bis Regulation, and if the court agrees that the couple's son is habitually resident in Slovenia, it will rule that it has jurisdiction under Article 8. The applicable law is *lex fori* as per Article 15 of the 1996 Hague Convention.

The jurisdiction for maintenance needs to be established referring to the Maintenance Regulation. Its Article 3 allows Julija to start the case in either Slovenia (if her and her son's habitual residence is considered to be there) or Belgium (habitual residence of the defendant).[43] The applicable law is Slovenian law under Article 4 of the 2007 Hague Maintenance Protocol (habitual residence of the creditor).

Finally, the Slovenian judge also needs to open the Matrimonial Property Regulation to determine whether or not it has jurisdiction under Article 5 as the jurisdiction to rule on the matrimonial property regime follows jurisdiction for divorce. As for applicable law, under Article 69 of the Matrimonial Property Regulation, rules on applicable law set in this instrument apply only to spouses who marry or specify the law applicable to the matrimonial property regime after 29 January 2019. Therefore, if the spouses have not concluded a choice-of-law agreement after this date, national Slovenian law has to be consulted.

What can be witnessed is that for a very typical divorce case all the EU private international family law instruments may need to be consulted. From one point of view this is a complex set of instruments and its application is a challenging task. This is particularly true if seen from a position of a national judge who, under national law, was used to dealing with divorce as one question (parental responsibilities, maintenance and the matrimonial property being elements of divorce) and applying national laws. Also to be noted, even though many instruments come into play, the set of instruments is the same whether the case is started in Slovenia, Belgium, Italy or Spain. This gives clarity to the parties, as consulting national conflict of law rules, especially for those who are not nationals of that state, is even more complicated.

8. CONCLUDING REMARKS

In 2011, Prof. González Beilfuss noted that if an outside observer were to look at the development of private international law in Europe during the last decade he or she would certainly be amazed at the amount of new EU legislation that has either already been passed or is currently being prepared.[44] She also underlined

---

[43] CJEU has ruled on relationship between divorce, parental responsibilities and child maintenance cases when interpreting Article 3(c) and Article 3(d) of the Maintenance Regulation (ancillary claims) in Case C-184/14, *A v B*, ECLI:EU:C:2015:479 and Case C-468/18, *R v P*, ECLI:EU:C:2019:666.

[44] CH. GONZÁLEZ BEILFUSS, 'The Unification of Private International Law in Europe: A Success Story?' in K. BOELE-WOELKI, J.K. MILES, J.M. SCHERPE (eds.), *The Future of Family Property in Europe*, Intersentia, Cambridge 2011, pp. 329–340.

the speed of development and progress made in the area of unification of family law in Europe.

Ten years later, her observations are equally correct. Indeed, it is fascinating how much was achieved in the area of private international family law. In the year 2000, the Brussels II Regulation started the era of European private international family law, and was revised by the Brussels II bis Regulation in 2003. After that, the Maintenance Regulation, the Rome III Regulation, and, most recently, the Matrimonial Property Regulation and Regulation on the Property Consequences of Registered Partnerships followed. In addition, cross-references were created with the instruments developed by the Hague Conference on Private International Law. Moreover, the Brussels II bis Recast was adopted in 2019 and will be applicable as of August 2022. The landscape of the family law in Europe has changed considerably.

The set of instruments of European private international family law seem to cover all of the major issues that arise to international couples. Nevertheless, as part of the instruments were adopted via enhanced cooperation mechanisms, the level of unification is not the same across Europe. The revision of the existing instruments or adoption of new ones might also be expected in the future as family law in Europe is developing faster than ever before.

THE TWIN REGULATIONS

Development and Adoption

Eglė Kavoliūnaitė-Ragauskienė[*]

1. Introduction 25
2. A Need for the EU Legislative Intervention 26
3. Harmonisation of Couples' Property Regimes in a Historical Perspective ... 30
4. Procedure of Adoption of the Twin Regulations 32
5. Concluding Remarks 37

1. INTRODUCTION

Even though for a long time, the EU did not adopt any rules in the field of family law, in the twenty-first century, a whole set of the EU private international family law instruments was developed.[1] While some of them were prepared and adopted comparatively smoothly, the field of cross-border family property regimes appeared to be a challenge. Nevertheless, as property effects of marriage and registered partnerships were excluded from the existing rules of the EU legislation, such as Brussels I Regulation (Article 1(2)(a)), Rome I Regulation (Article 1(2)(c)), Rome II Regulation (Article 1(2)(b)) and Rome III Regulation (Article 1(2)(e)), a respective regulation of property regimes was necessary. This necessity was accentuated in several programmes and framework documents as well as noted by academia.

Reacting to this, after long and intensive work, in 2016 the Matrimonial Property Regulation and the Regulation on the Property Consequences of Registered Partnerships (the Twin Regulations) were adopted. As significant discrepancies exist among the EU Member States on the legal recognition of couples' status, as well as different regimes applicable to matrimonial and partnership property, even setting aside the substantial provisions of family law,

---

[*] Eglė Kavoliūnaitė-Ragauskienė, PhD, is a Researcher at the Law Institute of the Lithuanian Centre for Social Sciences.
[1] See Chapter 1 of this volume in this regard.

it was challenging to harmonise the jurisdiction, applicable law and recognition, enforceability and enforcement of decisions in this field. As a result, only a partial agreement in the EU could be reached in the form of enhanced cooperation, meaning that not all the Member States, but only the ones wishing so, are bound by these instruments, and only some cross-border couples are thus able to invoke the rules set therein.

Similarly to other EU private international law instruments, the Twin Regulations do not harmonise or change any substantive national laws on marriage or registered partnership. They aim only to establish clear rules in cases of divorce or separation and bring an end to parallel and possibly conflicting proceedings in the various Member States.[2] The regulations either provide for default rules or enable cross-border couples to choose courts of a particular Member State to rule on their matrimonial (partnership) property or the law that applies to their property in case of divorce, separation or dissolution of a registered partnership. For registered partnerships with an international dimension, the EU rules enhance legal certainty as they take into account the different approaches in the Member States regarding this type of family formation. In general, the Twin Regulations bring clarity for international couples by setting coherent rules for identifying which country's court is competent and which law will apply and by increasing the predictability for couples by smoothing out the process for recognising judgments, decisions and titles throughout the EU.

This chapter overviews the road towards the adoption of the Twin Regulations. It first discusses the arguments supporting the need for regulation in the area of matrimonial and registered partnership property. It then presents the history of attempts to harmonise regulation for at least some aspects regulating matrimonial property. Finally, the chapter outlines the drafting procedure and the adoption of the Twin Regulations.

2. A NEED FOR THE EU LEGISLATIVE INTERVENTION

For an appreciable time, the EU considered family-related legal issues to be the responsibility of individual Member States. However, employing the possibilities granted by the Schengen area, people started moving from one state to another more actively, working in other countries and starting a life together with citizens of another state whom later they decide to marry or associate their daily life with.[3]

---

[2] L. VALENTOVÁ, 'Property Regimes of Spouses and Partners in New EU Regulations – Jurisdiction, Prorogation and Choice of Law' (2016) 16(2) *ICLR* 222.

[3] A.P. PÉREZ and M.C.J. GONZÁLEZ, 'Matrimonial property regimes in the absence of choice by the spouses under Regulation (EU) 2016/1103' in M.J.C. GONZÁLEZ, M. GIOBBI, J.K. ŠKERL, L. RUGGERI, S. WINKLER (eds.), *Property relations of cross border couples in the European Union*, Edizioni Scientifiche Italiane 2020, p. 29.

As the number of cross-border couples increased, the need for EU action eventually became clear. In this way, during the last 20 years, several EU private international family law instruments were adopted.

The adoption of the Twin Regulations was not a case of the legislation intrinsically stemming from the primary EU ideology and documents. It was a practical solution motivated merely by the need to fix the outcome brought by increased mobility of persons and enjoyment of free movement rights in the EU area.

According to the European Policy Evaluation Consortium (EPEC) study,[4] outlining different options to harmonise matrimonial and partnership related property regimes in the EU, already in 2007, approximately 122 million marriages existed in the EU. Of these, just over 20 million have been estimated to have at least one kind of 'international element' regarding their matrimonial property: around 16 million (13 per cent) were assumed to be international; 3.5 million married couples were assumed to be living abroad (in a country other than the one of their nationality); around 1 million married couples were assumed to have property abroad (in a country other than that of their habitual residence). Simultaneously, there were approximately 211,000 registered partnerships in the EU. Of these, just over 41,000 were estimated to have some kind of 'international element' regarding their patrimonial property: around 36,000 registered partnerships were assumed to be 'international' (i.e. involve partners from different countries), around 2,800 registered partnerships were assumed to be living abroad and around 2,500 registered partnerships were assumed to have property abroad. It was identified that many problems were experienced by cross-border married couples, *de facto* unions and partnerships.

Cross-border couples face many challenges when breaking up. In addition to typical psychological stress, they also have to deal with the legal issues related to the fact that more than one state might have jurisdiction to deal with their case, and the law of more than one state might apply. While many questions were answered by the Regulation Brussels II a, Rome II and other EU instruments, the questions of matrimonial property regimes remained unharmonised.

One of the 'classical' problems faced by cross-border couples in Europe arises from the fact that the recognition of the legal status of couples in the EU and the legal regulation linked to their family ties is very diverse. Taking an example of a same-sex relationship, in 2015, at the time of initiative for the Twin Regulations, a marriage of same-sex persons was recognised in 10 EU Member States,[5]

---

[4] EUROPEAN POLICY EVALUATION CONSORTIUM (EPEC). Impact Assessment Study on Community Instruments concerning matrimonial property regimes and property of unmarried couples with transnational elements. 2010, pp. 7–13. <https://op.europa.eu/en/publication-detail/-/publication/48820a62-4950-4ebb-a20c-d5bc9f35bd84>.

[5] Belgium, Denmark, Finland, France, Luxembourg, the Netherlands, Portugal, Spain, Sweden and the United Kingdom.

and partnership of same-sex persons was open in 17 Member States,[6] as well as in several autonomous communities in Spain. Naturally, the consequences of registered partnership differ significantly among the EU countries, even those recognising such types of family formation. It should be noted that the initiatives of registered partnership in the EU Member States have emerged in response to a specific need for legal recognition for same-sex couples.[7] Thus some states were (and still are) too conservative to allow registration of partnerships. Although the countries' legislative situation has changed since 2015, still, for example, six Member States[8] have not yet adopted the registered partnership model in their legislation and do not allow same-sex couples to marry or register a partnership. This means that regarding property consequences of same-sex couples in those countries, no legal regime exists at all. Moreover, in some countries[9] registration of the partnership is reserved exclusively for same-sex partners.

Many examples can be given on the divergence of rules in recognising different family formations. In Croatia, Slovenia and Hungary, the rules on the property consequences of registered partnerships are broadly in line with those laid down for marital regimes. There is a community of property unless the parties agree otherwise. In the Czech Republic, the registered partnership is only partially regulated as marriage. As far as the property consequences are concerned, unlike marriage, there is no community of property, and the parties can at most acquire assets in co-ownership. In Italy, the discipline of registered partnerships mirrors the marital one, despite some differences: for example, there is no obligation of mutual fidelity. Speaking about property consequences, the parties are subject to the community regime, as is the case in marriage, unless the parties opt for separation, the contractual community and/or the property fund.[10] The third group of the Member States allow registered partnership of same-sex couples but different rules than for the property consequences of marriage apply. For example, in Belgium and France, the effects of registered partnerships, although similar to marriage, do not entail personal obligations between the parties, which may be of the same or opposite sex. Unlike marriage, the parties to the registered partnership are subject to a

---

[6] Austria, Belgium, Croatia, the Czech Republic, Denmark, Estonia, Finland, France, Germany, Hungary, Ireland, Luxembourg, Malta, the Netherlands, Slovenia, Sweden and the United Kingdom.

[7] J.M. SCHERPE, 'The Past, Present and Future of Registered Partnerships' in J.M. SCHERPE and A. HAYWARD (eds.), *The Future of Registered Partnerships. Family Recognition Beyond Marriage?*, Intersentia, Cambridge 2017, p. 570.

[8] Bulgaria, Latvia, Lithuania, Poland, Romania and Slovakia.

[9] Croatia, the Czech Republic, Hungary, Italy and Slovenia.

[10] R. GARETTO, M. GIOBBI, F.G. VITERBO, L. RUGGERI, 'Registered partnerships and property consequences' in M.J.C. GONZÁLEZ, M. GIOBBI, J.K. ŠKERL, L. RUGGERI, S. WINKLER (eds.), *Property relations of cross border couples in the European Union*, Edizioni Scientifiche Italiane, 2020 p. 89.

system of separation of property unless they agree otherwise. In Cyprus, Greece, Luxembourg, Malta, the Netherlands and Estonia, the property regime of registered partnerships is similar to the marriage regime. In five Member States (Denmark, Finland, Germany, Ireland and Sweden), where same-sex couples are now granted the right to marry, partners in previously registered partnerships were given the option to convert the previous partnership into a marriage.[11]

Though EU instruments are not to unify the different approaches of the EU Member States to marriages or partnerships, nevertheless, the EU-wide conflict of law rules can assist in overcoming at least some legal uncertainties faced by cross-border couples due to such a variety of national laws. Therefore, it was expected that EU regulations in matrimonial and partnership property would be of particular benefit to couples by bringing more legal certainty (e.g. by establishing connecting factors that would not leave a cross-border couple in a legal vacuum situation).

Even leaving aside different union regimes in the Member States, differences of the Member States' property consequences of marriage and partnership bring a plethora of inconveniences and frustration to couples with a cross-border element, especially in relation to termination of the matrimonial or partnership related property regime. For those entering into a marriage or a registered partnership, the problem may be one of lack of awareness that legal complications might arise in the future when managing the common estate and lack of understanding of the possible options of legally arranging the family property to minimise the legal uncertainty. For those in cross-border marriages or partnerships who are divorcing or separating, many questions arise due to a variety of national laws and the possibility that several of them might be applicable to their situation. The differences in legislation might lead to parallel proceedings; dealing with the assets and their division may be overly complex. Even when the legal solution is reached, without common EU rules, decisions made by a court in one Member State may not be accepted in another. Finally, the surviving spouse/partner might become engaged in complicated court proceedings when matrimonial or partnership related property regimes are dissolved due to the death of a spouse or a partner.[12]

---

[11] In Sweden, registered partnerships are no longer allowed since 2009, in Denmark – since 2012, in Ireland – since 2015, in Finland and Germany – since 2017. On those dates couples in partnership were given the opportunity to convert their civil union into marriage, following the reform of the rules on marriage. In case they failed to do so, the registered partnership in any case remained valid and the respective property regime was continued being applied. R. GARETTO, M. GIOBBI, F.G. VITERBO, L. RUGGERI, 'Registered partnerships and property consequences' in M.J.C. GONZÁLEZ, M. GIOBBI, J.K. ŠKERL, L. RUGGERI, S. WINKLER (eds.), *Property relations of cross border couples in the European Union*, Edizioni Scientifiche Italiane 2020, pp. 88–90.

[12] EUROPEAN POLICY EVALUATION CONSORTIUM (EPEC), Impact Assessment Study on Community Instruments concerning matrimonial property regimes and property of unmarried couples with transnational elements. 2010, pp. 7–13. <https://op.europa.eu/en/publication-detail/-/publication/48820a62-4950-4ebb-a20c-d5bc9f35bd84>.

3. HARMONISATION OF COUPLES' PROPERTY REGIMES IN A HISTORICAL PERSPECTIVE

The first international legal documents to address matrimonial property issues were the 1905 Hague Convention relating to conflict of laws with regard to the effects of marriage on the rights and duties of the spouses in their personal relationship and with regard to their estates and the 1978 Hague Convention on the Law Applicable to Matrimonial Property Regimes. The 1905 Hague Convention dealt only with the law applicable to the personal relations and property of the spouses. The parties to this Convention were Germany, Belgium, France, Italy, the Netherlands, Poland and the free city of Gdansk, Portugal, Romania and Sweden. The Convention went into effect in all states by the end of February 1915, and then all the Contracting States stepped out of the treaty by August 1987. The 1978 Convention also dealt exclusively with the law applicable to matrimonial property regimes and was based on the universality principle. However, although the universality principle seemed promising for the creation of international cooperation and understanding, only a few states became Contracting States.[13] In essence, this Convention was in force only in France, Luxemburg and the Netherlands and thus lacked any significant international effect.

The initial idea of the Twin Regulations emerged from the 1998 Vienna Action Plan[14] and its priority – the adaptation of rules on matrimonial property regimes in need to address problems derived from the co-existence of different laws and jurisdictions. A year later, in 1999, the European Council meeting in Tampere endorsed the principle of mutual recognition of judgments and other decisions of judicial authorities as the cornerstone of judicial cooperation in civil matters.[15] It also invited the Council and the Commission to adopt a programme of measures to implement that principle.

A programme for implementation of the principle of mutual recognition of decisions in civil and commercial matters, common to the Commission and to the Council, was drafted in 2000.[16] The programme clearly identified

---

[13] L. VALENTOVÁ, 'Property Regimes of Spouses and Partners in New EU Regulations – Jurisdiction, Prorogation and Choice of Law' (2016) 16(2) *ICLR* 223.

[14] EUROPEAN COUNCIL, EUROPEAN COMMISSION, Action plan of the Council and the Commission on how best to implement the provisions of the Treaty of Amsterdam on an area of freedom, security and justice (OJ 1999, C 19, p. 1).

[15] EUROPEAN COUNCIL, Presidency Conclusions. 15–16 October 1999, Tampere. Draft programme of measures for implementation of the principle of mutual recognition of decisions in civil and commercial matters (OJ 2001, C 12, p. 1).

[16] EUROPEAN COUNCIL, Presidency Conclusions. 15–16 October 1999, Tampere. Draft programme of measures for implementation of the principle of mutual recognition of decisions in civil and commercial matters (OJ 2001, C 12, p. 1).

the exclusion of important sectors of private law from the scope of European regulations as one of the major obstacles to the creation of a European legal area, characterised by the mutual recognition of civil and commercial judgements. Together it identified measures relating to the harmonisation of conflict of laws rules as measures facilitating the mutual recognition of decisions and provided main principles for the drafting of instruments relating to wills and succession, to matrimonial property regimes and to the property consequences of the separation of unmarried couples.

A few years later, the European Council taking place in Brussels in November 2004 adopted a new programme – The Hague Programme: Strengthening Freedom, Security and Justice in the European Union.[17] The programme invited the Commission to present a Green Paper on the conflict of laws in matters concerning couples' property regimes, including the question of jurisdiction and mutual recognition, and stressed the need to adopt an instrument in this latter area. In 2006, through the publication of the Green Paper,[18] the Commission launched broad consultations on all aspects of the difficulties faced by couples in Europe regarding the liquidation of their common property and the legal remedies available. The Green Paper also addressed all issues of private international law encountered by couples in unions other than marriages, including couples with registered partnerships, and issues specific to them.

These previous actions were followed by The Stockholm Programme – An Open and Secure Europe Serving and Protecting Citizens.[19] In it, the European Council reaffirmed the priority of developing an area of freedom, security and justice and specified as a political priority the achievement of a Europe of law and justice, including in civil matters. The Stockholm Programme considered that mutual recognition should be extended to fields not yet covered but essential to everyday life, for example, succession and wills, matrimonial property rights and the property consequences of the separation of couples. It also underlined the need of taking into consideration Member States' legal systems, including public policy (*ordre public*) and national traditions in this area. Within the context of the Stockholm Programme, the European Council invited the Commission to assess whether there were grounds for consolidation and simplification to improve the consistency of existing Union legislation in

---

[17] EUROPEAN COUNCIL and EUROPEAN COMMISSION, Action Plan implementing the Hague Programme on strengthening freedom, security and justice in the European Union (OJ 2005, C 198, p. 1).

[18] COMMISSION OF THE EUROPEAN COMMUNITIES Green Paper on conflict of laws in matters concerning matrimonial property regimes, including the question of jurisdiction and mutual recognition [SEC(2006) 952], COM/2006/0400 final.

[19] EUROPEAN COUNCIL, The Stockholm Programme – An open and secure Europe serving and protecting citizens (OJ 2010, C 115, p. 1).

those areas of law.[20] EU Citizenship Report 2010: Dismantling the Obstacles to EU Citizens' Rights[21] delivered by the European Parliament further stressed the need for regulation. The request expressed by the European Council and the European Parliament led to the elaboration of different proposals by the Commission, including the Proposal for a Council Regulation on jurisdiction, applicable law and the recognition and enforcement of decisions in matters of matrimonial property regimes,[22] and the Proposal for a Council Regulation on jurisdiction, applicable law and the recognition and enforcement of decisions regarding the property consequences of registered partnerships[23] (Proposals for Twin Regulations). These two documents later resulted in the adoption of the current legal instruments that apply to matrimonial and registered partnerships property regimes, both having cross-border implications.[24]

4. PROCEDURE OF ADOPTION OF THE TWIN REGULATIONS

The codification process of European private international law is often described as 'creeping codification'. It involves the technique of adoption of a plurality of regulations on well-defined and limited issues, rather than a single source applicable to the whole field.[25] In this context, the Twin Regulations on matrimonial and partnership related property was meant to join a growing number of EU private international law instruments in international family law concerning divorce and legal separation (Brussels II a Regulation, Rome III Regulation), parental responsibilities (Brussels II bis Regulation), maintenance (Maintenance Regulation), and successions and wills (Succession Regulation).[26]

When drafting the Twin Regulations, the European institutions had in mind the unsatisfactory experience of the above-mentioned 1978 Hague Convention

---

[20] EUROPEAN COMMISSION, EU Citizenship Report 2010: Dismantling the obstacles to EU citizens' rights. [COM(2010) 603 final].

[21] EUROPEAN PARLIAMENT, Report on the EU Citizenship Report 2010: Dismantling the obstacles to EU citizens' rights (2011/2182(INI)).

[22] EUROPEAN COMMISSION, Proposal for a Council Regulation on jurisdiction, applicable law and the recognition and enforcement of decisions in matters of matrimonial property regimes. [COM(2011) 126 final].

[23] EUROPEAN COMMISSION, Proposal for a Council Regulation on jurisdiction, applicable law and the recognition and enforcement of decisions regarding the property consequences of registered partnerships. [COM(2011) 127 final].

[24] J.I.S De Mesa, 'Introduction' in M.J.C. González, M. Giobbi, J.K. Škerl, L. Ruggeri, S. Winkler (eds.), *Property relations of cross border couples in the European Union*, Edizioni Scientifiche Italiane 2020, pp. 6–8.

[25] M. Czepelak, 'Would We Like to Have a European Code of Private International Law?' (2010) 18 *European Review of Private Law* 705–728.

[26] See Chapter 1 of this volume on the interaction of those instruments.

on the applicable law to marital property regimes – even though the instrument seemed promising, it was ratified by very few states and only entered into force in 1992. The sensitive area of regulation was probably the main reason for the failure of this international convention. The EU institutions also had to take into account the restrictions in EU legislative powers on substantive issues of family matters which resulted in the fact that the aim of new legislative initiatives could not be the harmonisation of the rules of substantive law on family property. Moreover, the legal traditions and regulation of family law were very different in the EU Member States, which required compromise on all issues.

As a result, drafting the Twin Regulations was not a trivial undertaking. As Garetto, Giobi et al. put it:

> The path of the European Union in this area is marked by obstacles, forks and compromises caused by multiple factors: the failure to draft a European Constitutional Treaty, the progressive emergence of sovereign forces, the Brexit, the extreme fragmentation of domestic regulations in central issues such as the recognition of cohabitation, the conditions required by each individual State to consider a given cohabitation legally relevant, the provision of specific property regimes for couples, the identification of the rights in rem covered by these rules, the relationships within the couple and between the couple and third parties who are creditors of one or both partners.[27]

However, the EU was determined to regulate the cross-border aspects of matrimonial property and property of registered partnerships. More than ten years after the 1998 Vienna Action Plan, in March 2011, the Commission adopted Proposals for Twin Regulations.

Despite that, optimistic hopes to finally have the instruments passed failed. After considerations in the Parliament and having received its opinion, in 2015, the Council concluded that no unanimity could be reached for the adoption of the proposals for regulations on matrimonial property regimes and the property consequences of registered partnerships. It highlighted that in the situation as it was, the objectives of cooperation in this area could not be attained within a reasonable period by the EU as a whole.

The need for common rules, however, remained. Besides the previously mentioned 1905 Hague Convention relating to conflict of laws with regard to the effects of marriage on the rights and duties of the spouses in their personal relationship and with regard to their estates and the 1978 Hague Convention on the Law Applicable to Matrimonial Property Regimes, no international

---

[27] R. Garetto, M. Giobbi, F.G. Viterbo, L. Ruggeri, 'Registered partnerships and property consequences' in M.J.C. González, M. Giobbi, J.K. Škerl, L. Ruggeri, S. Winkler (eds.), *Property relations of cross border couples in the European Union*, Edizioni Scientifiche Italiane 2020, p. 43.

agreements were applicable to the property consequences of marriage. In the case of registered partnerships, the Convention on the Recognition of Registered Partnerships of 5 September 2007 of the International Commission on Civil Status applied. However, this Convention covered only the recognition of partnerships, and had not entered into force, so it was not likely to offer the solutions needed given the magnitude of the problems addressed by the drafts of the Twin Regulations. Therefore, it was evident for the Commission that, given the nature and the scale of the problems experienced by European citizens in the fields of matrimonial and registered partnerships property regimes, the objectives to be fulfilled by the Twin Regulations could only be achieved at the EU level. Furthermore, it was repeatedly underlined that the need for legal certainty and predictability called for clear and uniform rules and imposed the form of regulation. In fact, the objectives would have been compromised if the Member States had some discretion in implementing these rules.

As it was clear that the regulation of substantial law relating to the status of couples' and their property regimes throughout the EU was vastly different, and some Member States which did not recognise same-sex marriages and/or registered partnerships were worried that if they agreed with the initiative, they would be obliged to recognise such unions. This did not allow the unanimity to proceed with the initiative. Therefore, there was no other choice but to apply an enhanced cooperation model to adopt the Twin Regulations. Enhanced cooperation is open to all Member States, subject to compliance with any conditions of participation laid down by the authorising decision. It is also open to them at any other time, subject to compliance with the acts already adopted within that framework, in addition to those conditions.

In June 2016, after many delays and obstacles, the Twin Regulations were finally adopted via enhanced cooperation procedure. At present, the Twin Regulations are binding in their entirety and directly applicable only in the Member States participating in the enhanced cooperation defined by virtue of Decision (EU) 2016/954,[28] i.e. Belgium, Bulgaria, Cyprus, the Czech Republic, Germany, Greece, Spain, France, Croatia, Italy, Luxembourg, Malta, the Netherlands, Austria, Portugal, Slovenia, Finland and Sweden.

However, even with the enhanced cooperation, we can note that the adoption of the Twin Regulations required a compromise. The Matrimonial Property Regulation does not define the concept of 'marriage', which is left to be defined by the national laws of the Member States. By contrast, the Regulation on the Property Consequences of Registered Partnerships establishes a

---

[28] EUROPEAN COUNCIL, Decision (EU) 2016/954 of 9 June 2016 authorizing enhanced cooperation in the area of jurisdiction, applicable law and the recognition and enforcement of decisions on the property regimes of international couples, covering both matters of matrimonial property regimes and the property consequences of registered partnerships (OJ 2016, L 159, p. 16).

concept of 'registered partnership', which is defined solely for the purposes of the regulation. The actual substance of the concept remains defined in the national laws of the Member States. Nothing in the Regulation on the Property Consequences of Registered Partnerships obliges a Member State whose law does not have the institution of registered partnership to provide for it in its national law. This approach reveals the solid commitment of the EU to respect national systems of family law. However, given that the way in which forms of union other than marriage are provided for in the Member States' legislation differs from one state to another, the Regulation on the Property Consequences of Registered Partnerships draws a distinction between couples whose union is institutionally sanctioned and couples in *de facto* cohabitation. The Regulation on the Property Consequences of Registered Partnerships only considers registered partnerships that have an official character for the purposes of the rules it provides.[29]

As the EU lacks the competence to interfere in substantive law, in the field of family law, the EU efforts have been directed towards the creation of a uniform framework of conflict of law rules aimed at resolving those family issues that have cross-border implications.[30] Therefore, the Twin Regulations provide for enhanced cooperation on three basic issues: (i) determination of the competent court; (ii) determination of the applicable law; and (iii) recognition and enforcement of judgments in property regimes. It should be noted that the Twin Regulations repeatedly stress the need for predictability and legal certainty. It is important for the spouses and partners to know which court will have jurisdiction over their property relations and which law will be applicable to them. In this respect, the regulations also give a wide margin to the autonomy of the will in making this choice.[31]

The Twin Regulations do not change the rules of each Member State but instead help to determine the jurisdiction and law applicable to the matrimonial property regime for spouses who have entered into marriage on or after 29 January 2019 and have decided to choose the applicable law under Article 22.

---

[29] J.I.S DE MESA, 'Introduction' in M.J.C. GONZÁLEZ, M. GIOBBI, J.K. ŠKERL, L. RUGGERI, S. WINKLER (eds.), *Property relations of cross border couples in the European Union*, Edizioni Scientifiche Italiane 2020, pp. 9–10.

[30] A.M.P. VALLEJO, 'Matrimonial property regimes with cross-border implications: Regulation (EU) 2016/1103' in M.J.C. GONZÁLEZ, M. GIOBBI, J.K. ŠKERL, L. RUGGERI, S. WINKLER (eds), *Property relations of cross border couples in the European Union*, Edizioni Scientifiche Italiane 2020, p. 15.; M.J.C. GONZALEZ, 'Ley aplicable al régimen económico matrimonial después de la disolución del matrimonio tras la entrada en vigor del Reglamento UE 2016/1104' (2019) 21 International Journal of Doctrine and Jurisprudence 87–104.

[31] A.M.P. VALLEJO, 'Matrimonial property regimes with cross-border implications: Regulation (EU) 2016/1103' in M.J.C. GONZÁLEZ, M. GIOBBI, J.K. ŠKERL, L. RUGGERI, S. WINKLER (eds.), *Property relations of cross border couples in the European Union*, Edizioni Scientifiche Italiane 2020, p. 15.

In other words, the application of the Regulations results in a shift in the national rules on the resolution of 'international' or 'cross-border' disputes, as far as their material and temporal scope of application is concerned.[32] The proper functioning of a common area of justice, which respects the different legal systems and traditions of the Member States, is one of the aims of the European Union. Hereby the Regulations, continuing the tradition of preceding legal instruments, constitute further progress towards the unification of private international family law in Europe.

The adoption of the Twin Regulations was warmly welcomed at the EU political level. However, a big concern was raised that a significant number of couples are still left outside the scope of application of the Twin Regulations. The 18 Member States that joined the enhanced cooperation make up 70 per cent of the EU population and represent the majority of international couples who live in the EU.[33] The non-participating Member States continue applying their respective national laws (including their rules on private international law) to cross-border situations relating to matrimonial property regimes and the property consequences of registered partnerships. On this, the First Vice-President of the European Commission Frans Timmermans remarked:

> This is about giving certainty to thousands of European couples – whether married or in registered partnerships – about what happens to them and their families if their dream of a life together does not work out. I wish we had been able to take this forward with all Member States as the Commission had proposed, but today's proposals mean we can help at least some of the people concerned to manage at the most difficult times.

Similarly, Vera Jourová, the EU Justice Commissioner, observed that:

> In case of divorce or death of a partner, the lives of 16 million international couples can become even more difficult through burdensome administrative procedures and unclear legal situations: what will happen to my house if I divorce and my spouse is of a different nationality? Which court do I turn to? The new proposed rules will bring legal clarity and ease the complicated process of dividing up joint assets no matter where they are located. This will facilitate the lives of the couples concerned and help them save around €400 million a year of extra costs. Today we pave the way for those Member States willing to go forward with this important initiative.[34]

---

[32] P.C.G De Parada, 'Nuevos reglamentos europeos sobre regímenes matrimoniales y sobre efectos patrimoniales de las uniones registradas' (2018) 78 (XXI) *El Notario del Siglo*.

[33] EUROPEAN COMMISSION, Property regimes for international couples in Europe: new rules apply in 18 Member States as of today. <https://ec.europa.eu/commission/presscorner/detail/en/IP_19_681>.

[34] EUROPEAN COMMISSION, Commission goes ahead with 17 Member States to clarify the rules applicable to property regimes for Europe's international couples. <https://ec.europa.eu/commission/presscorner/detail/en/IP_16_449>.

Indeed, it is a big challenge, at least to some extent, to unify the European provisions striving for a more synergistic regulatory approach to property regimes. Unification and simplification of rules in the field of property consequences of registered partnerships, as discussed above, is an even more challenging goal.

5. CONCLUDING REMARKS

Free movement of people, ability to work in any EU country is both an opportunity and a challenge for EU citizens and couples. It might look paradoxically, however, the greater extent of personal liberties lead to the need for more extensive regulation as the new lifestyles do not fit the existing legal frameworks. The national legislation regulating family matters is insufficient, especially when it comes to conflict situations or termination of a relationship. Therefore, certain conflict of law rules which would govern the application of national substantial rules is necessary, and the adoption of the EU instruments was needed.

Although, theoretically, it seems not so difficult to draw a line between substantial and procedural family law rules, the issue of family property regime brings many challenges. First, taking into account that there are 27 different national attitudes on the marital property division, this issue was difficult not only from the creation of the rules perspective but even more so from the adoption process. The situation is even more complicated when the property that is supposed to be divided belongs to the registered partners.[35] Second, it is difficult to separate purely procedural rules from the material (substantial) family law rules, as in this regard, they are very interdependent. Procedural rules depend as well on the legal status of a couple, e.g. in case a country does not recognise a registered partnership, the applicability of the Regulation on the Property Consequences of Registered Partnerships becomes impossible.

The fact that the process of adoption of the Twin Regulations took more than 10 years, and these Regulations are applicable only in respect of some couples in the EU, might look not too promising. However, this step should be perceived as an achievement and a step forward, especially considering the former unsuccessful efforts to harmonise the related international procedural rules. More and more EU Member States adopt liberal regimes on couples' legal status and, taking into account that any Member State might join the framework of the Twin Regulations, this implies that further developments and broadening of the scope of application might be expected.

---

[35] L. VALENTOVÁ, 'Property Regimes of Spouses and Partners in New EU Regulations – Jurisdiction, Prorogation and Choice of Law' (2016) 16(2) *ICLR* 222.

PART II
ANATOMY OF THE TWIN REGULATIONS

MAIN CONCEPTS AND SCOPE OF APPLICATION OF THE TWIN REGULATIONS

María José Cazorla González and Mercedes Soto Moya[*]

1. Introduction 41
2. Defining the Main Concepts 42
3. Scope of Application of the Twin Regulations 48
   3.1. Material Scope of Application of the Twin Regulations 48
       3.1.1. Matters Falling under the Scope of Application of the Twin Regulations. 50
       3.1.2. Matters Excluded from the Application of the Twin Regulations. 51
   3.2. Personal Scope of Application of the Twin Regulations 53
   3.3. Temporal Scope of Application of the Twin Regulations 61
       3.3.1. Temporal Scope of Application of the Jurisdictional Provisions. 62
       3.3.2. Temporal Scope of Provisions on Recognition and Enforcement. 64
       3.3.3. Temporal Application of the Provisions on Applicable Law 64
   3.4. Territorial Scope of the Twin Regulations 66
4. Concluding Remarks 70

1. INTRODUCTION

The European Union has set itself the objective of maintaining and developing an area of freedom, security and justice in which the free movement of persons is ensured, in accordance with Article 81(2) of the Treaty on the Functioning of the EU (TFEU). In this regard, the Twin Regulations which are in a broader sense located within the framework of international cooperation regarding civil

---

[*] María José Cazorla González, Full Professor of civil law at the University of Almería, Spain. Mercedes Soto Moya, PhD, Full Professor of private international law at the University of Granada, Spain. María José Cazorla González is the author of Sections 1, 2, 3.1, 3.3, 3.4 and 4 and Mercedes Soto Moya is the author of Sections 2, 3.2 and 4 of this chapter.

matters with cross-border implications, constitute an important step towards the unification of private international family law.

As discussed in Chapter 2, the way towards the Twin Regulations was not easy and to have them adopted it was necessary to resort to the enhanced cooperation mechanism. The mechanism of enhanced cooperation is regulated in Article 20 of the Treaty on European Union (TEU) and Articles 326 et seq. of the TFEU; it requires the cooperation of a minimum of nine EU Member States.[1]

This chapter focuses on the main concepts and the scope of application of the Twin Regulations. In particular, it analyses the main concepts of the Regulations, such as 'marriage' 'registered partnership', 'matrimonial property regime', 'property consequences of a registered partnership', 'matrimonial property agreement' and 'partnership property agreement. It then discusses the material, personal, temporal and territorial scope of the Twin Regulations. A clear understanding as to in what cases, to whom and when the Regulations apply is essential for the proper interpretation and application of these instruments.

2. DEFINING THE MAIN CONCEPTS

The harmonisation and unification of family law in Europe is very complicated.[2] The reason for this can be found in the fact that each country has its own national regulations concerning the family, including its recognition, the property effects of the marriage (registered partnership), the procedures and causes for termination or dissolution of the relationship, and the rights of related third parties.

To be able to establish common rules, therefore, unification of some legal terms and their consistent usage on the European level is necessary. The Twin Regulations both contain Article 3, determining the main definitions of the relevant terms. As is common for other European terminologies, all of the terms have to be interpreted autonomously (separately from national understandings) when applied in practice.[3]

In part, the definitions are the same in both regulations (i.e. 'decision', 'authentic instrument', 'court settlement',[4] 'Member State of origin' and 'Member

---

[1] This procedure is designed to overcome paralysis, when a proposal is blocked by a single country or by a small group of countries that do not wish to participate in the initiative, thus creating a Europe of 'variable geometry'. Despite this, one cannot ignore the fact that rules adopted through this mechanism may indirectly affect those EU states that do not participate in the specific enhanced cooperation.

[2] See N. DETHLOFF, 'Arguments for the unification and harmonisation of family law in Europe' in K. BOELE-WOELKI (ed.), *Perspectives for the unification and harmonisation of family law in Europe*, Intersentia, Antwerp 2003, pp. 37–39.

[3] B. REINHARTZ, 'C. Article 3: Definitions' in U. BERGQUIST, D. DAMASCELLI, R. FRIMSTON, P. LAGARDE and B. REINHARTZ (eds.), *The EU Regulations on Matrimonial and Patrimonial Property*, Oxford University Press, Oxford 2019, p. 40.

[4] For more on 'authentic instrument' and 'court settlement' see Chapter 7 of this volume.

State of enforcement'). These include terms that have the same meaning in both regulations regardless of whether the couple concluded a registered partnership or got married. The definitions of those terms are the same, except for the part referring to the specific form of the relationship.[5] These terms are common for private international law in general and therefore also for other European regulations from that field; however, Article 3 defines them within the scope of the application of the Twin Regulations.

The rest of the terms in Article 3 of the Twin Regulations are different. They are tightly related to the specifics of the content of each regulation. The Matrimonial Property Regulation therefore additionally defines 'matrimonial property regime' and 'matrimonial property agreement', whereas the Regulation on the Property Consequences of Registered Partnerships defines 'registered partnership', 'property consequences of a registered partnership' and 'partnership property agreement'.

Interestingly, neither of the Twin Regulations contains the definition of the 'family', which is the basic foundation and the same time the main reason that legal instruments such as the Twin Regulations are needed.

The institution of family is constantly evolving within Europe and beyond, which makes it more difficult to define a single-family model. For this reason, neither the EU nor other international organisations are bound by a single concept of 'family', nor does this concept remain static. Rather, the objective is to protect all families and relationships. The basic principle of the international regulation can be found in Article 16 of the Universal Declaration of Human Rights, which refers to the right to marry, the right to start a family, and the equal rights of spouses.[6] Within this, the United Nations (UN) system is open to many non-traditional family structures. Among these, we can find single-parent families, intergenerational families, adoptive families, separated or divorced parents, and nuclear families regardless of whether they comprise persons of the same or different sex, even in the event of a change of sex by one of the partners in a marriage. Following a flexible and dynamic concept, the EU recognises the right to marry and the right to start a family according to the national laws of the EU Member States that regulate its exercise (Article 9 of the Charter of Fundamental Rights of the European Union), as well as the protection of the

---

[5] For example a term 'decision' is in the Regulation on the Property Consequences of Registered Partnerships defined as 'any decision in a matter of the property consequences of a registered partnership given by a court of a Member State, whatever the decision may be called, including a decision on the determination of costs or expenses by an officer of the court', whereas in the Matrimonial Property Regulation as 'any decision in a matter of a matrimonial property regime given by a court of a Member State, whatever the decision may be called, including a decision on the determination of costs or expenses by an officer of the court'.

[6] See for example the ECHR case, *Hämäläinen v Finland*, no. 37359/09. ECHR 2014\50. The case deals with a claim of a Finnish citizen against the Republic of Finland, for not being able to obtain full recognition of her new sex without converting her marriage into a civil union.

family in the legal, economic and social spheres (Article 33(1) of the Charter of Fundamental Rights of the European Union). Likewise, the General Comment No. 19 of the International Covenant on Civil and Political Rights states that the protection of the family requires recognition of the different types of family organisation or models, adding single-parent families and unmarried couples in Article 23.[7]

These legal instruments have been applied by courts and their interpretation has been evolving with the application of European principles.[8] Thus, in its judgments, the European Court of Human Rights (the ECtHR) has several times recognised a broad and flexible concept of family, centred on non-discrimination and the right to equality, based on respecting private and family life, as provided in Article 8 of the ECHR.[9]

Having all of this in mind, the progress that the Twin Regulations represent in this sensitive area, is considerably big. Their aim is to ensure legal certainty in the issues caused by the diverse national rules on private international law regarding the property regimes of cross-border couples. Both the matrimonial property regimes and the property consequences of registered partnerships are *sensu lato* part of family law.[10]

While the Twin Regulations do not define the term 'family', they do interpret some other important concepts that need to be inspected.

The Regulation on the Property Consequences of Registered Partnerships in its provision on definitions first mentions 'registered partnership' (Article 3(1)(a)). It is defined as 'a regime governing the shared life of two people which is provided for in law, the registration of which is mandatory under that law and which fulfils legal formalities required by that law for its creation'. The regulation itself does not specify whether this form of partnership includes same-sex or opposite-sex couples or both, leaving this to the specific national regulations of different states.[11]

---

[7] S. SANZ CABALLERO, *La familia en perspectiva international y europea*, Tirant lo Blach, Valencia 2006, p. 26, and S. SANZ CABALLERO, 'Familia (en derecho internacional y europeo)' in *Diccionario analítico de derechos humanos e integración jurídica* <http://opendata.dspace.ceu.es/bitstream/10637/7809/1/Familia_en%20derecho%20internacional%20y%20europeo.pdf>.

[8] K. BOELE-WOELKI, 'The principles of European family law: its aims and prospects' (2005) 2 *Utrecht Law Review* 161.

[9] European Convention on Human Rights. Rome, 4 November 1950.

[10] W. PINTENS, 'Union européenne et l'émergence d'un droit international de la famille – L'exemple des régimes matrimoniaux et des effets patrimoniaux des partenariats enregistrés' in C. CALLIESS (ed.), *Herausforderungen an Staat und Verfassung; Völkerrecht, Europarecht, Menschenrechte; Liber Amicorum für Torsten Stein zum 70. Geburtstag*, Nomos, Baden-Baden 2015, pp. 806–822.

[11] While this is surely a way to include all of the various national forms of partnerships, it can cause some uncertainty when determining the jurisdiction or the applicable law. For more see A. RODRIGUEZ BENOT, 'Definitions' in I. VIARENGO and P. FRANZINA (eds.), *The EU Regulations on the Property Regimes of International Couples, A Commentary*, Edward Elgar, Cheltenham 2020, pp. 38–39.

The Regulation on the Property Consequences of Registered Partnerships establishes three elements of the definition. These are: (i) a shared life of two people; (ii) the obligation to register the partnership; and its (iii) compliance with the legal formalities required by the law under which the partnership is registered.

The definition therefore explicitly requires the registration of a partnership. The existence of the partnership has to be attested by a public authority in a public register.[12] Consequently, the pair that only lives together, but has not registered a partnership, does not meet standards which are set in the Regulation on the Property Consequences of Registered Partnerships. This legal instrument, therefore, does not apply to de facto couples, who only live together, but have not registered their relationship (this is confirmed also in Recital 16). However, a registration, which is required for the existence of a 'registered partnership', is clearly not the same as a legal institution as marriage, even if the effects of both might in some Member States be substantially the same.

The need for a definition of the term 'registered partnership' lies in different and diverse approaches towards registered partnerships in the EU Member States. Nevertheless, the definition of a registered partnership can only be used for the purposes of the specific regulation itself, whereas its Recital 17 explicitly emphasises that the actual substance of the concept should remain defined in the national laws of the Member States. Moreover, not all national laws of EU Member States provide for such a legal form of a relationship. The Regulation on the Property Consequences of Registered Partnerships therefore explicitly emphasises that nothing in this regulation should oblige a Member State whose law does not have the institution of registered partnership to provide for it in its national law (Recital 17).

While the Regulation on the Property Consequences of Registered Partnerships defines the term 'registered partnership', on the contrary, the Matrimonial Property Regulation does not provide for a definition of the term 'marriage', although the term is used several times within the regulation. The Matrimonial Property Regulation explicitly emphasises that it does not define this specific term and that 'marriage' is defined by the national laws of the Member States only (Recital 17). While such a legal void might cause some uncertainty when applying the Matrimonial Property Regulation in practice, the term 'marriage' is certainly less problematic than the term 'registered partnership'. Marriage is an old and traditional form of a relationship and while the requirements for its conclusion and possibly, also its effects might partially differ among different states, the term has a globally more certain and unified

---

[12] A. RODRIGUEZ BENOT, 'Definitions' in I. VIARENGO and P. FRANZINA (eds.), *The EU Regulations on the Property Regimes of International Couples, A Commentary*, Edward Elgar, Cheltenham 2020, p. 36.

meaning compared to the term 'registered partnership'. The latter is a much newer form of formal relationship and it varies considerably among national regulations.

Additionally, the Twin Regulations define two terms that form the basis for their further provisions. These are the terms of 'matrimonial property regime' and 'property consequences of a registered partnership'. Their importance can be seen also in the fact that they are part of the titles of the Twin Regulations (Council Regulation (EU) 2016/1103 of 24 June 2016 implementing enhanced cooperation in the area of jurisdiction, applicable law and the recognition and enforcement of decisions in matters of *matrimonial property regimes* and Council Regulation (EU) 2016/1104 of 24 June 2016 implementing enhanced cooperation in the area of jurisdiction, applicable law and the recognition and enforcement of decisions in matters of the *property consequences of registered partnerships*).

The Matrimonial Property Regulation defines 'matrimonial property regime' as 'a set of rules concerning the property relationships between the spouses and in their relations with third parties, as a result of marriage or its dissolution'.[13] This is a rather broad definition. It does not give any precise instructions regarding the set of property questions that are included within the scope of this regulation. When interpreting the term, it is, therefore, necessary to take into consideration Recital 18 of the Matrimonial Property Regulation. It determines that all civil law aspects of matrimonial property regimes are included, which consist of the daily management of the matrimonial property on one hand and the liquidation of the regime on the other.

The term includes not only property arrangements envisaged by certain national legal systems in the case of marriage but also any property relationships between the spouses and in their relations with third parties, resulting directly from the matrimonial relationship, or the dissolution thereof. The respect of these general instructions can be seen in Article 27 of the Matrimonial Property Regulation, which determines the non-exhaustive set of circumstances that are covered with this definition. The law applicable to the matrimonial property regime pursuant to the Matrimonial Property Regulation shall therefore govern, inter alia: (i) the classification of property of either or both spouses into different categories during and after marriage; (ii) the transfer of property from one category to the other one; (iii) the responsibility of one spouse for liabilities and debts of the other spouse; (iv) the powers, rights and obligations of either or both

---

[13] In national laws of European states, the matrimonial property regime is typically understood as a set of mandatory and default rules which apply automatically to all couples married under the law of the state or who have elected the law of the state in a marriage contract (pre-nuptial or post-nuptial). The matrimonial property regime applied in particular country outlines the minimum duties and rights of the spouses in respect of the managing of and the administration of their property.

spouses with regard to property; (v) the dissolution of the matrimonial property regime and the partition, distribution or liquidation of the property; (vi) the effects of the matrimonial property regime on a legal relationship between a spouse and third parties; and (vii) the material validity of a matrimonial property agreement. When deciding whether a specific issue is covered by the scope of the Matrimonial Property Regulation, its Article 1 also plays an important role in that it determines the questions that are excluded from its scope. These are: revenue, customs or administrative matters; the legal capacity of spouses; the existence, validity or recognition of a marriage; maintenance obligations; the succession to the estate of a deceased spouse; social security; the entitlement to transfer or adjustment between spouses, in the case of divorce, legal separation or marriage annulment, of rights to retirement or disability pension accrued during marriage and which have not generated pension income during the marriage; the nature of rights *in rem* relating to a property; and any recording in a register of rights in immoveable or moveable property, including the legal requirements for such recording, and the effects of recording or failing to record such rights in a register.[14]

The term 'matrimonial property regime' is therefore not fully clear and remains ambiguous in its application. It should be interpreted autonomously (Recital 18), which will undoubtedly lead to different interpretations in the different Member States.

Parallel to the term 'matrimonial property regime' in the Matrimonial Property Regulation is the term 'property consequences of a registered partnership' in the Regulation on the Property Consequences of Registered Partnerships. It is defined as 'the set of rules concerning the property relationships of the partners, between themselves and in their relations with third parties, as a result of the legal relationship created by the registration of the partnership or its dissolution'. Due to the fact that the definition is materially the same as the one of the matrimonial property regime, the same that is written above regarding its interpretation is valid also here (see Recitals 18 and 19 and Articles 1 and 27 of the Regulation on the Property Consequences of Registered Partnerships).

Furthermore, both the Twin Regulations define similar terms 'matrimonial property agreement' and 'partnership property agreement'. Such an agreement is defined as an agreement between spouses/partners or future spouses/partners by which they organise their matrimonial property regime or the property consequences of their registered partnership. It is possible to conclude that such a term has therefore the same meaning in both regulations. The definitions are adjusted only to the proper terminology of each specific regulation. While on one side, parties can conclude a general agreement on different aspects related to the property (i.e. choose the property regime), they can also agree on applicable

---

[14] See Section 3.1.2 below.

law and competent court.[15] The Twin Regulations provide details regarding the material and procedural requirements that need to be fulfilled when concluding such an agreement.[16] This way it is easier and more certain for property rights acquired as a result of a property agreement to be accepted in the other Member States (Recital 48 of the Matrimonial Property Regulation).

Defining the main terms used in an EU instrument is very important from the perspective of the legislative process as it sets definitions common for all European regulations. It ensures that the basic concepts are as clear as possible before using them in a regulation of the specific legal field. Regardless of the depth and thoroughness of the definitions, problems always arise when interpreting and using the terms in practice. The same can also be expected regarding the terms and definitions listed in the Twin Regulations and the Court of Justice of the European Union (CJEU) will surely play an important role in interpreting them.

3. SCOPE OF APPLICATION OF THE TWIN REGULATIONS

After discussing the main concepts of the regulations, it is now necessary to define the scope of application of the Twin Regulations. In particular, the material, personal, temporal and territorial scope of the Twin Regulations are discussed in the sections below.

3.1. MATERIAL SCOPE OF APPLICATION OF THE TWIN REGULATIONS

The Twin Regulations are binding in their entirety and are directly applicable only in the Member States participating in enhanced cooperation in the field of jurisdiction, applicable law, recognition and enforcement of decisions on property regimes of international couples, both on matrimonial property regimes[17] and on the property consequences of registered partnerships.

---

[15] B. REINHARTZ, 'C. Article 3: Definitions' in U. BERGQUIST, D. DAMASCELLI, R. FRIMSTON, P. LAGARDE and B. REINHARTZ (eds.), *The EU Regulations on Matrimonial and Patrimonial Property*, Oxford University Press, Oxford 2019, pp. 41 and 281–282, differs among matrimonial/partnership property agreement in general and matrimonial/partnership property agreements choosing an applicable law. The background for both types of agreements can be found in Recitals 46 and 47 of the Regulation on the Property Consequences of Registered Partnerships and in Recital 48 of the Matrimonial Property Regulation.

[16] For more on agreements on the jurisdiction and the applicable law (also regarding the formal requirements for their validity) see Chapters 4 and 5 of this volume.

[17] U. BERQUIST, D. DAMASCELLI, R. FRIMSTON, P. LAGARDE, B. REINHARTZ, *The EU Regulations on matrimonial and patrimonial property*, Oxford University Press, Oxford 2019, pp. 56–57.

The scope of the material application of both regulations includes all civil law aspects of matrimonial property regimes[18] and the property consequences of registered partnerships. This includes relevant day-to-day administration of the property and also the liquidation of assets, in particular as a result of judicial separation, divorce, annulment of the marriage, the death of one of the spouses or one of the partners,[19] or the dissolution of the registered partnership.

Chapter I of both regulations (Scope and Definitions) consists of three articles that cover the scope of the Twin Regulations and the main concepts used therein. Guidelines as to their interpretation can also be found in the recitals.

For the purposes of the Matrimonial Property Regulation, the term 'matrimonial property regime' is to be interpreted autonomously. As explained in Recital 18, this term should encompass not only rules from which the spouses may not derogate but also any optional rules to which the spouses may agree in accordance with the applicable law, as well as any default rules of the applicable law. It includes not only property arrangements specifically and exclusively envisaged by certain national legal systems in the case of marriage but also any property relationships between the spouses and in their relations with third parties, resulting directly from the matrimonial relationship, or the dissolution thereof.

The Regulation on the Property Consequences of Registered Partnerships similarly interprets the property consequences of the registered partnership. These are defined as 'the set of rules concerning the property relationships of the partners, between themselves and in their relations with third parties, as a result of the legal relationship created by the registration of the partnership or its dissolution' (Article 3(1)(b)). This includes both the agreements between partners specifically if the partnership lasts and remains unchanged, as well as those resulting from their partnership.

---

[18] Ibid.

[19] See G. DI BENEDETTO, 'European certificate of succession and rights of the surviving spouse' in J. KRAMBERGER ŠKERL, L. RUGGERI and F. G. VITERBO (eds.), *Case studies and best practices analysis to enhance EU family and succession law. Working paper*, Quaderni degli Annali della Facoltà giuridica dell'Università di Camerino (2019) 3. In this publication, the author has analysed Article 1 of the Succession Regulation, determining that it must be interpreted as meaning that the provisions of a Member State governing matters relating to matrimonial property regimes for the period following the death of one of the spouses fall within its scope. Such conclusion is confirmed by the CJEU case C-558/16, *Doris Margret Lisette Mahnkopf v Sven Mahnkopf*, ECLI:EU:C:2018:138. It will therefore be possible to insert a right within the European succession certificate, the rationale of which is to compensate for the disadvantaged situation resulting from the interruption of the legal communion regime due to the death of the spouse. Moreover, this interpretation is not contradicted by the scope of application of the Matrimonial Property Regulation, which implements reinforced cooperation in matters of the matrimonial property regime. Although it was adopted to regulate all aspects of civil law regarding matrimonial property regimes (also with reference to the liquidation phase of the marital assets following the death of one of the spouses), the regulation expressly excludes the succession *causa mortis* of a spouse from its scope of application in Article 1.

Both regulations are binding in their entirety and directly applicable only in the Member States participating in enhanced cooperation in the field of jurisdiction, applicable law, recognition and enforcement of decisions on property regimes of international couples, both on matrimonial property regimes and on the property consequences of registered partnerships, pursuant to Decision (EU) 2016/954, or pursuant to a decision adopted in accordance with the second or third subparagraph of Article 331.1 of the TFEU (Recital 13).

On the other hand, the Regulations' temporal, material, territorial and personal scope of application will be determined by the provisions of the parties or, failing that, by applying the conflict rules introduced by the applicable regulation, considering the harmonising criteria that will be followed to determine the applicable law and the competent court.

One should bear in mind, however, that to guarantee the legal safeguarding of the transactions, and to prevent any change in the law applicable to the matrimonial property regime or to the property consequences of the registered partnership by choice, the parties must expressly manifest their wishes. The change decided upon by the spouses or partners must not have retroactive effects unless expressly provided otherwise. In any event, it may not prejudice the rights of third parties.

3.1.1. Matters Falling under the Scope of Application of the Twin Regulations

Articles 1(1) of the Twin Regulations, in a positive manner defining the material scope of application of the regulations, are very brief. They state only that the regulations shall apply to matrimonial property regimes or, respectively, to matters of the property consequences of registered partnerships. As mentioned earlier, Recital 18 of both regulations gives some general instructions regarding the matters falling under their scope. Such a general definition of the scope of application is then further specified by listing the matters excluded from the regulations (see Section 3.1.2 below).

It is important to underline that the Twin Regulations apply to matrimonial property regimes and to matters of the property consequences of registered partnerships having cross-border implications. Such a cross-border element arises when two or more national systems are involved and might be seen as competing (due to personal, territorial, or objective factors). For example, a case might concern a couple of different nationalities, residing in different countries or residing in a country other than that of their nationality.[20] Purely domestic cases fall under national law and the Twin Regulations do not apply. This is

---

[20] See also A. RODRIGUEZ BENOT, 'Article 1. Scope' in I. VIARENGO and P. FRANZINA (eds.), *The EU Regulations on the Property Regimes of International Couples, A Commentary*, Edward Elgar, Cheltenham 2020, p. 132.

confirmed by the Recital 14 of both regulations which state that, in accordance with Article 81 TFEU, the regulations should apply in the context of property regimes having cross-border implications.

3.1.2. Matters Excluded from the Application of the Twin Regulations

While the Twin Regulations are brief when noting the issues falling under their scope, they provide an extensive list of the matters that are excluded from their application.

First, Article 1(1) of the Twin Regulations stipulate that they do not apply to tax, customs, and administrative matters. These questions fall outside the scope of the regulations.

Secondly, the Twin Regulations do not apply to questions regarding the general legal capacity of the spouses or partners (Article 2(a)). This is a matter to be determined by national law. However, this exclusion is limited and therefore it should not cover the specific powers and rights of either or both spouses with regard to property, either between themselves or as regards third parties, as these powers and rights should fall under the scope of this Regulation (Recitals 20 of both regulations).

The exclusion also applies to preliminary questions, such as the existence, validity or recognition of a marriage or registered partnership (Article 2(b)). These matters remain governed by the national law of the Member States, including their rules on private international law (Recitals 21 of the Twin Regulation).

Maintenance obligations are also excluded from the Twin Regulations (Article 2(c)) as there exist separate instruments dealing with this area. In particular, the Maintenance Regulation and the 2007 Hague Maintenance Protocol applies in this regard. For the same reason, the Twin Regulations do not apply to the succession to the estate of a deceased spouse, as the Succession Regulation covers this issue (see also *Mahnkopf* case (C-558/16) in this regard).[21]

Moreover, the Twin Regulations do not apply to social security (Article 2(e)) which is left from the national law of the Member States. Issues of entitlements to transfer or adjustment between spouses of rights to retirement or disability pension, whatever their nature, accrued during the marriage and which have not generated pension income during the marriage are matters that are also excluded from the scope of the regulations (Article 2 f). However, as explained in Recital 23, this exclusion should be strictly interpreted and the regulations should govern in particular the issue of classification of pension assets, the

---

[21] See also A. PÉREZ VALLEJO, 'Notas sobre la aplicación del Reglamento (UE) 2016/1103 a los pactos prematrimoniales en previsión de la ruptura matrimonial' (2019) 21 *Revista Internacional de Doctrina y Jurisprudencia* 112.

amounts that have already been paid to one spouse during the marriage, and the possible compensation that would be granted in case of a pension subscribed with common assets.

The nature of rights *in rem* relating to a property[22] is also excluded from the scope of application of the regulations (Article 2(g)), same as for any recording in a register of rights in immoveable or moveable property, including the legal requirements for such recording, and the effects of recording or failing to record such rights in a register (Article 2(h)). It is for the law of the Member State in which the register is kept to determine whether the registering is, for instance, declaratory or constitutive in effect.

From this list, it should be remembered that, under the unity of the law applicable to the matrimonial property regime or the property consequences of registered partnerships, Articles 22 or 26 will apply to all property included in said regime, irrespective of where it is located, thus significantly increasing their possible scope of application, because both Regulations allow the creation or the transfer of a right in fixed or moveable assets resulting from the matrimonial property regime or the property relations of the registered

---

[22] See Case-218/16, *Aleksandra Kubicka v Przemysława Bac*, ECLI:EU:C:2017:755. In this case, a request for a preliminary ruling under Article 267 of the TFEU was submitted by the Sąd Okręgowy w Gorzowie Wielkopolskim, in the proceedings brought by Aleksandra Kubicka. Ms Kubicka, Polish national resident in Germany, wished to include in her will (which she wanted to conclude in Poland) a legacy 'by vindication', which was allowed by Polish law, in favour of her husband, concerning her share of ownership of the jointly-owned immovable property located in Germany. She wished to leave the remainder of her assets in accordance with the statutory order of inheritance, whereby her husband and children would inherit it in equal shares. She expressly intended to rule out recourse to an ordinary legacy (legacy 'by damnation'). The notary refused noting that creation of a will containing such a legacy is contrary to German legislation and case law relating to rights *in rem* and land registration. The Court noted that the Succession Regulation lists various matters that are excluded from the scope of that regulation, including, 'the nature of rights *in rem*' and 'the recording in a register of rights in immovable or movable property, including the legal requirements for such recording, and the effects of recording or failing to record such rights in a register'. Both the legacy 'by vindication', provided for by Polish law and the legacy 'by damnation', provided for by German law, constitute methods of transfer of ownership of an asset, namely, a right *in rem* that is recognised in both of the legal systems concerned. Therefore, the direct transfer of a property right by means of a legacy 'by vindication' concerns only the arrangement by which that right *in rem* is transferred at the time of the testator's death, which, according to Recital 15, is precisely what the Succession Regulation seeks to allow, in accordance with the law governing succession. Therefore, the Court held that Article 1(2)(k) of the Succession Regulation must be interpreted as precluding a refusal to recognise, in a Member State whose legal system does not provide for legacies 'by vindication', the material effects produced by such a legacy when succession takes place, in accordance with the law governing succession chosen by the testator. The Court stated that where a person invokes a right *in rem* to which he is entitled under the law applicable to the succession and the law of the Member State in which the right is invoked does not know the right *in rem* in question, that right shall, if necessary and to the extent possible, be adapted to the closest equivalent right *in rem* under the law of that state, taking into account the aims and the interests pursued by the specific right *in rem* and the effects attached to it.

partnership, as provided for in the law applicable to the property consequences of marriages or registered partnerships. However, it should not affect the limited number ('*numerus clausus*') of *in rem* rights recognised in the national law of some Member States, as seen in the Kubicka case, where adaptation to the closest equivalent *in rem* right under the law of that State is allowed, taking into account the objectives and interests pursued by that *in rem* right and the effects inherent in it in relation to the succession regulation. However, this does not imply that a Member State is obliged to recognise an *in rem* right relating to property situated in that Member State if the *in rem* right in question is not recognised in its law.[23]

3.2. PERSONAL SCOPE OF APPLICATION OF THE TWIN REGULATIONS

Similar to other EU private international family law instruments, the Twin Regulations apply regardless of the nationality, habitual residence or domicile of the spouses (in case of the Matrimonial Property Regulation) or partners (in case of the Regulation on the Property Consequences of Registered Partnerships). The Twin Regulations apply even if the spouses or partners are non-EU nationals or reside outside the EU. When the case has cross-border effects and is started in the Member State participating in the Twin Regulations, the provisions of the regulations are activated and must be taken into account. In other words, the court seised with a case has to check merely if jurisdictional and applicable law criteria set in the regulations are fulfilled, without any other connection criteria being required or applied.

> A recent case before the Court of Appeal of Arnhem-Leeuwarden (Gerechtshof Arnhem-Leeuwarden) dealt with the division of the joint property of two former spouses. In her application, the ex-wife (living in the Netherlands) applied to the court for the division of the property located in the Netherlands which was not divided during the divorce. It was established that the ex-husband has Nigerian nationality, does not reside in the Netherlands and (most likely) lives in Nigeria (therefore, the case had cross-border aspects).

> The court noted that the Matrimonial Property Regulation has an (unwritten) universal formal field of application with regard to the jurisdiction regime. It, therefore, does not matter for the applicability of the Regulation that the state concerned (Nigeria) is not an EU Member State. Therefore, the Court of Appeal assessed the jurisdiction of the Dutch court based on the Matrimonial Property Regulation.[24]

---

[23] I. VIARENGO and P. FRANZINA, *The EU regulations on the property regimes of international couples. A Commentary*, Edward Elgar, Cheltenham 2020, p. 22.
[24] Court of Appeal of Arnhem-Leeuwarden (Gerechtshof Arnhem-Leeuwarden), decision of 16 March 2021, No. 200.277.891 / 01 (ECLI: NL: GHARL: 2021: 2490).

In addition, it should be mentioned that it is not relevant where the couple's property is located. Even if the assets of the couple are located in a third country (whether an EU country not participating in the Twin Regulations, or a country outside the EU), a court of participating Member State seised with the case should apply the regulations. Such a rule applies both with regard to jurisdictional provisions and provisions on the applicable law. As Franzina notes, Article 13 on limitations of proceedings and Article 21 on the unity of the applicable law, among others, mirror precisely that understanding.[25]

If one imagines both Twin Regulations as secant circles, both marital and registered same-sex partnerships would be in the zone of convergence between the two. The fundamental reason for this is that, just as opposite-sex marriage is a consolidated institution that has remained intact and unquestioned over time, same-sex partnerships could be qualified as a 'liquid institution' (coining the central category on which the author built his conceptual edifice).[26] The old (solid) institutions are being replaced by more flexible ones.

In the area of same-sex partnerships, each country or even region (for example in the case of Spain) regulate them differently. For example, some countries do not allow same-sex couples to register, but only to marry (i.e. Finland and Sweden).[27] And since 1 October 2017, same-sex couples in Germany can no longer conclude a registered civil partnership,[28] but they can marry, although previously registered civil partnerships still exist and can be converted into marriage by the civil registry upon request.[29] Does the Regulation on the Property Consequences of Registered Partnerships apply in these countries to

---

[25] P. FRANZINA, 'Chapter I. Scope and Definitions', I. VIARENGO and P. FRANZINA (eds.), *The EU Regulations on the Property Regimes of International Couples, A Commentary*, Edward Elgar, Cheltenham 2020, pp. 14–16.

[26] Z. BAUMAN, *Liquid Modernity*, Polity Press, Cambridge 2000.

[27] The Swedish same-sex marriage law, which entered into force at the end of April 2009, repealed the Registered Partnership Act, which nevertheless continues to produce legal effects in respect of couples who registered their partnership before the end of April 2009 and have not converted their partnership into a marriage. In Finland, same-sex marriage has been possible since March 2017, according to the law passed by the parliament on 12 December 2014, which is why the Registered Partnership Act has also been repealed (*Lagom ändring av äktenskapslagen*, 156/2015. Available at <http://www.finlex.fi/sv/laki/alkup/2015/20150156>).

[28] Gesetz zur Einführung des Rechts auf Eheschließung für Personen gleichen Geschlechts (EheRÄndG k.a.Abk.), G. v. 20.07.2017 BGBl. I S. 2787 (Nr. 52); Geltung ab 01.10.2017 <https://www.buzer.de/gesetz/12739/index.htm> Amends the Civil Code in Articles 1309.3 and 1353.1.

[29] R. GARETTO, 'Uniones registradas y efectos patrimoniales' ['Registered partnerships and property consequences'] in L. RUGGERI, M. GIOBBI, M.J. CAZORLA GONZALEZ, J. KRAMBERGER ŠKERL, S. WINKLER (eds.), *Property relations of cross-border couples in the European Union*, Edizioni Scientifiche Italiane, p. 91. In the past, before same-sex couples were granted the right to marry, five other Member States (Denmark, Finland, Germany, Ireland and Sweden) allowed them to register their partnership and these registered partnerships remain valid in these Member States if the parties have not chosen to convert

same-sex couples registered in another state? In other words, do they consider the registered same-sex partnership to be an unrecognised institution and assimilate it into marriage or, conversely, do they consider that the Regulation on the Property Consequences of Registered Partnerships does apply to them?

On the contrary, in some other states (Croatia, Slovenia, Hungary, Italy and the Czech Republic) same-sex couples do not have access to marriage but can only form a registered partnership. The same applies in Italy or Austria with some differences with respect to Italy, for example.[30] In these countries, instead of creating a completely new institution, it was simply decided which rights the registered couples do not have that married couples do. Only same-sex couples can register, as different-sex couples can choose to marry or simply cohabit. Registration of the partnership produces effects equivalent to marriage in almost all areas.[31] In these cases, do the Regulation on the Property Consequences of Registered Partnerships or the Matrimonial Property Regulation apply to couples registered in these states, where they are assimilated into marriage?[32]

The choice of one or the other regulation is not a trivial matter, given the notable differences between the two regarding the applicable law and its possible connection with nationality and habitual residence. As seen above, the usage of the connecting factor of a habitual residence does not always guarantee the application of a law that, although closely linked to the couple, is known to the institution of the registered partnership. Hence, the Regulation on the Property Consequences of Registered Partnerships enables the application of the law of the state under whose law the registered partnership was created. This ensures the recognition of the institution of a registered partnership, and thus gives the parties greater legal certainty.

---

them into marriage. Furthermore, nine Member States also allow opposite-sex couples, in addition to same-sex couples, to register their partnership (Austria, Belgium, Cyprus, Estonia, France, Greece, Luxembourg, Malta, and the Netherlands). Differently, two Member States (Portugal and Spain) have not provided for the registration of common law couples, but allow same-sex couples to marry or unite (although in Spain, some of the Autonomous Communities have regulated it). Finally, six Member States (Bulgaria, Latvia, Lithuania, Poland, Slovakia and Romania) do not provide for any form of registered partnership and do not allow same-sex marriages.

[30] Italian Law 76/2016 on civil unions, (GU n.118 of 21-05-2016) and *Eingetrangene Partnershaft-Gesetz* (EPG), 30 December 2009, in Austria.

[31] F. SWEDDEN, and S. EGGERMONT, 'Same-sex Couples in Central Europe: Hop, Step and Jump' in *Legal Recognition of Same-Sex Relationships in Europe. National, Cross-border and European Perspectives*. Intersentia, Cambridge 2012, pp. 19–40.

[32] D. MARTINY, 'Die Kommissionsvorschläge für das internationale Ehegüterrrecht Bowie für das internationale Güterrrecht eingetrangener Partnerschaften', *IPRax*, 2011, pp. 443; S. MARINO, 'Strengthening European Civil Judicial Cooperation: The Property Effects of Family Relationships' (2017) 9 *Cuadernos de Derecho Transnacional* 265–284.

If it is accepted that EU rules may or may not be applied to the same union because of sexual orientation of its members, depending on the Member State where it is located, the intended uniformity is broken. From a private international law perspective, the continuity of legal relationships should be sought. Furthermore, it is necessary to avoid alterations of the personal status of the citizen within the Community area itself, as this is detrimental to the unitary approach to the desirable solutions.[33] Unquestionably, the solution would be a creation of autonomous concepts with which a unification of family law could be achieved. However, the EU does not currently have the jurisdiction to do so.[34] It has been considered that family law belongs to the hard core of civil matters that are resistant to unification.[35] It is deemed that such a solution would entail the disappearance of national private law and the creation of a new European law applicable to internal and intra-community situations without distinction. The creation of autonomous concepts is therefore currently unfeasible, and the absence of a substantive family law in the EU leads to great instability in the status of mobile couples.

However, in this matter, the CJEU has opened an interesting pathway through the complexities of the exclusive competence of states with the famous *Coman* case, which concerned the free movement of a same-sex married couple within the EU, the main thesis of which can, in the authors' view, be extrapolated to registered partnerships.[36] The CJEU has held that the civil status of persons, which includes rules on marriage, is a matter which falls within the exclusive jurisdiction of the Member States. The Member States are free to allow or refuse same-sex marriages in their legislation. However, in exercising this jurisdiction, they may not infringe the freedom of movement of EU citizens. In other words,

---

[33] E. ARTUCH IRIBERRI, 'La libertad individual y las parejas ante el Derecho internacional privado' (2002) 54(1) *Revista española de Derecho internacional* 41–65.

[34] On the unification of EU family law and the competence or incompetence of the EU to undertake this task, see M. ANTOKOLSKAIA, 'Would the Harmonisation of Family Law Enlarge the Gap between the Law in the Books and the Law in Action?' (2002) *FamPra.* 261–292; J. BASEDOW, 'Codification of Private Law in the European Union: the Making of a Hybrid' (2001) *ERPL* 35–49; G.R. DE GROOT, 'Auf dem Wege su einem europäischen (internationales) Familienrecht' (2001) *ZEuP* 617–627.

[35] See M. SOTO MOYA, 'Libre circulación por el territorio de la Unión Europea de los matrimonios del mismo sexo celebrados en España' (2012) 43 *Revista de Derecho Comunitario Europeo*, no. 43, Madrid, September/December 2012, pp. 807–847; W. PINTENS, 'Europeanisation of Family Law' in K. BOELE-WOELKI (ed.), *Perspectives for the Unification and Harmonisation of Family Law in Europe*, Intersentia, Antwerp 2003, p. 6.

[36] The CJEU case C-673/16, *Coman-Hamilton*, ECLI:EU:C:2018:385. This deals with the case of a Romanian national (Coman) who married an American national (Hamilton) in Brussels. Mr Hamilton wished to move to live in Romania with his spouse, Mr Coman, in accordance with Directive 2004/38/EC of 29 April 2004 on the right of Union citizens and their family members to move and reside freely within the territory of the Member States. The Romanian authorities refused Mr Hamilton's application for residence in Romania on the ground that the Romanian Civil Code prohibits same-sex marriages and does not recognise such marriages in Romania even if they have been validly entered into in other countries.

the CJEU requires the recognition of such a marriage only for the purpose of granting a derived right of residence to a third-country national, stating that this does not undermine the national identity or threaten the public order of the Member State concerned.[37]

The CJEU's argument can lead us to affirm that an institution validly constituted in one Member State must be recognised in another Member State, even if for the sole purpose of guaranteeing the free movement of people. In the case of the Regulation on the Property Consequences of Registered Partnerships, the question arises regarding its application to registered same-sex couples. And although this does not entail the unification of concepts or interference with the national family laws of each state, it does open the door to the obligation of recognising the existing institution. Through this indirect route a certain homogenisation of concepts in the EU may be generated.

It can be said that the Regulation on the Property Consequences of Registered Partnerships is a milestone in the construction of EU private international law, since never before has a regulation of this nature been drafted with registered partnerships as the protagonist. The diversity of institutions with which each state regulates partnerships has transferred private international law to a much more complex and varied terrain than in the past. It is no longer possible to speak of either universality of the institutions or uniformity of their content, unlike what has traditionally been the case with the institution of opposite-sex marriage. Precisely because regulating the property regime of registered partnerships within the EU is so novel, it is obvious that applying it is complex.

One of the most far-reaching and complicated interpretative issues concerns the scope of personal application. Before specifying which authority is competent, or which law applies in determining the couple's property regime, the legal authority has to establish whether Regulation on the Property Consequences of Registered Partnerships applies in a specific case.

---

[37] For an analysis of this judgment see, among others, S. ÁLVAREZ GONZÁLEZ, 'Same-sex marriage for the whole EU? Regarding the conclusions of the General Counsel in the Coman Affair' (2018) 56 *The European Union Law*; M. REQUENA CASANOVA, 'Free movement of same-sex marriages celebrated in the territory of the European Union: consequences of the Coman and others matter' (2019) 23(62) *Journal of European Community Law*, 41-79; P. JIMÉNEZ BLANCO, 'Cross-border mobility of same-sex marriages: the EU takes a step: Judgment of the CJEU of June 5, 2018, case C- 673/18: "Coman"' (2018) 61 *The European Union Law*; and STOPPIONI, 'Une analyze critique de l'arrêt Coman: déconstruction de la consécration de l'obligation de reconnaissance du droit de séjour du conjoint homosexuel' (27 February 2019) *European Papers, European Forum* 1 et seq. 377-388; V. STEHLÍK, 'The CJEU crossing the Rubicon on the same-sex marriages? Commentary on the Coman case' (2018) 18(2) *International and Comparative Law Review* 85-99; D. KOCHENOV and U. BELAVUSAU, 'Same-Sex Spouses: More Free Movement, but What About Marriage?', Coman: Case C-673/16, Coman et al. *v Inspectoratul General Pentru Imigrări*, Judgment of the CJEU of 5 June 2018, (2020) 57(1) *Common Market Law Review* 227–242.

The Regulation on Property Consequences of a Registered Partnership defines registered partnerships as: 'the regime governing the shared life of two people which is provided for in law, the registration of which is mandatory under that law and which fulfils the legal formalities required by that law for its creation' (Article 3(1)(a)). Furthermore, its Recital 16 limits the application of the regulation to 'couples whose union is institutionally sanctioned by the registration of their partnership with a public authority'. Therefore, it seems clear that any couple that is not registered does not fall within the scope of this EU regulation's personal application, completely ruling out unmarried couples, or perhaps more precisely, unregistered couples.[38] The reason, according to the regulation itself, is that its official nature allows its specificity to be considered and to proceed with its regulation in EU law. Some authors interpret the definition in Article 3 (1)(a) even more flexibly, understanding that 'what is important is that it is a regulated partnership with a more or less unitary property or asset regime, and that it is registered or has been formalised, vis-à-vis society, before the public authority'.[39]

However, this statement does not clarify many other questions that arise, such as the country of registration, the nature of the registration, or whether or not registered same-sex couples are included in its scope of application.

As indicated above, the sine qua non condition established by Article 3 (1)(a) for the Regulation on the Property Consequences of Registered Partnerships to be applied is the registration of the partnership. What is not clear is whether the couple has to register a partnership in one of the states bound by the regulation (remember that it is a rule of enhanced cooperation to which not all EU countries are party), or whether they can do that in other EU Member States, or even in any other state in the world.

The regulation's lack of specificity does not guide to any of the options. At first glance, its application would seem to be limited to couples registered in a state that is bound to the Regulation on the Property Consequences of Registered Partnerships. This solution, however, seems to be very restrictive and not in

---

[38] There are authors who consider that according to an ultimate interpretation, the partnerships that fall under the Regulation on the Property Consequences of Registered Partnerships are not so much those that are registered as those in which the members have expressly declared their intent to form a union, whether or not this declaration of intent has been registered, M. GARRIDO MELERO, 'Las uniones registradas en el ámbito del Reglamento europeo 1104/2016' of the Council of June 24, EU regulations 2016/1103 and 2016/1104 on matrimonial property regimes and property consequences of registered partnerships. Marcial Pons, 2020, pp.48–72, p.55.

[39] A. QUIÑONES ESCÁMEZ, 'Problemas generales de derecho internacional privado en los nuevos reglamentos europeos en materia de regímenes matrimoniales y efectos patrimoniales de las unions', International law and international relations courses in Vitoria-Gasteiz, 2018, pp. 245–335, 281. Available at <https://www.ehu.eus/documents/10067636/11188925/2017-Ana-Quinones-Escamez.pdf/65e2b82d-6523-557d-640a-bc348b600a4a?t=1545215928000>.

line with the spirit and purpose of the EU regulation. First, Article 3(1) of the Regulation on the Property Consequences of Registered Partnerships states that 'registered partnership is a regime of cohabitation of two persons regulated by law, the registration of which is compulsory under that law', but it does not add that it has to be the law of a Member State. The second argument in favour of extension is that the parallel Matrimonial Property Regulation does not limit its application to marriages celebrated in a Member State that is bound to it, but to marriages celebrated in any country in the world. Both regulations were drawn up at the same time and entered into force on the same day.[40] The content of both legal instruments are structured identically, dealing with jurisdiction, applicable law, recognition of decisions and documents, enforceability against third parties, and concluding with general and final provisions. In fact, it was initially intended that both subjects should be included in a single regulation, but this proved to be impossible and the two were split.[41] Taking into account all these circumstances, it does not seem unreasonable to think that, just as the Matrimonial Property Regulation applies to marriages celebrated in any country in the world, so the Regulation on the Property Consequences of Registered Partnerships applies to registered partnerships regardless of the state of registration.

Thirdly, it is necessary to remember the universal nature of the applicable law designated by the rules of the Regulation on the Property Consequences of Registered Partnerships (Article 20). It would be inconsistent for the competent authority of the state in question to be able to apply the law of any country in the world to settle a problem relating to a couple's property regime, but at the same time to restrict the regulation's application to couples registered in a Member State only.

---

[40] The Regulations came into force on 28 July 2016, 20 days after their publication in the Official Journal of the European Union (Art. 70 of both Regulations).

[41] The germ of these two legal instruments can be found in the Action Plan of the Council and the Commission on how best to implement the provisions of the Treaty of Amsterdam relating to the creation an area of freedom, security and justice (OJ C 19 of 25.01.1999). Although nothing was said at the time about partnerships, it was soon put on the agenda following the Draft measures for implementation of the principle of mutual recognition of decisions in civil and commercial matters (OJ C 12, 15.1.2001), which provided for the drafting of an instrument on jurisdiction and the recognition and enforcement of decisions concerning matrimonial property regimes and the property consequences of the separation of unmarried couples. The Stockholm Programme, adopted by the European Council on 11 December 2009, also stated that mutual recognition should be extended to matrimonial property regimes and the property consequences of the separation of unmarried couples. And in the 2010 Report on EU citizenship: removing obstacles to EU citizens' rights (COM (2010) 603), adopted on 27.10.2010, the Commission pointed out that uncertainty about the property rights of international couples was one of the main obstacles that EU citizens still face in their daily lives when exercising their EU rights across national borders. In the end, it was decided to split the regulation for marriages and registered partnerships.

Finally, it should be emphasised that there are other EU rules that have specifically limited their application to couples registered in a Member State. For example, Directive 2004/38 of the European Parliament and of the Council on the right of Union citizens and their family members to move and reside freely within the territory of the Member States.[42] Its Article 2(2)(b) allows free movement of persons with a character derived specifically from 'the partner with whom the Union citizen has entered into a registered partnership, *in accordance with the legislation of a Member State*' (emphasis added), a phrase that has not been included in the Regulation on the Property Consequences of Registered Partnerships.[43]

The inclusion or not of same-sex registered partnerships in the scope of the Regulation on the Property Consequences of Registered Partnerships has been the main bone of contention in the negotiations, and one of the main reasons why not all EU Member States have agreed to be part of it. All the strenuous efforts to dispel any doubts about the total freedom of countries to regulate 'the actual content of the concept of registered partnership' (Recital 17) did not help. It even renounces the creation of homogeneous content, which would be essential to provide the rule with a minimal degree of legal certainty.[44]

This *modus operandi* should come as no surprise, since the EU legislature does not usually elaborate autonomous concepts in the field of family law, but in most cases transfers this task to the legal systems of the Member States. This referral – also present in the Brussels II bis Regulation, the Maintenance Regulation, the Rome III Regulation and the Matrimonial Property Regulation – is the reason why each state interprets the concepts introduced into EU law according to its own criteria. Thus, there is an unavoidable heterogeneity in the material scope of EU law.[45]

The neutrality of the EU Regulation with regard to the inclusion of same-sex couples means that in all cases regarding their economic regime, it is essential to first resolve the question of whether or not they are included in its scope of application. Such a questions might be resolved differently depending on the EU Member State where the dissolution of the partnership takes place, the EU Member State which is dealing with the succession of one of the members of that partnership, the EU Member State where they wish to make an arrangement, etc.

---

[42] OJ L 158, 30 April 2004. Correction of mistakes, OJ L 229/35, 29.06.2004.
[43] See M. Soto Moya, 'El Reglamento 1104/2016 sobre régimen patrimonial de las parejas registradas: algunas cuestiones controvertidas de su puesta en funcionamiento en el sistema español de DIPr.' (December 2018) 35 *REEI*.
[44] In the words of A. Rodríguez Benot, 'The concept of a registered partner in Regulation 1104/2016 is merely functional as it can only be used for the purposes of that EU standard' in I. Viarengo, P. Franzin (coord), *Article 1: Scope, The EU regulations on the property regimes of international couples: A commentary*, Edward Elgar 2020, pp.17–28.
[45] An extensive analysis of the application of these EU Regulatios to same-sex unions can be found in M. Soto Moya, *Uniones transfronterizas entre personas del mismo sexo [Cross-border unions between people of the same sex]* Tirant Lo Blanch, Valencia 2013.

For example, Mr A, a Belgian national, and Mr B, a French national, marry in Belgium in January 2020. Shortly afterwards they move their habitual residence to Italy. In July 2021 they intend to divorce and liquidate their matrimonial property regime. Will the Italian authorities have jurisdiction? The preliminary question before determining if Regulations 2201/2003 and 1103/2016, respectively apply is whether the Italian authorities consider Mr A and Mr B to be spouses or not. In principle, each state is sovereign in deciding on the concept of spouses. Italy has not regulated same-sex marriages, so it will not apply Regulation 1103/2016 to this marriage concluded in Belgium. On the other hand, the Belgian authorities would do so. This results in a discontinuity of spatial relations and an obvious loss of legal safeguarding within the EU itself.

A lack of definition also results in problems regarding compatibility between the Matrimonial Property Regulation and the Regulation on the Property Consequences of Registered Partnerships.

3.3. TEMPORAL SCOPE OF APPLICATION OF THE TWIN REGULATIONS

One might notice that Articles 70 of the Twin Regulations differentiate between two different dates:

- The entry into force date, which is 20 days after publication of the regulations on 8 July 2016, that is to say, 28 July 2016.
- The date from which the provisions of the regulations apply, which is 29 January 2019.[46]

This difference between the entry into force of the instruments and the date of their application enabled the publication of the content of the regulations, the adaptation of the internal regulations of the Member States and possibly greater adherence to enhanced cooperation in matters such as this, where integration and unification are complicated.[47] In other words, the first date (the date of entry into force) is important for the Member States and their institutions responsible for the preparation of implementing national provisions. It bears little relevance for such practitioners as judges, lawyers, notaries or mediators. For them, the second date (the date of the application of the Twin Regulations) is of main

---

[46] An exception is made for Articles 63 and 64, which deal with the information that Member States must provide to the Commission, on the one hand, and the drawing up of lists, certificates, forms and consultation procedures to do so, on the other (Articles 65, 66 and 67).

[47] H. MOTA, 'Regímenes matrimoniales y sucesión después de la disolución por muerte de un matrimonio transfronterizo: un caso de estudio' (2019) 21 *Revista Internacional de Legislación y Jurisprudencia*, p. 58.

significance as it is the turning point from which the national provisions were changed by the imperative EU rules.

In general, the Twin Regulations apply as of 29 January 2019. However, the more precise rules of entry into application of the rules set in the Twin Regulations are established in Articles 69 (Transitional provisions). The main rule is that the regulations apply only to legal proceedings instituted, to authentic instruments formally drawn up or registered and to court settlements approved or concluded on or after 29 January 2019 (Article 69(1) of the Twin Regulations).

It is important to highlight that the transitional provisions in Article 69 concern only the application of the Twin Regulations towards the Member States participating in the enhanced cooperation at the moment the regulations came into effect. For the Member States that will join the enhanced cooperation at some later date, the decision of the Commission will be issued which will establish adapted transitional provisions taking into account the agreement with such state. This is a standard practice in case of enhanced cooperation instruments (see e.g. Commission decision on Estonia joining the Rome III Regulation[48]) and could also be compared with specific dates of entry into application of EU instruments towards the states newly acceding to the EU (e.g. Brussels II bis regulation entered into application on 1 March 2005, but for Croatia which joined the EU on 1 July 2013 it is applicable as of this date).

It should also be noted that Recital 69 of the Matrimonial Property Regulation and Recital 67 of the Regulation on the Property Consequences of Registered Partnerships establish that Regulation No 1182/71 of the Council of 3 June 1971 determining the rules applicable to periods, dates and time limits[49] applies for calculating the periods and time limits provided for in the Twin Regulations.

3.3.1. Temporal Scope of Application of the Jurisdictional Provisions

The freedom of choice of court and jurisdiction rules must take account of the temporal scope of the two Regulations. They will therefore only apply to proceedings initiated after the Regulations' entry into force, unless the partners in the marriage or registered partnership have entered into a choice-of-law agreement, the validity of which is subject to the provisions of the Regulations, or of the published provisions that came into force previously.

---

[48] Commission Decision (EU) 2016/1366 of 10 August 2016 confirming the participation of Estonia in enhanced cooperation in the area of the law applicable to divorce and legal separation [2016] C/2016/5137, OJ L 216.
[49] OJ L 124, 8.6.1971.

Thus, the jurisdictional rules in cross-border relationships are strongly related to the temporal scope of the Twin Regulations. The possible scenarios are the following:

Time frame of Proceedings	Application of the Twin Regulations
Proceedings instituted and resolved (also authentic instruments formally drawn up or registered and to court settlements approved or concluded) before 29 January 2019	International jurisdiction had to be established under the national rules of the Member State without applying the Twin Regulations.
Proceedings instituted (also authentic instruments formally drawn up or registered and to court settlements approved or concluded) on or after the entry into force of the Twin Regulations	Jurisdictional rules set in the regulations fully apply in the Member States participating in the enhanced cooperation.

A question might arise how the wording 'proceedings instituted on or after the entry into force of the regulation' should be understood, especially in a case when an appeal is brought later. As notes Biagoni, in the absence of any clarification in Article 69, regard is to be had to the institution of the first instance proceedings.[50] Moreover, in Article 14 defining the moment of seising a court (by listing the procedural steps to be taken into account), the Twin Regulations provide clarity to the term 'instituting proceedings'. In this regard, even though Article 14 was adopted having in mind the rules on *lis pendens* and related actions, it is also relevant to assess whether the Twin Regulations are to be applied.[51] It is also worth noting that it is the date of instituting the main proceedings that matters – the date when an ancillary claim, a counterclaim, a request for a protective or provisional measure is filed is of little relevance for the application of the Twin Regulations.

Since the Twin Regulations entered into force comparatively recently, in practice the questions as to the temporal scope of application of jurisdictional provisions still arise.

> The County Court in Zagreb in its decision of 8 July 2020 had to rule whether the Croatian courts had jurisdiction for determining the matrimonial property of Croatian nationals located in Austria. The plaintiff indicated in the appeal that the Croatian court should declare itself competent based on provisions of the Matrimonial Property Regulation. The County Court, however, correctly held that the case does not fall into the temporal scope of application of the Matrimonial Property Regulation, since the proceedings were instituted in 2017. Given that the proceedings were instituted before 29 January 2019, to establish jurisdiction, national private international law provisions were held to be applicable.[52]

---

[50] G. BIAGONI, 'Article 69. Transitional Provisions' in I. VIARENGO and P. FRANZINA (eds.), *The EU Regulations on the Property Regimes of International Couples, A Commentary*, Edward Elgar, Cheltenham 2020, pp. 484–488.
[51] Ibid.
[52] County Court in Zagreb (Croatia), decision of 8 July 2020, No. Gž Ob 1137/2019-2.

On the contrary, in a decision of 16 March 2021, the Court of Appeal of Arnhem-Leeuwarden (Gerechtshof Arnhem-Leeuwarden) noted that since the claim was filed with the court after January 29, 2019, the Matrimonial Property Regulation also applies temporally (Article 69 paragraph 1).[53]

3.3.2. Temporal Scope of Provisions on Recognition and Enforcement

When proceedings were instituted before the entry into force of the Twin Regulations, those instruments will not be applicable to establish jurisdiction or applicable law. However, if the decision in such a case has been taken after 29 January 2019, the provisions of the Twin Regulations regarding recognition and enforcement will apply as long as the rules of jurisdiction that were applied comply with those set out in Chapter II of the regulations.

For national rules of jurisdiction to comply with the ones set in Chapter II of the regulations, it seems to be sufficient that the national rules would grant jurisdiction to the same court as the rules of the Twin Regulations. In case the jurisdiction of the court was based on the choice-of-court agreement, it is important that the choice-of-court agreement would be valid under Article 7 of the Twin Regulations.[54]

Time frame of Proceedings	Application of the Twin Regulations
Proceedings instituted before 29 January 2019 but resolved on or after this date	Decisions rendered after 29 January 2019 are being recognised and enforced in accordance with Chapter IV of the Twin Regulations. This is possible as long as the applied rules of jurisdiction comply with those set out in Chapter II of the Twin Regulations (Article 69(2) of the Twin Regulations). Naturally, this is possible only for the states that participate in enhanced cooperation.
Proceedings instituted or after 29 January 2019	With no exceptions, decisions rendered after 29 January 2019 are recognised and enforced in accordance with the Twin Regulations.

While in the long term such transitional arrangements will become less important, for some years after the entry into force of the Twin Regulations they remain relevant.

3.3.3. Temporal Application of the Provisions on Applicable Law

In accordance with Article 69(3), Chapter III (Applicable law) applies only to spouses (partners) who marry (register their partnership agreement) or

---

[53] Court of Appeal of Arnhem-Leeuwarden (Gerechtshof Arnhem-Leeuwarden), decision of 16 March 2021, No. 200.277.891/01 (ECLI: NL: GHARL: 2021: 2490).
[54] See in this regard G. BIAGONI, 'Article 69. Transitional Provisions' in I. VIARENGO and P. FRANZINA (eds.), *The EU Regulations on the Property Regimes of International Couples, A Commentary*, Edward Elgar, Cheltenham 2020, pp. 484–488.

who specify the law applicable to their property regime after 29 January 2019 (the day on which both regulations came into force). Such limitation results in four different scenarios that might arise in practice:[55]

Time frame of the Conclusion of the Marriage or Registered Partnership	Application of the Twin Regulations
A marriage or a registered partnership concluded before 29 January 2019 without an agreement on the choice of applicable law or with an agreement concluded before this date	In such a case, the national rules of private international law apply.
A marriage or a registered partnership concluded before 29 January 2019 in which a choice-of-law agreement is concluded on or after this date	In such a case, the courts shall consider the choice-of-law agreement under the Twin Regulations in so far as the agreement is valid (validity to be established under the provisions of the regulations).
A marriage or a registered partnership concluded on or after 29 January 2019, but the choice-of-law agreement was concluded before this date	In this case, the courts must apply the Twin Regulations and consider whether a choice-of-law agreement meets the requirements established under EU law.
A marriage or a registered partnership concluded on or after 29 January 2019 with no choice-of-law agreement or with choice-of-law agreement concluded after this date	Any marriage or registered partnership with cross-border effects, concluded on or after 29 January 2019, is subject to the Twin Regulations. The Twin Regulations apply for a choice-of-law agreement if it is concluded within this timeframe.

It is apparent, that the applicable law rules of the Twin Regulations are linked not to the date of institution of the proceedings (as jurisdictional rules) but to the date of the establishment of legal relationship.[56] The idea of such choice is linked to the need for legal certainty and predictability: the couple should know in advance what law applies to their property regime. If the couple formalises their relationship after the Twin Regulations became applicable, it conforms to their legal expectations that this instrument will regulate law applicable to their property regime. If, however, they married or registered their partnership earlier, when the Twin Regulations do not apply to their situation and national conflict of law rules will apply instead (what the couple reasonably expected at the time of formalisation of their relationship).

Articles 69(3) also provides that Chapter III of the Twin Regulation apply to couples who 'specify the law applicable to the matrimonial or partnership

---

[55] On temporal scope of application for registered partnerships see also F. DOUGAN and J. KRAMBERGER ŠKERL, 'Model clauses for registered partnerships under Regulation (EU) 2016/1104' in M. J. CAZORLA GONZÁLEZ and L. RUGGERI (eds.), *Guidelines for practitioners in cross-border family property and succession law (a collection of model acts accompanied by comments and guidelines for their drafting)*, Dykinson, Madrid 2020, p. 38.

[56] Similar principle applies in other instruments on applicable law, for instance the Succession Regulation.

property regime after 29 January 2019'. In other words, the regulations apply also to couples who formalised their relationship earlier but the choice-of-law agreements were concluded in the period of time when the Twin Regulations were already applicable. Moreover, in the doctrine, it is argued that the term 'specify' also implies that the Twin Regulations also apply to the situations where the choice-of-law agreement is amended or supplemented after this date.[57] Naturally, such regulation is in line with legitimate expectations of the spouses and partners and such provision was needed for the consistency of the instruments.

3.4. TERRITORIAL SCOPE OF THE TWIN REGULATIONS

The Twin Regulations are binding and directly applicable only in the Member States participating in enhanced cooperation, pursuant to Decision (EU) 2016/954: namely, Belgium, Bulgaria, the Czech Republic, Cyprus, Germany, Greece, Spain, France, Croatia, Italy, Luxembourg, Malta, the Netherlands, Austria, Portugal, Slovenia, Finland and Sweden. This is the principle stemming from Article 20(4) of the Treaty on the European Union, which provides that acts adopted in the framework of enhanced cooperation shall bind only participating the Member States.[58]

The other EU Member States are considered to be third states for the application of the regulation. When a case on matrimonial property regime arises before the court of EU Member States not participating in the enhanced cooperation, they apply their national law to establish jurisdiction, applicable law, or recognition and enforcement rules.

> For example, a recent case before Klaipėda regional court (Lithuania, a country not participating in the enhanced cooperation), concerned spouses that were Lithuanian citizens. They were residents in Germany for many years and then returned to Lithuania with their child where they started a divorce case. The court established its jurisdiction for divorce, parental responsibilities and maintenance in accordance with relevant EU regulations. As to matrimonial property, it ruled that since there is no EU regulation that could be applied for property relations of the couple (Lithuania not being party to the Matrimonial Property Regulation), the court had to proceed applying national law.[59]

---

[57] G. BIAGONI, 'Article 69. Transitional Provisions' in I. VIARENGO and P. FRANZINA (eds.), *The EU Regulations on the Property Regimes of International Couples, A Commentary*, Edward Elgar, Cheltenham 2020, pp. 484–488.

[58] In addition, acts adopted in the framework of enhanced cooperation are not regarded as part of the *acquis*, which has to be accepted by candidate States for accession to the EU.

[59] Klaipėda regional court (Lithuania), decision of 20 May 2021, No. e2A-728-896/2021.

It should be noted that although, Recitals 11 of the Twin Regulations determines that territorial jurisdiction is fully applicable only in 18 countries participating in the enhanced cooperation, the law of any other EU Member State or even a third country can be applied within the framework of the Twin Regulations due to the principle of universal application (Articles 20 of the Twin Regulations). Articles 62 of both regulations emphasise that neither of them shall affect the application of the bilateral or multilateral conventions in force, except those between the Member States, prevailing over them. Moreno argues[60] that concerning the applicable law, this refers mainly to the Hague Convention of 1978,[61] which continues to apply in France, the Netherlands and Luxembourg, as well as the relevant conventions signed by the Scandinavian countries.

Finally, it's possible to apply the territorial scope under the choice of applicable law or attending to connecting factor as the habitual residence or nationality.

In the first scope and in light of the above, it would appear that the parties may choose the applicable law of any Member State by applying Article 20, and based on the principle of free choice regulated by Article 22 in each Regulation, including the law of a non-participating Member State; however, in such a case, it will be necessary to take into account the limitations that the article itself establishes referring to the law of the state participating (or not) in the enhanced cooperation, and referenced in the first section of this chapter (Section 1.3.1).

Consequently, the free choice of applicable law would be reduced to a maximum of six different national legal systems if the parties have dual nationality; and to four, if they only have one each.[62] Nationalities of Member States other than for the case law of the CJEU[63] must be on an equal footing, without a Member State being able to give preference to its nationality based on its national rules, because there is only one option for each nationality and place of habitual residence different from each other. These options may be reduced for same-sex marriages in thirteen EU Member States that do not contemplate their regulation: Croatia, the Czech Republic, Cyprus, Slovenia, Greece, Hungary, Italy, Latvia, Lithuania, Poland, Slovakia, Bulgaria and Romania; likewise for registered partnerships, which are not regulated in the last six Member States mentioned.

---

[60] G. PALAO MORENO, 'Forum necessitatis' in I. BUIGUES and G. PALAO MORENO (eds.), *Régimen económico matrimonial y efectos patrimoniales de las uniones registradas en la Unión Europea*, Tirant lo Blanch, Valencia 2019, pp. 131–134.

[61] A. RODRIGUEZ BENOT, 'Los efectos patrimoniales de los matrimonios y de las uniones registradas en la unión europea' (2019) 1 *Cuadernos de Derecho Transnacional 9*.

[62] S. DE VIDO, 'The relevance of dual nationality in conflict-of-law issues relating to divorce and legal separation in Europe' *Cuadernos de Derecho Transnacional*, March 2012, 4, N° 1, pp. 222–232.

[63] Judgment of 7 July 1992. Case C-369/90. <https://curia.europa.eu/juris/showPdf.jsf?docid=97581&doclang=ES>.

Based on the possible options and some studies that have been carried out within the PSEFS project framework,[64] three possible scenarios that might affect marriages or registered partnerships in determining the applicable law must be addressed. They differ regarding whether or not a Member State participating in an enhanced cooperation is involved. The possibilities are that both parties are from nationals of the EU Member States participating in the enhanced cooperation (see Recitals 11 of the Twin Regulations); that only one of the spouses or partners is a national of such a state and the other is not; and neither is a national of such a state. In the latter case, the Rome III Regulation and the relevant national rules will apply to marriages, and only the latter as far as registered partnerships are concerned.

The territorial scope of application, though simple in appearance, contains asymmetries that will have to be clarified in accordance with the provisions of Article 26 (1) of either of the regulation in each specific case.[65] The relevant connecting factors are:[66] the place of residence, nationality or closest connection for the spouses; and the law of the state where the union was created for registered partnerships. For the latter, the connection with a nationality or habitual residence is avoided, as this could imply applying a law that does not recognise the registered partnership institution, even though the applicable law is universal in nature.

Consequently, the parties may have formed their union in one state and at that time or subsequently have their habitual residence in another state. Regardless of whether spouses or partners are of the same or different sex, all European citizens and their family members have the right to cross-border mobility within the Community territory for themselves and their family members. This may be a situation that is complicated in terms of formal validity, since a union must be registered, and therefore a formal act before a public authority is required, and in many legal systems no prior period of cohabitation is required.

On the other hand, the territorial scope is based on the connecting factors of habitual residence or nationality.

It should be noted that circumstances of residence or habitual residence are variable and can therefore cause some distortion, either because there are indeterminate circumstances such as the definition of both terms, or because the time for determining residence will vary depending on the country.

---

[64] Justice Project 'Personalized Solution in European Family and Succession Law (PSEFS)' No. 800821-JUST-AG- 2017/JUST-JCOO-AG-2017 <https://www.euro-family.eu>. See Atlas <https://www.euro-family.eu/atlas>.

[65] M. SOTO MOYA: 'Ámbito de aplicación personal del Reglamento 2016/1104 sobre régimen patrimonial de la pareja registrada' (December 2020) 23 *Revista internacional de doctrina y jurisprudencia* 7–8.

[66] S. DE VIDO, 'The relevance of dual nationality in conflict-of-law issues relating to divorce and legal separation in Europe' *Cuadernos de Derecho Transnacional*, March 2012, 4, Nº 1, pp. 222–232.

In case C-523/07,[67] the CJEU ruled that the habitual residence corresponds to the place where the person has some integration in a social and family environment. The national judicial body must therefore determine the state of the habitual residence in the specific case based on the specific circumstances.

There are differences in the legislation of different EU Member States when determining habitual residence:

- The first difference is found when we approach the indeterminacy of the term residence/domicile, we find different solutions. While in Portugal[68] and Poland[69] the domicile is where the habitual residence is, in Ireland a domicile of origin equivalent to the concept of habitual residence and a domicile of choice, which is identified with the place where there is a permanent or indefinite intention to reside.[70] The difficulty can spring from the uncertainty of determining a person's intention of the available facts, or it may result from the application of the legal principles relating to domicile (e.g., the rules relating to domicile of dependency or domicile of origin). These uncertainties may compel those concerned with, for instance, administration of estates to have recourse to legal proceedings to settle the matter. In Italy,[71] the domicile is the place where the person's professional activity and interests are, which does not have to coincide with the residence (where he or she habitually lives).
- Additionally, the requirements regarding the length of residence vary depending on the country, ranging from 40 days of residence prior to the application filing in Scotland or to the three months of prior residence required in Cyprus, or 12 months required in Belgium or Malta. However, the last residence or domicile is also indeterminate, as in Greece, England or Wales, where it is sufficient to have a domicile in the territory.

Nevertheless, all European countries have something in common. They all deem a residence or a domicile and a nationality as close connecting elements when regulating rules on private international law. These factors are therefore used for determining the competent international body that must resolve conflicts arising from property consequences of marriages or registered partnerships, in disputes with members of different nationalities, and in the division of assets due to annulment, separation, divorce/dissolution, or death.

---

[67] Case C-523/07, A., ECLI:EU:C:2020:531.
[68] <https://ec.europa.eu/immigration/country-specific-information/portugal/family-member_en>.
[69] <https://ec.europa.eu/immigration/country-specific-information/poland/family-member_en>.
[70] P. ROGERSON, 'Habitual Residence: The New Domicile?' (2000) 49(1) *The International and Comparative Law Quarterly* 90. The author considers that is necessary settle intention of the person.
[71] <https://ec.europa.eu/social/main.jsp?catId=1116&langId=en&intPageId=4629>.

Finally, we must highlight connecting factors that exist with the Succession Regulation: Article 4 of the 'twin' regulations, when the succession of a member of a registered partnership or of a spouse is brought before a court of a Member State under Regulation (EU) No 650/2012, but this matter is covered in another chapter.

4. CONCLUDING REMARKS

The harmonisation of family law in Europe advances with the adoption of the Twin Regulations, which represents a step forward for cross-border families, in the interests of the harmonious functioning of justice. Both Regulations represent a development in European private law, within the enhanced cooperation framework and with the flexibility of an universal application of their Article 20.

In this regard, the new private international, procedural and civil instruments contribute to providing solutions to the issues derived from the mobility of people of different nationalities within Europe, from the material, temporal and personal scope, following the provisions for the determination of the competent court and the law applicable to the specific case, and with special attention to states with more than one legal system, such as Spain. So harmonised conflict of law rules have been introduced in order to avoid contradictory results, because the main rule should ensure that the matrimonial property regime or the effective partnership property is governed by a predictable law with which it is closely connected. Such instruments as the territorial, temporal, personal and material scope are determined by respecting the principle of free movement as a right regulated in the EU when establishing the residence of the registered partnership members or the spouses, regardless of whether they are same-sex or different-sex couples.

In conclusion, the Twin Regulations constitute a further step towards the unification of private international family law, aimed at the creation of a uniform framework of conflict rules to resolve cross-border issues arising within the family and not at the unification of its substantive rules. The Twin Regulations apply only to cross-border situations and not to purely national cases. To determine whether the Twin Regulations apply in a specific case, their temporal, territorial and material scope needs to be studied and taken into account. All of these are determined by respecting the principle of free movement as a right regulated in the EU. Lastly, it should be remembered that both regulations came fully into force on 29 January 2019, and from that moment on, the private international law of the Member States, participating in the enhanced cooperation does not apply.

JURISDICTIONAL PROVISIONS IN THE TWIN REGULATIONS

Ivana Kunda and Agnė Limantė*

1. Introduction 71
2. Concentration of Jurisdiction as the Key Principle 73
   2.1. Concentration in the *Forum Successionis* 74
   2.2. Concentration in the *Forum Divortii* 78
3. Jurisdiction in 'Other Cases' 82
   3.1. *Forum Prorogatum Expressum* 82
   3.2. *Forum Prorogatum Tacitum* 84
   3.3. The Default Rules 85
4. Remaining Jurisdiction Rules 88
   4.1. *Forum Alternativum* 88
   4.2. Limitation of Proceedings 90
   4.3. *Forum Subsidiarium* 91
   4.4. *Forum Necessitatis* 92
   4.5. Forum for Counterclaims 93
   4.6. Forum for Provisional Measures 94
5. Coordination Among Concurrent Proceedings in Different Member States 95
   5.1. Time When the Court is Seised 96
   5.2. *Lis Pendens* 97
   5.3. Related Actions 98
6. Concluding Remarks 99

1. INTRODUCTION

Spouses or registered partners, who are of different nationalities, live in two or more states as a couple, or have their property situated in two or more countries,

---

* Ivana Kunda, Full Professor and Head of the International and European Private Law Department at the Faculty of Law of the University of Rijeka.
Agnė Limantė, MA, PhD, is a Chief Researcher at the Law Institute of the Lithuanian Centre for Social Sciences.

are faced with various questions pertaining to the matrimonial property regime in case they find themselves in a situation of dividing their property for the reason of managing it or breaking up as a couple or in case one of them dies.[1] The first of those questions is that of the court jurisdiction. Often, the couple is not sure in which state they can commence the proceedings and whether division of property can be settled together with some other issues (e.g. divorce or maintenance). In the Member States participating in the enhanced cooperation on matters of matrimonial property regimes and the property consequences of registered partnerships, the Twin Regulations provide the answers.

The Matrimonial Property Regulation and the Regulation on the Property Consequences of Registered Partnerships should be read along each other, including when it comes to jurisdictional rules which are outlined in Chapter II, Articles 4–19 of both Regulations. Articles 4 and 5 lay down the hierarchically dominant jurisdictional rules, while Article 6 provides for jurisdictional rules in 'other cases', complemented by Article 7 on a limited party autonomy to choose competent courts of a Member State and Article 8 on jurisdiction deriving from the appearance of the defendant. Further jurisdictional rules include alternative and subsidiary jurisdiction (Articles 9 and 10), *forum necessitatis* (Article 11), counterclaims (Article 12), limitation of proceedings (Article 13) and provisional measures (Article 19). Moreover, Chapter II addresses some procedural issues different from jurisdiction, such as the time of seising a court (Article 14), examination as to jurisdiction and admissibility (Articles 15–16), *lis pendens* (Article 17) and related actions (Article 18). These rules are of mandatory application, and the court may not decline the jurisdiction conferred to it under the Twin Regulations, unless a particular provision to that effect permits so (e.g. Articles 9 and 13).[2] Likewise, a court of a Member State seised with a matter of matrimonial property regime over which it has no jurisdiction under the Twin Regulations, has to declare of its own motion that it has no jurisdiction according to Article 15.

Prior to discussing the jurisdictional rules, certain structural annotations seem appropriate. First, save for variations in Articles 5 and 6, the provisions on jurisdiction in the Matrimonial Property Regulation and the Regulation on the Property Consequences of Registered Partnerships are equivalent.

---

[1] The notion of 'matrimonial property' in the European private international law is a broad one and draws on its civil law origins. W. PINTENS, 'Matrimonial Property Law in Europe' in K. BOELE-WOELKI, K. MILES and J. SCHERPE (eds.), *The Future of Family Property in Europe*, Intersentia, Cambridge 2011, p. 20. With respect to the same concept in the Matrimonial Property Regulation see P. QUINZÁ REDONDO, 'Matrimonial Property Regimes' in I. VIARENGO and F.C. VILLATA (eds.), *Planning the Future of Cross Border Families: A Path Through Coordination*, Hart Publishing, Oxford 2020, p. 105.

[2] P. FRANZINA, 'Article 13. Limitation of Proceedings' in I. VIARENGO and P. FRANZINA (eds.), *The EU Regulations on the Property Regimes of International Couples. A Commentary*, Edward Elgar, Cheltenham 2020, p. 132.

Therefore, throughout this chapter the references to the Matrimonial Property Regulation should be understood also to refer to the Regulation on the Property Consequences of Registered Partnerships, except where stated otherwise. Likewise, references to spouse(s) or matrimonial property matters should be understood as references to registered partner(s) or matters of property consequences of registered partners, and similar. Second, similar to some other EU private international law instruments, the jurisdictional rules in the Twin Regulations govern international jurisdiction of Member States' courts, without pointing to a concrete court within a Member State. Consequently, national rules as to territorial and subject matter jurisdiction in a Member State determined by the Matrimonial Property Regulation or Regulation on the Property Consequences of Registered Partnerships are to be consulted to establish the actual court that will deal with the case. Third, the reference to a 'Member State' is limited to Member States participating in the enhanced cooperation established by the Twin Regulations. In the non-participating Member States instead of the Twin Regulations, courts apply national rules which fall outside the scope of this chapter.[3] Finally, the reference to the term 'court' should, along the lines of Recital 29 of the Twin Regulations, be understood as reference to not only courts *stricto sensu*, but also to other competent bodies or persons entrusted with judicial functions like or instead of courts, such as notaries and legal professionals in some Member States.[4]

2. CONCENTRATION OF JURISDICTION AS THE KEY PRINCIPLE

As discussed in Chapter 2, the EU has adopted a number of separate regulations covering different aspects of family private international law resulting in an atomised approach – different legal instruments regulate jurisdiction in matrimonial matters, parental responsibility, child abduction, maintenance, and succession. They each tend to set their own jurisdictional rules with diverse grounds of jurisdiction. In addition, certain family law matters are not captured by the unified EU legal instruments at all, such as jurisdiction for matters of personal status or termination of registered partnerships. Employing a variety of EU and national instruments is further complicated by the fact that there are few cross-references between those instruments

---

[3] See Chapter 3 of this volume.
[4] In France this is entrusted to notaries, while in Italy these decisions are made by civil registrars and lawyers. See L. RUGERRI, 'Registered Partnerships and Property Consequences. Jurisdiction' in M.J. CAZORLA GONZÁLEZ, M. GIOBBI, J. KRAMBERGER ŠKERL, L. RUGGERI and S. WINKLER (eds.), *Property Relations of Cross Border Couples in the European Union*, Edizioni Scientifiche Italiane, Napoli 2020, p. 59.

and in particular jurisdictional rules.[5] The Twin Regulations are distinctive in this regard as they partially rest on the unified EU jurisdictional rules in matters of succession[6] and matrimonial matters[7] and national jurisdictional rules in matters of dissolution or annulment of registered partnership. Appearing only later in the line of EU family private international law regulations,[8] the Twin Regulations recognise the benefits of interconnection between EU family law instruments, in particular of the concentration of jurisdiction.[9] Articles 4 and 5 are both mandatory in their respective realms of application and take primary place in the Twin Regulations' jurisdictional architecture, above the other jurisdictional rules. As a result, the courts of any Member State different from the ones competent under Articles 4 or 5, as the case may be, have to declare of their own motion, pursuant to Article 15, that they have no jurisdiction.[10]

2.1. CONCENTRATION IN THE *FORUM SUCCESSIONIS*

Article 4 of the Matrimonial Property Regulation concentrates jurisdiction for matrimonial property in case of the death of one of the spouses before the courts of the Member States where the succession proceedings are commenced. It provides that the courts of a Member State seised in matters of the succession of a spouse pursuant to the Succession Regulation (*forum successionis*) also have jurisdiction to rule on matters of the matrimonial property regime arising in connection with that succession case. In addition to assuring procedural

---

[5] Reference from one EU instrument to another is envisaged between maintenance and parental responsibility, while reference from an EU instrument is made to a national law between maintenance and personal status. See Article 3(c) and (d) of the Maintenance Regulation. Reference within an instrument links (by means of prorogation of jurisdiction) the jurisdiction in parental responsibility matters to the matrimonial matters in Article 12(1) of the Brussels II bis Regulation.

[6] See the Succession Regulation.

[7] See the Brussels II bis Regulation, to be replaced as of 1 August 2022 by the Brussels II ter Regulation.

[8] The private international law rules on matrimonial property regimes were planned already in The Hague Programme: strengthening freedom, security and justice in the European Union, OJ C 53, 3.3.2005, pp. 1–14, especially p. 13. See C. Honorati, 'Verso una competenza della Comunità europea in materia di diritto di famiglia?' in S. Bariatti (ed.), *La famiglia nel diritto internazionale privato communitario*, Guiffrè editore, Milano 2007, p. 21.

[9] See Recital 32 of the Matrimonial Property Regulation. See also A. Limantė and N. Pogorelčnik Vogrinc, 'Party Autonomy in the Context of Jurisdictional and Choice of Law Rules of Matrimonial Property Regulation' (2020) 13 *Baltic Journal of Law & Politics* 135, 142.

[10] I. Kunda, 'Novi međunarodnoprivatnopravni okvir imovine bračnih i registriranih partnera u Europskoj uniji: polje primjene i nadležnost' ['New Private International Law Framework for Matrimonial and Registered Partner's Property in the European Union: Scope of Application and Jurisdiction'] (2019) *Hrvatska pravna revija [Croatian Law Review]* 27, 31.

economy and efficiency, such concentration is also intended to avoid potential difficulties or incoherent outcomes arising out of the interconnectedness between issues of succession and matrimonial property regimes.[11] This solution certainly appears to be purely logical as, under the laws of many countries, the liquidation of the matrimonial property regime precedes the decision on succession, and succession only covers the assets of the deceased and not the surviving spouse. Thus, concentration of jurisdiction takes into account close links between the issues of succession and matrimonial property, allowing for reasonable management of the two proceedings. It is nevertheless limited to international jurisdiction of a particular Member State, whereas the application of its national rules on intra-state territorial and subject matter jurisdiction may still result in the succession proceedings and the matrimonial property proceedings being handled separately by two different courts in a Member State.[12] The advantage of concentration is still not lost as the coherence and coordination is surely maintained to a much higher degree within a single legal system, than among two different ones.

The jurisdictional rule in Article 4 is mandatory, tolerates no exceptions and cannot be derogated by parties' will, as explained above. The requirements triggering its application are straightforward, trifold and cumulative: (i) the court in a Member State is seised with the succession case concerning a deceased spouse; (ii) the jurisdiction of that court is established pursuant to the Succession Regulation; and (iii) the matters of the matrimonial property regime are connected with that succession case.[13] The requirements have been given a broad interpretation in the literature, in particular the requirement of connectedness which should encompass not only the matrimonial property cases in which issues of preliminary nature to the succession proceedings are to be resolved, but also issues such as taking of evidence which could contribute to

---

[11] A. BONOMI, 'Article 4. Jurisdiction in the Event of the Death of One of the Spouses [Partners]' in I. VIARENGO and P. FRANZINA (eds.), *The EU Regulations on the Property Regimes of International Couples. A Commentary*, Edward Elgar, Cheltenham 2020, pp. 52–53.

[12] P. FRANZINA, 'Jurisdiction in Matters related to Property Regimes under EU Private International Law' (2017/2018) 19 *Yearbook of Private International Law* 159, 169. For criticism see P. MANKOWSKI, 'Internationale Zuständigkeit nach EuGüVO und EuPartVO' in A. DUTTA and J. WEBER (eds.), *Die Europäischen Güterrechtsverordnungen*, C. H. Beck, München 2017, p. 14.

[13] Compare A. BONOMI, 'Article 4. Jurisdiction in the event of the death of one of the spouses [partners]' in I. VIARENGO and P. FRANZINA (eds.), *The EU Regulations on the Property Regimes of International Couples. A Commentary*, Edward Elgar, Cheltenham 2020, p. 56, who accepting the requirement under b) states that 'it is not entirely clear from the text'. It is submitted here that the wording 'a court of a Member State is seised in matters of the succession of a spouse pursuant to Regulation (EU) No 650/2012' is clear and leaves no room for other interpretation than that the condition under b) is straightforward.

the procedural economy.[14] It is upon the court seised with the particular case to assess the connectedness in the light of Article 4.[15]

Where a Member State court is seised with such succession case, the matters of matrimonial property follow attracted to the same jurisdiction by the force of ancillary connection. Due to the principle of *perpetuatio jurisdictionis*, the concentration of jurisdiction remains even if the succession case is ended following the commencement of the matrimonial property case, because it is finally decided, settled or otherwise.[16] Conversely, if the court is seised with the matrimonial property case after the succession case is already ended, Article 4 will not be applicable and Article 6 et seq. should be applied instead.

Application of Article 4 means that jurisdiction as regards matrimonial property matters directly depends on the jurisdiction grounds laid down in the Succession Regulation. Unlike in Article 5 as will be seen below, no distinction is made in Article 4 among the grounds of jurisdiction in the Succession Regulation.[17] The general jurisdictional rule in Article 4 establishes jurisdiction of the courts of the Member State in which the deceased had his or her habitual residence at the time of death, which was subject to recent interpretation by the Court of Justice of the European Union (CJEU) in the case *E.E.*[18]

> E.E. is a Lithuanian national whose mother married K.-D.E., a German national. Together with his mother, E.E., still a minor child, moved to live in Germany. In 2013, E.E.'s mother drew up a will at the notary office in Garliava (Lithuania) and named her son E.E. as sole heir to her entire estate. Following her mother's death which occurred in Germany, E.E. requested notary office in Kaunas (Lithuania) to open the succession and issue a certificate of succession rights in 2017. The notary refused to do so, convinced that the deceased's habitual residence at the time of her death was in Germany, despite the fact that E.E.'s mother was a Lithuanian national who had never severed her links with her homeland. While the Supreme Court of Lithuania did not directly ask about the habitual residence of the deceased (at the time of

---

[14] P. FRANZINA, 'Jurisdiction in Matters related to Property Regimes under EU Private International Law' (2017/2018) 19 *Yearbook of Private International Law* 159, 171.

[15] R. FRIMSTON, 'Article 4: Jurisdiction in the Event of Death of One of the Spouses' in U. BERGQUIST, D. DAMASCELLI, R. FRIMSTON, P. LAGARDE and B. REINHARTZ, *The EU Regulations on Matrimonial and Patrimonial Property*, Oxford University Press, Oxford 2019, p. 49.

[16] P. FRANZINA, 'Jurisdiction in Matters related to Property Regimes under EU Private International Law' (2017/2018) 19 *Yearbook of Private International Law* 159, 166; A. BONOMI, 'Article 4. Jurisdiction in the event of the death of one of the spouses [partners]' in I. VIARENGO and P. FRANZINA (eds.), *The EU Regulations on the Property Regimes of International Couples. A Commentary*, Edward Elgar, Cheltenham 2020, p. 55.

[17] P. MANKOWSKI, 'Internationale Zuständigkeit nach EuGüVO und EuPartVO' in A. DUTTA and J. WEBER (eds.), *Die Europäischen Güterrechtsverordnungen*, C. H. Beck, München 2017, p. 15.

[18] Case C-80/19, *E.E.*, EU:C:2020:569.

death), the CJEU provided certain guidelines incidentally. The CJEU underlined that the Succession Regulation is built on the concept of a single habitual residence of the deceased ruling out the possibility of considering a person habitually resident in several states.[19] Referring to Recitals 23 and 24 of the Regulation, the CJEU set the criteria for establishing habitual residence of the deceased. The authority dealing with the succession should make an overall assessment of the circumstances of the life of the deceased during the years preceding his or her death and at the time of his death, taking account of all relevant factual elements, in particular the duration and regularity of the deceased's presence in the state concerned and the conditions and reasons for that presence. Afterwards, the authority should verify where the centre of interests of the deceased person's family and social life was. Where this is still insufficient to establish habitual residence of the deceased, the secondary set of criteria – nationality and location of assets – should be taken into account.[20]

As noted by Bonomi, when the jurisdiction in succession case is based on the habitual residence of the deceased under Article 4 of the Succession Regulation, the concentration of jurisdiction in the matrimonial property case within the same Member State is foreseeable and usually close to the surviving spouse.[21] There is also a necessary proximity between the matrimonial property matters and the court seised with the succession matters such as for the purpose of taking evidence. The link is, according to Bonomi, weaker when the jurisdiction for succession matters is based on other grounds, e.g. Article 10 of the Succession Regulation providing for subsidiary jurisdiction and listing nationality, previous habitual residence and location of the assets as jurisdiction grounds.[22] Besides, Article 5 of the Succession Regulation allows the parties concerned to choose the court of the Member State whose law was chosen by the deceased to govern his or her succession under Article 22 of the Succession Regulation. This has been characterised by some as a 'striking influence of the heirs' over the jurisdiction which extends to matrimonial property matters because of putting the surviving spouse in an unforeseen and impractical position.[23] It does not seem to be an actual concern at least in those circumstances in which

---

[19] Case C-80/19, *E.E.*, EU:C:2020:569, para 40.
[20] For a detailed comment on this case see A. LIMANTĖ, 'The E.E. Decision (C-80/19) Sheds Light on Notaries Acting as "Courts" and on a Few Other Notions within the Context of the Succession Regulation' (2021) 6 *European Papers* 45–55.
[21] A. BONOMI, 'The Regulation on Matrimonial Property and Its Operation in Succession Cases – Its Interaction with the Succession Regulation and Its Impact on Non-participating Member States' (2020) 26 *Problemy Prawa Prywatnego Międzynarodowego [Issues in Private International Law]* 71, 81 <https://doi.org/10.31261/PPPM.2020.26.07>.
[22] A. BONOMI, 'Article 4. Jurisdiction in the Event of the Death of One of the Spouses [Partners]' in I. VIARENGO and P. FRANZINA (eds.), *The EU Regulations on the Property Regimes of International Couples. A Commentary*, Edward Elgar, Cheltenham 2020, p. 64.
[23] J. GRAY and P. QUINZÁ REDONDO, 'The Coordination of Jurisdiction and Applicable Law' in J.-S. BERGÉ, S. FRANCQ and M. GARDEÑES SANTIAGO (eds.), *Boundaries of European Private International Law*, Bruylant, Bruxelles 2015, p. 642.

one of the heirs is the surviving spouse. Namely, prorogation agreement under Article 5 of the Succession Regulation has to be concluded by the concerned parties, meaning that all parties having an interest in succession are necessary parties to the prorogation agreement. In case one of them was not party to the agreement, such as the surviving spouse, the chosen court will retain jurisdiction only if such parties external to the agreement enters an appearance without contesting the jurisdiction of the court pursuant to Article 9 of the Succession Regulation.[24]

It should be underlined that the rule of concentration laid down in Article 4 applies only where the court seised with the succession case is located in a Member State participating in both the Matrimonial Property Regulation or the Regulation on the Property Consequences of Registered Partnerships, as the case may be, and the Succession Regulation. While all Member States that are bound by the Twin Regulations are also bound by the Succession Regulation, the number of countries bound by the Succession Regulation (all Member States, except Denmark and Ireland) is higher than that bound by the Twin Regulations (18 Member States). If the court in, for instance Lithuania, Poland or Hungary which are not bound by the Twin Regulations, is seised with the succession case, there is a potential conflict of jurisdiction for matrimonial property matters between those Member States where such jurisdiction may be established under national rules and other Member States where such jurisdiction may be established pursuant to Article 6 of the Matrimonial Property Regulation.[25]

2.2. CONCENTRATION IN THE *FORUM DIVORTII*

Resembling Article 4, Article 5 of the Twin Regulations is designed to concentrate jurisdiction in one Member State – that of the *forum divortii*. It provides that the courts of the Member States seised with an application for divorce, legal separation or marriage annulment under the Brussels II bis Regulation (to be replaced by the Brussels II ter Regulation) also have jurisdiction to rule on matters of matrimonial property arising in connection with that application. As matrimonial property issues nowadays typically arise in consequence of the marriage dissolution, Article 5 will probably be the most commonly used jurisdictional rule in the Twin Regulations.

---

[24] I. Kunda and D. Vrbljanac, 'Choice of Court and Applicable Law under Regulation (EU) 650/2012' in M.J. Cazorla González and L. Ruggeri (eds.), *Guidelines for Practitioners in Cross-Border Family Property and Succession Law*, Dykinson, Madrid 2020, p. 51.

[25] See also A. Bonomi, 'The Regulation on Matrimonial Property and Its Operation in Succession Cases – Its Interaction with the Succession Regulation and Its Impact on Non-participating Member States' (2020) 26 *Problemy Prawa Prywatnego Międzynarodowego [Issues in Private International Law]* 71, 85 <https://doi.org/10.31261/PPPM.2020.26.07>.

Mirroring Article 4, the requirements triggering the application of Article 5 are cumulative: (i) the court in a Member State is seised to decide on the application for a matrimonial matter (divorce, legal separation or marriage annulment); (ii) the jurisdiction of that court is established pursuant to the Brussels II bis Regulation; and (iii) the matters of the matrimonial property regime are connected with that application in a matrimonial case. The above comments related to the requirements under Article 4 are *mutatis mutandis* applicable under Article 5 as well.

However, Article 5 of the Matrimonial Property Regulation has additional feature: it foresees two different tracks for the concentration of the jurisdiction. In certain cases, concentration of jurisdiction is automatic (unqualified), in others, consent of spouses as to the concentration of jurisdiction is required.[26] Whether the consent is required depends on the ground of jurisdiction in the Brussels II bis Regulation relied on in the divorce case. Automatic extension of jurisdiction is foreseen for the cases where jurisdiction for divorce is based on the first four criteria in Article 3(1)(a) of the Brussels II bis Regulation also referred to as the 'strong' jurisdiction grounds:[27] the current or last common habitual residence of spouses, the habitual residence of the respondent and the habitual residence of either of them in the event of a joint application.

> Two Italian nationals are married and live in Spain. If one of them commences divorce proceedings in Spain, Spanish courts will have jurisdiction to decide the divorce case pursuant to Article 3(1)(a), first indent of the Brussels II bis Regulation. According to Article 5 of the Matrimonial Property Regulation or the Regulation, Spanish courts will automatically have jurisdiction to rule on the matters of matrimonial property of the spouses as well.

Where jurisdiction for divorce is based on 'weak jurisdiction grounds'[28] in Article 3(1)(a), fifth and sixth indent of the Brussels II bis Regulation, concentration of jurisdiction for a matrimonial property matter in the respective Member State is subject to the spouses' agreement. This is because the cited provisions allow one of the spouses to choose jurisdiction closer to him or

---

[26] In contrast to Article 5 of the Matrimonial Property Regulation, in case of registered partnerships under Article 5(2) of the Regulation on the Property Consequences of Registered Partnerships, the agreement between partners is always needed for concentration of jurisdiction in the *forum dissolutionis*. This is justified by the fact that as jurisdiction in proceedings for dissolution of registered partnerships is based on the national rules of private international law (the Brussels II bis Regulations applies to marriages only) and thus may differ among the Member States.

[27] P. Franzina, 'Jurisdiction in Matters related to Property Regimes under EU Private International Law' (2017/2018) 19 *Yearbook of Private International Law* 159, 172.

[28] Ibid., 159, 172.

her and as such suffer from 'legitimacy deficit'.[29] In particular, they enable the applicant to choose jurisdiction of the Member State in which the applicant had resided for at least a year immediately before the application was made or six months in case of a Member State of his or her nationality (and which, as a result, might have no link at all with the respondent). By requiring spouses' consent in such cases, the Matrimonial Property Regulation aims to assure fairness so that the choice by one spouse of closer jurisdiction for divorce will not result in the choice of jurisdiction for the matrimonial property.[30] In other words, it is important to limit the benefits of the forum shopping, resulting from the alternative nature[31] of the jurisdiction criteria in Article 3 of the Brussels II bis Regulation.[32] Spouses' agreement to concentrate jurisdiction is also required in cases where the jurisdictional rule for conversion of legal separation into divorce in Article 5 or residual jurisdiction in 7 of the Brussels II bis Regulation is relied on. If such an agreement is not reached, Article 6 of the Matrimonial Property Regulation will be applicable.

> A Croatian husband and an Italian wife live in Croatia. After a few years, the wife receives a job offer in Brussels and moves there. The husband remains in Croatia. After one year in Brussels, the wife files for divorce there. Under Article 3(1)(a), fifth indent of the Brussels II bis Regulation, Belgian courts would have jurisdiction for divorce. However, the matters of matrimonial property will fall under Belgian courts' jurisdiction only if the husband agrees to such concentration pursuant to Article 5(2)(a) of the Matrimonial Property Regulation. In the absence of the husband's agreement on the concentration of jurisdiction, Belgian courts would decide on the application for divorce, while the court having jurisdiction to decide on the dissolution of matrimonial property will be determined with reference to Article 6.

According to Article 5(3) of the Matrimonial Property Regulation, if the agreement on concentration of jurisdiction for matrimonial property with jurisdiction for divorce under the Brussels II bis Regulation is concluded before the court is seised to rule on the matrimonial property, the agreement has to comply with Article 7(2) of the Matrimonial Property Regulation. The same is provided in Article 5(2) of the Regulation on the Property Consequences

---

[29] P. Mankowski, 'Internationale Zuständigkeit nach EuGüVO und EuPartVO' in A. Dutta and J. Weber (eds.), *Die Europäischen Güterrechtsverordnungen*, C.H. Beck, München 2017, p. 18.
[30] A. Limantė and N. Pogorelčnik Vogrinc, 'Party Autonomy in the Context of Jurisdictional and Choice of Law Rules of Matrimonial Property Regulation' (2020) 13 *Baltic Journal of Law & Politics* 135, 145.
[31] See Case C-168/08, *Hadadi*, EU:C:2009:474, para. 48.
[32] W. Pintens and J.M. Scherpe, 'Matrimonial Property' in J. Basedow et al. (eds.), *Encyclopedia of Private International Law*, vol. 2, Edward Elgar, Cheltenham 2017, p. 1239.

of Registered Partnerships with reference to Article 7 thereof. According to Frimston, the notion of 'agreement' should be construed in an autonomous manner as a binding declaration of the parties conferring jurisdiction over the matrimonial property to the courts of the Member State having jurisdiction to rule on the application for a divorce or other matter.[33] The agreement may be concluded at any time before the court is seised, but it is also possible that the parties accept that the court seised with the dissolution of marriage or partnership has jurisdiction to rule on matrimonial property matters, expressing such agreement when the case is already pending before the court. In this context Viarengo suggests that, lacking any indication to the contrary in the Twin Regulations, it would be reasonable to assume that they permit also tacit acceptance of the jurisdiction of the seised court, according to the relevant (procedural) rules in force in the forum Member State.[34] Although the concentration of various related proceedings before the courts of a single Member State is an important goal of the Twin Regulations,[35] the above conclusion on tacit acceptance is difficult to reconcile with both the overall system of the Twin Regulation provisions operating as self-sufficient set of rules (except where the residual jurisdiction is explicitly provided for) and the specific wording of Article 5 which explicitly refers to Article 7, but not to Article 8 on *prorogatio tacita*.[36] It derives that, in the interest of legal certainty and foreseeability and support for the informed party's decisions, an explicit agreement, where required, is necessary under Article 5 and cannot be replaced by the tacit submission let alone pursuant to national procedural rules. With respect to the requirements pertaining to the form of an agreement the reference here is made to the section below dealing with Article 7.[37]

---

[33] R. FRIMSTON, 'Article 5: Jurisdiction in Case of Divorce, Legal Separation or Marriage Annulment' in U. BERGQUIST, D. DAMASCELLI, R. FRIMSTON, P. LAGARDE and B. REINHARTZ, *The EU Regulations on Matrimonial and Patrimonial Property*, Oxford University Press, Oxford 2019, p. 57.

[34] I. VIARENGO, 'Article 5 Jurisdiction in Cases of Divorce, Legal Separation or Marriage Annulment [in Cases of Dissolution or Annulment]' in I. VIARENGO and P. FRANZINA (eds.), *The EU Regulations on the Property Regimes of International Couples. A Commentary*, Edward Elgar, Cheltenham 2020, p. 76.

[35] See Recital 32 of the Twin Regulations.

[36] The same is true in the parallel provision in Article 4(2) of the Proposal for a Council Regulation on jurisdiction, applicable law and the recognition and enforcement of decisions in matters of matrimonial property regimes, COM/2011/0126 final – CNS 2011/0059, which reads: 'Such an agreement may be concluded at any time, even during the proceedings. If it is concluded before the proceedings, it must be drawn up in writing and dated and signed by both parties.' These form requirements necessarily entail explicit agreement, and were not altered in the final version of the provisions, but merely nomotechnically replaced by the reference to Article 7 where the same requirements pertaining to the form are detailed.

[37] See below Section 3.1. of this chapter.

3. JURISDICTION IN 'OTHER CASES'

The Twin Regulations clearly prioritise unity of jurisdiction for the related cases and coordination among different legal instruments. However, concentration of jurisdiction cannot be achieved in certain situations in which the application of Articles 4 and 5 fails. Jurisdiction in such situations is established under the default rules of jurisdiction in Article 6 if no forum is chosen by the parties under Article 7 and no tacit submission to jurisdiction took place under Article 8.

3.1. *FORUM PROROGATUM EXPRESSUM*

Article 7 of the Twin Regulations, opening the door for party autonomy to choose the competent court (*prorogatio fori*), comes into play only if the application of Articles 4 and 5 fails and concentration of jurisdiction is thus not possible.[38] According to Article 7 of the Matrimonial Property Regulation, the parties (note that the term 'parties' and not 'spouses' is used) may agree that exclusive jurisdiction to rule on matters of their matrimonial property regime is conferred on either (i) the courts of the Member State of the *lex causae* (under Articles 22, 26(1)(a) or (b) of the Matrimonial Property Regulation or Articles 22 and 26(1) of the Regulation on the Property Consequences of Registered Partnerships); or (ii) the courts of the Member State of the *locus celebrationis*. The choice among different *lex cause* unfolds into four possible options depending on the spouses' habitual residences and nationalities at the time the agreement on the choice of law is concluded, thus amounting to five potential court-related connection choices for the parties which are increased wherever a spouse has double or multiple nationalities.

Such limited options result from the balancing between party autonomy and legal security (foreseeability especially).[39] These options are further limited by the fact that the parties may choose only the courts of a participating Member State. If the parties are married in a third state (or a non-participating Member State) or choose the law of such state as applicable to their matrimonial property, an agreement in favour of the courts of such third state would not be valid under the Matrimonial Property Regulation and the default rules in Article 6 would apply.[40] On the other hand, a valid agreement on prorogation

---

[38] See also E. Lein, 'Article 7. Election de for' in A. Bonomi and P. Wautelet (eds.), *Le droit européen des relations patrimoniales de couple: Commentaire des Règlements n°s 2016/1103 et 2016/1104*, Bruylant, Bruxelles 2021, p. 433.
[39] Ibid., pp. 430–431.
[40] See also P. Franzina, 'Article 7. Choice of Court' in I. Viarengo and P. Franzina (eds.), *The EU Regulations on the Property Regimes of International Couples. A Commentary*, Edward Elgar, Cheltenham 2020, pp. 86 et seq.

of jurisdiction of the courts of a particular Member State under Article 7, derogates the jurisdiction of the courts of any other Member State based on the grounds in Article 6.

> One partner, a double Croatian and Bosnian and Herzegovinian national, living in Slovenia, and the other partner, a German and Polish national living in Luxembourg, who registered their partnership in Spain, own properties in Croatia, France, Germany and Luxembourg. They intend to choose the court which will have jurisdiction to rule on the property consequences of their registered partnership. Their options are as follows: (i) Slovenian courts featuring as the *forum residentiae habitualis* for one partner; (ii) Luxembourgian courts as the *forum residentiae habitualis* for the other partner; (iii) Croatian courts as the *forum nationalis* for one partner; (iv) German courts as the *forum nationalis* for the other partner; or (v) Spanish courts as the *forum celebrationis*. Bosnian and Herzegovinian nationality of one partner and Polish nationality of the other are irrelevant since the former country is not a Member State, while the latter is not a participating Member State. French courts are also not on the list of available courts since location of property is not a relevant factor for choosing the courts.

It is important to note that the Twin Regulations refer to the choice of 'the courts of the Member State' and not to the choice of a particular court in the chosen Member State. If an agreement includes an indication of a concrete court, that would necessitate interpretation. It is likely that in such a case, the courts would hold that the parties agreed on the courts of the Member State to which the indicated court belongs, while the validity of the choice of the venue (indicated court) would be decided based on the national rules of the Member State in question.

The question might arise as to who in particular should or could conclude an agreement under Article 7. The provision itself and Recital 36 use the terms 'parties' and 'parties concerned', respectively. Mankowski states that a third person may be a party to such an agreement given that some matrimonial property disputes potentially involve parties other than spouses.[41] The term 'parties' aims at a flexible solution which, according to Firmston, depends on the nature and extent of the proceedings.[42] For instance, the 'concerned parties' may be the heirs by operation of law and potential legal heirs identified in a will as well as other parties that claim a certain right to the estate, such as beneficiaries of a legacy or an executor (but not creditors who only have a claim against the estate).[43]

---

[41] P. MANKOWSKI, 'Internationale Zuständigkeit nach EuGüVO und EuPartVO' in A. DUTTA and J. WEBER (eds.), *Die Europäischen Güterrechtsverordnungen*, C. H. Beck, München 2017, p. 22.
[42] R. FRIMSTON, 'Article 7: Choice of Court' in U. BERGQUIST, D. DAMASCELLI, R. FRIMSTON, P. LAGARDE and B. REINHARTZ, *The EU Regulations on Matrimonial and Patrimonial Property*, Oxford University Press, Oxford 2019, p. 63.
[43] Ibid., p. 64.

Article 7(2) of the Twin Regulations governs the form of a choice-of-court agreement and requires it to be 'expressed in writing and dated and signed by the parties'. A communication by electronic means is considered to be in writing if it provides a durable record of the agreement.[44] Such strict requirements as to the form, as Franzina notes, ensure that the will of the parties can be established with sufficient certainty, based on appropriate evidence. Moreover, it also serves to strengthen informed choice of the parties and well-considered arrangement of their interests.[45]

The wording of Article 7(3) of the Matrimonial Property Regulation indicates that no restrictions exist as to the time when the agreement is entered into, enabling the parties to conclude that such agreement may be entered into before, at the time or after the marriage is concluded in a form of a clause in the pre-nuptial agreement or matrimonial property agreement or in a separate agreement, but also before, at the time or after the commencement of the court proceedings.[46]

3.2. FORUM PROROGATUM TACITUM

The courts of a Member State that otherwise have no jurisdiction based on an explicit agreement or default provisions can also have jurisdiction based on the silent agreement of the parties (*prorogatio tacita*). The provision of Article 8 of the Twin Regulations is worded according to the previous models, in particular Article 26 of the Brussels I bis Regulation.[47] Thus, it requires that a defendant enters an appearance before a court of the participating Member State which is seised with the matrimonial property matter, without contesting the court's

---

[44] One might question how, in the case of the exchange of emails, the requirement of signature could be fulfilled. It seems natural that electronic signature should be accepted; however, most likely if an agreement is signed, scanned and then sent by email, such exchange should suffice for an agreement to fulfil Article 7(2) requirements.

[45] P. FRANZINA, 'Article 7. Choice of Court' in I. VIARENGO and P. FRANZINA (eds.), *The EU Regulations on the Property Regimes of International Couples. A Commentary*, Edward Elgar, Cheltenham 2020, p, 90.

[46] If concluding an agreement quite in advance to these events, the spouses are not certain if their choice-of-court agreement will apply because there is no certainty that the matrimonial property matter will be dealt with at the same time as the succession proceedings of one of them, or their divorce, marriage annulment or legal separation. See A. LIMANTĖ and N. POGORELČNIK VOGRINC, 'Party Autonomy in the Context of Jurisdictional and Choice of Law Rules of Matrimonial Property Regulation' (2020) 13 *Baltic Journal of Law & Politics* 135, 146.

[47] Provisions requiring defendant's consent in some matrimonial property matters may be found in national laws, such as Article 59(2) of the former Croatian Dissolution of Conflict of Laws with the Laws of Other Countries in Certain Relations Act (*Zakon o rješavanju sukoba zakona s propisima drugih zemalja u određenim odnosima*), NN 53/91 and 88/01.

jurisdiction. However, the Twin Regulations add an additional requirement intended to promote the principle of proximity as well as convergence of *forum* and *ius*:[48] (i) only the court of the Member State of the *lex causae* (under Articles 22, 26(1)(a) or (b) of the Matrimonial Property Regulation or Articles 22 and 26(1) of the Regulation on the Property Consequences of Registered Partnerships) or (ii) the courts of the Member State of the *locus celebrationis* may acquire jurisdiction in this manner.

In holding with its role model in Article 26(2) of the Brussels I bis Regulation addressing the position of weaker parties (such as consumers or employees), Article 8 provides that, prior to assuming jurisdiction, the court has to 'ensure that the defendant is informed of his right to contest the jurisdiction and of the consequences of entering or not entering an appearance'. This provision attempts to assure that that the defendant's acceptance does not result from the lack of information about his or her procedural situation. Informed consent has to be given irrespective of whether the defendant is represented by an attorney or received qualified legal advice.[49] The proper time to receive the information is not defined in the Twin Regulations but logically has to occur prior to the moment in which the court is establishing its jurisdiction, ideally at the time the defendant is served with the documents initiating the proceedings, if feasible.[50]

3.3. THE DEFAULT RULES

In the absence of a valid agreement on the choice of court in 'other cases' pursuant to Article 7 or tacit submission to the jurisdiction of certain courts pursuant to Article 8, Article 6 is called into play. It provides for a cascade of jurisdiction grounds which evolve around habitual residence and nationality. As stated in Recital 35 of the Twin Regulations, these connecting factors are set to ensure that a genuine connection exists between the spouses and the Member State in which jurisdiction is exercised.

In particular, jurisdiction under Article 6 is conferred to the courts of a Member State in the following hierarchical order (next jurisdiction ground may

---

[48] S. CORNELOUP, 'Article 8. Jurisdiction based on the Appearance of the Defendant' in I. VIARENGO and P. FRANZINA (eds.), *The EU Regulations on the Property Regimes of International Couples. A Commentary*, Edward Elgar, Cheltenham 2020, pp. 93 and 96.

[49] P. MANKOWSKI, 'Internationale Zuständigkeit nach EuGüVO und EuPartVO' in A. DUTTA and J. WEBER (eds.), *Die Europäischen Güterrechtsverordnungen*, C. H. Beck, München 2017, p. 31.

[50] E. LEIN, 'Article 8. Compétence fondée sur la comparution de défendeur' in A. BONOMI and P. WAUTELET (eds.), *Le droit européen des relations patrimoniales de couple: Commentaire des Règlements n°s 2016/1103 et 2016/1104*, Bruylant, Bruxelles 2021, p. 455.

be used provided the requirements in an earlier one are not fulfilled): (i) in whose territory the spouses are habitually resident at the time the court is seised (*forum residentiae habitualis communis*);[51] (ii) in whose territory the spouses were last habitually resident, insofar as one of them still resides there at the time the court is seised; (iii) in whose territory the respondent is habitually resident at the time the court is seised (embodying the principle *actor sequitur forum rei*); and (iv) of the spouses' common nationality at the time the court is seised (*forum nationalis communis*). In addition to the above jurisdictional grounds, Article 6 of the Regulation on the Property Consequences of Registered Partnerships adds the fifth step – (v) jurisdiction of the courts of the Member State under whose law the registered partnership was created (*forum celebrationis*). The additional ground is owed to the fact that not all Member States recognise registered partnerships; therefore, granting jurisdiction to the courts of the state where the partnership was registered, ensures that at least in that Member State the partnership will be recognised and thus it will be possible to terminate it.

> Two Slovenians met and got married in Amsterdam, where they both studied. Subsequently, the husband moved to France in pursuit of better employment with the intention to advance in his career. The wife also left the Netherlands as she began working in Brussels where she hopes to remain. A year later, the wife instituted the divorce proceedings in a Belgian court, which has jurisdiction under Article 3(1)(a), fifth indent of the Brussels II bis Regulation. For the Belgian court to have the concentrated jurisdiction to rule on the dissolution of the spouses' matrimonial property, the husband's consent is required. If the husband fails to agree, jurisdiction has to be established under Article 6 of the Matrimonial Property Regulation. First to be verified is whether the spouses have a common habitual residence. In the case at hand they do not have a common habitual residence, as one is living in Belgium, and the other in France, with the intention to stay there. The next jurisdictional ground similarly fails to result in jurisdiction as neither spouse is resident in the Netherlands any longer. On the third ground, only French courts (if the husband, as the respondent, is habitually resident there) or, if that fails, on the last ground, Slovenian courts (by the spouses' common nationality) would have jurisdiction to rule on the spouses' matrimonial property.

While the definition of 'habitual residence' is not contained in the Twin Regulations, or other EU regulations for that matter,[52] most likely it will be interpreted along the same lines as the concept of habitual residence under the

---

[51] The requirement of habitual residence in one Member State only refers to the same country of residence, which means that it is not necessary that the spouses (partners) actually live together for this requirement to be fulfilled.

[52] The only definitions of 'habitual residence' relate to that of the legal persons and natural persons acting in the course of their business in Article 19 of the Rome I Regulation.

Brussels II bis Regulation.[53] In EU private international law, the term 'habitual residence' is given an autonomous interpretation and its elements are detailed in the case law of the CJEU.[54] For a habitual residence to be established, physical presence in a Member State is essential, and it should be clear that the presence is not in any way temporary or intermittent.[55] Although stability and presence are important, a person's intention to establish habitual residence is also relevant especially in cases where the residence is of a relatively short time, provided it is manifested by certain tangible steps.[56] Either way, the concept of habitual residence is to be established on a case-to-case basis taking account of the particular facts of a case.

As for the last jurisdictional ground, it is important to underline that only common nationality of the spouses matters. If the spouses are of different nationalities, this jurisdictional ground would fail right away. If, however, the spouses share more than one common nationality, the issue has been raised as to whether the judgment in *Hadadi* may be applied by analogy. Invoking Recital 50 of the Matrimonial Property Regulation and Recital 49 of the Regulation on the Property Consequences of Registered Partnerships, Franzina contends that, regrettably, the option to resort to the *Hadadi* principle has been explicitly excluded.[57] It is not clear how this conclusion can be extended to jurisdiction since these Recitals are clearly set in the context of applicable law only, not jurisdiction.[58] Such policy is logical for the applicable law, as there cannot be

---

[53] See R. FRIMSTON, 'Article 6: Jurisdiction in Other Cases' in U. BERGQUIST, D. DAMASCELLI, R. FRIMSTON, P. LAGARDE and B. REINHARTZ, *The EU Regulations on Matrimonial and Patrimonial Property*, Oxford University Press, Oxford 2019, pp. 60–61; T. KRUGER, 'Finding a Habitual Residence' in I. VIARENGO and F.C. VILLATA (eds.), *Planning the Future of Cross Border Families: A Path Through Coordination*, Hart Publishing, Oxford 2020, pp. 117–132.

[54] So far, in the context of private international family law, most of the cases relate to a child's habitual residence. See e.g. Case C-523/07, *A.*, EU:C:2009:225, paras. 34–35; Case C-497/10 PPU, *Mercredi*, EU:C:2010:829, paras. 45–46. However, the case C-501/20, *M.P.A.*, which concerns interpretation of the habitual resident of adults who often move between jurisdictions (diplomats), is currently pending before the CJEU.

[55] Case C-376/14 PPU, *C.*, EU:C:2014:2268, para. 51; Case C-499/15, *W. and V.*, EU:C:2017:118, para. 60; Case C-111/17 PPU, *O.L. v P.Q.*, EU:C:2017:436, para. 43; Case C-512/17, *H.R.*, EU:C:2018:513, para. 41; and Case C-393/18, *UD v XB*, EU:C:2018:835, para. 50.

[56] Case C-497/10 PPU *Mercredi*, EU:C:2010:829, paras. 50–51.

[57] P. FRANZINA, 'Article 6. Jurisdiction in Other Cases' in I. VIARENGO and P. FRANZINA (eds.), *The EU Regulations on the Property Regimes of International Couples. A Commentary*, Edward Elgar, Cheltenham 2020, pp. 82–84. These Recitals state that the issue of multiple nationalities falls outside the scope of the Regulation and is left to be resolved by the national law, applicable international conventions and general principles of EU law.

[58] This is evident from the structure of the preamble which in case of the Matrimonial Property Regulation holds guidelines on jurisdiction and procedural matters in general up to Recital 41, while the applicable law matters are dealt with in Recital 43 and onwards. In addition, the last sentence in Recital 50 of the Matrimonial Property Regulation refers to applicable law as well. Such structure is replicated in the Regulation on the Property Consequences of Registered Partnerships, with slightly different numeration.

more than one law applicable at the same time. On the contrary, courts with competing elective jurisdiction are common in EU private international law and the CJEU in *Hadadi* found this outcome acceptable. In its judgment in *Hadadi*, the CJEU rejected the concept of 'effective nationality' existing in many national Member States' private international laws, worrying about verification of jurisdiction being subject to ambiguous criteria and becoming onerous, which in practical terms would translate into potentially fierce litigation already at the stage of determining jurisdiction.[59] For these reasons it is submitted that as far as the jurisdiction under Article 6 of the Twin Regulations is concerned, the *Hadadi* principle should inform the courts in interpreting the spouses' common nationality as the jurisdiction ground and their double, triple, etc. common nationalities should be deemed equal.[60] Hence, the courts of both (or more) Member States of which spouses are common nationals would have jurisdiction, the choice belonging to the party instigating the proceedings.[61] Thus, where parallel proceedings are brought before the courts of different Member States, Article 17 of the Twin Regulations may be used to resolve a conflict between these competing jurisdictions.[62]

4. REMAINING JURISDICTION RULES

The above main jurisdictional rules are complemented by the set of other rules aimed at dealing with particular situations imaginable in the cross-border matrimonial property cases. Alternative, subsidiary and necessary jurisdiction may be important in ensuring access to justice or proper administration thereof. By providing two separate options for declining the jurisdiction, the Twin Regulations additionally ensure protection of domestic family legal systems or coordination with third countries.

4.1. *FORUM ALTERNATIVUM*

Article 9 Matrimonial Property Regulation provides rules on alternative jurisdiction, which apply by way of exception, if a court of the Member State that has jurisdiction pursuant to Article 4, 6, 7 or 8 but holds that, 'under its private

---

[59] See Case C-168/08, *Hadadi*, EU:C:2009:474, para. 55.
[60] See also S. MARINO, *I rapporti matrimoniali della famiglia nella operazione giudiziaria civile dell' Unione europea*, Giuffrè Francis Lefebvre, Milano 2019, 143.
[61] In Case C-168/08, *Hadadi*, EU:C:2009:474, para. 58.
[62] A. BONOMI, 'Article 6. Compétence dans des affaires de divorce, de séparation de corps ou d'annulation du mariage' in A. BONOMI and P. WAUTELET (eds.), *Le droit européen des relations patrimoniales de couple: Commentaire des Règlements n°s 2016/1103 et 2016/1104*, Bruylant, Bruxelles 2021, p. 427.

international law, the marriage in question is not recognised for the purposes of matrimonial property regime proceedings'. Likewise, Article 9 of the Regulation on the Property Consequences of Registered Partnerships provides such rules when a court of the Member State, that has jurisdiction pursuant to Article 4, 5, or 6(a), (b), (c) or (d), holds that 'its law does not provide for the institution of registered partnership'. In such situations the court may (but need not) decline jurisdiction. However, this Article is not applicable if the marriage ended in divorce, legal separation or annulment or when the parties have obtained a dissolution or annulment of a registered partnership, as the case may be, which is capable of being recognised in the Member State of the forum.

The reasons for this unique provision in EU private international law to offer an 'exit strategy' whereby the courts in the participating Member States whose national laws cannot recognise certain marriages, such as same-sex marriages, may 'elegantly withdraw from the role conferred on them'.[63] In that vein the participating Member States are safe from loosing the power over recognition of a couple's relationship, where a particular type of the relationship is not known in that legal system.[64] In fact, laws of some Member States do not provide for same-sex marriages but provide for registered partnerships for same-sex couples, while some do not provide for either.[65]

If the court, which has jurisdiction to resolve the matter under the respective Regulation, decides to decline its jurisdiction pursuant to Article 9, it has to do so without undue delay so as to enable the couple to seek another forum (*forum alternativum*). To prevent situations in which such couples are left without access to courts as a result of declined jurisdiction,[66] the parties may agree to confer jurisdiction to the courts of any other participating Member State in accordance with Article 7. Where no such agreement is reached, jurisdiction lies with the courts of any other participating Member State pursuant to Article 6 or 8, or the courts of the Member State of the conclusion of the marriage. Recital 38 of the Matrimonial Property Regulation and Recital 36 of the Regulation on the Property Consequences of Registered Partnerships clarify

---

[63] I. KUNDA, 'Novi međunarodnoprivatnopravni okvir imovine bračnih i registriranih partnera u Europskoj uniji: polje primjene i nadležnost' ['New Private International Law Framework for Matrimonial and Registered Partner's Property in the European Union: Scope of Application and Jurisdiction'] (2019) *Hrvatska pravna revija [Croatian Law Review]* 27, 34.

[64] P. FRANZINA, 'Article 9. Alternative Jurisdiction' in I. VIARENGO and P. FRANZINA (eds.), *The EU Regulations on the Property Regimes of International Couples. A Commentary*, Edward Elgar, Cheltenham 2020, p. 108.

[65] For a complete overview of the type of relationships between couples recognised in different Member States see L. RUGGERI, I. KUNDA and S. WINKLER (eds.), *Family Property and Succession in EU Member States National Reports on the Collected Data*, University of Rijeka, Faculty of Law, Rijeka 2019.

[66] P. FRANZINA, 'Jurisdiction in Matters related to Property Regimes under EU Private International Law' (2017/2018) 19 *Yearbook of Private International Law* 159, 185.

that the otherwise present hierarchy among grounds of jurisdiction in these provisions (Article 6 and 8) does not apply when any of them is resorted to as the *forum alternativum*.

4.2. LIMITATION OF PROCEEDINGS

In addition to the option in Article 9 of the Twin Regulations, Article 13 provides grounds for the court to partially decline its jurisdiction, although, only with respect to individual property items. The reason underlying this option is coordination with jurisdiction of the third states. In the absence of a general scheme to coordinate situations which involve connection with a third state like in the Brussels I bis Regulation, this option is intended to protect parties' interests when there is a specific type of connection with a third state. Operating as an exception, this provision pierces the principle of the unity of assets which, besides being written out with respect to applicable law,[67] is also a structural element in the architecture of the jurisdictional rules.

Such limitation of the scope of the proceedings is available to the court seised to rule on the matrimonial property regime where: (i) the estate of the deceased, whose succession falls under the Succession Regulation, comprises assets located in a third state; (ii) one of the parties made the request for the limitation of the proceedings; and (iii) it may be expected that the decision of this court in respect of one or more of such assets will not be recognised and, where applicable, declared enforceable in that third state. Resemblance with Article 12 of the Succession Regulation is by no way accidental; the two provisions are functionally related because the issues of matrimonial property are often preliminary to the ones in the succession proceedings. Therefore, equivalent conditions contained in the provisions allow for the combined and coherent outcomes where the same asset located in a third state is subject to both types of issues. This having been said, the outcomes of application of the two provisions need not be the same in all cases because courts of different Member States may have jurisdiction in the separate proceedings, one on a matrimonial property matter and the other on a matter of succession. Furthermore, the decisions on limitation of the two proceedings are formally separate and it may be the case that the conditions are not fulfilled in respect to one matter but are fulfilled in respect to the other.[68]

The third requirement seems to be the central theme for the court seised. It entails assessment of the hypothetical situation in which the decision of the

---

[67] See Chapter 5 of this volume.
[68] A. BONOMI, 'Article 13. Limitation de la procédure' in A. BONOMI and P. WAUTELET (eds.), *Le droit européen des relations patrimoniales de couple: Commentaire des Règlements n*^{os} *2016/1103 et 2016/1104*, Bruylant, Bruxelles 2021, p. 507.

court seised would be rendered and attempted to be recognised (and enforced) in the third state where the assets are located. Such assessment should be carried out taking account of the factual and legal elements of the case before the seised court and rules on recognition (and enforcement) in the third state in question. The third requirement will be fulfilled where the court seised finds that its potential decision would not be recognised in the third state, for instance, because such matter falls within the exclusive competence of the courts in the third state.[69]

The court's discretion to limit the proceedings under the Twin Regulations does not affect the right of the parties under the *lex fori* to limit the scope of the proceedings.

4.3. FORUM SUBSIDIARIUM

Resort to the national rules on international jurisdiction is permitted by virtue of Article 10 on subsidiary jurisdiction (*forum subsidiarium*), modelled after Article 10(2) of the Succession Regulation.[70] This avenue is available under very strict conditions: (i) no court of a Member State has jurisdiction pursuant to Articles 4, 5, 6, 7 or 8, or all the courts pursuant to Article 9 have declined jurisdiction and no court has jurisdiction pursuant to Article 9(2); and (ii) the immoveable property of one or both spouses is located in the territory of the forum Member State.

> Registered partners are nationals of Norway and United States, respectively. They concluded their partnership in 2007 in Norway, and have been living in in Lithuania since 2013. They own several properties in different countries. One of them is registered as the owner of an apartment in a Spanish coastal village. In 2020, she sells it to a third party. In the attempt to invalidate this contract, the other partner commences the proceedings in Spain asking the court also to render a declaratory judgment establishing that they co-own the apartment. Does Spanish court have jurisdiction to hear the action seeking declaratory relief? Since this case is not related to succession of a registered partner or dissolution of registered partnership, Articles 4 and 5 are inapplicable. The same is true for Articles 7 and 8 since the partners have neither expressly nor tacitly agreed on the jurisdiction of any court. Likewise, Article 6 is inapplicable given that the partners are habitually resident in Lithuania (which is a non-participating Member State), they never habitually resided in any of the participating Member States, they do not have a common nationality and their

---

[69] See ibid., p. 513 (mentioning common law systems); P. FRANZINA, 'Article 13. Limitation of Proceedings' in I. VIARENGO and P. FRANZINA (eds.), *The EU Regulations on the Property Regimes of International Couples. A Commentary*, Edward Elgar, Cheltenham 2020, p. 134 (mentioning Tunisian law).

[70] See also the provision on subsidiary jurisdiction in Article 6 of the Maintenance Regulation.

registered partnership was created under Norwegian law (which is a non-Member State). Article 9 was not at issue here since no declining of jurisdiction was possible as no courts of a participating Member State have jurisdiction. Consequently, the answer to the question on the jurisdiction of Spanish court is affirmative because the immoveable (allegedly) owned by at least one of the registered partners is located in Spain.

The scope of thus established jurisdiction is limited only to the immoveable property in that Member State, thus presenting the other point where the principle of the unity of assets is pierced when it comes to jurisdictional rules.[71] As a result of the territorial principle, if more such property items are located in two or more participating Member States, courts of each such state have jurisdiction to adjudicate only the matter related to the immoveable in the forum state. Scholarly opinions, however, seem to differ on the question of the notion of 'immoveable'. While some advocate applicability of *lex rei sitae* for determining the moveable or immoveable nature of the asset,[72] others tend to favour Euroautonomous interpretation by reference to the same notion in other areas of EU law.[73]

4.4. FORUM NECESSITATIS

Echoing some other EU regulations,[74] Article 11 of the Twin Regulations provides for the *forum necessitatis* as the last resort and on exceptional basis because it weakens the principles of proximity and legal certainty (especially foreseeability). In order to establish jurisdiction on this ground the following requirements have to be fulfilled: (i) no court of a Member State has jurisdiction pursuant to Article 4, 5, 6, 7, 8 or 10, or all the courts pursuant to Article 9 have declined jurisdiction and no court of a Member State has jurisdiction pursuant to Article 9(2) or Article 10; (ii) the proceedings in matrimonial property matter cannot reasonably be brought or conducted or would be impossible in a third state with which the case is closely connected; and (iii) the case has a sufficient connection with the forum Member State.

---

[71] Other such instance concerns Article 13. See above Section 4.2. of this chapter.

[72] P. Mankowski, 'Internationale Zuständigkeit nach EuGüVO und EuPartVO' in A. Dutta and J. Weber (eds.), *Die Europäischen Güterrechtsverordnungen*, C. H. Beck, München 2017, p. 40; A. Bonomi, 'Article 13. Limitation de la procédure' in A. Bonomi and P. Wautelet (eds.), *Le droit européen des relations patrimoniales de couple: Commentaire des Règlements n°s 2016/1103 et 2016/1104*, Bruylant, Bruxelles 2021, p. 482.

[73] P. Franzina, 'Article 10. Subsidiary Jurisdiction' in I. Viarengo and P. Franzina (eds.), *The EU Regulations on the Property Regimes of International Couples. A Commentary*, Edward Elgar, Cheltenham 2020, p. 113.

[74] See e.g. Article 7 of the Maintenance Regulation and Article 11 of the Succession Regulation.

Whereas the first requirement is deductible following step-by-step the provisions referred to therein, the second requirements may present considerable difficulty to the court seised with the matrimonial property matter. Recital 41 of the Matrimonial Property Regulation and Recital 40 of the Regulation on the Property Consequences of Registered Partnerships explain that such impossibility may exist in a situation of civil war in a third state, or when a spouse cannot reasonably be expected to initiate or conduct proceedings in that state. The former belongs to the situations of absolute impossibility because the judiciary ceased to function due to the circumstances of war or other circumstances, including natural disaster or state of dangerous epidemic, or because of the lack of any grounds on which jurisdiction could be based in the case in question. Relative impossibility is present in situations such as seriously deficient procedural standards exposing the parties to discriminatory treatment.[75] Likewise, the impossibility would exist where the third state recognises neither same-sex marriages nor property consequences thereof.[76]

While the third requirement has been identified as difficult to interpret, it is common ground that it is to be assessed in the light of the particular circumstances of each case. Possible elements of connection are any of the connecting factors mentioned in the other provisions of the Twin Regulations, where they fail to result in jurisdiction of courts in any of the participating Member States pursuant to any of the previously addressed jurisdiction-conferring provisions.[77]

4.5. FORUM FOR COUNTERCLAIMS

A well established rule in EU private international law[78] has been included in the Twin Regulations in Article 12, whereby the court in which the proceedings are pending pursuant to any Article (4, 5, 6, 7, 8, 9 (2), 10 or 11) also has

---

[75] A. BONOMI, 'Article 11. *Forum necessitatis*' in A. BONOMI and P. WAUTELET (eds.), *Le droit européen des relations patrimoniales de couple: Commentaire des Règlements n°s 2016/1103 et 2016/1104*, Bruylant, Bruxelles 2021, pp. 492–493.

[76] See I. VIARENGO, 'Effetti patrimoniali delle unioni civili transfrontaliere e la nuova disciplina europea' (2018) 54 *Rivista di diritto internazionale privato e processuale* 33, 46; G. BIAGIONI, 'Article 11. *Forum necessitatis*' in I. VIARENGO and P. FRANZINA (eds.), *The EU Regulations on the Property Regimes of International Couples. A Commentary*, Edward Elgar, Cheltenham 2020, p. 119.

[77] A. BONOMI, 'Article 11. *Forum necessitatis*' in A. BONOMI and P. WAUTELET (eds.), *Le droit européen des relations patrimoniales de couple: Commentaire des Règlements n°s 2016/1103 et 2016/1104*, Bruylant, Bruxelles 2021, p. 495.

[78] See e.g. Article 8(3) of the Brussels I bis Regulation and Article 4 of the Brussels II bis Regulation.

jurisdiction to rule on a counterclaim.[79] Counterclaim is admissible as long as it falls within the scope *ratione materiae* of the respective Regulation,[80] meaning that it has to concern the matrimonial property or a property consequence of registered partnership. It should also be within the scope *ratione temporis* of the Regulations. It has been submitted in the commentaries that the counterclaim must also fall within the scope of the jurisdiction of the court in question. By way of example, where the court has subsidiary jurisdiction the counterclaim has to concern the immoveable in the forum Member State.[81]

Although the provision of Article 12 fails to specify further requirements, commentaries suggest that certain connection between the main claim and the counterclaim has to be verified.[82] However, this does not seem to be provided as a particular requirement since the connection seems to be sufficiently assured by means of the requirement that the counterclaim falls within the scope of the Regulation in question, because the entire regulation concerns the same type of matters. This is also the case with the provision on counterclaims in Article 4 of the Brussels II bis Regulation which likewise requires that it falls within the scope of that Regulation. On the contrary, the Brussels I bis Regulation encompasses a variety of different types of matters, hence its provision in Article 8(3) defines in more detail the elements of connection requiring that it arises from 'the same contract or facts on which the original claim was based'.

4.6. FORUM FOR PROVISIONAL MEASURES

In already a traditional manner,[83] Article 19 of the Twin Regulations provides that application may be made to the courts of a Member State for such

---

[79] The notion of a 'counterclaim' has been previously interpreted by the CJEU in the context of the Brussels Convention and Brussels I Regulation, the predecessors of the Brussels I bis Regulation. See Case C-341/93, *Danværn Production A/S v Schuhfabriken Otterbeck GmbH & Co.*, EU:C:1995:239, para. 18; Case C-185/15, *Marjan Kostanjevec v F&S Leasing, GmbH.*, EU:C:2016:763, paras. 32–33.

[80] See above Chapter 3 of this volume.

[81] P. FRANZINA, 'Jurisdiction in Matters related to Property Regimes under EU Private International Law' (2017/2018) 19 *Yearbook of Private International Law* 193; A. BONOMI, 'Article 12. Demandes reconventionnelles' in A. BONOMI and P. WAUTELET (eds.), *Le droit européen des relations patrimoniales de couple: Commentaire des Règlements n°s 2016/1103 et 2016/1104*, Bruylant, Bruxelles 2021, pp. 499, 500–501.

[82] P. MANKOWSKI, 'Internationale Zuständigkeit nach EuGüVO und EuPartVO' in A. DUTTA and J. WEBER (eds.), *Die Europäischen Güterrechtsverordnungen*, C. H. Beck, München 2017, p. 43; P. FRANZINA, 'Jurisdiction in Matters related to Property Regimes under EU Private International Law' (2017/2018) 19 *Yearbook of Private International Law* 193.

[83] See e.g. Article 35 of the Brussels I bis Regulation, Article 20 of the Brussels II bis Regulation, Article 14 of the Maintenance Regulation and Article 54 of the Succession Regulation.

provisional, including protective, measures[84] as may be available under the law of that state, even if, under the respective Regulation, the courts of another Member State have jurisdiction as to the substance of the matter. Thus, courts of any participating Member State having jurisdiction on the merits under the Twin Regulations also have direct jurisdiction to grant provisional measures. This is the natural extension of the court's competence to decide on the merits. Additionally, provisional jurisdiction to grant such measures is conferred upon the courts of the participating Member State whose law provides for a particular measure applied for. This is a reference to the national rules, both on the substance and domestic jurisdiction pertaining to the provisional measures.[85]

> A couple of mixed nationalities, French and German, with habitual residence in Brussels, is divorcing and as a corollary matter resolving their matrimonial property issues. One of their valuable immoveables is located in Croatia. In order to protect her interests in that immoveable, the wife applies to the Croatian courts for the provisional measure pursuant to Croatian law which consists in the prohibition of sale or other disposal of the immmoveable in question, along with the entry of the prohibition in the Land Registry and temporarily entrusting the management of the immoveable to the wife or a third party.

Article 19 is a practical route to preserve factual or legal situation before the courts of the very Member State where the measure will have to be enforced. Its efficiency lays not only in the direct enforceability avoiding the exequatur but also in maintaining the surprise effect where the *lex fori* provides for it.[86]

5. COORDINATION AMONG CONCURRENT PROCEEDINGS IN DIFFERENT MEMBER STATES

One of the important issues related to judicial coordination among courts of different Member States is the one concerning concurrent proceedings. For this purpose, the Twin Regulations define priority rules where parallel or

---

[84] The notion of 'provisional, including protective, measures' has been elaborated in the CJEU case law. See e.g. C-261/90, *Mario Reichert, Hans-Heinz Reichert and Ingeborg Kockler v Dresdner Bank AG.*, EU:C:1992:149, para. 31.

[85] S. MIGLIORINI, 'Article 19. Mesures provisoires et conservatoires' in A. BONOMI and P. WAUTELET (eds.), *Le droit européen des relations patrimoniales de couple: Commentaire des Règlements n°s 2016/1103 et 2016/1104*, Bruylant, Bruxelles 2021, p. 556.

[86] L. SANDRINI, 'Article 19. Provisional, Including Protective, Measures' in I. VIARENGO and P. FRANZINA (eds.), *The EU Regulations on the Property Regimes of International Couples. A Commentary*, Edward Elgar, Cheltenham 2020, p. 173.

related proceedings are pending before the courts of two or more participating Member States. These rules determine the chronological order in which the seised courts are each to decide on their own jurisdiction following the principle *prior in tempore, potior in iure*. The aim is to minimise the risk of concurrent proceedings because this may result in conflicting or irreconcilable decisions and consequently hinder their free circulation among the participating Member States. In preventing territorial separation of the European judicial area wide respect for the principle of mutual recognition is of fundamental importance. It presupposes the existence of mutual trust among Member States,[87] in the matrimonial property cases of the participating Member States. On the more practical side, in order to make the coordination system functional, it was also necessary to provide autonomous rules on the time when a court is deemed seised.

5.1. TIME WHEN THE COURT IS SEISED

By taking account of the variety of procedural solutions in different Member States and drawing on its predecessors,[88] Article 14 of the Twin Regulations defines when a court is deemed seised by referring either to the 'the document instituting the proceedings or an equivalent document', or 'opening the proceedings' or 'registering the case' as the case may be. If the proceedings are commenced by the parties, the court is deemed seised: (i) at the time when the document is lodged with the court; or (ii) if the document has to be served before being lodged with the court, at a time when it is received by the authority responsible for service. It is important that any subsequent steps are taken if necessary under the *lex fori*. If the proceedings are opened on the court's own motion the court is deemed seised (iii) at the time when the decision to open the proceedings is taken by the court, or, where such a decision is not required, at the time when the case is registered by the court.

Article 16 defines steps which the court of a participating Member State seised has to take if a defendant habitually resident in another state does not enter an appearance. The purpose is to safeguard his or her right to defence under the principle of *audiatur et altera pars*.[89]

---

[87] K. LENAERTS, 'The Principle of Mutual Recognition in the Area of Freedom, Security and Justice', The Fourth Annual Sir Jeremy Lever Lecture, University of Oxford, 30 January 2015, <www.law.ox.ac.uk>, p. 4.

[88] See e.g. Article 32 of the Brussels I bis Regulation, Article 16 of the Brussels II bis Regulation, Article 9 of the Maintenance Regulation and Article 14 of the Succession Regulation.

[89] The references are made here to Article 19 of the Regulation (EC) No 1393/2007 of the European Parliament and of the Council of 13 November 2007 on the service in the Member States of judicial and extrajudicial documents in civil or commercial matters

5.2. LIS PENDENS

Article 17 defines *lis pendens* as the situation in which proceedings involving the same cause of action and between the same parties are brought before courts of different Member States. The notions of the 'same cause of action' and the 'same parties' have been repeatedly elucidated by the CJEU within the Brussels I bis Regulation and its predecessors, relying on autonomous, systematic and teleological interpretation. Namely, those rules are designed to preclude, in so far as is possible and from the outset in the European judicial area, the possibility of a situation resulting in a non-recognition of a judgment in one Member State on account of its irreconcilability with a judgment given in a dispute between the same parties in the other Member State in which recognition is sought.[90]

Based on the autonomous interpretation, the notion of 'cause of action' comprises both the 'cause of action', i.e. the facts and the rule of law relied on as the basis of the action, and the 'object of the action' (or 'subject matter') which means the ends the action has in view.[91] Thus, the different nature of the claims under the applicable national law is not in itself an obstacle for the proceedings to be considered the 'same cause of action'. For instance, the proceedings for the declaration of invalidity of a matrimonial property agreement and the proceedings for the enforcement of the same agreement by means of separation of assets would be considered as having the same cause of action because the validity of the agreement lies in the heart of both claims.[92] However, deciding on the *lis pendens* in the proceedings subject to the Brussels II bis Regulation, the CJEU held that *lis pendens* cannot exist where one action is for provisional measure and the other action is for the resolution on the merits.[93]

(service of documents), and repealing Council Regulation (EC) No 1348/2000, OJ L 324, 10.12.2007, pp. 79–120, which as of 1 July 2022 will be replaced by the Regulation (EU) 2020/1784 of the European Parliament and of the Council of 25 November 2020 on the service in the Member States of judicial and extrajudicial documents in civil or commercial matters (service of documents) (recast), OJ L 405, 2.12.2020, pp. 40–78, or Article 15 of the Hague Convention of 15 November 1965 on the service abroad of judicial and extrajudicial documents in civil or commercial matters.

[90] See e.g. Case C-144/86, *Gubisch Maschinenfabrik KG v Giulio Palumbo*, EU:C:1987:528, paras. 8 and 11; Case C-406/92, *The owners of the cargo lately laden on board the ship 'Tatry' v the owners of the ship 'Maciej Rataj'*, EU:C:1994:400, paras. 30 and 32. On the grounds for refusal of recognition and enforcement see below Chapter 6 of this volume.

[91] Case C-406/92, *The owners of the cargo lately laden on board the ship 'Tatry' v the owners of the ship 'Maciej Rataj'*, EU:C:1994:400, paras. 38 and 40. See also Case C-144/86, *Gubisch Maschinenfabrik KG v Giulio Palumbo*, EU:C:1987:528, para. 14 et seq.

[92] See by analogy Case C-144/86, *Gubisch Maschinenfabrik KG v Giulio Palumbo*, EU:C:1987:528, paras. 16–17.

[93] Case C-296/10, *Bianca Purrucker v Guillermo Vallés Pérez (Purrucker II)*, EU:C:2010:665, para. 69.

The notion of the 'same parties' has been interpreted, not only that the parties may be in the reverse procedural positions,[94] but also beyond its literal meaning to mean the parties on whom the *res iudicata* effect of the decision rendered against one party extends, provided that their interests are identical and indissociable.[95] In the Twin Regulations in particular, the possibility that a third party participates in the proceedings is recognised in the definitions related to their respective scopes. Thus, in the definition of the 'matrimonial property regime' in Article 3(1)(a) of the Matrimonial Property Regulation the reference is made not only to 'the property relationships between the spouses' but also 'their relations with third parties'. The latter reference is to be found in Article 3(1)(b) of the Regulation on the Property Consequences of Registered Partnerships as well.

The steps to be taken by the two courts where the proceedings are pending simultaneously are as follows: any court later seised has to of its own motion stay its proceedings until the jurisdiction of the court first seised is established. A court later seised is in no position to verify or decide on the jurisdiction of the court first seised and always has to wait for such decision of the court first seised.[96] This decision is binding upon courts in other Member States.[97] Two different scenarios are possible: (i) if the court first seised finds that it has jurisdiction, the second court must decline its jurisdiction *ex officio* without examining the first court's decision; or (ii) if the court first seised finds that it does not have jurisdiction, the court later seised may resume its proceedings (and determine its jurisdiction). To facilitate the efficiency of the coordination between parallel proceedings, there is an obligation, upon request, of prompt communication between the courts of different Member States concerning the date when it was seised.

5.3. RELATED ACTIONS

Article 18 of the Twin Regulations defines related actions as actions pending in the courts of different Member States which are so closely connected

---

[94] Case C-144/86, *Gubisch Maschinenfabrik KG v Giulio Palumbo*, EU:C:1987:528, para. 19.
[95] Case C-351/96, *Drouot assurances SA v Consolidated metallurgical industries (CMI industrial sites), Protea assurance and Groupement d'intérêt économique (GIE) Réunion européenne*, EU:C:1998:242, para. 25.
[96] C-351/89, *Overseas Union Insurance and Others v New Hampshire Insurance Company*, EU:C:1991:279, para. 25.
[97] The courts in other Member States are bound by the earlier decisions on jurisdiction of the court first seised, including its findings in *obiter*. See Case C-456/11, *Gothaer Allgemeine Versicherung AG and Others v Samskip GmbH*, EU:C:2012:719; I. KUNDA and D. VRBLJANAC, 'Lis Pendens' in C. HONORATI (ed.), *Jurisdiction in Matrimonial Matters, Parental Responsibility and International Abduction. A Handbook on the Application of Brussels IIa Regulation in National Courts*, Giappichelli and Peter Lang, Torino 2017, pp. 219, 232–233.

that it is expedient to hear and determine them together to avoid the risk of irreconcilable decisions resulting from separate proceedings. Migliorini distinguishes two elements to this definition.[98] First is the substantive element concerning the close connection between the proceedings, which manifests in common questions that need to be answered in both proceedings. The second element of the definition is latent because it is related to the risk of irreconcilable decisions, which may only be assessed by imagining various outcome scenarios in the two proceedings and comparing them. The notion of 'irreconcilability' needs to be construed autonomously and in a wider sense when read in the context of Article 18 (in comparison to Article 37)[99] so as to cover situations of risk of conflicting decisions, even if the decisions could be separately enforced and their legal consequences are not mutually exclusive.[100] The operation of this provision is triggered only upon an application of one of the parties.

Unlike in situations of *lis pendens* where the courts' actions are strictly prescribed, in situations of two related actions the later seised court enjoys certain discretion to stay its proceedings or not. This discretion is limited by the following considerations: (i) the related actions are pending at the first instance; (ii) there is the application of one of the parties asking the court to decline its jurisdiction; (iii) the court first seised has jurisdiction over the actions in question; and (iv) the law of the court first seised permits consolidation of the actions in question.

6. CONCLUDING REMARKS

The above analysis of the jurisdictional rules in the Twin Regulations proves what has been noted before – they display 'a remarkable degree of complexity'.[101] Thus they present an extension of the nomotechnical approach employed in the Succession Regulation while their overall structure follows other regulations in the area of cooperation in civil matters. The said complexity in the legislative technique is evident both on the surface and underneath it. Instead of one or two articles with several basic connections for matrimonial property matters (and matters of property consequences of registered partnerships), which are typically found in national private international law of the Member States,

---

[98] S. MAGLIORINI, 'Article 18. Connexité' in A. BONOMI and P. WAUTELET (eds.), *Le droit européen des relations patrimoniales de couple: Commentaire des Règlements n*os *2016/1103 et 2016/1104*, Bruylant, Bruxelles 2021, pp. 549, 551.

[99] See below Chapter 6 of this volume.

[100] Case C-406/92, *The owners of the cargo lately laden on board the ship 'Tatry' v the owners of the ship 'Maciej Rataj'*, EU:C:1994:400, para. 55.

[101] P. FRANZINA, 'Jurisdiction in Matters related to Property Regimes under EU Private International Law' (2017/2018) 19 *Yearbook of Private International Law* 193.

the Twin Regulations introduce a multi-layered and highly specialised architecture of the jurisdictional rules. The set of fundamental principles informing the structural elements of the system of jurisdictional rules, including the selection of jurisdictional grounds, consist of legal certainty, foreseeability, proximity, unity of assets as well as convergence of *forum* and *ius*. Against this background, the rules (and exceptions) are shaped in various manners, exposing different features, having diverse scopes, listing specific requirements, and standing in different interrelationships of structures and functions.

This complexity may hinder straightforward prediction of the competent courts by the parties and defy simple and rapid analysis of jurisdiction by the courts. Application in practice of the system of jurisdictional rules in the Twin Regulations requires deep appreciation for both private international law and EU law and is thus reserved primarily for the legal specialists. It is unlikely that lay parties will be able to rely on these rules without professional legal advice, irrespective of how much this is supported by the European Commission as evident in the funds allocated to the creation of such hands-on and ready-to-use tools in recent years.[102] In particular, choice of courts, which – although limited – is intended to help organise couples' property relations, is largely dependent on the awareness of the concerned parties (in the same vein as in the Succession Regulation), but also on the awareness of those from whom they receive legal advice. A whole set of new clauses and legal documents will have to be developed in order for couples to take the full advantage of the party autonomy option in the Twin Regulations and to fulfil the legislators' aspirations that the everyday life of relocating EU citizens and families will become less obscure since they will be able to organise in advance their family property relations.

---

[102] This is primarily done by means of the EU Justice Programme whereby the Commission funds projects intended not only towards training of professionals but also bringing the rules closer to the parties themselves. See e.g. Personalized Solution in European Family and Succession Law – PSEFS (br. 800821-JUST-AG-2017/JUST-JCOO-AG-2017), <www.euro-family.eu>.

APPLICABLE LAW IN THE TWIN REGULATIONS

Neža Pogorelčnik Vogrinc*

1. Introduction 102
2. Connecting Factors in the Absence of an Agreement on the Choice of Law 102
    2.1. General Remarks 102
    2.2. The Law of the State of the Spouses' First Common Habitual Residence 103
    2.3. The Law of the State of Spouses' Common Nationality 107
    2.4. The Law of the State of the Closest Connection 108
    2.5. The Law of the State under Whose Law the Registered Partnership was Created 109
3. Rules Supporting and Supplementing the Application of Connecting Factors 110
    3.1. The Immutability Rule and Escape Clause 110
    3.2. Unity of the Applicable Law 113
    3.3. Public Policy and Overriding Mandatory Provisions 114
        3.3.1. Overriding Mandatory Provisions 114
        3.3.2. Public Policy 116
    3.4. Exclusion of *Renvoi* 117
4. Agreement on the Choice of Law 118
    4.1. Connecting Factors 118
    4.2. Formal Requirements 120
    4.3. Consent and Material Validity 121
    4.4. Change of an Agreement on the Choice of Law 123
    4.5. Effects in Respect of Third Parties 124
5. Case Study 126

---

* Neža Pogorelčnik Vogrinc, PhD, Assistant Professor of civil and commercial law at the Faculty of Law, University of Ljubljana, and researcher at the Institute for Comparative Law at the Faculty of Law in Ljubljana, Slovenia.

1. INTRODUCTION

The Matrimonial Property Regulation and the Regulation on the Property Consequences of Registered Partnerships (the Twin Regulations) establish a consistent set of rules regulating the determination of applicable law for matrimonial property and property of registered partners. In particular, the Regulations are designed to cover two possible situations regarding the applicable law: (i) situations where the parties have agreed on the law that should apply to their property relations; and (ii) situations where no such agreement was made. The Twin Regulations establish detailed rules regulating these two situations. In this chapter, we shall analyse these rules seeking to present an in-depth analysis of them.

The Twin Regulations put 'party autonomy' as the main connecting factor for the establishment of applicable law (see Articles 22 of both Regulations). In such a way it is presumed that parties tend to conclude an agreement on the choice of law. Only subsequently (see Articles 26 of both Regulations) do the Twin Regulations anticipate the option of determining applicable law in the absence of the parties' choice. In practice, however, the reality is different. While agreements on the matrimonial property regime are gaining in popularity, the majority of couples, even cross-border ones, still do not conclude an agreement on the choice of law. The chapter, therefore, starts with the connecting factors to decide on the applicable law in the absence of such an agreement (Section 2) and the supplementary rules that are of an important value when determining and applying a relevant law (Section 3). It then proceeds to requirements to the parties' choice-of-law agreement (Section 4), in which it examines the relevant connecting factors, the requirements regarding the formal and material validity of the agreement, and its effect on third persons. The chapter finishes with a case study in which it shows that the couple's decision for a specific form of their relationship can have far-reaching consequences.

2. CONNECTING FACTORS IN THE ABSENCE OF AN AGREEMENT ON THE CHOICE OF LAW

2.1. GENERAL REMARKS

As presented below, though the Twin Regulations are in most cases similar to each other, they provide for completely different sets of connecting factors for the establishment of applicable law in case the choice was not made. While the Matrimonial Property Regulation includes three different cascading connecting factors, the Regulation on the Property Consequences of Registered Partnerships determines only one. However, the difference is not only in the number of connecting factors, but also in the content of the connecting factors.

In matters of matrimonial property regimes, the applicable law is either: (i) the law of the state of the spouses' first common habitual residence after the conclusion of the marriage;[1] (ii) the law of the state of the spouses' common nationality at the time of the conclusion of the marriage; or (iii) the law of the state with which the spouses jointly have the closest connection at the time of the conclusion of the marriage. Under the Regulation on the Property Consequences of Registered Partnerships, in the absence of an agreement on the choice of law, the applicable law shall be the law of the state under whose law the registered partnership was created. This major difference between both sets of rules can be attributed to the protection of registered partnerships due to the uncertain position and distinct consequences that they have in different countries. Habitual residence and nationality are less proper connecting factors in the case of registered partnerships as they might refer to the law which does not recognise registered partnerships at all or grant them limited protection. Nevertheless, both sets of connecting factors fulfil their primary role of eliminating ambiguity in the absence of an agreement on the choice of law and ensuring legal certainty.

The applicable law determined under the Twin Regulations applies whether or not it is the law of a Member State (Articles 20 of the Twin Regulations). As a consequence, a law of an EU Member State participating in the enhanced cooperation, a law of an EU Member State not participating in the enhanced cooperation, or a law of a third state (a non-EU Member State) can apply. A competent court in a Member State bound by the Twin Regulations can therefore apply the law of any state as determined according to the conflict of law rules of the Twin Regulations.

2.2. THE LAW OF THE STATE OF THE SPOUSES' FIRST COMMON HABITUAL RESIDENCE

The first connecting factor for determining the applicable law for matrimonial property regimes is the spouses' first common habitual residence after the conclusion of the marriage (Article 26(1)(a) of the Matrimonial Property Regulation). This being the first connecting factor in the Matrimonial Property Regulation is a continuation of the legal tradition. Already Regulation's predecessor, the Hague Convention of 14 March 1978 on the Law Applicable to Matrimonial Property Regimes, provided for the same connecting factor as a primary one.

---

[1] The term 'conclusion of the marriage' is the term used in the Twin Regulations to refer to when a marriage begins, so that is the term that will be used in this chapter as well.

The use of a habitual residence as a connecting factor increasingly flourished in the range of European regulations and other legal sources in the area of private international law. The EU has moved away from nationality as the typical connecting factor used in private international law of European states.[2] The habitual residence as a connecting factor is used to determine the jurisdiction or applicable law, as is the case in the Matrimonial Property Regulation (see Articles 5(2) and 6), and also in the Regulation on the Property Consequences of Registered Partnerships (see Article 6) and other[3] European instruments of international private law.

While it is common that EU legal instruments do not define 'habitual residence', there is no question that this concept has to be interpreted autonomously and independently regardless of the national concepts. The Court of Justice of the European Union (CJEU) has slowly built up the content of the term in its case law.[4] Generally, it represents the place where a person has the centre of his or her interests. Additionally, the CJEU emphasised that 'a person may have the centre of his interests in a Member State in which he or she does not habitually reside, in so far as other factors, such as the pursuit of professional activity, may establish the existence of a particularly close link with that State'.[5] As argued in legal theory[6] and evidenced in national case law,[7] some specific factual circumstances might be vital for 'finding' a 'habitual residence' in a certain state. These are the minimum physical presence of a person in a certain place,[8] his or her integration into the social environment, his or her intention

---

[2] R. SCHULZ, 'Choice of law in relation to matrimonial property in the 21st Century' (2019) 15 *Journal of Private International Law* 10–11.

[3] For habitual residence as a connecting factor for determining jurisdiction, see e.g. the Brussels II bis Regulation (or its Recast), the Maintenance Regulation, and the Succession Regulation. For habitual residence as a connecting factor for determining the applicable law, see, for example, the Rome III Regulation, the Rome I Regulation, and the Succession Regulation.

[4] See e.g. Case C-523/07, *A*, ECLI:EU:C:2009:225; Case C-393/18 PPU, *UD v XB*, ECLI:EU:C:2018:835; Case C-512/17, *HR*, ECLI:EU:C:2020:585; and Case C-253/19, *MH, NI v OJ, Novo Banco SA*, ECLI:EU:C:2020:585.

[5] Joined Cases C-509/09 and C-161/10, *eDate Advertising GmbH v X and Olivier Martinez, Robert Martinez v MGN Limited*, ECLI:EU:C:2011:685, para. 49. It is important to emphasise, this is not a family law case. Nevertheless, its definition is used to show the meaning of 'habitual residence' as has been interpreted within different CJEU cases.

[6] K. HILBIG-LUGANI, '"Habitual residence" in European family law: The diversity, Coherence and Transparency of a Challenging Notion' in K. BOELE-WOELKI, N. DETHLOFF, and W. GEPHART (eds.), *Family Law and Culture in Europe*, Intersentia, Cambridge 2014, p. 252.

[7] Due to the relative novelty of the Twin Regulations, there is not much national case law using them. At the time of writing, in Slovenia for example there is no relevant case law using the Twin Regulations. However, there are Slovenian court decisions deciding on habitual residence when using other European regulations. See e.g. decision of Ljubljana High Court IV Cp 2535/2018, decision of Ljubljana High Court IV Cp 1054/2018, and decision of the Koper High Court Cp 141/2010.

[8] It is difficult to determine the length of an individual period of stay in a specific state to establish habitual residence. The Succession Regulation, for example, mentions a period of

to reside there, the fact that a person was learning a language of a current residence, the reasons for moving to the state, and the frequency and intensity of contacts with people in other states. However, it is speculated that the term might have different meanings in different legal contexts. Its interpretation within one EU instrument, therefore, might need modifications when used in the context of another EU instrument. Therefore, the 'habitual residence' needs to be established individually in each case within the specific EU instrument concerning its specific provisions.[9] Nevertheless, it is possible to conclude that finding the actual centre of someone's life (*Lebensmittelpunkt*) is common to all interpretations of habitual residence.[10] Additionally, it is unquestionable that when using the Matrimonial Property Regulation, the term 'the spouses' first common habitual residence' must be interpreted uniformly in all Member States.

This connecting factor in the Matrimonial Property Regulation is even more complex than in other European legal sources. It is formulated as the 'first common habitual residence' of both spouses. This does not require that the spouses live together at the same address; however, it is necessary that they both have habitual residences within a single state.[11] It is additionally necessary that such a habitual residence is the first one established after the conclusion[12] of the marriage.[13] At the same time, the Matrimonial Property Regulation does not specify within what amount of time after the happy event the common

---

five years. Differently, the Matrimonial Property Regulation does not give a similar hint. However, for its purposes, a stay of much less than five years is needed. Perhaps it would be more suitable to look at the Brussels II bis Regulation, which mentions six-month and one-year periods in relation to the length of habitual residence (see Article 3(1)(a)). However, at least some presence is needed in a specific state. The CJEU has in this regard stated: 'Thus, the determination of a child's habitual residence in a given Member State requires at least that the child has been physically present in that Member State.' See the CJEU case C-499/15, *W and V v X*, ECLI:EU:C:2017:118, para. 61.

[9] See CJEU case C-523/07, *A*, ECLI:EU:C:2009:225, paras. 36 and 37. D. MARTINY, 'Applicable law in the absence of choice by the parties' in I. VIARENGO and P. FRANZINA (eds.), *The EU Regulations on the Property Regimes of International Couples, A Commentary*, Edward Elgar, Cheltenham 2020, p. 247. For more details, see also K. HILBIG-LUGANI, '"Habitual residence" in European family law: The diversity, Coherence and Transparency of a Challenging Notion' in K. BOELE-WOELKI, N. DETHLOFF, and W. GEPHART (eds.), *Family Law and Culture in Europe*, Intersentia, Cambridge 2014, p. 252.

[10] A further explanation of the term 'habitual residence' exceeds the scope of this chapter. For more, see D. MARTINY, 'Applicable law in the absence of choice by the parties' in I. VIARENGO and P. FRANZINA (eds.), *The EU Regulations on the Property Regimes of International Couples, A Commentary*, Edward Elgar, Cheltenham 2020, pp. 248-249.

[11] J. DOLŽAN, 'Uredbi (EU) glede premoženjskopravnih razmerij za mednarodne pare – kolizijska pravila' (2019) 90 *Odvetnik* 111.

[12] The moment, of the conclusion of the marriage is determined with regard to the national law of the state in which the event happens.

[13] This does not mean that such a residence cannot already be established prior to the conclusion of the marriage, however the crucial situation is the one after.

habitual residence must be established. Since newlyweds generally start living together after the conclusion of the marriage, the question does not arise often. However, it is possible, especially with cross-border couples, that spouses do not live in the same state after they marry. The only help can be found in Recital 49, which states that the first common habitual residence of the spouses should be established shortly after the conclusion of the marriage. While it is clear that no specific time limit is determined, the court in each individual case is the one to interpret the term 'shortly'. It can encompass a period from a few weeks to a few months, possibly a year or two, but probably not more.[14] Therefore, it is hard to agree with the opinion that the period within which the spouses should establish their first common residence should be unrestricted.[15]

The reason behind such a primary connecting factor is that usually there is a strong connection between a couple and the place in which they first live after the conclusion of the marriage.[16] If the spouses' first common habitual residence is established sometime after the conclusion of the marriage, and a dispute regarding the matrimonial property regime arises after that, the law of that state applies from the moment of the conclusion of the marriage. In such a situation, it does not matter that the habitual residence was not established immediately after the conclusion of the marriage. However, if a dispute arises in the interim period – after the wedding but before the establishment of a common habitual residence – the connecting factors of Article 26(1) (b, c) apply.[17]

There is only one first common habitual residence of a couple. Subsequent changes in their lives can lead to a discrepancy between their first and current habitual residence. This can produce a situation in which the applicable law is unsuitable for the spouses, as they have no relation anymore to the state of their first habitual residence.

---

[14] Legal theory recommends an acceptable period of between three months and a year. See D. MARTINY 'Applicable law in the absence of choice by the parties' in I. VIARENGO and P. FRANZINA (eds.), *The EU Regulations on the Property Regimes of International Couples, A Commentary*, Edward Elgar, Cheltenham 2020, p. 249.

[15] See e.g. D. DAMASCELLI, 'Applicable law, jurisdiction, and recognition of decisions in matters relating to property regimes of spouses and partners in European and Italian private international law' (2018) 0 *Trusts & Trustees* 4.

[16] D. MARTINY, 'Applicable law in the absence of choice by the parties' in I. VIARENGO and P. FRANZINA (eds.), *The EU Regulations on the Property Regimes of International Couples, A Commentary*, Edward Elgar, Cheltenham 2020, p. 246.

[17] D. MARTINY, 'Applicable law in the absence of choice by the parties' in I. VIARENGO and P. FRANZINA (eds.), *The EU Regulations on the Property Regimes of International Couples, A Commentary*, Edward Elgar, Cheltenham 2020, p. 249, P. LAGARDE, 'Applicable Law: Articles 20–35' in U. BERGQUIST, D. DAMASCELLI, R. FRIMSTON, P. LAGARDE and B. REINHARTZ, *The EU Regulations on Matrimonial and Patrimonial Property*, Oxford University Press, Oxford 2019, p. 112.

2.3. THE LAW OF THE STATE OF SPOUSES' COMMON NATIONALITY

If the applicable law cannot be determined by referring to the spouses' first common habitual residence after the conclusion of the marriage, the spouses' common nationality comes into play (Article 26(1)(b) of the Matrimonial Property Regulation). The relevant moment to determine this factor is the time of the conclusion of the marriage. Subsequent changes are not relevant. The Matrimonial Property Regulation does not provide guidance on how to identify spouses' nationalities.[18] Relevant national and international provisions thus apply. However, identifying common nationality seems easier than identifying common habitual residence. As it is much more difficult to lose or change nationality compared to relocating to another state, the law of the state of the spouses' common nationality is a much more stable connecting factor.

It should be noted that spouses' common nationality can also be a nationality of a third state. The application of a law of a third state is in line with the principle of universal application (Articles 20 of the Twin Regulations).

If, at the relevant moment, the spouses do not share a common nationality, this connecting factor is not used. The same is true when the spouses have more than one common nationality at the time of the conclusion of the marriage. This corresponds to the CJEU's opinion on the equality of nationalities,[19] the principle of non-discrimination, and the refusal to favour the nationality of the *lex fori*.[20] When the spouses share more than one common nationality, the Matrimonial Property Regulation states that this connecting factor becomes inapplicable and only the other two connecting factors established by Article 26(1) should be used (Article 26(2)). Such instructions are not entirely consistent. If the applicable law is to be determined using the connecting

---

[18] For the situation regarding stateless persons and refugees that are not mentioned in the Matrimonial Property Regulation, see D. MARTINY, 'Applicable law in the absence of choice by the parties' in I. VIARENGO and P. FRANZINA (eds.), *The EU Regulations on the Property Regimes of International Couples, A Commentary*, Edward Elgar, Cheltenham 2020, p. 251.

[19] If spouses share more than one common nationality, it would be discriminative that the forum would have an option to choose among them when choosing an applicable law and would always choose *lex fori* if possible. To avoid that, a rule in the Matrimonial Property Regulation therefore equally treats all nationalities and prevent preferring one of them. See also S. MARINO, 'Strengthening the European civil judicial cooperation: the patrimonial effects of family relationships' (2017) 9 *Cuadernos de Derecho Transnacional* 280.

[20] This is different than for determining jurisdiction in divorce cases under the Brussels II bis Regulation. See Case C-168/08, *Laszlo Hadadi v Csilla Marta Mesko*, ECLI:EU:C:2009:474, and Case C-148/02, *Carlos Garcia Avello v Belgian State*, ECLI:EU:C:2003:539. For more, see D. MARTINY, 'Applicable law in the absence of choice by the parties' in I. VIARENGO and P. FRANZINA (eds.), *The EU Regulations on the Property Regimes of International Couples, A Commentary*, Edward Elgar, Cheltenham 2020, p. 252, and S. MARINO, 'Strengthening the European civil judicial cooperation: the patrimonial effects of family relationships' (2017) 9 *Cuadernos de Derecho Transnacional* 280.

factor of common nationality (Article 26(1)(b)), this undoubtedly signifies that possibility to use the connecting factor of common habitual residence (Article 26(1)(a)) failed. Referral back to this provision is not correct. If the spouses have more than one common nationality, the only option is therefore to apply the law with which the spouses jointly have the closest connection at the time of the conclusion of the marriage (Article 26(1)(c)).

2.4. THE LAW OF THE STATE OF THE CLOSEST CONNECTION

If none of the previous connecting factors can be used, the law applicable to the matrimonial property regime shall be the law of the state with which the spouses jointly have the closest connection (Article 26(1)(c) of the Matrimonial Property Regulation).[21] This is a rather undefined and unsubstantiated term.[22] The Regulation's only guidance is that the closest connection should be determined taking into account all the circumstance. Therefore, the whole situation with all its factual details has to be considered relevant. There is no list of suitable circumstances; however, the following are most certainly among them: the (common) nationalities of the spouses, their residence, and the location of their assets. Some scholars argue that these relevant circumstances need to be linked to the marriage and the matrimonial property relations of the spouses,[23] which can be argued. More proper explanation would be that it is necessary to find the closest connection between each of the spouses, on one hand, and a specific state, on the other. There is no need that the connection derives from their marriage or its property consequences. It can thus also be a language or religious beliefs.

The competent court determines the closest connection that existed at the moment of the conclusion of the marriage. The specific connecting factor is therefore unchangeable no matter the subsequent changes in the circumstances

---

[21] The same connecting factor is used also in Article 21(2) of the Succession Regulation and Article 4(4) of the Rome I Regulation. For the differences regarding the specific connecting factor in the Matrimonial Property Regime compared to the that used in the Hague Convention of 14 March 1978 on the Law Applicable to Matrimonial Property Regimes, see P. LAGARDE, 'Applicable Law: Articles 20–35' in U. BERGQUIST, D. DAMASCELLI, R. FRIMSTON, P. LAGARDE and B. REINHARTZ, *The EU Regulations on Matrimonial and Patrimonial Property*, Oxford University Press, Oxford 2019, p. 114.

[22] Poretti is of the opinion that the main reason for its open meaning is its possibility to be used for all of the many different cases in which neither the first nor the second connecting factor can be used. See P. PORETTI, 'Odlučivanje o imovinskim odnosima bračnih drugova u ostavinskim postupcima sukladno Uredbi 2016/1103 o bračnoimovinskom režimu' (2017) 38 *Zbornik Pravnog fakulteta Sveučilišta u Rijeci* 463.

[23] D. MARTINY, 'Applicable law in the absence of choice by the parties' in I. VIARENGO and P. FRANZINA (eds.), *The EU Regulations on the Property Regimes of International Couples, A Commentary*, Edward Elgar, Cheltenham 2020, p. 254.

of the case.[24] While this provides for some stability and certainty, it can at the same time lead to the application of a law that does not correspond to the spouses' situation at the time of the court procedure.

> A German man and a Spanish woman meet when studying in Belgium. After the end of the studies, she moves back home, while he stays in Belgium. Shortly after they get married, however, they do not move in together. He works and stays in Belgium, while she is offered a job in France and moves there. She starts a procedure and obtains German citizenship and they plan to move together to Germany. However, after few years of long-distance marriage they decide to divorce. In this specific case, they have never lived together after the marriage and therefore the connecting factor of a first common habitual residence cannot be used. Regardless of the fact that she obtained a German citizenship, they did not have a common nationality at the time of the conclusion of the marriage. The applicable law is therefore determined using the connecting factor of the closest connection at the time of the conclusion of the marriage. In this specific case this might be Belgium, however she did not live there at the time of the conclusion of the marriage. The second option is German, however, she never lived there, she only obtained citizenship, but only after the wedding. It is possible to conclude that the relevant law are not those of the France or Spain as he has no ties to these states. As can be seen, determining the closest connection is not a straightforward and easy task for a competent court.

2.5. THE LAW OF THE STATE UNDER WHOSE LAW THE REGISTERED PARTNERSHIP WAS CREATED

While the Matrimonial Property Regulation provides for a set of cascading connecting factors, with the aim of finding the perfect solution regarding the applicable law, the principle in the Regulation on the Property Consequences of Registered Partnerships is different. It determines only one possibility to decide on the applicable law if no agreement on the choice of law exists. In such a situation, the law applicable to the property consequences of registered partnerships shall be the law of the state under whose law the registered partnership was created (Article 26(1)). A connecting factor with such content offers a reliable guarantee and certainty for registered partners. It is realistic to expect that a state that legally enables the registration of a partnership[25]

---

[24] M. GEČ KOROŠEC, *Mednarodno zasebno pravo: Splošni del*, Uradni list Republike Slovenije, Ljubljana 1994, p. 115, sees these unchangeable connecting factors as a guarantee of legal certainty.

[25] For the dilemma on which law should be used to decide on the moment of the registration, see S. MARINO, 'Strengthening the European civil judicial cooperation: the patrimonial effects of family relationships' (2017) 9 *Cuadernos de Derecho Transnacional* 281–282.

legally recognises this form of relationship. Consequently, the determination of the applicable law is always possible and simple. On the contrary, using nationality or residence as a connecting factor might lead to the application of the law of a state that does not legally know or recognise registered partnerships (for example, Romania, Poland, and Bulgaria).

Determining the applicable law using only one very precise circumstance (i.e. the law of the state under whose law the registered partnership was created) is very fixed and reliable. It allows no space for interpretation and therefore it does not depend on the way of its application by the competent court (as is the case for the connecting factors of the habitual residence or the closest connection). Consequently, forum shopping is disabled as parties have no interest in starting the court procedure in a specific state.

3. RULES SUPPORTING AND SUPPLEMENTING THE APPLICATION OF CONNECTING FACTORS

3.1. THE IMMUTABILITY RULE AND ESCAPE CLAUSE

An essential factor in conflict of law rules is the time or period to which a connecting factor is bound. Often this is the time of the beginning of the court procedure or the time when a specific dispute arose, or if this is not possible, the time shortly before that.[26] Such a rule ensures the connection and closeness between the parties, on one hand, and the applicable law, on the other.

A different approach is taken in the Twin Regulations. The Twin Regulations determine that the moment of the conclusion of the marriage or the registration of the partnership is decisive. It has to be noted that the application of the connecting factors that are tied to the beginning of the marriage or registered partnership might not correspond to the couple's situation at the beginning of the court procedure. This is particularly likely to happen if the latter begins years or decades after the wedding or registration. The couple may have moved, had children, changed jobs, or even acquired new nationalities. The circumstances

---

[26] See Article 8 of the Rome III Regulation. It fixes the connecting factor of common habitual residence to the time the court is seised. If this does not exist, the law of the state where the spouses were last habitually resident is applied. This could easily also be used in the Matrimonial Property Regulation. It would resolve the problems of a couple's subsequent moves and ensure the closeness between the couple and the applicable law. Moreover, such a solution would enable the application of the law of the same state for several reciprocal disputes of the spouses, i.e. divorce, the classification of the property of the spouses into different categories, the dissolution of the matrimonial property regime, and the partition, distribution, or liquidation of the property. Additionally, this would resolve the difficult task of separating individual questions, which is otherwise highly important due to the application of the proper law.

of the day of the wedding or registration might be long forgotten and passé. The application of the first habitual common residence after the conclusion of the marriage or the state of the registration of the partnership for deciding on the applicable law might no longer be suitable. It can even surprise parties who do not expect the application of such a law. Additionally, it could entail that the competent court[27] has to apply foreign law.[28] Such an immutability rule, therefore, has several disadvantages, but from the other perspective, it also entails also some advantages. It enables parties to rely on the fixed past circumstances and predict which law is applicable no matter the subsequent developments in their lives.

Obviously, the EU places an essential value on legal certainty and stability, and therefore a rigid immutability rule is enacted in many European legal sources. To avoid its application, parties can conclude an agreement on the choice of law. However, the Twin Regulations additionally provide another solution to bypass such an inconvenience. This is the application of an escape clause. To avoid using the connecting factor of Article 26(1)(a) of the Matrimonial Property Regulation[29] or of Article 26(1) of the Regulation on the Property Consequences of Registered Partnerships, a party can propose the application of the law of the state of their last common habitual residence (Article 26(3)) of the Matrimonial Property Regulation or Article 26(2) of the Regulation on the Property Consequences of Registered Partnerships). It is not necessary that the latter directly follows their first common habitual residence, which is normally applied when using the Article 26(1)(a) of the Matrimonial Property Regulation. It is also not mandatory that such a last common habitual residence still exists when the claim is made.[30] It is only required that one of the spouses

---

[27] There are other options to determine a court's competence, for example the existence of an agreement of the parties on the jurisdiction or the merger of a procedure regarding the property regime with a succession or divorce procedure. However, the application of Articles 6 of the Twin Regulations leads to the competent court of the state in which the couple is habitually resident at the time the court is seised. If the couple no longer lives in the place of their first common habitual residence, a situation entailing a divergence between the competent court and the applicable law arises.

[28] The opposite is the mutability rule, in which the connecting factor is bound to some fact, and with a change thereof there is an automatic change in the applicable law. For more on this, see A. BONOMI, 'The Proposal for a Regulation on Matrimonial Property: A Critique of the Proposed Rule on the Immutability of the Applicable Law' in K. BOELE-WOELKI, N. DETHLOFF, and W. GEPHART (eds.), *Family Law and Culture in Europe*, Intersentia, Cambridge 2014, p. 233. For the system of partial mutability or modified mutability, see R. SCHULZ, 'Choice of law in relation to matrimonial property in the 21st Century' (2019) 15 *Journal of Private International Law* 11–12, 47–48.

[29] An escape clause can be used only when the connecting factor of the first common habitual residence is used (see Article 26(3) of the Matrimonial Property Regulation).

[30] P. LAGARDE, 'Applicable Law: Articles 20–35' in U. BERGQUIST, D. DAMASCELLI, R. FRIMSTON, P. LAGARDE and B. REINHARTZ, *The EU Regulations on Matrimonial and Patrimonial Property*, Oxford University Press, Oxford 2019, p. 116. The same can also be found in C. RUDOLF, 'European Property Regimes Regulations – Choice of Law and the Applicable Law in the Absence of Choice by the Parties' (2019) 11 *Lexonomica* 144.

or partners proposes to use the last common habitual residence of the couple as a connecting factor to establish applicable law. The application of such law not only entails the application of a law that is close to the couple, but it furthermore enables that the law of the same state is possibly used for several different legal issues. The same connecting factor for deciding on the applicable law (i.e. the last habitual residence of the deceased) namely also appears in the Succession Regulation.[31]

To justify such a proposal, the spouse or partner asking to apply the law of last habitual residence must demonstrate the existence of two elements. First, he or she must prove that – in the case of a registered partnership – the couple had their last common habitual residence in another state for a significantly long period. In the case of marital relations, this period must be significantly longer than the period they spent at their first common habitual residence. The partially different conditions for using an escape clause for spouses and partners derive from the different connecting factors that are determined for the two groups.[32] For registered partners, the initial connecting factor for determining the applicable law does not include another residence. The competent court therefore only needs to decide whether the period of stay in such a state is significantly long. This is easier than deciding on similar conditions regarding spouses. In the case of spouses, the court has to decide what is a significantly longer period compared to the period of time spent at the first common habitual residence. Some opine that spending two-thirds of the time as habitual residents in another state compared to spending one-third in the state of first habitual residence fulfils the conditions for using an escape clause.[33] However, it is impossible to give a theoretically precise answer. It is up to the competent court to consider the circumstances of the specific case and decide on the term 'significantly long(er)'.

Secondly, the party must prove that both spouses or partners had relied on the law of that other state when arranging or planning their property relations. It is not sufficient that only one of them relied on the law of another state. This enables a couple to apply a law according to its expectations. Both of them had to rely on the law of the same (another) state when concluding financial or other transactions. A spouse or a partner, proposing the application of such rule, has an easier task when the other spouse or partner agrees with the application of the law of another state.

---

[31] Such a solution gives the same result as already provided in Articles 4 and 5 of the Twin Regulations, i.e. a concentration of court procedures regarding different matters in the same (competent) state and the application of the law of the same state for different matters.

[32] Compare with Articles 26(2) of both Twin Regulations.

[33] D. MARTINY, 'Applicable law in the absence of choice by the parties' in I. VIARENGO and P. FRANZINA (eds.), *The EU Regulations on the Property Regimes of International Couples, A Commentary*, Edward Elgar, Cheltenham 2020, p. 257.

Additionally, there is another important requirement related only to the application of an escape clause for registered partners. The law of the state of last common habitual residence can apply and govern the property consequences of a registered partnership if it attaches property consequences to the institution of registered partnership. The reason for such a rule is the same as the reason for the limited set of connecting factors in Article 26 (1) of the Regulation on the Property Consequences of Registered Partnerships, i.e. the protection of registered partners. However, in the opinion of some scholars, it suffices that the applicable law is only acquainted with the institute of a registered partnership.[34]

A law determined using an escape clause generally applies *ex tunc* from the conclusion of the marriage or the creation of the registered partnership. The aim is the application of only one law for all of the couple's legal transactions regardless of the time of the conclusion thereof. The law determined using an escape clause, therefore, applies retroactively unless one spouse or partner disagrees. In the latter case, the law of the state of the last common habitual residence shall have effect from the establishment of the habitual residence there.

The application of an escape clause and therefore the law of another state might have a negative impact on the legal certainty and predictability of third parties who assumed that the primary connecting factor is and will be used. The Twin Regulations, therefore, determine that the application of an escape clause shall not adversely affect the rights of third parties deriving from the law applicable pursuant to the primary connecting factor. On the contrary, such protection is not needed if the third party knew or, in the exercise of due diligence, should have known of that law (see Article 28).[35]

The application of connecting factors and the related application of an escape clause are unquestionably under influence of the court's discretion. Ultimately, spouses can avoid this simply by concluding a suitable agreement (see Section 4 below).

3.2. UNITY OF THE APPLICABLE LAW

When the applicable law is determined (using Articles 26 of the Twin Regulations or by the couple's agreement on the choice of law), it is used for the spouses' entire property regardless of the location of the assets (Articles 21 of the

---

[34] C. RUDOLF, 'European Property Regimes Regulations – Choice of Law and the Applicable Law in the Absence of Choice by the Parties' (2019) 11 *Lexonomica* 146.
[35] P. LAGARDE, 'Applicable Law: Articles 20–35' in U. BERGQUIST, D. DAMASCELLI, R. FRIMSTON, P. LAGARDE and B. REINHARTZ, *The EU Regulations on Matrimonial and Patrimonial Property*, Oxford University Press, Oxford 2019, p. 117.

Twin Regulations).³⁶ It applies to property located in all countries in the world regardless of the type or nature of the assets. The aim is to avoid the fragmentation of the matrimonial property regime (Recital 43 of the Matrimonial Property Regulation and Recital 42 of the Regulation on the Property Consequences of Registered Partnerships).

3.3. PUBLIC POLICY AND OVERRIDING MANDATORY PROVISIONS

The principle of the unity of the applicable law is limited by the overriding mandatory provisions (Articles 30 of the Twin Regulations) and public order (Articles 31 of the Twin Regulations). These can cause that a specific provision of applicable law does not apply in a specific case. The main goal is to protect the fundamental legal principles of the law of the forum and to offer a 'general correction mechanism'.³⁷ Nevertheless, they differ as to their application.

3.3.1. Overriding Mandatory Provisions

Overriding mandatory provisions are provisions that an individual Member State deems must be respected in order to safeguard its public interests. The mandatory provisions are applicable to any situation falling within the scope of the Twin Regulations (see Articles 30(2)).³⁸ The overriding mandatory provisions of the law of the forum (*lex fori*) therefore apply regardless of the provisions in the otherwise applicable law.³⁹ A law determined according to the conflict of law provisions of the Twin Regulations, therefore, does not apply in this part. It is up to the competent court to assess the overriding mandatory nature of a national legal provision and to decide on the application thereof.⁴⁰ This is a difficult task, because national legislation rarely explicitly labels a specific national provision as

---

[36] A similar principle can be found in the Succession Regulation (see Article 23(1)).
[37] L. M. van Bochove, 'Overriding Mandatory Rules as a Vehicle for Weaker Party Protection in European Private International Law' (2014) 3 *Erasmus Law Review* 148.
[38] The option to apply overriding mandatory provisions in international private law primary derives from the Rome I Regulation. On the contrary, other regulations from the same legal field as the Twin Regulations, for example the Succession Regulation and the Rome III Regulation, do not provide for such an option.
[39] The Rome I Regulation furthermore provides the application of the overriding mandatory provisions of other states, not only of the law of the state of the forum (see Article 9). On the contrary, the Twin Regulations do not include such a possibility.
[40] K. Bogdzevič, 'Overriding Mandatory Provisions in Family Law and Names' (2020) *ELTE Law Journal* 60, emphasises the similarities of the relevant provision of the Twin Regulations to the relevant provision on overriding mandatory rules in the Rome I Regulation. She therefore concludes that the articles should be interpreted similarly. Therefore, the relevant case law of the CJEU on contractual and non-contractual matters should furthermore be used for interpretation of the provisions on overriding mandatory rules of the Twin Regulations.

having such a strict nature. Additionally, not all national overriding mandatory provisions should be used when deciding on a case in the frame of the Twin Regulations. Those not dealing with the matrimonial property regime or matters regarding the property consequences of registered partnerships are not relevant and therefore cannot be applied.[41] Only overriding mandatory provisions of national family law and related fields shall be considered. The application of an overriding mandatory provision of the law of the competent court undoubtedly requires the application of two different legal orders in the same procedure.

The Twin Regulations mention the political, social, or economic organisation of the state as an example of public interest that can be considered crucial and therefore requires safeguarding.[42] The legal theory emphasises that overriding mandatory provisions protect more specific values. An example is 'precise norms allowing or forbidding something'.[43] Furthermore, Recital 52 of the Regulation on the Property Consequences of Registered Partnerships and Recital 53 of the Matrimonial Property Regulation give an example of the protection of a family home as a rule of an imperative nature that is encompassed by the concept of overriding mandatory provisions.[44] However, the Recitals emphasise that the application of the overriding mandatory rules must be interpreted strictly in order to remain compatible with the general objective of the Twin Regulations.[45]

---

[41] M. GEBAUER, 'Overriding mandatory provisions', I. VIARENGO and P. FRANZINA (eds.), *The EU Regulations on the Property Regimes of International Couples, A Commentary*, Edward Elgar, Cheltenham 2020, pp. 300–301.

[42] L. RUGGERI, 'Registered partnerships and property consequences' in M. JOSÉ CAZORLA GONZÁLEZ, M. GIOBBI, J. KRAMBERGER ŠKERL, L. RUGGERI, S. WINKLER (eds.), *Property relations of cross border couples in the European Union*, Edizioni Scientifiche Italiane, Napoli 2020, pp. 83–84, suggests that these might also be national provisions adopted during the Covid-19 pandemic on travel, transport or supply contracts. Their goal namely was to protect public health or the national economy, which can be treated as higher goals, when in need of protection by overriding mandatory rules.

[43] K. BOGDZEVIČ, 'Overriding Mandatory Provisions in Family Law and Names' (2020) *ELTE Law Journal* 53.

[44] Such a mandatory provision on the protection of the family home is, for example, also provided in the French Civil Code (Article 215/3), the German Civil Code (Article 1568a), and the Slovenian Family Code (Article 59). See F. DOUGAN, 'Nova evropska pravila o pristojnosti, pravu, ki se uporablja, ter priznavanju in izvrševanju odločb na področju premoženjskih razmerij mednarodnih parov' in D. MOŽINA (ed.), *Liber Amicorum Ada Polajnar Pavčnik, Razsežnosti zasebnega prava*, Pravna fakulteta Univerza v Ljubljani, Ljubljana 2019, p. 243, and B. NOVAK, *Družinski zakonik z uvodnimi pojasnili*, Uradni list Republike Slovenije, Ljubljana 2017, p. 72.

[45] M. GEBAUER, in I. VIARENGO and P. FRANZINA (eds.), *The EU Regulations on the Property Regimes of International Couples, A Commentary*, Edward Elgar, Cheltenham 2020, p. 298 emphasises that it is a challenge to interpret the term 'strict interpretation'. This will most certainly lead to divergent national approaches to the application of national mandatory provisions.

3.3.2. Public Policy

While the Twin Regulations, in Articles 30, provide for the application of certain national provisions regardless of the content of the provisions of the applicable law, they additionally also enable the rejection of the application of a certain provision of the applicable law (Articles 31). This applies if the application of such a provision (and not the provision itself) is manifestly incompatible with the public policy of the state of the competent court.

Several other European private law regulations know and use a public policy exception. The same provision can, for example, be found in the Succession Regulation (Article 35). The relevant provisions of the Rome I Regulation, the Rome III Regulation, and Regulation No 864/2007 of the European Parliament and of the Council of 11 July 2007 on the law applicable to non-contractual obligations (Rome II) are likewise similar. The possibility of preventing the application of a certain provision of an otherwise applicable foreign law is therefore not unusual in private international law. Despite the similarity of the relevant provision on public policy exceptions of the Twin Regulations to the ones found in other instruments, it is clear that the values that are protected in the court procedures under the Twin Regulations are different.[46] Recital 53 of the Regulation on the Property Consequences of Registered Partnerships and Recital 54 of the Matrimonial Property Regulation give important instructions. They determine that the courts should not apply a public policy exception in order to set aside the law of another state when doing so would be contrary to the Charter of Fundamental Rights of the European Union, in particular Article 21 on the principle of non-discrimination. Such an instruction limits courts' refusals to apply a provision of an applicable law if such a refusal would create inequality between spouses or partners based on personal circumstance, i.e. gender, nationality or religion.[47] The public policy exception shall be applied in exceptional circumstances only. Its wide application might otherwise weaken the efficiency of the conflict of law rules.[48]

A public policy exception provides for the exclusion of the application of a foreign provision; however, it does not give a solution as to which provision applies instead. The legal theory speculates about two possible options. First, the possibility exists that there is no need to apply another provision instead of a refused foreign one. In such a situation, the competent court uses all of the other

---

[46] M. GEBAUER, in I. VIARENGO and P. FRANZINA (eds.), *The EU Regulations on the Property Regimes of International Couples, A Commentary*, Edward Elgar, Cheltenham 2020, p. 307.
[47] P. LAGARDE, 'Applicable Law: Articles 20–35' in U. BERGQUIST, D. DAMASCELLI, R. FRIMSTON, P. LAGARDE and B. REINHARTZ, *The EU Regulations on Matrimonial and Patrimonial Property*, Oxford University Press, Oxford 2019, p. 129.
[48] M. GEBAUER, in I. VIARENGO and P. FRANZINA (eds.), *The EU Regulations on the Property Regimes of International Couples, A Commentary*, Edward Elgar, Cheltenham 2020, p. 308.

provisions of the applicable law. Secondly, if the non-application of a specific legal provision requires the application of another one, two contradictory solutions exist. It is possible that the gap is filled with another provision of an otherwise applied legal order[49] or that such a provision is searched for within the *lex fori*.[50] To avoid the simultaneous application of several legal orders, the first solution is better. If possible, the solutions should be found in the applicable law. If this does not bring the desired result, the *lex fori* might be used subsidiarily.

3.4. EXCLUSION OF *RENVOI*

The Twin Regulations provide for the exclusion of *renvoi* without any exceptions (see Articles 32). The application of the law of any state determined by the rules of the Twin Regulations, therefore, entails the application of the rules of the law in force in that state except for its rules of private international law.[51] Such a rule eliminates the possible danger of complications when conflict of law rules refer back or forward, whereupon one of the subsequent laws refers to a law that had already been considered. Such exclusion of *renvoi* is common in European instruments on private international law. It can, for example, be found in the Rome III Regulation, the Rome II Regulation, and the Rome I Regulation. On the contrary, the Succession Regulation provides for partial *renvoi* (see Article 34).

There are contradictory opinions in legal theory regarding the effects of such a provision on legal certainty and predictability, on the one hand, and party autonomy, on the other. Some opine that the exclusion of *renvoi* is understandable when a couple did agree on the applicable law, but not otherwise.[52] Others are of the opinion, that the exclusion of *renvoi* protects (also) the expectations of a couple that did not choose the applicable law.[53]

---

[49] M. GEBAUER, in I. VIARENGO and P. FRANZINA (eds.), *The EU Regulations on the Property Regimes of International Couples, A Commentary*, Edward Elgar, Cheltenham 2020 above n. 9, p. 311.

[50] P. LAGARDE, 'Applicable Law: Articles 20–35' in U. BERGQUIST, D. DAMASCELLI, R. FRIMSTON, P. LAGARDE and B. REINHARTZ, *The EU Regulations on Matrimonial and Patrimonial Property*, Oxford University Press, Oxford 2019, p. 129.

[51] Additionally, exceptions regarding the overriding mandatory rules and public order as described above are applied.

[52] P. LAGARDE, 'Applicable Law: Articles 20–35' in U. BERGQUIST, D. DAMASCELLI, R. FRIMSTON, P. LAGARDE and B. REINHARTZ, *The EU Regulations on Matrimonial and Patrimonial Property*, Oxford University Press, Oxford 2019, p. 132, sees the exclusion of *renvoi* as a surprise to a couple that did not conclude an agreement on the choice of law.

[53] M. GEBAUER, in I. VIARENGO and P. FRANZINA (eds.), *The EU Regulations on the Property Regimes of International Couples, A Commentary*, Edward Elgar, Cheltenham 2020, p. 315. Similarly, see also C. KOHLER, p. 200, who sees a negative effect for couples choosing the law of a non-Member State or a non-participating Member State, as it can entail the 'application of a law, which is not applicable according to its own conflict-of-laws rules'.

4. AGREEMENT ON THE CHOICE OF LAW

Interpreting the Twin Regulations using the literal method of interpretation, it is possible to conclude that all of the above-described rules regarding the determination of the applicable law are applicable subsidiarily. Partners or spouses are initially expected to conclude an agreement choosing the law that is to be applied for all civil law aspects of their matrimonial property regime or the property consequences of their registered partnership.

4.1. CONNECTING FACTORS

When choosing the applicable law, partners and spouses are relatively limited and cannot choose a law of just any state.[54] They can choose either the law of the state of habitual residence[55] of one or both of them, or the law of a state of the nationality[56] of either of them (Articles 22 of the Twin Regulations). Both connecting factors are bound to the time of the conclusion of the agreement.

The set of connecting factors that spouses may choose from is similar to that provided in the Matrimonial Property Regulation in situations when they have not concluded an agreement. Nevertheless, those connecting factors that spouses may choose from when concluding a choice-of-law agreement are noticeably wider compared to those in Article 26. The latter enables only the application of the law of the residence or nationality of both spouses, while under Article 22 they can also agree on the application of the law of the state of the residence or nationality of one of them. The set of connecting factors when concluding an agreement is therefore doubled and the spouses have a wider list of options to choose from.

Registered partners also have wider options when choosing a law by themselves compared to the situation when a law is determined with regard to the conflict of law rules of the Regulation on the Property Consequences of Registered Partnerships. The connecting factors of nationality and residence are not an option in Article 26 of the Regulation on the Property Consequences of Registered Partnerships. The reason is the same as the reason for a third connecting factor in Article 22(1) of the Regulation on the Property Consequences of Registered Partnerships. There exists a risk that neither the state of the habitual residence of the partners nor the state of their

---

[54] Compare, for example, with the autonomy of parties in international contract law, i.e. the Rome I Regulation.
[55] See Section 2.2 for more on the term 'habitual residence'.
[56] For more on the agreement on the choice of the law of the state of the nationality of one or both parties, see N. POGORELČNIK VOGRINC, 'Applicable law in matrimonial property regime disputes' (2019) 40 *Zbornik Pravnog fakulteta Sveučilišta u Rijeci* 1088–1089.

nationalities legally provides for the institution of registered partnership and does not regulate its legal consequences.[57] The Regulation on the Property Consequences of Registered Partnerships, therefore, provides for an additional connecting factor. Partners or future partners may agree to designate the law of the state under whose law the registered partnership was created (compare with Article 26 of the same Regulation). This is a safety net, which ensures that the partners always have at least one option when concluding an agreement on the choice of law. At the same time, it is a reliable connecting factor because it is independent of possible subsequent changes in the partners' lives.[58]

Where the connecting factors in Articles 22 and 26 of each of the Twin Regulations overlap, it is possible to conclude that an agreement on the choice of law is not needed. Spouses can choose the law of the state of the spouses' common habitual residence or the law of the state of the spouses' common nationality. If at the time of the conclusion of the agreement they still live in the same state, or in a case in which the first connecting factor does not apply and they have the same nationalities as at the time of the conclusion of the marriage, they can choose the same law as would apply without their agreement, i.e. with the application of the conflict of law rules of the Matrimonial Property Regulation. The situation is the same when partners agree on the application of the law of the state under whose law the registered partnership was created, which is otherwise used also when a special agreement does not exist. However, the conclusion of an agreement does have the advantage of ensuring parties reliability and security. Furthermore, it has another consequence. If an agreement on the choice of law exists, the possibility of applying an escape clause is excluded.

Spouses and partners can conclude a choice-of-law agreement during a marriage or registered partnership, before concluding the marriage or registered partnership, or even just before the break up (regardless of the reason, i.e. divorce, legal separation, dissolution, or annulment). It is realistic to expect that at the same time they will also agree on the choice of the competent court[59] and potentially on the matrimonial/partnership property regime.[60]

---

[57] There is a question whether the chosen law should ensure property consequences with regard to registered partnerships or if it is sufficient if it only recognises the institute of a registered partnership. For more on this, see C. RUDOLF, 'European Property Regimes Regulations – Choice of Law and the Applicable Law in the Absence of Choice by the Parties' (2019) 11 Lexonomica 138–139.

[58] C. KOHLER, in I. VIARENGO and P. FRANZINA (eds.), *The EU Regulations on the Property Regimes of International Couples, A Commentary*, Edward Elgar, Cheltenham 2020, pp. 207–208.

[59] See Chapter 4 of this volume.

[60] If they do not also choose a property regime, the default matrimonial regime provided by the chosen national law applies. See E. A. OPREA, 'Party autonomy and the law applicable to the matrimonial property regimes in Europe' (2018) 10 *Cuadernos de Derecho Transnacional* 590. The same in P. LAGARDE, 'Applicable Law: Articles 20–35' in U. BERGQUIST, D. DAMASCELLI, R. FRIMSTON, P. LAGARDE and B. REINHARTZ, *The EU Regulations on Matrimonial and Patrimonial Property*, Oxford University Press, Oxford 2019, p. 100.

4.2. FORMAL REQUIREMENTS

The Twin Regulations set identical provisions regarding the formal conditions that need to be fulfilled for the agreement on the choice of law to be valid. The couple's agreement has to be made in writing (either in handwriting or typed and printed), dated, and signed by both (Articles 23). The Twin Regulations also reflect the current trends regarding electronic communications and stipulate that any communication by electronic means that provides a durable record of the agreement is equivalent to writing. However, the form of a customary electronic message (email) is not sufficient. Secure electronic signatures of both parties are needed.[61] The requirements are similar to those in other European regulations on international private law – see e.g. Article 7 of the Rome III Regulation. Fulfilling these formal requirements ensures that spouses and partners are aware of the seriousness of the agreement and its consequences (Recitals 47 of the Twin Regulations). The described requirements are the same as those determined in the Twin Regulations for a choice-of-court agreement and an agreement[62] on the matrimonial/partnership property regime. Parties can thus agree on all three together in one document. Nevertheless, additional national requirements need to be fulfilled if they exist.

For an agreement on the choice of law to be valid, the Twin Regulations require the fulfilment of the legal requirements of the Member State in which both spouses or partners have their habitual residence at the time of concluding such agreement. This is a reasonable requirement, as parties normally seek information regarding the required form of an agreement in the place where they live.[63] If they are habitually resident in different Member States and the laws of those states determine different formal requirements, the agreement has to satisfy the requirements of either of those laws. If only one of the parties is habitually resident in a Member State, its national requirements regarding matrimonial/partnership property agreements shall apply. The Twin Regulations do not specify special rules when neither of the partners has a habitual residence

---

[61] C. KOHLER, in I. VIARENGO and P. FRANZINA (eds.), *The EU Regulations on the Property Regimes of International Couples, A Commentary*, Edward Elgar, Cheltenham 2020, p. 216, emphasises that an electronic form substitutes for a written form of an agreement, but not also for the requirement that it be dated and signed. The latter can only be fulfilled with a qualified electronic signature as determined by Regulation (EU) No 910/2014 of the European Parliament and of the Council of 23 July 2014 on electronic identification and trust services for electronic transactions in the internal market and repealing Directive 1999/93/EC. The typed names of the parties at the end of such an agreement in electronic form is not sufficient.

[62] For the relevant national rules applied to an agreement on the matrimonial/partnership property regime, see Articles 25 of the Twin Regulations.

[63] R. SCHULZ, 'Choice of law in relation to matrimonial property in the 21st Century' (2019) 15 *Journal of Private International Law* 27.

in a Member State. It is possible to conclude that in such a situation only the requirements of the Twin Regulations apply.⁶⁴

The potentially stricter national requirements of the Member State of habitual residence compared to those in the Twin Regulations, therefore, need to be fulfilled. A typical example is a requirement that a choice-of-law agreement has to be concluded in the form of a notarial deed. When concluding such an agreement, the parties, therefore, need to find out which national law is relevant and consequently which formal requirements they need to fulfil. This can be different from the law they have agreed to be applicable for their matrimonial property or property of registered partnership. This is the case when they agree on a law that is different from that of a state of habitual residence of either of them.

When an agreement on the choice of law does not fulfil the formal requirements of the Twin Regulations or national legislation, such agreement is not valid. The competent court then uses Article 26 of the relevant Twin Regulation to decide on the applicable law. In the author's opinion, the strict rules regarding the formal requirements for a choice-of-law agreement demonstrate that a silent agreement with such content is not possible.⁶⁵

4.3. CONSENT AND MATERIAL VALIDITY

The Twin Regulations furthermore include a provision regarding the material validity of an agreement on the choice of law (Articles 24 of the Twin Regulations).⁶⁶ It has the same goal as formal requirements, i.e. ensuring the informed choice of the parties and therefore better legal certainty. While the Twin Regulations themselves provide few formal requirements for the choice-of-law agreements (see Articles 23(a)), they use different approach regarding the material validity. They themselves provide for all the requirements that have to be respected when concluding an agreement on the choice of law and none of the relevant national requirements need to be respected (compare Articles 23 and 24 of both Regulations). The existence and validity of an agreement shall be

---

[64] See E. A. OPREA, 'Party autonomy and the law applicable to the matrimonial property regimes in Europe' (2018) 10 *Cuadernos de Derecho Transnacional* 591–592. She questions if such a regulation is suitable.

[65] For an opposing view, see C. RUDOLF, 'Kolizijske norme Uredbe Sveta (EU) 2016/1104 za premoženjskopravne posledice registriranih partnerskih skupnosti' in D. MOŽINA (ed.), *Liber Amicorum Ada Polajnar Pavčnik, Razsežnosti zasebnega prava*, Pravna fakulteta Univerza v Ljubljani, Ljubljana 2019, p. 276. Similarly, C. KOHLER, in I. VIARENGO and P. FRANZINA (eds.), *The EU Regulations on the Property Regimes of International Couples, A Commentary*, Edward Elgar, Cheltenham 2020, p. 201, is of the opinion that the Twin Regulations are not clear regarding the need for the parties' will to be expressed explicitly.

[66] Related to this, it is necessary to emphasise that the Twin Regulations do not apply to, inter alia, the legal capacity of spouses and partners (Articles 1(2)(a) of both regulations).

determined by the chosen law if the agreement was valid. Some critics wonder how an agreement can be examined under the chosen law if it is not proven that the choice is valid.[67] However, such a provision is not entirely new, and has been previously used in other European instruments.[68] It is an easy rule for partners and spouses to apply[69] and provides certainty and stability.

An exception exists if a spouse or a partner wishes to establish that he or she did not consent to the choice of law. In such a case, he or she may rely upon the law of the state in which he or she has his or her habitual residence at the time the court is seised.[70] This is possible if it appears from the circumstances that it would not be reasonable to determine the effect of his or her conduct in accordance with the chosen law. This provision plays an essential role in regulations when parties can conclude an agreement implicitly. In these cases it can thus happen that one of them did not consent (i.e. did not reply to the other party's proposal), however, his or her act was deemed to be an agreement.[71] Because[72] the Twin Regulations require an explicit expression of will, the party will have a difficult task proving that his or her explicit expression of will on the applicable law is not his or her consent.[73] The Twin Regulations provide that in such a case a party can rely upon the law of the state in which he or she has his or her habitual residence at the time the court is seised. Interestingly, in such

---

[67] L. RADEMACHER, 'Changing the past: retroactive choice of law and the protection of third parties in the European regulations on patrimonial consequences of marriages and registered partnerships' (2018) 10 *Cuadernos de Derecho Transnacional* 18; C. GRIECO, 'The role of party autonomy under regulations on matrimonial property regimes and property consequences of registered partnerships. Some remarks on the coordination between the legal regime established by the new regulations and other relevant instruments of European private international law' (2018) 10 *Cuadernos de Derecho Transnacional* 475.

[68] See e.g. the Succession Regulation, the Rome I Regulation and the Rome III Regulation.

[69] E. A. OPREA, 'Party autonomy and the law applicable to the matrimonial property regimes in Europe' (2018) 10 *Cuadernos de Derecho Transnacional* 590.

[70] For criticism of such rule, see N. POGORELČNIK VOGRINC, 'Applicable law in matrimonial property regime disputes' (2019) 40 *Zbornik Pravnog fakulteta Sveučilišta u Rijeci* 1092.

[71] C. KOHLER, in I. VIARENGO and P. FRANZINA (eds.), *The EU Regulations on the Property Regimes of International Couples, A Commentary*, Edward Elgar, Cheltenham 2020, p. 230, reminds that 'if a declaration of a party has been made under error or misrepresentation, or if the consent of that party is the result of coercion or undue influence, a remedy will normally be available under the hypothetical *lex causae* according to Article 24(1)'.

[72] Different opinions exist, as described above. C. RUDOLF, 'European Property Regimes Regulations – Choice of Law and the Applicable Law in the Absence of Choice by the Parties' (2019) 11 *Lexonomica* 140, is of the opinion that Articles 24(2) of the Twin Regulations are the exact reason that enable the conclusion that an implied choice of law is admissible. However, she acknowledges (also citing other legal theorists) that there are no criteria for an implied choice of the applicable law and that further clarification must come from the CJEU. However, it is possible to conclude to the contrary. As there is no mention of an implied agreement on the choice of law in the Twin Regulations, this is not an option.

[73] See C. KOHLER, in I. VIARENGO and P. FRANZINA (eds.), The EU Regulations on the Property Regimes of International Couples, A Commentary, Edward Elgar, Cheltenham 2020, p. 230.

a situation the connecting factor of habitual residence is bound to the time of the beginning of the court procedure and not the time of the conclusion of the agreement, as is often found at other times.[74] The reason for that is uncertainty and ambiguity regarding the moment of the agreement's conclusion when there is a dispute whether the parties even concluded one. However, the party cannot be sure that he or she will really be able to use the law of the state of his or her habitual residence. This is a decision of the competent court that is considering whether it would be unreasonable to determine the effect of a party's conduct in accordance with the chosen law. The Twin Regulations do not give any further instructions regarding these circumstances, which can lead to different interpretations in different Member States.

4.4. CHANGE OF AN AGREEMENT ON THE CHOICE OF LAW

As it is always possible that spouses or partners conclude an agreement on the choice of law for the first time any time during their marriage or partnership or even just before it has ended, it is also possible that they change an earlier agreement. A subsequent change or the conclusion of a new agreement undoubtedly entails the application of a law that is different from that determined based on the conflict of law rules (i.e. Articles 26 of the Twin Regulations) or that derives from the previous agreement. Such a 'new' law applies from the conclusion of the (new) agreement.

Articles 22 of the Twin Regulations are namely uniform in determining that a change in the applicable law shall generally have prospective effect. Such a rule aims to protect legal certainty and predictability; however, it also has some serious negative consequences. The *ex nunc* application of a choice-of-law agreement necessarily means that the legal regulations of two different states are applied for matters regarding the matrimonial property regime or the property consequences of a registered partnership of one couple. This can lead to a couple being confused about their legal situation and entails a difficult task for the court deciding in a court procedure.

However, spouses and partners have greater autonomy when changing an agreement and can avoid a prospective application only if such is an intention.[75] The Twin Regulations allow them to explicitly agree on the retroactive effect of an agreement. This eliminates the consequences of the application of two

---

[74] C. KOHLER, in I. VIARENGO and P. FRANZINA (eds.), *The EU Regulations on the Property Regimes of International Couples, A Commentary*, Edward Elgar, Cheltenham 2020, p. 230.

[75] A. LIMANTE and N. POGORELČNIK VOGRINC, 'Party autonomy in the context of jurisdictional and choice of law rules of matrimonial property regulation' (2020) 13 *Baltic Journal of Law & Politics*, 147 et seq.

(or even more) legal systems. However, this solution may also have significant negative implications. It might negatively affect the right of third persons relying on the content of the existing agreement or the use of the conflict of law rules provided for in the Twin Regulations.[76] Therefore, the Twin Regulations explicitly provide for their protection. The Regulations require that the retroactive effect of a new agreement on the choice of law shall not adversely affect the rights of third parties deriving from that law (Articles 22(3) of the Twin Regulations). There are no additional provisions in the Twin Regulations on the solution of such a complication. One option is the simultaneous application of both laws, where the previous one is used exclusively regarding the acquired rights of a third person.[77] On one hand, this ensures the realisation of the couple's wish to use the law subsequently agreed upon for their whole legal relationship. On the other hand, such a solution protects the rights of third persons relying on the application of the previously applicable law. While it is easy to propose such a solution in theory, it is much harder to implement it in practice. Courts, therefore, face a difficult task when trying to satisfy all the interests.

4.5. EFFECTS IN RESPECT OF THIRD PARTIES

The Twin Regulations explicitly require that the retroactive effect of an agreement on the choice of law must not have a negative impact on the rights of third parties. However, this is not the only protection of third persons. As provided in Articles 28 of both Regulations, the otherwise applicable law may not be invoked by a spouse or a partner against a third party in their dispute unless the third party knew or, in the exercise of due diligence, should have known of that law. This applies to any applicable law regardless of the fact whether it is determined by reference to the conflict of law rules of the Twin Regulations or the couple agreed on it. Articles 28, therefore, determine the so-called negative conflict of law rule.[78] As a consequence thereof, it is possible that the otherwise applicable law does not apply in certain relations between a spouse or a partner and a third person.

---

[76] *Ex tunc* effect can furthermore have an adverse impact on the previous transactions between spouses and partners themselves. While a proposal of the Twin Regulations included a provision preventing such a consequence, the current text of the Twin Regulations does not. For more on this, see C. KOHLER, in I. VIARENGO and P. FRANZINA (eds.), *The EU Regulations on the Property Regimes of International Couples, A Commentary*, Edward Elgar, Cheltenham 2020, pp. 209–210.

[77] L. RADEMACHER, 'Changing the past: retroactive choice of law and the protection of third parties in the European regulations on patrimonial consequences of marriages and registered partnerships' (2018) 10 *Cuadernos de Derecho Transnacional* 16.

[78] J. M. CARRUTHERS, in I. VIARENGO and P. FRANZINA (eds.), *The EU Regulations on the Property Regimes of International Couples, A Commentary*, Edward Elgar, Cheltenham 2020, p. 277.

The Twin Regulations explicitly determine the circumstances in which a third party is deemed to possess knowledge of the law applicable to the matrimonial property regime. This is true in two different situations. The first relates to the law itself and its relation to the circumstances of a specific legal transaction. These are cases when the relevant law is the law of: the state whose law is applicable to the transaction between a spouse and the third party; the state where the contracting spouse and the third party have their habitual residence; or, in cases involving immovable property, the state in which such property is situated. The national law is believed to be so evident to the third person that its application is justifiable and no need for special protection exists. The second set of circumstances relates to the disclosure or registration of the matrimonial property regime or the property consequences of the registered partnership. The third person is deemed to possess knowledge of the applicable law if either spouse or partner has complied with the requirements for its disclosure or registration specified by the law of the relevant state, i.e. the state whose law is applicable to the transaction between a spouse and the third party; the state where the contracting spouse and the third party have their habitual residence; or in cases involving immovable property, the state in which the property is situated. The assumption that a third person knows which law applies if a couple has disclosed or registered an agreement is questionable. If the law of the relevant state obliges a couple only to register an agreement but not also to publicly disclose its content, a third person will only know that an agreement on the choice of law exists, but will not know its content. It remains a question whether a legal basis exists enabling a third person to require a couple to also disclose the specific content of their agreement.

It is not clear at what moment a third person is supposed to possess knowledge of the applicable law. It is possible to conclude that the relevant time is the moment of the conclusion of the legal transaction.[79] Furthermore, it is essential to know whether a third person should possess knowledge of which state's law applies for a certain relation, or if he or she also should know the content of the relevant provisions of the applicable law.[80] The first solution is more realistic. It is unrealistic to expect a spouse or partner, let alone a third person, to know the content of the relevant provisions of the applicable law.

A rule on effects in respect of third parties makes their legal situation much easier. When concluding a legal transaction with someone who is married or in a registered partnership, a third person does not have to spend money or time finding out the relevant applicable law. If he or she is not aware of it through no fault of his or her own, such a law will not apply for a specific legal relation.

---

[79] J. M. CARRUTHERS, in I. VIARENGO and P. FRANZINA (eds.), *The EU Regulations on the Property Regimes of International Couples, A Commentary*, Edward Elgar, Cheltenham 2020, p. 278.

[80] Ibid.

5. CASE STUDY

When deciding how to formalise their relationship, partners consider different circumstances and personal wishes. On the one hand, an institution of marriage has a long tradition and therefore a general belief exists that marriage is a stronger form of formalisation of the relationship as compared to registered partnership. On the other hand, young people are often more inclined to a new approach and therefore sometimes prefer the registration of a partnership to a marriage. Additionally, legal possibilities offered in a specific state (i.e. can a same-sex couple marry or can an opposite-sex couple register a partnership) play an important role in a couple's decision.

In such a situation, normally partners do not foresee that their decision regarding the form of formalisation of the relationship that they choose will affect their life in many aspects. Amongst others, it will influence the instruments that are used to decide on jurisdiction and conflict of law rules of their property relations in case of break up.

Let us take as an example a Portuguese–Belgian couple who met and fell in love at the student exchange in the Netherlands.

Scenario 1

In the first situation, they get married in the Netherlands and move to Slovenia because of the work opportunity that one of them got there. They live in Slovenia for few years and buy a house in Ljubljana and a flat in Piran (as a variation, they buy a flat in Croatia). A few years later, they divorce. Each of them moves back to their home country, one to Portugal and the other to Belgium. One of the ex-spouses wants to start a court procedure regarding their property regime.

Jurisdiction

The first question is the court of which state has jurisdiction. There is no related court procedure regarding the succession of a spouse (Article 4 of the Matrimonial Property Regulation) or regarding divorce, legal separation or marriage annulment (Article 5 of the Matrimonial Property Regulation) and the ex-spouses have not concluded an agreement regarding the jurisdiction for those matters. The jurisdiction is therefore determined according to the general rules of Article 6 of the Matrimonial Property Regulation.

The first connecting factor of Article 6 of the Matrimonial Property Regulation is the state in whose territory the spouses are habitually resident at the time the court is seised. In this specific case, it cannot be used as at the beginning of the court procedure the ex-spouses did not have habitual residence in the same Member State (as they moved back to their home states).

The second connecting factor of Article 6 of the Matrimonial Property Regulation is the state in whose territory the spouses were last habitually resident, insofar as one of them still resides there at the time the court is seised. Similarly this connecting factor cannot be used because neither of the ex-spouses still live in Slovenia, where they had their last habitual residence as a couple.

The third connecting factor of Article 6 of the Matrimonial Property Regulation is the state in whose territory the respondent is habitually resident at the time the court is seised. In regard to the fact of who the respondent is, either Belgian or Portuguese courts have international jurisdiction to decide on the house and flat, regardless of their location.

Applicable law

The spouses did not conclude an agreement on the choice of law. The applicable law is therefore determined according to Article 26 of the Matrimonial Property Regulation.

The first connecting factor is the spouses' first common habitual residence after the conclusion of the marriage. As they moved to Slovenia after they married, the applicable law is Slovenian law.

The rule of Article 26 of the Matrimonial Property Regulation is used for the applicable law to be determined, no matter which court has international jurisdiction. That means that Belgian as well as Portuguese courts have to use the same connecting factor. They both apply the law of the state of the spouses' first common habitual residence after the conclusion of the marriage, i.e. Slovenian law.

Scenario 2

In the second situation, the same Portuguese–Belgian couple decides to register their partnership rather than getting married. They register their partnership in the Netherlands and move to Slovenia for work reasons immediately after the registration. They live there for a couple of years. They buy a house and flat in Slovenia (as a variation, the flat is in Croatia). After few years, they dissolve the partnership and move back to their home states. One of them wants to start a court proceeding regarding the property matters.

Because they registered their partnership, the Regulation on the Property Consequences of Registered Partnerships applies.

Jurisdiction

There is no court procedure regarding the succession procedure of a registered partner (Article 4 of the Regulation on the Property Consequences of Registered Partnerships) and no court procedure regarding the dissolution or annulment of the partnership (Article 5 of the Regulation on the Property Consequences of Registered Partnerships). There is also no agreement of the registered partners on international jurisdiction. The international jurisdiction is therefore determined according to the general Article 6 of the Regulation on the Property

Consequences of Registered Partnerships. It provides four connecting factors (Article 6(1) a–d), that are the same as for the marriage and as explained above, the connecting factor of the state in whose territory the respondent is habitually resident at the time the court is seised exists. The same as when the couple got married, Belgian or Portuguese courts have an international jurisdiction.

Applicable law

Article 26 of the Regulation on the Property Consequences of Registered Partnerships is used to determine the applicable law. No agreement on the choice of law exists. The law applicable to the property consequences of registered partnerships would therefore be the law of the state under whose law the registered partnership was created. In the specific case, the applicable law is the law of the Netherlands. Belgian or Portuguese courts therefore have to apply the law of different states only on the basis of the fact if the couple married or registered the partnership.

Commentary

When conflict as to the property of a couple arises, the outcome regarding the jurisdiction and the applicable law is significantly different depending on the fact whether the couple got married or registered a partnership. Couples deciding to take the next step in their relationship, therefore, need to think more broadly and take into account also the wider consequences of their decision, something not exactly romantic, but practical in the long term.

RECOGNITION, ENFORCEABILITY AND ENFORCEMENT OF DECISIONS UNDER THE TWIN REGULATIONS

Jerca KRAMBERGER ŠKERL*

1. Introduction 130
   1.1. Which Decisions can Circulate under the Rules of the Twin
        Regulations? 131
   1.2. Issuing Authorities. 133
   1.3. Territorial and Temporal Scope of Application 134
   1.4. Material Scope of Application 135
2. Recognition 136
3. The Declaration of Enforceability (*Exequatur*). 138
   3.1. The Admissibility of the Application for *Exequatur* 139
   3.2. First Instance Proceedings 141
   3.3. Appeal(s) against the Declaration of Enforceability 142
   3.4. Provisional, Including Protective, Measures Before and During
        Exequatur Proceedings 144
   3.5. Costs of *Exequatur* Proceedings. 145
4. Grounds for Refusal of Recognition and Enforcement. 146
   4.1. The Public Policy Exception (*Ordre Public*) 147
   4.2. The Lack of Service of the Introductory Document in the
        Proceedings. 150
   4.3. Irreconcilability of Judgments 152
   4.4. Further Guidance on the Examination of the Grounds for
        Refusal 153
5. Concluding Remarks 153

---

* Jerca Kramberger Škerl, Associate Professor of Private International Law, Civil Procedure and French Legal Language, Vice Dean of the Law Faculty of the University of Ljubljana, Slovenia.

1. INTRODUCTION

The first mention of the EU plan to enable the free circulation of decisions within its borders can be found in the conclusions of the European Council meeting in Tampere of October 1999,[1] which endorsed the principle of mutual recognition of judgments and other decisions of judicial authorities as the cornerstone of judicial cooperation in civil matters and invited the Council and the Commission to adopt a programme of measures to implement that principle. In the Draft Programme of Measures of 2001,[2] action is called for specifically in areas of family law not covered by the then existing instruments. The need for progress in this field was reiterated in the Hague Programme[3] and further specified in the Stockholm Programme, adopted at a European Council meeting in December 2009.[4] The latter specified that the forthcoming rules needed to respect the 'Member States' legal systems, including public policy (*ordre public*), and national traditions in this area'.

These plans and programmes were followed by legislative action and several regulations were adopted which considerably broadened the EU unification of rules on recognition and enforcement of decisions in the field of family law. While the Brussels II bis Regulation,[5] the Maintenance Regulation[6] and the Succession Regulation[7] are applicable in the territory of the whole EU,[8] the most recent Matrimonial Property Regulation[9] and the Regulation on the Property

---

[1] Tampere European Council 15 and 16 October 1999 Presidency Conclusions, <https://www.europarl.europa.eu/summits/tam_en.htm#c>.
[2] Draft programme of measures for implementation of the principle of mutual recognition of decisions in civil and commercial matters [2001] OJ C12.
[3] The Hague Programme: Strengthening Freedom, Security and Justice in The European Union [2005] OJ C53.
[4] The Stockholm Programme – An open and secure Europe serving and protecting citizens [2010] OJ C115.
[5] Council Regulation (EC) 2003/2201 of 27 November 2003 concerning jurisdiction and the recognition and enforcement of judgments in matrimonial matters and the matters of parental responsibility, repealing Regulation (EC) 2000/1347 [2003] OJ L338.
[6] Council Regulation (EC) 4/2009 of 18 December 2008 on jurisdiction, applicable law, recognition and enforcement of decisions and cooperation in matters relating to maintenance obligations [2009] OJ L7.
[7] Council Regulation (EU) 650/2012 of the European Parliament and of the Council of 4 July 2012 on jurisdiction, applicable law, recognition and enforcement of decisions and acceptance and enforcement of authentic instruments in matters of succession and on the creation of a European Certificate of Succession [2012] OJ L201.
[8] With the exception of Denmark, which is not bound by the Brussels II bis and the Succession Regulation, and Ireland, which is not bound by the Succession Regulation.
[9] Council Regulation (EU) 2016/1103 of 24 June 2016 implementing enhanced cooperation in the area of jurisdiction, applicable law and the recognition and enforcement of decisions in matters of matrimonial property regimes [2016] OJ L183.

Consequences of Registered Partnerships[10] (the Twin Regulations) are currently applicable in the majority, but not all EU Member States. Like the Rome III Regulation beforehand (which does not, however, deal with the recognition and enforcement of decisions),[11] the Twin Regulations were adopted under the system of enhanced cooperation,[12] in view of the lack of a possible consensus 'within a reasonable period by the Union as a whole'.[13] Eighteen Member States joined the enhanced cooperation regarding these Regulations.[14]

Before entering into analysis of the different aspects of the recognition and enforcement of decisions, basic information on the applicability of the Twin Regulations must be provided in this introductory section, i.e. on the definitions of the term 'decision', the authorities which had to issue such decision, and the contours of the territorial, temporal and material scope of application.

1.1. WHICH DECISIONS CAN CIRCULATE UNDER THE RULES OF THE TWIN REGULATIONS?

The Regulations use the term 'decisions', like the Succession Regulation, and not 'judgments', like the Brussels I bis Regulation.[15] This can be useful in determining which acts can circulate under the rules of the Twin Regulations. While the term 'judgment' implies that the issuing authority was the court, the term 'decision' seems more open as to the issuing body, which can, under the Twin Regulations, also be a notary or another authority or profession vested with judicial powers in the material scope of application of the Regulations.[16] Bearing this in mind, the term 'decision' and 'judgment' will be used interchangeably in this chapter.

Article 3(1)(d) of the Matrimonial Property Regulation provides: ' "decision" means any decision in a matter of a matrimonial property regime given by a court of a Member State, whatever the decision may be called, including a decision on

---

[10] Council Regulation (EU) 2016/1104 of 24 June 2016 implementing enhanced cooperation in the area of jurisdiction, applicable law and the recognition and enforcement of decisions in matters of the property consequences of registered partnerships [2016] OJ L183.
[11] Council Regulation (EU) 1259/2010 of 20 December 2010 implementing enhanced cooperation in the area of the law applicable to divorce and legal separation [2010] OJ L343.
[12] The possibility of the adoption of a regulation within the enhanced cooperation is provided for in Article 326 and the following articles of the Consolidated Version of the Treaty on the Functioning of the EU [2012] OJ C326.
[13] Recital 10 of the Regulation on the Property Consequences of Registered Partnerships.
[14] As of 8 June 2021, the participating Member States are: Belgium, Bulgaria, the Czech Republic, Germany, Greece, Spain, France, Croatia, Italy, Luxembourg, Malta, the Netherlands, Austria, Portugal, Slovenia, Finland, Sweden, and Cyprus.
[15] Regulation (EU) 1215/2012 of the European Parliament and of the Council of 12 December 2012 on jurisdiction and the recognition and enforcement of judgments in civil and commercial matters (recast) [2012] OJ L351.
[16] For more on the issuing authorities, see the next section.

the determination of costs or expenses by an officer of the court'. Article 3(1)(e) of the Regulation on the Property Consequences of Registered Partnerships contains an identical provision, naturally with the reference to matters of the property consequences of a registered partnership.

While it is clear that decisions on the substance of the dispute are eligible, it might be important to emphasise that provisional and protective measures are not exempt. This was clarified by the Court of Justice of the EU (CJEU) in the *Denilauler* judgment concerning the Brussels Convention, where the Court, however, demanded that such 'judgments' be issued in contradictory proceedings.[17] The Court later further developed that case law, for example in the *Van Uden*[18] and *Mietz*[19] cases. With the recast of the Brussels I Regulation in 2012, the matter was finally expressly regulated. A specific rule was added laying down conditions for the recognition and enforcement of provisional and protective measures (Article 2(1)(a) of the Brussels I bis Regulation). In particular, besides the need for the defendant to be 'summoned to appear' or at least be served with the decision prior to enforcement, such measures needed to be issued by the court competent as to the substance of the matter. Since the Twin Regulations do not expressly address the provisional and protective measures in the context of the recognition and enforcement of decisions, an analogy can be drawn with the Brussels regime.[20]

This means that provisional and protective measures issued on the basis of Article 19 of the Twin Regulations by courts other than the court having jurisdiction to judge on the substance of the dispute, will only have effects in the Member State of their origin. This prevents a sort of '*forum shopping*' for provisional and protective measures, where parties could seek out a Member State where they could obtain a measure in their favour, even though such state would not have any real connection with the dispute, and then seek the enforcement of the measure either in the Member State where proceedings as to the substance would be conducted (but where a similar measure could not be obtained) or in yet another Member State.

Additionally, the defendant should have the possibility to participate in the proceedings for the issuance of the provisional or protective measure, or else be notified of the existence of such a measure prior to enforcement. This means that the 'surprise effect' of the provisional and protective measures cannot be obtained via the circulation of decisions regime of the Twin Regulations.

---

[17] Case 125/79, *Bernard Denilauler v SNC Couchet Frères*, ECLI:EU:C:1980:130.
[18] Case C-391/95, *Van Uden Maritime BV, trading as Van Uden Africa Line v Kommanditgesellschaft in Firma Deco-Line and Another*, ECLI:EU:C:1998:543.
[19] Case C-99/96, *Hans-Hermann Mietz v Intership Yachting Sneek BV*, ECLI:EU:C:1999:202.
[20] For the analogy between the Twin Regulations and the Brussels I bis Regulation, cf. M. ANDRAE, *Internationales Familienrecht*, Nomos, Baden Baden, 2019, p. 402.

The cross-border circulation of court settlements and authentic instruments is regulated separately from that of the 'decisions' and will be described in the next chapter of this book. It must, however, be noted that the characterisation issue is not entirely avoided by the definitions of the Twin Regulations, especially in light of all the different effects national legislations vest in these two categories of official documents. In authentic instruments, a question could arise as to the delimitation of when a notary performs judicial functions and when not. In court settlements, one could wonder whether they could not fall into the category of 'decisions' where they produce, in the Member State of origin, the same effects as a judgment, i.e. they acquire the *res judicata* effect and are enforceable in the same way as judgments.[21] The wording of the Regulations seems to hardly allow such interpretation; however, it is suggested that the question is relevant, since the actual effects of an official document should prevail over its title when determining the regime of cross-border circulation.

1.2. ISSUING AUTHORITIES

Recital 29 of the Matrimonial Property Regulation calls for the respect of the different systems for dealing with matters of the matrimonial property regime in the Member States. For the purposes of the Regulation:

> the term 'court' should therefore be given a broad meaning so as to cover not only courts in the strict sense of the word, exercising judicial functions, but also for example notaries in some Member States who, in certain matters of matrimonial property regime, exercise judicial functions like courts, and the notaries and legal professionals who, in some Member States, exercise judicial functions in a given matrimonial property regime by delegation of power by a court.

Article 3(2) of the Matrimonial Property Regulation provides that, for the purposes of the Regulation:

> the term 'court' means any judicial authority and all other authorities and legal professionals with competence in matters of matrimonial property regimes which

---

[21] Such is, for example, the case in Slovenia, where court settlements have the same effects as final judgments (there is no ordinary appeal available, just an extraordinary one, the 'action for annulment of a court-settlement' (Sl. *tožba za razveljavitev sodne poravnave*) under Articles 392 and 393 of the Slovenian Civil Procedure Act (*Zakon o pravdnem postopku*), consolidated version, Official Gazette of the Republic of Slovenia, No. 73/2007, with further amendments. Under Slovenian national rules, a foreign court settlement is recognised and enforced under the same rules as a foreign judgment (Article 94(2) of the Private International Law and Procedure Act (*Zakon o mednarodnem zasebnem pravu in postopku*), Official Gazette of the Republic of Slovenia, No. 56/1999, with further amendments.

exercise judicial functions or act by delegation of power by a judicial authority or under its control, provided that such other authorities and legal professionals offer guarantees with regard to impartiality and the right of all parties to be heard, and provided that their decisions under the law of the Member State in which they operate: (a) may be made the subject of an appeal to or review by a judicial authority; and (b) have a similar force and effect as a decision of a judicial authority on the same matter.

The Regulation on the Property Consequences of Registered Partnerships contains an identical rule regarding the property of registered partnerships.

The defining feature of the 'court' is therefore the exercise of judicial functions, and not the name or the type of the authority exercising such functions. The most common type of authorities, which are not courts in the strict sense of the term, but can, in many Member States, exercise (also) judicial functions, are notaries which are also expressly mentioned in the Regulations. Recital 30 of the Twin Regulations further explains that the Regulations do not interfere with the competences of the notaries under national law. It is, however, important, that when the notarial acts fall in the scope of the Regulations, the notaries respect the jurisdictional rules set out by the Regulations.

Member States had to notify the Commission of the other authorities and legal professionals referred to above.[22] While notaries frequently join the courts in succession matters, the notifications interestingly show that only Portugal and the Czech Republic vest judicial powers in notaries in the field of couples' property relations. Some Member States notified other legal professions, for example, Italy notified 'lawyers and civil registrars acting under the assisted negotiation (It. *negoziazione assistita*) procedure'.[23] The majority of participating countries, however, notified that no other professions or authorities apart from the courts were competent to issue decisions with regard to the Regulations.

1.3. TERRITORIAL AND TEMPORAL SCOPE OF APPLICATION

Being adopted within the system of enhanced cooperation, the rules on recognition and enforcement of decisions from the Twin Regulations only apply in the Member States participating in the enhanced cooperation, and only to decisions issued in the participating Member States. If a judgment originates in an EU Member State which does not participate in the enhanced cooperation or

---

[22] As of 10 June 2021, Malta and Slovenia have not yet sent their notifications.
[23] Sweden notified the 'executors' (*bodelningsförrättare*), estate administrators (*boutredningsman*), and, in summary proceedings concerning payment orders or assistance, the Enforcement Authority (*Kronofogdemyndigheten*). Portugal notified (beside the notaries) civil registry offices (*Conservatórias do Registo Civil*). Finland notified the 'executor, appointed by the court'.

recognition and enforcement is required in such a Member State, national rules on recognition and enforcement of foreign judgments apply, just as in the case of a decision from a non-EU state. For the purposes of clarity, this limitation in the territorial scope of application of the Twin Regulations is not repeated throughout the chapter, and the term Member States is used to refer to the participating Member States.

Regarding the temporal scope of application, the Twin Regulations apply to the recognition and enforcement of decisions issued in legal proceedings instituted on or after 29 January 2019. It is important to emphasise that the important date is that of the beginning of the court proceedings, and, in principle, not the date of the issuance of the judgment. However, the regulations allow for the recognition and enforcement of judgments issued after their entry into application, under their rules, even in the event the proceedings started before their entry into force, if the jurisdiction of the competent court was based on a rule compliant with the rules on jurisdiction from the regulation.[24]

1.4. MATERIAL SCOPE OF APPLICATION

The material scope of application relevant for the recognition and enforcement of decisions is laid out in Articles 1 and 3 of the Regulations, while the recitals are also of help in the interpretation. The term 'marriage' is not defined by the Matrimonial Property Regulation and is to be interpreted under national laws of participating Member States (see Recital 17). Also, pursuant to Recital 64 of the Matrimonial Property Regulation: '[t]he recognition and enforcement of a decision on matrimonial property regime under this Regulation should not in any way imply the recognition of the marriage underlying the matrimonial property regime which gave rise to the decision.' Article 1(2) of the Regulation expressly excludes from its scope of application 'the existence, validity or recognition of a marriage'. The Regulation on the Property Consequences of Registered Partnerships, on the other hand, defines 'registered partnerships' as 'the regime governing the shared life of two people which is provided for in law, the registration of which is mandatory under that law and which fulfils the legal formalities required by that law for its creation'. The Regulation, however, does not apply to the existence, validity or recognition of a registered partnership

---

[24] This system is analogous to that from the Brussels I Regulation of 2000. For more on the issues that arise regarding such a system, see J. KRAMBERGER ŠKERL, 'The application 'ratione temporis' of the Brussels I regulation (recast)' in D. DUIĆ and T. PETRAŠEVIĆ (eds.), *EU and Comparative Law Issues and Challenges: Procedural Aspects of EU Law*, Faculty of Law Osijek, Osijek, 2017, pp. 341–363, <www.pravos.unios.hr/download/eu-and-comparative-law-issues-and-challenges.pdf>. For more on the rules on jurisdiction in the Matrimonial Property Regimes Regulation, see N. POGORELČNIK VOGRINC, 'Mednarodna pristojnost v sporih glede premoženjskih razmerij med zakoncema' (2020) 1 *Podjetje in delo* 178–203.

(Article 1(2)), and Recital 63 of the Regulation on the Property Consequences of Registered Partnerships states: 'The recognition and enforcement of a decision on the property consequences of a registered partnership under this Regulation should not in any way imply the recognition of the registered partnership which gave rise to the decision.'

Because of these exclusions, it can happen that one participating Member State will apply one of the Regulations in determining jurisdiction, but another Member State will not recognise the ensuing judgment under the same Regulation; the other Twin Regulation will be applied, or even national law.[25] If the judgment comprises decisions on several issues, only those regarding the property relations between spouses or registered partners are recognised and enforced under the Twin Regulations.[26]

2. RECOGNITION

The rules on the recognition in the Twin Regulations mimic the system under the Brussels I Regulation of 2000,[27] later also adopted (with some notable exceptions) in the Succession Regulation and the Maintenance Regulation. This is very welcome since the practitioners and the legislatures of the Member States have experience in dealing with such rules. Also, importantly, the case law of the CJEU and of national courts, adopted on the basis of the Brussels I Regulation (and, before that, the Brussels Convention), is able to serve as an instrument of interpretation.[28]

The recognition of judgments from other Member States is thus 'automatic' (*ipso iure*), i.e. without any verifications in the Member State of recognition. The effects of the judgment, issued in a participating Member State, are automatically broadened to other participating Member States. In other participating Member States, the binding force of such judgment is equal to that of the domestic judgments (but not broader than in the Member State of origin).

---

[25] Cf. M. ANDRAE, *Internationales Familienrecht*, Nomos, Baden Baden 2019, p. 401, who gives the example where the court in the Member State of the origin of the judgment determines its jurisdiction on the basis of the Matrimonial Property Regulation, but the Member State of enforcement enforces the judgment under the Regulation on the Property Consequences of a Registered Partnership.

[26] If, for example, the judgment comprises a decision on maintenance, as well as a decision on the division of the common property of the divorced spouses, the first part will be recognised and enforced under the Maintenance Regulation, and the latter part under the Matrimonial Property Regulation. Cf. ibid.

[27] Council Regulation (EC) 2001/44 of 22 December 2000 on jurisdiction and the recognition and enforcement of judgments in civil and commercial matters [2001] OJ L12.

[28] Cf. U. BERGQUIST in U. BERGQUIST, D. DAMASCELLI, R. FRIMSTON, P. LAGARDE and B. REINHARTZ, *The EU Regulations on Matrimonial Property*, Oxford University Press, Oxford 2019, p. 140.

There is, however, a difference between a decision from another participating Member State and a domestic judgment. Namely, the 'presumption of regularity'[29] of a judgment from another Member State is rebuttable if grounds for refusal of recognition are proven to exist.

In order to ensure legal certainty for the party relying on the effectiveness of the foreign decision, the 'presumption of regularity' can be confirmed in special recognition proceedings under the Regulations, so as to become unrebuttable (Article 36(2) of the Twin Regulations). These proceedings are conducted pursuant to the rules on proceedings for the declaration of enforceability in the same regulations. The decision on recognition is of a declaratory nature, since the judgment produced effects in all Member States at the same time as in the Member State of origin.[30] The opposing party in such proceedings can invoke grounds for refusal of recognition and, in case of success, prevent the foreign judgment to take effect in the country addressed.

In contrast to the declaration of enforceability, recognition can also (and mostly will) be decided upon as a preliminary question in the proceedings on another main subject (incidental recognition, Article 36(3) of the Twin Regulations). In such a case, every court having jurisdiction in the main matter can also decide on the recognition of a foreign judgment, the effects of which were invoked in the proceedings. Such recognition, in turn, only becomes final (unrebuttable) in such proceedings and not *erga omnes* (i.e. a different decision can still be taken in the stand-alone recognition proceedings mentioned above or in other incidental proceedings).

Just as in the Brussels I Regulation, the Twin Regulations do not provide for an application for non-recognition, which could, in some cases, be of interest for one of the parties to the original proceedings (the Brussels II bis Regulation, for example, provides for such option in Article 21(3)).[31] The party which deems that grounds for refusal exist, must thus wait until the other party asserts the effects of the judgment in another Member State, to be able to object and demand the refusal of recognition.

If stand-alone proceedings for recognition are instituted, the competent court can stay the proceedings if 'an ordinary appeal against the decision has been lodged in the Member State of origin' (Article 41 of the Twin Regulations).

---

[29] Cf. M. ANDRAE, *Internationales Familienrecht*, Nomos, Baden Baden 2019, p. 401, who speaks about a 'legal presumption in favour of recognition' (*Rechtsvermutung zu Gunsten der Anerkennung*).

[30] T. IVANC in M. REPAS and V. RIJAVEC (eds.), *Mednarodno zasebno pravo Evropske unije*, Uradni list, Ljubljana 2018, p. 554, U. BERGQUIST in U. BERGQUIST et al. *The EU Regulations on Matrimonial Property*, Oxford University Press, Oxford 2019, pp. 144, 146.

[31] The same option is provided in Article 30(3) of the Brussels II ter Regulation (Council Regulation (EU) 2019/1111 of 25 June 2019 on jurisdiction, the recognition and enforcement of decisions in matrimonial matters and the matters of parental responsibility, and on international child abduction (recast) [2019] OJ L178).

According to the case law of the CJEU regarding the Brussels Convention, the term 'ordinary appeal' must be interpreted autonomously.[32] The logical consequence of such regulatory provision is that the judgments, contrary to the requirements in numerous national legal systems, do not have to be final (*res judicata*) to be able to be recognised under the Regulations.[33] The 'fate' of the stayed proceedings is determined by the national law of the Member State of recognition and is not addressed by the Regulations. Undoubtedly, if the judgment is annulled in the Member State of origin, the recognition procedure should be terminated, given that the recognition should only 'broaden' the effects of the judgment which exist in the Member State of origin and a judgment cannot produce more effects abroad than in its country of origin.[34]

3. THE DECLARATION OF ENFORCEABILITY (*EXEQUATUR*)

The Twin Regulations enable the enforcement of judgments from other Member States if such judgments are enforceable in the Member State of origin and if they were declared enforceable in the Member State of enforcement.

The Regulations provide several procedural rules to be respected in proceedings with the application for a declaration of enforceability, but leave broad autonomy to the national laws to regulate other procedural issues. Information on some of these issues (e.g. the jurisdiction of courts and other authorities within the Member States and the type and availability of legal remedies) is available in all official EU languages on the website of the European Judicial Atlas in civil matters, under the tabs Matters of Matrimonial Property Regimes and Matters of the Property Consequences of Registered Partnerships.[35]

---

[32] In the *Industrial Diamond* judgment, the CJEU held: '(A)ny appeal which is such that it may result in the annulment or the amendment of the judgment which is the subject-matter of the procedure for recognition or enforcement under the Convention and the lodging of which is bound, in the State in which the judgment was given, to a period which is laid down by the law and starts to run by virtue of that same judgment constitutes an "ordinary appeal" …', Case 43/77, *Industrial Diamond Supplies v Luigi Riva*, ECLI:EU:C:1977:188.

[33] Cf. T. Franzmann and Th. Schwerin in R. Geimer and R. Schütze (eds.), *Europäische Erbrechtsverordnung*, C.H. Beck, Munich 2016, p. 364.

[34] This fundamental rule in the field of recognition and enforcement of foreign judgments was already mentioned in the 'Jenard Report' concerning the Brussels Convention of 1968. Jenard Report on the Convention on jurisdiction and the enforcement of judgments in civil and commercial matters (Signed at Brussels, 27 September 1968) [1979] OJ C59, p. 43. It was later endorsed by the CJEU case law, e.g. in Case 145/86, *Horst Ludwig Martin Hoffmann v Adelheid Krieg*, ECLI:EU:C:1988:61, and Case C-420/07, *Meletis Apostolides v David Charles Orams, Linda Elizabeth Orams*, ECLI:EU:C:2009:271.

[35] <https://e-justice.europa.eu/content_european_judicial_atlas_in_civil_matters-321-en.do>. All information on national legal systems, if not referenced otherwise, was accessed on this website.

It must be emphasised that national rules can only complement the rules of the Regulations; while it is clear that the rules of the Regulations have higher hierarchical value than any national provisions on the same subject matter, it is also important that the complementary national provisions do not deprive the EU rules of their full effect (*effet utile*) (thus, for example, national law cannot provide for additional grounds for the refusal of a declaration of enforceability beside the ones provided by the regulations).[36]

3.1. THE ADMISSIBILITY OF THE APPLICATION FOR *EXEQUATUR*

The application for a declaration of enforceability must be submitted to the court or competent authority of the Member State of enforcement, which that Member State communicated to the Commission. Thus, for example, Italy communicated the jurisdiction of the Court of Appeal (*Corte di Appello*), Spain of the Court of First Instance (*Juzgado de Primera Instancia*), Croatia of the municipal court (*općinski sud*), and Slovenia of the district court (*okrožno sodišče*).[37] The territorial (local) jurisdiction is determined by the Regulations and lies with the court of the place of domicile of the party against whom enforcement is sought, or the court of the place of enforcement.[38] The determination of the domicile is made under the national law of the Member State of enforcement.[39] It may be useful to note that this notion is different from the 'habitual residence' in the chapters of the Regulations which concern jurisdiction and applicable law and which is to be interpreted autonomously.[40]

The Regulations preclude the states from obliging the applicant to have a postal address or an authorised representative in the Member State of enforcement. For the purposes of an easier service of court documents, many national civil

---

[36] See e.g. CJEU judgment in Case C-157/12, *Salzgitter Mannesmann Handel GmbH v SC Laminorul SA*, ECLI:EU:C:2013:597 (regarding the Brussels I Regulation), where the Court held that 'the list of grounds for non-enforcement is exhaustive'.

[37] As of June 2021, Slovenia had not yet communicated the competent courts on the basis of the Property Regimes Regulations. However, since the procedure is identical to the Succession Regulation and to the 'original' Brussels I Regulation, the author deems that the same courts should hold jurisdiction.

[38] The relevant time for assessing the domicile of the defendant is the time of the lodging of the application for *exequatur*; any changes of domicile after that time are irrelevant (*perpetuatio fori*). U. BERGQUIST in U. BERGQUIST et al. *The EU Regulations on Matrimonial Property*, Oxford University Press, Oxford 2019, p. 188.

[39] For example, in Slovenia, this will be the so-called 'permanent residence' (*stalno prebivališče*) and in Germany the so-called 'ordinary residence' (*Wohnsitz*), as is indicated in the translations of the regulations into Slovenian and German.

[40] U. BERGQUIST in U. BERGQUIST et al. *The EU Regulations on Matrimonial Property*, Oxford University Press, Oxford 2019, p. 185.

procedural rules namely provide for such an obligation for parties with domicile abroad.[41] In the EU, however, the Service Regulation[42] facilitates the service to and from other Member States, and therefore the aforementioned procedural obligation can be omitted and thus time and money saved. On the other hand, even if the Regulations obviously intend to simplify the proceedings for the applicant by relieving them of the obligatory representation, it is highly probable that most applicants will nevertheless choose to be represented by an attorney in the Member State of enforcement. The proceedings will namely be conducted in the language of that state (which is an important practical issue, despite translation) and the *lex fori*, best known to 'domestic' lawyers, will determine many important procedural questions. Thus, the questions of representation and of the address for service are, in most cases, connected, since many national laws provide for the service to be made to the attorney (only).[43]

Several prerequisites are determined in the Twin Regulations, which the applicant must fulfil in order for the application to be admissible. The applicant must provide: (i) a copy of the decision which satisfies the conditions necessary to establish its authenticity; and (ii) the attestation issued by the court or competent authority of the Member State of origin using the appropriate form.[44] If the applicant does not produce the latter form, the court may set a time limit for its production or even decide on the application without such a form, if the applicant produces an 'equivalent document' or if the court deems that it has sufficient information to decide. This is a sensible decision of the European legislature, since the attestation is not a part of the judgment and is intended to simplify the work of the court in the Member State of enforcement by providing the most important information about the judgment on a form which is identical in all official EU languages and thus does not need translation.[45] If the court, however, has the information needed for its decision, insisting on the official form would be superfluous.

Translation and/or transliteration of the documents is not obligatory, but is subject to the demand of the court. In case of such demand, it is very important

---

[41] See e.g. Article 146 of the Slovenian Code of Civil Procedure (*Zakon o pravdnem postopku*), Official Gazette of the Republic of Slovenia, No. 26/1999, as amended.

[42] Regulation (EC) 2007/1393 of the European Parliament and of the Council of 13 November 2007 on the service in the Member States of judicial and extrajudicial documents in civil or commercial matters (service of documents), and repealing Council Regulation (EC) 2000/1348 [2007] OJ L324.

[43] See e.g. Article 137(1) of the Slovenian Code of Civil Procedure.

[44] Annex I of the Commission Implementing Regulation (EU) 2018/1935 of 7 December 2018 establishing the forms referred to in Council Regulation (EU) 2016/1103 implementing enhanced cooperation in the area of jurisdiction, applicable law and the recognition and enforcement of decisions in matters of matrimonial property regimes [2018] OJ L314.

[45] It is also possible to invoke in the *exequatur* proceedings that the content of the form is wrong. Cf. CJEU, Case C-619/10, *Trade Agency Ltd v Seramico Investments Ltd.* ECLI:EU:C:2012:531. Thus, the presumption of regularity is rebutted: U. BERGQUIST in U. BERGQUIST et al. *The EU Regulations on Matrimonial Property*, Oxford University Press, Oxford 2019, p. 192.

to emphasise that the court should only require the translation of the text which was inserted into the form by the foreign authority, and not of the form itself, since the form is already available in all EU official languages. The translator should therefore use the available form in the target language and insert the translation of the added text. It goes without saying that only the translation of the added text can be billed and considered a justified procedural cost.

If translation is required, it must be done by 'a person qualified to do translations in one of the Member States' (Article 46(2)). Thus, the court cannot demand the translation necessarily to be made by a translator from the Member State of enforcement, but must accept a translation made by a translator 'qualified' in another Member State. The Regulations do not further define the term 'qualified' and the doctrine is divided regarding the question of whether the translator must have an official authorisation to translate legal documents.[46] Since the quality of the translation is of crucial importance in cross-border disputes, it is this author's opinion that the translator must fulfil the conditions for translating judicial documents in relevant languages under the national law of at least one of the Member States.

3.2. FIRST INSTANCE PROCEEDINGS

Proceedings for the declaration of enforceability are, at first, unilateral (*ex parte*). The opposing party is thus not notified of the lodging of the application. The court only verifies the fulfilment of the formal requirements from the Regulations and from the national procedural law (e.g. concerning the representation of minors). It is very important to emphasise that the court does not verify on its own motion any of the grounds for refusal of enforcement, namely the contradiction to the public policy of the Member State of enforcement, the lack of service of the introductory document to the proceedings, and the irreconcilability of decisions.

If the admissibility requirements are met, the court declares the judgment enforceable. This decision will then be notified to both parties. The Regulations provide that the court must serve on the opposing party ('the party against whom enforcement is sought') also the judgment, if such has not yet been served on that party. It might be surprising that the Regulations envisage the possibility of the judgment not to have been served on the defendant, as enforceability usually follows such service.[47] In such cases, the defendant will be able to invoke that

---

[46] U. BERGQUIST in U. BERGQUIST et al. *The EU Regulations on Matrimonial Property*, Oxford University Press, Oxford 2019, p. 195.

[47] This is, however, not the case in all Member States: U. BERGQUIST in U. BERGQUIST et al. *The EU Regulations on Matrimonial Property*, Oxford University Press, Oxford 2019, p. 200.

they could not exhaust all legal remedies in the Member State of origin and will thus be able to assert certain grounds for refusal, most importantly the lack of service of the introductory document in the proceedings (Article 37 b) of the Twin Regulations) if such a document was also not served on them.

As is usual in the field of recognition and enforcement of foreign judgments, partial enforceability is also envisaged in the Regulations. Such partial enforceability can be granted either following the request by the applicant or on the court's own motion, '(w)here a decision has been given in respect of several matters and the declaration of enforceability cannot be given for all of them'. For example, partial enforceability can be the consequence of the fact that grounds for refusal exist only as to certain part(s) of the judgment, or else because certain parts of the judgment fall outside the scope of application of the Regulations (in the latter case, two or more partial decisions on enforceability will be issued on the ground of different legal acts).[48] For partial enforceability to be possible, the judgment must be 'divisible'.[49]

3.3. APPEAL(S) AGAINST THE DECLARATION OF ENFORCEABILITY

At least one appeal is possible against the declaration of enforceability. It can be lodged by either party, depending on the result of the proceedings with the application. The proceedings with the appeal must guarantee the possibility of participation for both parties (the principle of adversary proceedings).

Member States had to notify the competent courts for the decision on such an appeal. For example, Italy communicated the jurisdiction of the Supreme Court of Cassation (*Suprema Corte di Cassazione*), Spain the jurisdiction of the Provincial Court (*Audiencia Provincial*), Croatia the jurisdiction of the municipal courts, and Slovenia the jurisdiction of the district courts. The decision of Slovenia and Croatia to nominate the same courts as competent for the *exequatur* proceedings and for the appeal might seem surprising, but this follows the system established in the national laws of these countries regarding

---

[48] U. BERGQUIST in U. BERGQUIST et al. *The EU Regulations on Matrimonial Property*, Oxford University Press, Oxford 2019, pp. 219, 220.

[49] U. BERGQUIST in U. BERGQUIST et al. *The EU Regulations on Matrimonial Property*, Oxford University Press, Oxford 2019, p. 221. The 'divisibility' of the judgment means that its operative part can be divided in two or more independent parts, e.g. there is an obligation to pay a certain sum of money, and an obligation to deliver specific property: if the decision regarding the money does not pass the control in the Member State of enforcement (i.e. one or more grounds for refusal exist), the decision on the delivery of property will still be able to be enforced, if no grounds for refusal exist regarding that part.

proceedings for the recognition of foreign judgments.[50] In Slovenia, the first (unilateral) stage of the proceedings is handled by a single judge, and the (first) appeal by a panel of three judges of the same first instance court.

The time limit for lodging an appeal is 30 days from the service of the declaration of enforceability (or of the refusal of such a declaration) for the appellants domiciled in the Member State of enforcement, and 60 days for appellants domiciled in another Member State. No extension of this deadline can be granted on account of distance (but it can be granted on other grounds if the national law of the Member State of enforcement so provides). The Twin Regulations do not expressly mention the applicants domiciled in third states. Bergquist, citing several authors, deems that the 30-day time limit applies in those cases, but that an extension can be granted under national law.[51]

Member States have the possibility of granting another appeal (although no more than one), which is, however, not obligatory. To take as an example the states cited above, Italy, Spain and Slovenia provide for such an additional appeal before the highest national courts. Croatia, however, does not provide for a second appeal under the Twin Regulations, but provides for such an appeal under the Succession Regulation (which is, interestingly, decided upon either by the first instance court if it decides to modify the decision, or else by the second instance court).

The existence of the grounds for refusal of the declaration of enforceability (Articles 37, 38 and 39 of the Twin Regulations) will first be verified by the court in the appellate proceedings. They can further be scrutinised on the basis of the second appeal if such is provided in the Member State of enforcement. If a ground for refusal is found to exist, the court has to refuse recognition or the declaration of enforceability and does not have a discretion to do or not do so.[52] The Regulations demand that the courts decide on the appeals without delay, although, as is usually the case regarding the actions of the courts, no specific deadline is fixed.

Another guarantee is provided for the defendant. If, in the country of origin, the enforceability of the decision is suspended because a suspensive legal remedy has been lodged, then the court deciding on the first or second appeal against the declaration of enforceability stays the proceedings following the application

---

[50] For Slovenia, see e.g. J. KRAMBERGER ŠKERL, 'The recognition and enforcement of foreign judgments in Slovenia: national law and the Brussels I (recast) Regulation' (2018/19) 20 *Yearbook of Private International Law* 281–314.

[51] U. BERGQUIST in U. BERGQUIST et al. *The EU Regulations on Matrimonial Property*, Oxford University Press, Oxford 2019, p. 204.

[52] N. POGORELČNIK VOGRINC in M.J. CAZORLA GONZÁLES, M. GIOBBI, J. KRAMBERGER ŠKERL, L. RUGGERI, S. WINKLER, *Property relations of cross border couples in the European Union*, Edizioni Scientifiche Italiane, Naples 2020, p. 149.

of the opposing party (Article 52 of the Twin Regulations). In contrast to the recognition proceedings, where a stay is optional, such stay is obligatory in *exequatur* proceedings, if the opposing party so demands. The court will thus wait for the result of the proceedings in the state of origin, since, just as in the case of recognition, a judgment cannot produce more effects in the state of enforcement than in the state of origin, i.e. it cannot be enforceable in another state, if it is not enforceable in the state of origin.

3.4. PROVISIONAL, INCLUDING PROTECTIVE, MEASURES BEFORE AND DURING *EXEQUATUR* PROCEEDINGS

The Twin Regulations provide that provisional, including protective, measures (offered by the law of the state of enforcement)[53] are available to the person applying for the declaration of enforceability before a final decision on that issue is adopted. The applicant can apply for protective measures even before lodging an application for the declaration of enforceability, the basis for that being that the decision was already automatically recognised in the Member State of the future or possible enforcement (Article 53(1) of the Twin Regulations). The element of surprise, often aspired to by the applicant, will be ensured, if the protective measures are granted before the defendant is served with the court's decision on the declaration of enforceability, since the proceedings with the application for *exequatur* are at first unilateral and the defendant is usually not aware of them. When the declaration of enforceability becomes final (e.g. at the end of the time limit for lodging the (first) appeal or when the decision on such an appeal becomes final), the applicant will have access to (actual) enforcement.

Article 53 of the Twin Regulations thus refers to the issuance of the provisional measures requested in the Member State of (the future) enforcement on the basis of the decision from another Member State, of which the enforcement is or will be sought. This article does not, however, deprive Article 19 of its effect, which gives jurisdiction to courts of any Member State to issue provisional and protective measures. The only provisional and protective measures which will, however, be able to circulate in the EU and thus be enforced also in the Member State of enforcement of the judgment on the substance of the dispute, are those issued in contradictory proceedings by the court having jurisdiction as to the substance of the dispute (see the Section 1.1 on the interpretation of the term 'decision').

---

[53] U. BERGQUIST in U. BERGQUIST et al. *The EU Regulations on Matrimonial Property*, Oxford University Press, Oxford 2019, pp. 216, 217.

3.5. COSTS OF *EXEQUATUR* PROCEEDINGS

Given that the costs of *exequatur* proceedings can be quite high in certain Member States,[54] the provision of the Twin Regulations on legal aid is important (Article 55). It states that the right of the applicant who benefited from legal aid or exemption from costs or expenses in the main proceedings in the Member State of origin of the judgment is 'stretched' also to encompass proceedings for the declaration of enforceability in the Member State of enforcement.[55] Given that the legal aid systems differ considerably,[56] the broadest legal aid provided by the national law of the Member State of enforcement must be guaranteed (which is not necessarily the same in substance and/or ambit as the legal aid in the Member State of origin). The applicant must assert and prove that they benefited from legal aid in the Member State of origin.[57] Point 7 of the attestation form (Annex I of the implementing regulations) provided by the Commission is dedicated to such information.

Furthermore, no additional deposit or caution (*cautio judicatum solvi*, *cautio actoris*) should be imposed on the applicant on the basis of their foreign nationality or domicile abroad. This rule encompasses both the *exequatur* proceedings and the (actual) enforcement.[58]

It is important to emphasise that the Twin Regulations do not provide for an 'extension' of the right to legal aid beyond the proceedings for recognition (on the basis of Article 36(2) of the Twin Regulations) and *exequatur*, e.g. the proceedings regulated in these acts. If legal aid is needed in the (actual) enforcement proceedings, the national law of the state of enforcement applies fully.[59] On the other hand, the fact that the applicant did not benefit from legal aid in the Member State of origin does not preclude them from applying for legal aid in the Member State of enforcement under the national rules of that

---

[54] A study of the costs of *exequatur* proceedings under the Brussels I Regulation found that the average cost of a simple (i.e. the applicant is successful with the application, no appeal is lodged) *exequatur* proceeding was 2,208 EUR in 2009; these costs include the costs of translation, lawyer's fees and court fees: Commission Staff Working Paper, SEC(2010) 1547 final, 14 December 2010, p. 53.

[55] Rudolf speaks of 'the principle of continuity and extension of legal aid'. C. RUDOLF in A. DEIXLER-HÜBNER and M. SCHAUER (eds.), *EuErbVO Kommentar zur Eu-Erbrechtsverordnung*, Manz, Vienna 2015, p. 405.

[56] The right to legal aid for those who lack sufficient resources for effective access to justice must, however, be guaranteed in all Member States on the basis of Article 47/3 of the Charter of Fundamental Rights of the EU [2012] OJ C326.

[57] U. BERGQUIST in U. BERGQUIST et al. *The EU Regulations on Matrimonial Property*, Oxford University Press, Oxford 2019, p. 225.

[58] U. BERGQUIST in U. BERGQUIST et al. *The EU Regulations on Matrimonial Property*, Oxford University Press, Oxford 2019, p. 227 and other authors cited there.

[59] U. BERGQUIST in U. BERGQUIST et al. *The EU Regulations on Matrimonial Property*, Oxford University Press, Oxford 2019, p. 225 and other authors cited there.

state. The principle of non-discrimination in granting legal aid in cross-border disputes is enshrined in the EU Legal Aid Directive.[60]

In most Member States, a court fee is imposed for the instituting of *exequatur* proceedings. The Regulations do not preclude such fees, although they must not be calculated by reference to the value of the matter at issue, as is common in other court proceedings. Cross-border proceedings tend to concern issues of a non-negligible value, at least to the parties (otherwise the parties would not bother to institute them), and therefore such provision is welcome. It is also justified, since the courts' task consists only of formal verifications (which can be more or less complicated, unrelated to the value of the original dispute). It must be emphasised that this rule applies only to 'proceedings for the issue of a declaration of enforceability' (and, by analogy as determined in the regulations, to recognition proceedings), but not to other stages of the *exequatur* proceedings,[61] nor to proceedings regarding provisional measures.[62]

The Twin Regulations only mention legal aid for the applicant, whereas the defendant might also need it when he or she lodges the appeal(s). Such legal aid is regulated by the national law of the Member State of enforcement, naturally in respect of the above-mentioned supranational rules.[63]

4. GROUNDS FOR REFUSAL OF RECOGNITION AND ENFORCEMENT

Grounds for refusal of recognition and of the declaration of enforceability are regulated in Article 37 of the Twin Regulations. Identical grounds for refusal are thus foreseen in both situations, which should be borne in mind throughout this section. The said article provides that a decision shall not be recognised, if it is manifestly contrary to public policy, if, in default judgments, the defendant was not properly served with the introductory document in the proceedings, and if the judgment is irreconcilable with an already existing judgment issued in the

---

[60] Article 4 of the Council Directive 2002/8/EC of 27 January 2003 to improve access to justice in cross-border disputes by establishing minimum common rules relating to legal aid for such disputes [2003] OJ L26.

[61] The proceedings with the appeal(s) no longer consist only of the verification of formalities, since grounds for refusal had to be invoked by the applicant, some of which (especially the public policy ground) can demand a thorough substantial and procedural scrutiny of the appellate authority (for more on that, see the chapter dealing with the grounds for refusal).

[62] U. Bergquist in U. Bergquist et al. *The EU Regulations on Matrimonial Property*, Oxford University Press, Oxford 2019, p. 229, and other authors cited there.

[63] In its order in the Case C-156/12, *GREP GmbH v Freitstaat Bayern*, ECLI:EU:C:2012:342, the CJEU decided that the appeal against the declaration of enforceability under the Brussels I Regulation constituted an exercise of EU law in the sense of Article 51 of the EU Charter of Fundamental Rights, and that the obligation to provide legal aid from Article 47(3) of the Charter was applicable.

Member State of enforcement or, under certain conditions, in another state. It is important to note that these are the only grounds for refusal that can be applied; the Member States cannot provide other or additional grounds for refusal.[64]

Article 38 further provides that Article 37 of the Twin Regulations shall be applied by the courts and other competent authorities of the Member States in observance of the fundamental rights and principles recognised in the EU Charter of Fundamental Rights, in particular in Article 21 thereof regarding the principle of non-discrimination. Article 39 prohibits the review of jurisdiction of the court of origin, as well as the application of the public policy defence to the rules on jurisdiction set out in Articles 4–12.[65] Lastly, Article 40 emphasises the general rule that under no circumstances may a decision given in a Member State be reviewed as to its substance.

4.1. THE PUBLIC POLICY EXCEPTION (*ORDRE PUBLIC*)

Under the Twin Regulations, a decision shall not be recognised if it is manifestly contrary to public policy in the Member State in which recognition is sought. The public policy clause is a legal standard that has to be filled with content by the courts in each individual case. Doctrine and case law provide guidance for the sometimes tough decision to what extent a difference between the solution adopted by a foreign judge or the proceedings conducted abroad, on the one hand, and the view of domestic law, on the other hand, is acceptable for the state of enforcement and where it becomes unacceptable. Generally speaking, public policy contains fundamental values and vital interests of the requested state, which must stay intact in order to preserve the coherence of the legal and social order of that state. Naturally, such values and interests also encompass those originating in supranational legal instruments and in the membership of the Member States in international organisations, such as the EU, the Council of Europe, and others.[66]

When deciding on recognition and enforcement of a foreign judgment, one speaks of a 'mitigated public policy' (*ordre public attenué*), which means that

---

[64] Andrae speaks of 'exclusive grounds for refusal (*ausschließliche Anerkennungsversagungsgründe*)': M. ANDRAE, *Internationales Familienrecht*, Nomos, Baden Baden 2019, p. 402.

[65] In the 2019 judgment in the Case C-386/17, *Stefano Liberato v Luminita Luisa Grigorescu*, ECLI:EU:C:2019:24, regarding the interpretation of a similar rule from the Brussels I Regulation and the Brussels II bis Regulation, the CJEU decided that this prohibition stretches also to the rule on *lis pendens*, i.e. that the violation of this rule by the court of origin of the judgment cannot constitute a reason for refusing the recognition of a judgment on the basis of the public policy defence.

[66] For more on the 'European' parts of the national public policy, see J. KRAMBERGER ŠKERL, 'European public policy (with an emphasis on *exequatur* proceedings)' (2011) 3 *Journal of Private International Law* 461–490.

acquired rights and the connection of the legal relationship with the requested state (the so-called *Inlandsbeziehung*) must be taken into account. Therefore, put simply, the authority deciding on *exequatur* must be even more reserved in applying the public policy exception than when deciding on the application of a foreign law.

Fears about possible arbitrary use of this legal standard emerge regarding any plans for reform of the rules on recognition and enforcement of foreign judgments. Such fears have, however, proven unfounded, since it is widely accepted in doctrine and case law that the public policy defence has to be used as a tool of 'last resort'. It must be interpreted strictly and only sanction the truly unacceptable solutions in the contents of the foreign decision (the so-called 'substantial public policy'), or else in the proceedings leading to the issuing of such decisions (the so-called 'procedural public policy'). The procedural part of the public policy control was expressly included by the CJEU in its famous *Krombach* judgment in 2000,[67] after a time of speculation whether the public policy from the Brussels Convention was to be interpreted in a strict way, so as to exclude any procedural issues, the only such issue being separately regulated as the ground for refusal number two, i.e. the lack of service of the introductory document in case of a default judgment (same as in the Twin Regulations).

The question whether the scope of the public policy defence is entirely interpreted by the Member States (because the relevant article in the regulations expressly mentions 'the public policy in the Member States') or else is to be interpreted autonomously by the CJEU (because it is a notion from the EU legislation, which has to be applied uniformly throughout the EU), is resolved since the CJEU *Maxicar* case of 2000.[68] Very knowingly, the CJEU adopted a compromise solution in that the interpretation remains with the national authorities of the Member States; the CJEU, however, exercises the control of the EU acceptability of such interpretation. To put it simply, the CJEU controls whether the Member States have gone too far in their interpretations, either in that they did not find a contradiction to their public policy where they should have, or else their interpretation was too broad and resulted in an unacceptable restriction of the free circulation of judgments.

As other EU regulations before them, the Twin Regulations contain, in Article 40, a prohibition of review of a decision from another Member State as to its substance. Such review is to be made 'under no circumstances'. It is important to explain this interdiction in light of the public policy control, in order to ensure full effects of both provisions. In short, the prohibition of review means that the

---

[67] Case C-7/98, *Dieter Krombach v André Bamberski*, ECLI:EU:C:2000:164.
[68] Case C-38/98, *Régie nationale des usines Renault SA v Maxicar SpA and Orazio Formento*, ECLI:EU:C:2000:225.

authority in the Member State of enforcement, competent for examining the application for *exequatur*, must not play the role of a higher instance court to the court which issued the judgment. The control under the Regulations is namely an example of a 'limited control' of a foreign judgment (*contrôle limité*) and not of a 'full control' (*revision au fond*). Hence, the control performed in order to accept the effects of the foreign judgment is a specially designed control with a specific purpose, not intended to 'confirm' or 'repair' the foreign judgment; its aim is to establish whether the foreign judgment can produce effects in the domestic legal order, without damaging its coherence and its fundamental values. Therefore, the control must not be focused on the question of whether the court of origin correctly established the facts of the case, on whether they correctly applied the applicable procedural and substantial law, and even less on the question of whether the same result would have been achieved if the case was adjudicated in the state of enforcement. The control must focus on the existence of the possible contrariety of, first, the substantial legal result the judgment contains, and second, of the proceedings that led to the issuance of the judgment, to the public policy of the requested state.

The purpose of the control that is exercised must, however, not be confused with the method of performing this control. In order to examine the conformity of the judgment to the public policy, the competent authority will, in most cases, have no other choice than to examine the substance of the judgment. It is mostly by attentively reading the whole judgment, i.e. especially the explanation of motives for the adopted decision, that it will be possible to establish whether rights of defence have been trumped or whether the defendant is condemned to pay a certain sum of money for a reason which is perhaps shocking for the state of enforcement.[69]

Also, the wording of the Twin Regulations that the contrariety to public policy must be 'manifest', must not induce us to think that the authority deciding on *exequatur* is not allowed to thoroughly examine the judgment. The manifest nature of the public policy breach must be in the intensity of the clash with the fundamental values of the state of enforcement, and not (necessarily) in the fact that it is apparent at first glance of the judgment.

---

[69] For example, a judgment obliging one party to pay a certain sum of money to the other party is an everyday case in all Member States and thus nothing special or shocking. However, the reason why this payment is due can be unacceptable and contrary to the public policy of the Member State of enforcement. Therefore, it is important that the court in the Member State of enforcement also examines the motives of the judgment and that it refuses the enforcement if it establishes that, for example, the payment is due because of the application of a discriminatory rule, which attributes a larger part of the former common property to one of the spouses only on the basis of, for example, their gender.

4.2. THE LACK OF SERVICE OF THE INTRODUCTORY DOCUMENT IN THE PROCEEDINGS

Arguably the most important procedural guarantee in civil proceedings is the due service of the introductory document in the proceedings. It is a crucial point in any court proceedings, establishing a three-part relationship between the parties and the court. Due service of the introductory document is a prerequisite for the effective right to be heard (i.e. the principle of contradiction) and, further, for the equality of arms, both essential parts of the right to a fair trial from Article 6 of the European Convention of Human Rights and Fundamental Freedoms (ECHR), as well as from national constitutions and procedural legislation of the EU Member States.

The Twin Regulations provide that the recognition and enforcement can be refused, where the judgment 'was given in default of appearance, if the defendant was not served with the document which instituted the proceedings or with an equivalent document in sufficient time and in such a way as to enable him to arrange for his defence unless the defendant failed to commence proceedings to challenge the decision when it was possible for him to do so'.

With the already mentioned *Krombach* judgment of 2000, the CJEU definitely resolved the dilemma of whether the lack of due service of the introductory document in the proceedings was the only procedural issue that could result in the refusal of recognition and enforcement of a judgment under the Brussels Convention. Pursuant to that judgment, other violations of the fundamental procedural guarantees (for example, the violation of the right to be heard during the proceedings, after a successful service of the introductory document) can be sanctioned via the public policy exception. Undoubtedly, this interpretation has to be stretched to all EU regulations with the same or similar wording of the grounds for refusal, and thus also to the Twin Regulations. The fact that EU regulations adopted in this field after the issuance of the *Krombach* judgment still contain a separate mention of the lack of service of the introductory document, despite it being a part of the procedural public policy now encompassed by the public policy exception, might be surprising. While such separate mention can no longer be interpreted as described above, it can now be seen as an emphasis of the importance of this element of procedural public policy, with welcome precisions about the possibility of invoking it in the *exequatur* proceedings, which is thus not left to the interpretation of national courts. If the interpretation of the contents of the public policy largely remains in the sphere of the Member States, the text of the second ground for refusal does not contain any mention of the Member States and the autonomous interpretation could fully be taken over by the CJEU.

The CJEU case law on the interpretation of the same ground for refusal from the Brussels I bis Regulation is abundant and should be followed by the courts when they interpret the Twin Regulations. Thus, the criteria under which the introductory document must be served on the defendant in sufficient time and in a way that enable them to prepare their defence, can be met, although the service was not regular according to the national procedural rules of the Member State of origin.[70] For instance, even if the procedural rules demand that the defendant be served personally, i.e. their signature is needed on the certificate of service, but the service was actually made to the defendant's roommate, this will not be a problem under the Regulations, if it is proven that the defendant did, in fact, receive the introductory document with sufficient information and had enough time to prepare their defence.

A very important emphasis is made in the Regulations regarding the limits of invoking said ground for refusal. Namely, if the defendant had the chance to invoke the lack of adequate service in the Member State of origin, they can no longer rely on the Member State of recognition to remedy such procedural violation. This is in line with the general principle that the states should have the possibility to repair their mistakes before an international mechanism kicks in, but also with the principle of efficient and expedient civil proceedings, where parties are required to actively protect their rights throughout the proceedings (and not retroactively if the result of the proceedings is unfavourable for them). The court must ensure that the parties had the possibility to participate in the proceedings and defend their rights, but the parties must bear the consequences if they do not do so, even if they could. This is why it is so important to clarify whether the passive stance of a party was actually their choice, or was the consequence of the fact that the party did not know the proceedings were started or did not have sufficient time to respond adequately. In *ASML*, the CJEU further specified that the defendant is only considered to have had the opportunity to object to the lack of service of the claim, if they were later not only aware of the existence of the default judgment, but also acquainted with the grounds of that judgment. This is in line with another procedural principle that judgments have to have reasons, which enable the parties to file a reasoned appeal and the appellate courts to conduct a review.

That said, it is important to reiterate that due service is interpreted autonomously, which also entails the possibility of the Member State of enforcement (or of the CJEU, if asked) to establish that a service made in respect of the rules of the Member State of origin was not made in such a way and in sufficient time for the defendant to prepare their defence. The defendant can thus complain, in *exequatur* proceedings, about inadequacies of the service of the introductory document they were unable to invoke in the Member State of origin.

---

[70] Case C-283/05, *ASML Netherlands BV v Semiconductor Industry Services GmbH (SEMIS)*, ECLI:EU:C:2006:787.

4.3. IRRECONCILABILITY OF JUDGMENTS

The third ground for refusal of recognition and enforcement from the Regulations is the irreconcilability or incompatibility of decisions. Again, interpretation of the same rule in other EU Regulations can provide guidance. Two situations are presented. First, that the judgment from another Member State contradicts a judgment issued in the Member State of recognition or enforcement, and second, that the judgment is incompatible with a judgment from another Member State or a third state (i.e. not the state where recognition or enforcement is sought).

In the case of a contradicting domestic judgment, the latter must have been issued in proceedings between the same parties, but not necessarily regarding the same subject matter. Andrae gives the example of a domestic judgment on the personal status, which is incompatible with a property relations judgment from another Member State based on a different personal status of the parties.[71] Also, the Regulations do not require that the domestic judgment be issued prior to the issuance of the judgment from another Member State. This is somewhat contradictory to the *ipso iure* recognition of judgments in all participating Member States, where in principle, the judgments take effects in all such states at the same time. On the other hand, the interested party could have invoked a prior foreign judgment in the domestic proceedings (the court would have recognised it incidentally). If this was not done in time, the Regulation does not impose on the Member States the prevalence of a foreign judgment over a final domestic one.

In the case of an incompatible judgment from another Member State or from a third state, the latter must have been issued prior to the judgment for which recognition is sought and between the same parties, and must involve the same cause of action, as well as fulfil the conditions for recognition in the requested state. The prevalence of a judgment from other states thus requires the fulfilment of stricter conditions as those set out for domestic judgments. First, such judgment must be issued prior to the judgment of which the recognition or enforcement is sought. Second, such judgment must concern not only the same parties, but also the same 'cause of action'. And thirdly, such judgment must be capable of recognition in the addressed Member State. If such judgment is issued in another participating Member State, the recognition is automatic and no conditions exist. On the other hand, if the judgment originates in one of the non-participating EU Member States or in a third state, national rules on the recognition of foreign judgments must be applied.

---

[71] Cf. M. ANDRAE, *Internationales Familienrecht*, Nomos, Baden Baden 2019, p. 402.

4.4. FURTHER GUIDANCE ON THE EXAMINATION OF THE GROUNDS FOR REFUSAL

The Regulations first emphasise that the grounds for refusal should be examined in a manner respecting the fundamental rights. This is probably self-evident, but there is no harm in such provision, which might possibly prevent an interpretation departing from commonly accepted standards of human rights, such as contained in the EU Charter of Fundamental Rights,[72] as well as in the ECHR, of which all Member States of the EU are parties. This can be especially important in the interpretation of the public policy exception, as was most prominently demonstrated in the CJEU *Krombach* case, where the Court also included in the scope of the public policy defence the protection of the procedural public policy, which, at the time, was not a unanimous doctrinal stance, but was, however, in line with Article 6 of the ECHR.

Contrary to the Brussels I bis Regulation,[73] the Twin Regulations do not allow for any review of jurisdiction of the court of origin of the judgment.[74] This further promotes the free circulation of judgments, as one possible ground for refusal is abolished. However, this can seem surprising, since the very liberal system of recognition and enforcement was, in EU regulations, traditionally linked to the respect of the provisions on jurisdiction from the same regulations, and at least the non-respect of the most important jurisdictional rules could result in the refusal of recognition and enforcement abroad. This author nevertheless supports this legislative decision, since there are in principle no weaker parties to be protected, and the jurisdiction is often joined to other related proceedings, such as proceedings for divorce and those regarding succession. In such cases, it is mostly in the interest of the parties to prevail themselves of the joinder, and the public interest is arguably less pronounced than, for instance, in exclusive jurisdictions under Article 24 of the Brussels I bis Regulation.

5. CONCLUDING REMARKS

The Twin Regulations provide the rules on 'recognition, enforceability and enforcement of decisions' in Chapter IV. The recognition happens *ipso iure*, whereas enforcement is only possible after the declaration of enforceability (*exequatur*) is obtained in special proceedings conducted in the Member State of enforcement. These rules are largely identical and follow the system well

---

[72] In this regard, Andrae emphasises the respect of the prohibition of discrimination: M. ANDRAE, *Internationales Familienrecht*, Nomos, Baden Baden 2019, p. 402.
[73] Article 45(1) e) of the Brussels I bis Regulation.
[74] See e.g. CJEU judgment in *Liberato v Luminita Luisa Grigorescu*, ECLI:EU:C:2019:24.

known to European lawyers from the Brussels I Regulation, which already served as a matrix for the rules on recognition and enforcement of judgments in the Succession Regulation, as well as in the Maintenance Regulation, when enforcement is sought of a judgment issued in a Member State not bound by the 2007 Hague Protocol (Chapter IV, Section 2). Paul Lagarde wrote: 'The property regimes Regulations follow a sort of European common law on (the recognition and enforcement of decisions and authentic instruments).'[75] Also, Recital 55 of the Regulation on the Property Consequences of Registered Partnerships (and Recital 56 of the Matrimonial Property Regulation) emphasises this connection:

> In the light of its general objective, which is the mutual recognition of decisions given in the Member States in matters of the property consequences of registered partnerships, this Regulation should lay down rules relating to the recognition, enforceability and enforcement of decisions similar to those of other Union instruments in the area of judicial cooperation in civil matters.

The (actual) enforcement, following the declaration of enforceability, will always be conducted under the national procedural rules of the Member State of enforcement. In principle, the EU regulations do not interfere with these rules. They regulate the phase of 'the transition' of the foreign judgment into the domestic legal system, i.e. the phase prior to the (actual) enforcement proceedings, which will be the same as for domestic judgments. Deciding on the application for (actual) enforcement, the enforcement authority will thus no longer verify the existence of the grounds for refusal from the Regulations: the decision on the *exequatur*, issued in the (necessarily)[76] separate *exequatur* proceedings is binding on all domestic authorities. It could be argued that, to avoid confusion, it would have been clearer if the EU regulations in the field of 'recognition and enforcement' spoke only of the 'enforceability' of decisions from other Member States and not of 'enforcement', with the exception of cases where the rules refer to the (actual) enforcement, for example to a possible stay thereof.

Looking into the future, the general goals of the EU make it relatively safe to predict that, eventually, judgments in property relations of couples will not only be automatically recognised, but also automatically enforceable in other Member States. Time will tell whether the first step of the development will be attracting more, and possibly all, Member States to join the enhanced cooperation in this field, or whether the currently participating Member States will continue their

---

[75] P. Lagarde in U. BERGQUIST et al. *The EU Regulations on Matrimonial Property*, Oxford University Press, Oxford 2019, p. 12.
[76] Unlike some national laws (for example in Slovenia), the Regulations do not envisage an incidental declaration of enforceability within enforcement proceedings.

proper path towards an even more liberal circulation of judgments system. Since the system currently provided by the Twin Regulations is already very accepting in substance and very well tested in practice, this author's preference would be for the first option, i.e. trying to get more Member States to join. To do that, it is important to gather and demonstrate good practices and 'success stories', in order to persuade those still doubting of the efficacy and relative simplicity of the system established by the Regulations, as well as to emphasise the respect that the Regulations show towards the national family law notions of each participating Member State.

AUTHENTIC INSTRUMENTS AND COURT SETTLEMENTS UNDER THE TWIN REGULATIONS

Ivana Kunda and Martina Tičić*

1. Introduction 158
2. The Notions of 'Authentic Instrument' and 'Court Settlement' 161
   2.1. Definition of 'Authentic Instrument' 161
       2.1.1. Involvement of Public Authority 163
       2.1.2. Role of Public Authority 165
       2.1.3. Paper or Electronic Form 166
   2.2. Features of 'Authentic Instrument' 167
       2.2.1. Form-Related and Content-Related Elements 167
       2.2.2. Distinction from 'Decision' 169
       2.2.3. Distinction from 'Public Document' under
              Regulation 2016/1191 169
   2.3. Definition of 'Court Settlement' 170
       2.3.1. Settlement between the Parties 171
       2.3.2. Involvement of the Court 172
       2.3.3. Distinction from 'Consent Judgments' 173
3. Extending the Effects of Authentic Instruments and Court Settlements 175
   3.1. 'Acceptance' of Authentic Instruments 176
       3.1.1. The Notion of 'Acceptance' 176
       3.1.2. Extension of Evidentiary Effects 177
       3.1.3. Optional Standardised Form 179
       3.1.4. Challenges as Obstacles to 'Acceptance' 180
       3.1.5. Public Policy as the Ground for Refusal of 'Acceptance' 180
       3.1.6. Incompatibility with Other Authentic Instruments,
              Court Settlements or Decisions 181

---

* Ivana Kunda, Full Professor and Head of the International and European Private Law Department at the Faculty of Law of the University of Rijeka.
Martina Tičić, doctoral candidate at the University of Rijeka, Faculty of Law, funded by the Croatian Science Foundation.

3.2. 'Declaration of Enforceability' of Authentic Instruments and
Court Settlements. 182
3.2.1. Enforceability in the Member State of Origin. 183
3.2.2. Procedure for Declaring the Enforceability in the
Member State of Enforcement. 183
3.2.3. Legal Remedies against the Declaration of
Enforceability. 186
4. Concluding Remarks 187

1. INTRODUCTION

Authentic instruments are of particular practical importance for family property matters, including matrimonial property matters and matters related to the property consequences of registered partners.[1] As means of assuring preventive justice, they enable preventive legal control through authentication of documents for legal transactions of high economic or personal concern to the interest of the public or individual parties.[2] Together with court settlements, authentic instruments also present an important category of enforceable titles, at least in most of the Member State jurisdictions.[3] The court settlements are usually considered as enforceable titles provided they are registered or witnessed by a court. On the other hand, authentic instruments are usually regarded as enforceable titles in civil law jurisdictions, less so in common law or Scandinavian ones.[4] Even in states where both authentic instruments and court

---

[1] Proposal for a Council Regulation on jurisdiction, applicable law and the recognition and enforcement of decisions in matters of matrimonial property regimes, COM/2011/0126 final – CNS 2011/0059, p. 10; Proposal for a Council Regulation on jurisdiction, applicable law and the recognition and enforcement of decisions regarding the property consequences of registered partnerships, COM/2011/0127 final – CNS 2011/0060, p. 9. See also Proposal for a Regulation of the European Parliament and of the Council on jurisdiction, applicable law, recognition and enforcement of decisions and authentic instruments in matters of succession and the creation of a European Certificate of Succession, COM/2009/0154 final – COD 2009/0157, p. 7.

[2] COUNCIL OF THE NOTARIATS OF THE EUROPEAN UNION, *Comparative Study on Authentic Instruments National Provisions of Private Law, Circulation, Mutual Recognition and Enforcement, Possible Legislative Initiative by the European Union – United Kingdom, France, Germany, Poland, Sweden*, European Parliament, Brussels 2008, <https://www.europarl.europa.eu/RegData/etudes/STUD/2008/408329/IPOL-JURI_ET(2008)408329_EN.pdf>, p. iv.

[3] W. KENNETT, *The Enforcement of Judgments in Europe*, Oxford University Press, Oxford 2000, p. 65.

[4] Report (JLS/2004/C4/03) on the application of the Brussels I Regulation in the Member States presented by B. Hess, Th. Pfeiffer and P. Schlosser, Study JLS/C4/2005/03, Final version September 2007, Ruprecht-Karls-Universität Heidelberg, <http://courtesa.eu/wp-content/uploads/2019/03/study_application_brussels_1_en.pdf>, p. 276; J. FITCHEN, 'Authentic instruments and European private international law in civil and commercial matters: Is now time to break new ground?' (2011) 7 *Journal of Private International Law* 33; J. FITCHEN,

settlements present an enforceable title, a number of differences exist between the issuing authorities, the instruments themselves or procedures for their enforcement.

In order to achieve an efficacious cross-border judicial cooperation, it is necessary to establish a system which facilitates free movement of authentic instruments and court settlements from the Member State of origin to other Member States. This was established early on, in the 1968 Brussels Convention on jurisdiction and the enforcement of judgments in civil and commercial matters[5] and later in the 1988 Lugano Convention on jurisdiction and the enforcement of judgements in civil and commercial matters.[6] Some Member States went as far as concluding bilateral agreements to facilitate the free flow of foreign authentic instruments, e.g. France and Germany.[7] Newer EU regulations,[8] including the Twin Regulations, move away from somewhat confusing notions employed in previous regulations[9] and acknowledge their particular nature.

Mirroring the innovative terminology employed in the parallel provisions in the Succession Regulation,[10] the Twin Regulations seem to be opening the path to more direct and easier reliance especially on the authentic instruments in situations with cross-border implications, and hence strengthening the mutual recognition among Member States, as a horizontal component of the overarching principle of mutual trust.[11]

In general, the Twin Regulations provide that particular effects of authentic instruments and court settlements, originating from one Member State,

---

'"Recognition", Acceptance and Enforcement of Authentic Instruments in the Succession Regulation' (2012) 8 *Journal of Private International Law* 323, 331.

[5] Brussels Convention on jurisdiction and the enforcement of judgments in civil and commercial matters, Consolidated version CF 498Y0126(01) [1968] OJ L 299, 31.12.1972.

[6] Lugano Convention from 1988 on jurisdiction and the enforcement of judgements in civil and commercial matters [1988] OJ L 319, 25.11.1988, now replaced by the 2007 Lugano Convention on jurisdiction and the recognition and enforcement of judgments in civil and commercial matters [2007] OJ L 339, 21.12.2007.

[7] Abkommen vom 13 September 1971 zwischen der Bundesrepublik Deutschland und der Französischen Republik über die Befreiung öffentlicher Urkunden von der Legalisation Bundesgesetzblatt BGBl. 1974 II S. 1075, <https://www.bgbl.de>.

[8] See Articles 59–61 of the Succession Regulation.

[9] This particularly refers to the notion of 'recognition' of authentic instruments. See e.g. Articles 58–60 of the Brussels I bis Regulation, Article 46 of the Brussels II bis Regulations (to be replaced by the Brussels II ter Regulation as of 1 August 2022), Article 48 of the Maintenance Regulation. See also Articles 24 and 25 of the Regulation (EC) No 805/2004 of the European Parliament and of the Council of 21 April 2004 creating a European Enforcement Order for uncontested claims [2004] OJ L 143, 30.4.2004. The notion of 'recognition' was in regular use before, see e.g. Ch. PAMBOUKIS, *L'acte public étrangere ed droit international privé*, LGDJ, Paris 1993, p. 97.

[10] See Articles 59–61 of the Succession Regulation.

[11] I. KUNDA, 'Međunarodno privatnopravni odnosi' ['Private International Law Relations'] in E. MIŠĆENIĆ (ed.), *Europsko privatno pravo: posebni dio [European Private Law: Special Part]*, Školska knjiga, Zagreb 2021, p. 495.

may be extended to other Member States. This chapter focuses on the basic notions, including 'authentic instrument', 'court settlement', 'authenticity', and mechanisms, being the 'acceptance' and the 'declaration of enforceability'. It further contains comments on the number of unified procedural rules which are applicable in the proceedings relating to extension of effects.

Prior to entering into detail, it is important to emphasise that the Twin Regulations apply *ratione teritorii* only where the Member State of origin of an authentic instrument or a court settlement and the Member State of enforcement[12] within the meaning of Article 3(1)(g) and (h) are both Member States participating in the enhanced cooperation established by the Twin Regulations. This, of course, does not entail that such instruments need to be known in the law of the participating Member State of enforcement. Regardless of whether it is possible or not to create an authentic instrument under the national law of the participating Member State of enforcement, such instrument has to be accepted and/or enforced in that Member State if created in the participating Member State of origin.[13] Furthermore, the Twin Regulations apply *ratione temporis* to authentic instruments formally drawn up or registered and to court settlements approved or concluded on or after 29 January 2019. Finally, authentic instruments and court settlements to be captured *ratione materiae* by one or the other of the Twin Regulations have to be in a matter of matrimonial property or in a matter of the property consequences of a registered partnership, respectively.[14] Otherwise, they are captured by another EU private international law instrument or, failing that, by the rules of international agreement, if applicable, or national laws.

Furthermore, several technical notes seem appropriate at this point. Due to parallelism between the Twin Regulations, the references to the Matrimonial Property Regulation in this chapter should be understood also to refer to the Regulation on the Property Consequences of Registered Partnerships, except where indicated otherwise. In the same vein, references to spouse(s) or matrimonial property matters should be understood as references to registered partner(s) or matters of property consequences of registered partners, and similar. Moreover, the reference to a 'Member State' is limited to Member

---

[12] The term 'the Member State of enforcement' is used in this chapter consistently with the Twin Regulations where it entails, not only the Member State where the authentic instrument or court settlement is to be declared enforceable, but also the Member State in which authentic instruments is to be accepted.

[13] See in the context of the Brussels I Regulation, where the situation was less complex because all Member States were involved, see Report (JLS/2004/C4/03) on the application of the Brussels I Regulation in the Member States presented by B. Hess, Th. Pfeiffer and P. Schlosser, Study JLS/C4/2005/03, Final version September 2007, Ruprecht-Karls-Universität Heidelberg, <http://courtesa.eu/wp-content/uploads/2019/03/study_application_brussels_1_en.pdf>, p. 276.

[14] See Articles 3(1)(d) of the Twin Regulations.

States participating in the enhanced cooperation established by the Twin Regulations.[15]

2. THE NOTIONS OF 'AUTHENTIC INSTRUMENT' AND 'COURT SETTLEMENT'

The analysis of the basic notions of 'authentic instrument' and 'court settlement', their differentiation from other notions such as 'decision' (or 'judgment') and putting their basic features under scrutiny are deemed as necessary steps prior to opening the discussion on their legal effects which are extended to other Member States by virtue of the mechanisms envisaged in the Twin Regulations.

2.1. DEFINITION OF 'AUTHENTIC INSTRUMENT'

Drawing on the definition in Article 3(1)(i) of the Succession Regulation, 'authentic instrument' is defined in Article 3(1)(c) of the Matrimonial Property Regulation and Article 3(1)(d) of the Regulation on the Property Consequences of Registered Partnerships as a document in a matter of a matrimonial property regime/the property consequences of a registered partnership which has been formally drawn up or registered as an authentic instrument in a Member State and the authenticity of which: (i) relates to the signature and the content of the authentic instrument; and (ii) has been established by a public authority or other authority empowered for that purpose by the Member State of origin. While the latter requirement demands the effective involvement of the public authority, the former concerns the qualitative capacity of that involvement. The two requirements are cumulatively applicable and relate to the quality of an 'authentic instrument' when drafted or registered pursuant to the law of the Member State of origin. This having been said, the cited provisions are not intended to impose any unified form-related (*instrumentum*) requirements[16] as to the 'authentic instruments' in the Member States. While the Member States' power to regulate form-related requirements remains intact, the notion of 'authenticity' in the Twin Regulations is interpreted autonomously from any national meanings.[17] Its function is to serve as a criterion to extend the effects

---

[15] See above Chapters 2 and 3 of this volume.
[16] About these features see below Section 2.2. of this chapter.
[17] Recital 59 of the Matrimonial Property Regulation and Recital 58 of the Regulation on the Property Consequences of Registered Partnerships, which are modelled upon Recital 62 of the Succession Regulation. Although autonomous, the notion of 'authentic instruments' is built on parallel national definitions. See e.g. Article 1369 of the French Civil Code (*Code civil* en vigueur au 26 mai 2021 – l'article 1369 comme modifié par Ordonnance n°2016-131 du 10 février 2016 dans l'article 4) which provides that an authenticated instrument

of the documents which, created under a national law of a Member State, are considered 'authentic interments' also under the Twin Regulations.

This twofold-requirement scheme departs from the definition in other EU private international legislation which also list the third cumulatively applicable requirement – enforceability of the instrument. Based on the texts of the provisions, analysis of their respective contexts, the system of the regulations in question and preparatory work documents, three requirements which need to be fulfilled in order for a document to be characterised as authentic were formerly identified by the Court of Justice of the European Union (CJEU).[18] Originating from the Jenard-Möller Report on the Lugano Convention,[19] the threefold-requirement scheme consists of the following: (i) the authenticity of the instrument should have been established by a public authority; (ii) this authenticity should relate to the content of the instrument and not only, for example, the signature; and (iii) the instrument has to be enforceable in itself in the Member State in which it originates.[20] While all three are mandatory in some legislation belonging to the EU private international law,[21] only two are

---

(*l'acte authentique*) is one which has been received, with the requisite formalities, by a public official having the power and the function to draw it up. Likewise, Article 230 of the Croatian Civil Procedure Act (*Zakon o parničnom postupku*, Službeni list SFRJ 4/77, 36/77, 6/80, 36/80, 43/82, 69/82, 58/84, 74/87, 57/89, 20/90, 27/90 and 35/91, and Narodne novine 53/91, 91/92, 58/93, 112/99, 88/01, 117/03, 88/05, 02/07, 84/08, 96/08, 123/08, 57/11, 148/11, 25/13, 89/14 and 70/19), defines public document (which is a broader notion than the authentic instrument) as a document which is issued in the prescribed form by the state authority within the boundaries of its competence and the document which is issued in such a form by the legal or natural person in performing acts of public authority which is entrusted to her by an act or instrument based on an act. Article 3(2) of the Croatian Public Notaries Act (*Zakon o javnom bilježništvu*, Narodne novine, 78/93, 29/94, 162/98, 16/07, 75/09, 120/16), provides that public notaries' documents issued pursuant to the Act have the force of public documents provided that in their composing and issuing the essential formal requirements under the Act have been fulfilled.

[18] See e.g. Case C-260/97, *Unibank A/S v Flemming G. Christensen*, EU:C:1999:312, paras. 17–20.

[19] Jenard-Möller Report on the Convention on Jurisdiction and the Enforcement of Judgments in Civil and Commercial Matters done at Lugano 16 September 1988 [1990] OJ C189/57, 28.7.1990.

[20] Ibid., p. 80.

[21] See e.g. Article 58 of the Brussels I bis Regulation, Article 46 of the Brussels II bis Regulation and Article 2(3)(a) of the Maintenance Regulation. See also, *K.H.K.*, which was decided under the Regulation (EU) No 655/2014 of 15 May 2014 establishing a European Account Preservation Order procedure to facilitate cross-border debt recovery in civil and commercial matters [2014] OJ L 189, 27.6.2014. The question referred to the CJEU was whether a particular order for payment under Bulgarian law, that of a monetary claim which has not yet become enforceable, constitutes an 'authentic instrument' within the meaning of Article 4(10) of the Regulation 655/2014. The CJEU found that, in the absence of the explicit wording, it is apparent from the analysis of the context of the provision and the objective pursued Regulation 655/2014 and the *travaux préparatoires* for the Regulation that, in order to be regarded as a 'judgment', 'court settlement' or 'authentic instrument' within the meaning of that Regulation, an instrument must be enforceable in the Member State of origin. In the case at hand, the order for payment was not yet enforceable; therefore, it did not amount to an authentic instrument.

necessary for the legal instrument to be characterised as 'authentic' under the Succession Regulation[22] or the Twin Regulations:[23] the involvement of public authority and its role in creation of an authentic instrument. This does not entail an essential difference in the definition, rather the enlargement of the types of effects to be extended. Initially, the effects of 'authentic instruments' could only be extended by declaration of 'enforceability', whereas recently it has been possible to also extend their effects by 'acceptance'. Naturally, it is not possible to declare as enforceable an 'authentic instrument' which under the law of the Member State of origin does not produce such an effect. After all, it is not the creation, but the extension of the effects that the Chapter V of the Twin Regulations entails.[24]

2.1.1. Involvement of Public Authority

Turning back to the twofold-requirement scheme under the Twin Regulations, the CJEU case law offers some guidance despite the fact that the interpretations are provided within the threefold-requirement scheme. The requirement demanding the involvement of the public authority was dealt with in *Unibank*.

> *Unibank* concerned the Danish legal institute of *Gældsbrev*, standing for an acknowledgement of indebtedness. The question which was central to the dispute on the national level and made its way to the CJEU was whether a *Gældsbrev* could be considered an authentic instrument under the Brussels Convention. The CJEU recalled the Jenard-Möller Report on the Lugano Convention, which expounded on the question of authentic instruments under the Lugano Convention.[25] The judgment in *Unibank* went on to establish these requirements as a norm within the context of the Brussels Convention.[26] As the cumulative requirements for determining the authenticity of a certain document, they led the CJEU to conclude that the *Gældsbrev* did not constitute an authentic instrument. This was due to the failure of the *Gældsbrev* to meet the requirement of the effective involvement of the public authority in authenticating the document. Given that the document in question was privately drafted and its authenticity was not 'established by a public authority or other authority empowered for that purpose by that State', it did not amount to an authentic instrument.[27]

---

[22] P. WAUTELET, 'Article 3. Définitions' in A. BONOMI and P. WAUTELET (eds.), *Le droit européen des successions, Commentaire du règlement (UE) No 650/2012, du 4 juillet 2012*, 2nd ed., Bruylant, Brussels 2016, p. 168; H.-P. MANSEL, 'Article 59. Acceptance of Authentic Instruments' in A.-L. CALVO CARAVACA, A. DAVÍ and H.-P. MANSEL (eds.), *The European Succession Regulation, A Commentary*, Cambridge University Press, Cambridge 2016, p. 637.
[23] See e.g. Case C-658/17, *WB v Notariusz Przemysława Bac*, EU:C:2019:444, paras. 66–72.
[24] Further on this see below Section 3 of this chapter.
[25] Case C-260/97, *Unibank A/S v Flemming G. Christensen*, EU:C:1999:312, para. 16.
[26] Case C-260/97, *Unibank A/S v Flemming G. Christensen*, EU:C:1999:312, paras. 17–20.
[27] Case C-260/97, *Unibank A/S v Flemming G. Christensen*, EU:C:1999:312, para. 21.

As the involvement of the public authority is a prerequisite for a document to be qualified as an 'authentic instrument', it is important to clarify the notion of 'public authority or other authority empowered for that purpose by the Member State of origin' as stated in the definition of 'authentic instrument' in the Twin Regulations. The public authorities possessing the powers to draft an authentic instrument are certainly the courts and the public notaries, in so far as authorised to that effect under their national law, such as in Croatia in which both the court and notary are alternative public authorities to authenticate the Croatian type of an agreement as to succession – agreement on transfer and distribution of property during lifetime.[28]

Generally, according to the Croatian Public Notaries Act, the notary public service consists of 'the official composing and issuing of public documents on legal affairs, statements and facts on which the rights are based, the official certification of private documents, the receipt for safekeeping of documents, money and valuables for delivery to other persons or authorities, and in performing, by order of courts or other public bodies, procedures determined by law', while also performing other tasks provided by the Act itself.[29] Similarly, the German Federal Code of Notaries describes notaries as 'independent holders of a public office who are appointed in the *Länder* to record legal acts ('notarial recording') and to perform other tasks in the field of the preventive administration of justice'.[30] While there are important variances between the powers that the notaries hold depending on the Member State in which they are appointed,[31] in some Member States the competence of notaries is exclusive,[32]

---

[28] Article 106(2) of the Succession Act (*Zakon o nasljeđivanju*), Narodne novine 48/03, 163/03, 35/05, 127/13, 33/15 and 14/19. More on the agreement see I. GLIHA, 'Chapter 4. Acts *Inter Vivos* Related to the Estate' in P. ŠARČEVIĆ, T. JOSIPOVIĆ, I. GLIHA, N. HLAČA and I. KUNDA, *Family Law In Croatia*, Kluwer Law International, Rijnland in Leiden, 2011, pp. 280–286.

[29] Article 2 of the Croatian Public Notaries Act (*Zakon o javnom bilježništvu*, Narodne novine, 78/93, 29/94, 162/98, 16/07, 75/09, 120/16).

[30] Article 1 of the German Federal Code of Notaries, *Bundesnotarordnung* in der im Bundesgesetzblatt Teil III, Gliederungsnummer 303-1, veröffentlichten bereinigten Fassung, die zuletzt durch Artikel 5 des Gesetzes vom 4. Mai 2021 (BGBl. I S. 882) geändert worden ist.

[31] In the context of the Brussels I Regulation and the European Enforcement Order Regulation, the CJEU showed that the classification of the notaries as the 'courts' in performing specific tasks may not be as clear-cut. See Case C-551/15, *Pula parking d.o.o. v Sven Klaus Tederahn*, EU:C:2017:193; Case C-484/15, *Ibrica Zulfikarpašić v Slaven Gajer*, EU:C:2017:199. The CJEU judgments in these cases led to the reform of the national enforcement legislation. See Article 39a(4) of the Croatian Enforcement Act (*Ovršni zakon*, Narodne novine 112/12, 25/13, 93/14, 55/16, 73/17 and 131/20), newly introduced by the Amendments to the Enforcement Act (*Zakon o izmjenama i dopunama Ovršnog zakona*, Narodne novine 131/2020).

[32] COUNCIL OF THE NOTARIATS OF THE EUROPEAN UNION, *Comparative Study on Authentic Instruments National Provisions of Private Law, Circulation, Mutual Recognition and Enforcement, Possible Legislative Initiative by the European Union – United Kingdom, France, Germany, Poland, Sweden*, European Parliament, Brussels 2008, <https://www.europarl.europa.eu/RegData/etudes/STUD/2008/408329/IPOL-JURI_ET(2008)408329_EN.pdf>, p. 32.

as they are in principle the only authorities with the power to create authentic instruments. However, as witnessed above, this role need not always be exclusively reserved for the notaries.

Exclusive or not, in civil law countries notaries are regarded as playing a 'complementary role to that of a judge.'[33] However, caution is needed as they may also act in other capacity – perform judicial function, and thus be considered 'courts' within the meaning of Article 3(2) of the Twin Regulations. The Preambles offer explanation: When notaries exercise judicial functions they are bound by the rules of jurisdiction set out in the Twin Regulations, and the decisions they give circulate in accordance with the provisions of the Twin Regulations on recognition, enforceability and enforcement of decisions in Chapter IV thereof. In contrast, when notaries do not exercise judicial functions they are not bound by those rules of jurisdiction, but by those of national (or international) law only, and the authentic instruments they issue circulate in accordance with the provisions of the Twin Regulations on authentic instruments in Chapter V thereof.[34]

2.1.2. Role of Public Authority

The other requirement for 'authentic instrument' goes beyond the mere involvement of the public authority and concerns the role of the public authority *in concreto*. This requirement was particularly dealt with by the CJEU in *WB*,[35] decided under the Succession Regulation. Given that the Succession Regulation contains the provision defining the 'authentic instrument' which is inbuilt verbatim into the Twin Regulations, the former Regulation may perfectly inform the interpretation of the notion of 'authentic instrument' in the later Regulations. The only difference between the definitions relates to the respective material scopes of the Regulations, which is irrelevant to the characterisation of an instrument as 'authentic'.

> The dispute in *WB* concerned the definition of an 'authentic instrument' as opposed to the 'decision' in a matter of succession under the Succession Regulation. The instrument in question in *WB* was a national instrument certifying the status of heir, specifically the Polish deed of certification of succession drawn up by a notary in accordance with a non-contentious (unanimous) application by all the parties to the certification proceedings. The CJEU differentiated between the notions of 'authentic instrument' and 'decision'. In its judgment, the CJEU states that the deed does not constitute a 'decision' since the notary was not the 'court' within the meaning of the provision of Article 3(2) of the Succession Regulation because of the fact that the Polish notary does not exercise judicial function when issuing the Polish

---

[33] Ibid., p. 4.
[34] Recital 31 of the Twin Regulations.
[35] Case C-658/17, *WB v Notariusz Przemysława Bac*, EU:C:2019:444.

national deed of certification of succession following the unanimous application by all the parties concerned.[36] On the other hand, the CJEU concluded that such a deed constitutes an 'authentic instrument', as it satisfies both requirements of the two-fold scheme.[37] By stating that the Polish notaries have the power to draw up instruments relating to a succession and the deed of certification of succession is formally registered as an authentic instrument,[38] the CJEU refers to the requirement for an authentic instrument concerned with the involvement of the public authority. To that effect, the CJEU further states that the Polish national deed of certification of succession is registered and produces, according to Polish law, the same effects as the final order establishing succession.[39] Moreover, the CJEU makes the reference to the role-related requirement by affirming that, pursuant to Polish law, a notary is required to carry out checks of its own motion, such as to the jurisdiction of the national courts, the content of applicable foreign law, the identity of the heir, the amount of the shares in the inheritance, and, where the testator has made a legacy 'by vindication', as to the person to whom the testator made the bequest 'by vindication' and the subject matter thereof. Since, these notary's findings lead to his or her refusal to draw up the deed of certification of succession, the authenticity of that instrument relates to both its signature and its content.[40]

2.1.3. Paper or Electronic Form

Lastly, in keeping up with the digitalisation of all spheres of life, including the legal one, it is important to note that, while it is inherent in the notion of an authentic instrument that it must be a written document, both paper-based and electronic are equally acceptable under the Twin Regulations. This also applies to the signatures contained therein, as they may be handwritten or electronic.[41] Some Member States explicitly address this question in their national laws, such as France. Its Civil Code lays down that an authentic instrument may be drawn up in electronic medium if it is created and stored under the conditions fixed by decree of the Conseil d'État,[42] which are essentially intended to enable identification of the person from whom it originates and guarantee the document's integrity.

---

[36] Case C-658/17, *WB v Notariusz Przemysława Bac*, EU:C:2019:444, para. 61. See e.g. M. WILDERSPIN, 'The Notion of "Court" under the Succession Regulation' [2020] *Problemy Prawa Prywatnego Międzynarodowego* 45–56 (welcoming the decision for bringing teleological consistence and coherence within the scheme of the Regulation). See also Chapters 3 and 6 of this volume.

[37] Case C-658/17, *WB v Notariusz Przemysława Bac*, EU:C:2019:444, para. 71.

[38] Case C-658/17, *WB v Notariusz Przemysława Bac*, EU:C:2019:444, para. 69.

[39] Case C-658/17, *WB v Notariusz Przemysława Bac*, EU:C:2019:444, para. 69.

[40] Case C-658/17, *WB v Notariusz Przemysława Bac*, EU:C:2019:444, paras. 58 and 70.

[41] P. FRANZINA, 'Article 58. Acceptance of Authentic Instruments' in I. VIARENGO and P. FRANZINA (eds.), *The EU Regulations on the Property Regimes of International Couples: A Commentary*, Edward Elgar, Cheltenham 2020, p. 437.

[42] Article 1369(2) of the French Civil Code (*Code civil* en vigueur au 26 mai 2021 – l'article 1369 comme modifié par Ordonnance n°2016-131 du 10 février 2016 dans l'article 4).

2.2. FEATURES OF 'AUTHENTIC INSTRUMENT'

To better understand this key concept, the Preambles to the Twin Regulations explain and separate the form-related (*instrumentum*) and the content-related (*negotium*) features of 'authentic instruments'. On the side of the form, the notion of 'authenticity', adhering to the Latin notary structure typical to civil law legal systems,[43] covers elements, such as the genuineness of the instrument, the formal prerequisites of the instrument, the powers of the authority drawing up the instrument, the procedure under which the instrument is drawn up and the factual elements recorded in the authentic instrument by the authority concerned. The latter elements include the fact that the parties indicated appeared before that authority on the date indicated and that they made the declarations indicated.[44]

2.2.1. Form-Related and Content-Related Elements

Elements related to the form are primarily of procedural nature and, consequently, subject to the law of the Member State whose public authority acts in the context of creation of the instrument. Pursuant to Article 58(2) of the Twin Regulations, a party wishing to challenge an authentic instrument in relation to its 'authenticity' may do so only under the law of the Member State of origin. This conflict rule is reinforced by the rule of jurisdiction in the same article providing for the exclusive jurisdiction of the courts of the Member State of origin.[45]

Content-wise, the notion of 'legal acts or legal relationships recorded in an authentic instrument' refers to the substance of the instrument.[46] A case in point is the agreement between the spouses as to matrimonial property regime to be applied between them (the matrimonial property agreement), whose formal validity is regulated by the minimum standards rule in Article 25(1) of the Matrimonial Property Regulation, whereas Article 25(2)–(3) permits cumulative application of the higher standards of the country of the *lex residentiae*

---

[43] In the context of succession see M. WELLER, 'Article 3. Definitions' in A.-L. CALVO CARAVACA, A. DAVÍ and H.-P. MANSEL (eds.), *The European Succession Regulation, A Commentary*, Cambridge University Press, Cambridge 2016, p. 121.

[44] Recital 59 of the Matrimonial Property Regulation and Recital 58 of the Regulation on the Property Consequences of Registered Partnerships, which are modelled upon Recital 62 of the Succession Regulation.

[45] See also P. WAUTELET, 'Article 58. Acceptation des actes authentiques' in A. BONOMI and P. WAUTELET (eds.), *Le droit européen des successions, Commentaire du règlement (UE) No 650/2012, du 4 juillet 2012*, 2nd ed., Bruylant, Brussels 2016, pp. 1221–1222.

[46] Recital 60 of the Matrimonial Property Regulation and Recital 59 of the Regulation on the Property Consequences of Registered Partnerships, which are modelled upon Recital 63 of the Succession Regulation.

habitualis of the spouse(s) at the time the agreement is concluded and the *lex causae*.[47] If this law requires the form of a notary deed, the document may qualify as an 'authentic instrument'. Such legal acts and legal relations can also include the agreement between the spouses on the division of their matrimonial property, the agreement on gift, or another declaration of intent which may affect the rights concerning the matrimonial property.

Elements related to the content are subject to the law applicable according to Chapter III of the Twin Regulations.[48] Although formal validity of an authentic instrument is asserted under the national law of the issuing public authority, *lex causae* is deemed applicable to the challenge of an 'authentic instrument' with regard to the *negotium*.[49] The reason for the applicability of the *lex causae* is in the essence of a dispute which is a matter of a matrimonial property regime or the property consequences of a registered partnership, as the case may be. The conflict rule in Article 58(3) of the Twin Regulations is complemented by the one on jurisdiction which states that jurisdiction for any challenge relating to the 'legal acts or legal relationships' recorded in an authentic instrument lays with the courts having jurisdiction under each of these Regulations.[50] This is a reference to the complex system of jurisdiction as elaborated above.[51]

It is also possible that the outcome of the matters of proceedings on matrimonial property or the property consequences of a registered partnership depends upon resolving the question raised *incidenter*, in relation to the content of the authentic instrument. In such case, the court having jurisdiction to decide on the principal matter also has jurisdiction over the incidental question which is contained in the authentic instrument.[52] As in the case when the content-related matter is the principle question of the proceedings, the applicable law to resolve it as an incidental question is determined in accordance with the Twin Regulations, namely its Chapter III.[53]

---

[47] See further in Chapter 6 of this volume.
[48] See further in Chapter 6 of this volume.
[49] J. FITCHEN, '"Recognition", Acceptance and Enforcement of Authentic Instruments in the Succession Regulation' (2012) 8 *Journal of Private International Law* 323, 327.
[50] See to the contrary in P. BEAUMONT, J. FITCHEN and J. HOLLIDAY, The evidentiary effects of authentic acts in the Member States of the European Union, in the context of successions, European Parliament, Brussels 2016, <https://www.europarl.europa.eu/RegData/etudes/STUD/2016/556935/IPOL_STU(2016)556935_EN.pdf>, p. 34.
[51] Further on this see Chapter 4 of this volume.
[52] Article 58(4) of the Twin Regulations.
[53] It seems that this is also confirmed by Franzina who, after discussing procedural matters related to principal and incidental questions, states in general what the applicable law is. P. FRANZINA, 'Article 58. Acceptance of Authentic Instruments' in I. VIARENGO and P. FRANZINA (eds.), *The EU Regulations on the Property Regimes of International Couples: A Commentary*, Edward Elgar, Cheltenham 2020, p. 443.

2.2.2. Distinction from 'Decision'

The distinction between a 'decision' (or a 'judgment') on the one hand, and an 'authentic instrument' on the other, was intensely discussed in the scholarly writings. The *res judicata* effect is mentioned as the crucial factor of delineation. While the decisions and judgments derive their executory force from their property of *res judicata*, the authentic instruments are devoid of such an effect.[54] This is also related to another feature of an authentic instrument, which regardless of the fact that it is drawn up by a public authority, possesses a certain private component.[55] As a consequence, its contents are contestable even after the enforcement. The same does not normally apply to decisions and judgments as they may be challenged only for a limited period of time,[56] upon which they become final and possibly subject only to extraordinary legal remedies.

2.2.3. Distinction from 'Public Document' under Regulation 2016/1191

Important to note is that various documents certifying elements of a legal status, such as birth, name, kinship, marriage, registration of partnership, marital status, divorce, dissolution of partnership, annulment of marriage or registered partnership, death, nationality, domicile, residence are not included in the definition of an 'authentic instrument'. Rather, their cross-border effects among Member States are governed by the Regulation 2016/1191.[57] This Regulation applies to public documents issued by the authorities of a Member State in accordance with its national law which have to be presented to the authorities of another Member State, the primary purpose of which is to establish one or more of the above listed facts. Thus, it simplifies the administrative requirements relating to the presentation of such public documents to ensure their free circulation within the EU and promote the free movement of EU citizens.

Careful delimitation between 'authentic instruments' within the meaning of the Twin Regulations and 'public documents' within the meaning of the Regulation 2016/1191 might prove necessary in some situations. In fact, there

---

[54] J. FITCHEN, 'Authentic instruments and European private international law in civil and commercial matters: Is now time to break new ground?' (2011) 7 *Journal of Private International Law* 33, 40.

[55] J. FITCHEN, '"Recognition", Acceptance and Enforcement of Authentic Instruments in the Succession Regulation' (2012) 8 *Journal of Private International Law* 323, 327.

[56] J. FITCHEN, 'Authentic instruments and European private international law in civil and commercial matters: Is now time to break new ground?' (2011) 7 *Journal of Private International Law* 33, 40.

[57] Regulation (EU) 2016/1191 of the European Parliament and of the Council of 6 July 2016 on promoting the free movement of citizens by simplifying the requirements for presenting certain public documents in the European Union and amending Regulation (EU) No 1024/2012 [2016] OJ L 200, 26.7.2016.

is a potential for confusion between the two notions, especially when court or notarial documents are at stake.[58] The criteria such as the contents of the document and the responsibility of the public authority in the creation of the document could play a decisive role. Thus, a document which certifies the fact that there is a marriage between two persons is subject to Regulation 2016/1191, while a document containing the statement by one of the spouses on the gift to the other spouse could qualify as an 'authentic instrument' provided other requirements under the Matrimonial Property Regulation are met as well. In the same vein, if the notary only authenticates the spouses' signatures on the document it would fall under Regulation 2016/1191, whereas the notary's responsibility, for instance, to check the contents of the spouses' dispositions in the document against the legal requirements and to inform the spouses of their legal situation and the effects of their legally relevant actions, would render such document an 'authentic instrument' under the Twin Regulations, provided other requirements are met as well.

As stated by Fitchen, an authentic instrument can generally be described as a 'public document by which an agent of the state in question formally and authoritatively records declarations made by the parties so as to constitute those declarations as legal obligations.'[59] Such document is considered to be of a 'higher evidentiary value' than, for instance, a document with a certified signature.[60] The reason for 'value' differentiation lays in the necessary fulfilment of form-related and content-related requirements verified by the public authority, which in turn provide the instrument and its holder with an elevated level of legal certainty and security.

2.3. DEFINITION OF 'COURT SETTLEMENT'

As in the case of authentic instruments, the definition of a 'court settlement' in Article 3(1)(e) of the Matrimonial Property Regulation and Article 3(1)(f) of the Regulation on the Property Consequences of Registered Partnerships is

---

[58] See the list in Article 3(1) of the Regulation 2016/1191.
[59] J. FITCHEN, 'Authentic instruments and European private international law in civil and commercial matters: Is now time to break new ground?' (2011) 7 *Journal of Private International Law* 33.
[60] COUNCIL OF THE NOTARIATS OF THE EUROPEAN UNION, *Comparative Study on Authentic Instruments National Provisions of Private Law, Circulation, Mutual Recognition and Enforcement, Possible Legislative Initiative by the European Union – United Kingdom, France, Germany, Poland, Sweden*, European Parliament, Brussels 2008, <https://www.europarl.europa.eu/RegData/etudes/STUD/2008/408329/IPOL-JURI_ET(2008)408329_EN.pdf>, p. 64; P. BEAUMONT, J. FITCHEN and J. HOLLIDAY, The evidentiary effects of authentic acts in the Member States of the European Union, in the context of successions, European Parliament, Brussels 2016, <https://www.europarl.europa.eu/RegData/etudes/STUD/2016/556935/IPOL_STU(2016)556935_EN.pdf>, pp. 21 and 32.

taken verbatim from the Succession Regulation,[61] which was taken from the earlier EU legislation in private international law.[62] Thus, the 'court settlement' means 'a settlement in a matter of matrimonial property regime/the property consequences of a registered partnership which has been approved by a court, or concluded before a court in the course of proceedings'.

This notion, which is subject to Euroautonomous interpretation,[63] consists of two basic requirements: (i) there has to be a settlement between the parties; and (ii) it has to be approved by a court, or concluded before a court in the course of proceedings.[64]

2.3.1. Settlement between the Parties

The notion of 'settlements' would include, for instance, the agreement of the spouses on the division of their matrimonial property,[65] or agreement with a third party on the right of the third party which is affected by the matrimonial property regime applicable between the spouses. Instructive in understanding the concept of the 'settlement' is the delineation between a 'judgment' and a 'court settlement'. This issue was deliberated early on in *Solo Kleinmotoren*.[66]

> The preliminary question referred to the CJEU was whether court settlements can be included in the notion of judgments under Article 27(3) of the Brussels Convention, which was in force at the time. The CJEU made a strict distinction, stating that 'settlements in court are essentially contractual in that their terms depend first and foremost on the parties' intention' whereas judgments must 'emanate from a judicial body ... deciding on its own authority on the issues between the parties'.[67]

---

[61] Article 3(1)(h) of the Succession Regulation.
[62] See e.g. Article 2(e) of the Brussels I bis Regulation.
[63] In the context of the Brussels I bis Regulation see X. KRAMER, in U. MAGNUS and P. MANKOWSKI (eds.), *Brussels Ibis Regulation: Commentary*, Otto Schmidt, Köln 2016, p. 986.
[64] Although subject to autonomous interpretation, the notion of 'court settlement' has strong similarities to same notion in some Member States' legal systems, such as German. According to Article 794 of the German Code of Civil Procedure (*Zivilprozessordnung* in der Fassung der Bekanntmachung vom 5. Dezember 2005 (BGBl. I S. 3202; 2006 I S. 431; 2007 I S. 1781), die zuletzt durch Artikel 7 des Gesetzes vom 4. Mai 2021 (BGBl. I S. 882) geändert worden ist), enforcement is possible based on settlements concluded by the parties, or between one of the parties and a third party, in order to resolve the legal dispute either in its full scope or as regards a part of the subject matter of the litigation, before a German court or before a dispute-resolution entity established or recognised by the Land department of justice (*Landesjustizverwaltung*), as well as based on settlements that have been recorded pursuant to Article 118(1), third sentence, or Article 492(3) for the record of the judge.
[65] In the context of succession see M. WELLER, 'Article 3. Definitions' in A.-L. CALVO CARAVACA, A. DAVÍ and H.-P. MANSEL (eds.), *The European Succession Regulation, A Commentary*, Cambridge University Press, Cambridge 2016, p. 121.
[66] Case C-414/92, *Solo Kleinmotoren GmbH v Emilio Boch*, EU:C:1994:221.
[67] Case C-414/92, *Solo Kleinmotoren GmbH v Emilio Boch*, EU:C:1994:221, paras. 17–18.

Apparently, the latter condition is not met in case of court settlements; regardless of the fact that such settlement may bring the court proceedings to the end. The CJEU also expressed that court settlements are governed explicitly by Article 51 of the Brussels Convention containing specific rules for their enforcement.[68]

Therefore, the first requirement pertaining to the 'court settlement' is the agreement between parties, as opposed to the decision of a court. However, the court's involvement is necessary, as the private agreement between parties does not fall under the scope of 'court settlements'. This leads to the second requirement.

2.3.2. Involvement of the Court

The court's involvement may take either of the two forms: (i) the settlement of the parties is reached outside the court and the court proceedings have been initiated for the purpose of formal *ex post* approval of the settlement; or (ii) the court is seised with the proceedings in which the matter ends by an agreement of the parties concluded in these proceedings before the court. In the former case, the courts are under the laws of some Member States able to certify the parties' declarations made in the settlements. This operates as an exception to the exclusive competence of notaries to authenticate declarations of the parties, as explained above.[69] However, courts are able to produce authentic instruments only in some Member States and in specific matters. In Germany, Article 127a of the German Civil Code, entitled 'Court Settlement', provides that in the event of a court settlement, the recording of declarations in a court record drawn up in accordance with the provisions under the Code of Civil Procedure (*Zivilprozessordnung*) replaces notarial recording.[70] When the court acts by approving the settlement, it is necessary that the court's involvement consists in active reviewing of the settlement.[71] By analogy with the notion of

---

[68] Case C-414/92, *Solo Kleinmotoren GmbH v Emilio Boch*, EU:C:1994:221, para. 22.
[69] COUNCIL OF THE NOTARIATS OF THE EUROPEAN UNION, *Comparative Study on Authentic Instruments National Provisions of Private Law, Circulation, Mutual Recognition and Enforcement, Possible Legislative Initiative by the European Union – United Kingdom, France, Germany, Poland, Sweden*, European Parliament, Brussels 2008, <https://www.europarl.europa.eu/RegData/etudes/STUD/2008/408329/IPOL-JURI_ET(2008)408329_EN.pdf>, p. 32.; P. BEAUMONT, J. FITCHEN and J. HOLLIDAY, The evidentiary effects of authentic acts in the Member States of the European Union, in the context of successions, European Parliament, Brussels 2016, <https://www.europarl.europa.eu/RegData/etudes/STUD/2016/556935/IPOL_STU(2016)556935_EN.pdf>, p. 19.
[70] Bürgerliches Gesetzbuch in der Fassung der Bekanntmachung vom 2. Januar 2002 (BGBl. I S. 42, 2909; 2003 I S.738), das zuletzt durch Artikel 1 des Gesetzes vom 9. Juni 2021 (BGBl. I S. 1666) geändert worden ist).
[71] X. KRAMER, in U. MAGNUS and P. MANKOWSKI (eds.), *Brussels Ibis Regulation: Commentary*, Otto Schmidt, Köln 2016, p. 987.

'authentic instrument',[72] the said activity should be related both to the signature and the contents.

2.3.3. Distinction from 'Consent Judgments'

A question may arise as to whether the *res iudicata* effect of the court settlement may disqualify it from the definition under Article 3(1)(e) of the Matrimonial Property Regulation and Article 3(1)(f) of the Regulation on the Property Consequences of Registered Partnerships, because such effect is the essence of the decision. There is no straightforward answer to this question in the definition of the 'court settlement'. In addition, nowhere in the Twin Regulations the effect of *res iudicata* is mentioned either to include it or to exclude it from the definition of the notion of 'court settlement'. This creates difficulties in the interpretation as the legal systems of different Member States ascribe diverse effects to the parties' settlements concluded with the participation of the courts.

In the Heidelberg Report concerned with the Brussels I Regulation, 'consent judgments', as they are termed there according to this concept in English law, are not considered court settlements in the sense of Article 58 of the Regulation, but must be qualified as judicial decisions which are recognised under Article 32 thereof.[73] By analogy, the same effect of *res iudicata* would qualify the 'consent judgments' in matrimonial property matters and matters of property consequences of registered partnerships as 'decisions' within the meaning of Article 3(1)(d) of the Matrimonial Property Regulation and 3(1)(e) of the Regulation on the Property Consequences of Registered Partnerships, rather than 'court settlements'.

The lack of *res iudicata* effect as the reason mentioned for such conclusion seems convincing if taking account of the fact that the system of recognition and enforcement of judgments in the Brussels I Regulation, and its successor – the Brussels I bis Regulation – lists the irreconcilability with another judgment among the grounds for refusal of recognition and enforcement,[74] whereas provisions on court settlements permit refusal to declare their enforceability on no other ground but manifest violation of public policy of the Member State

---

[72] The public authority has to authenticate the instrument with regard to both the signature and the content. See above Section 2.1.
[73] Report (JLS/2004/C4/03) on the application of the Brussels I Regulation in the Member States presented by B. Hess, Th. Pfeiffer and P. Schlosser, Study JLS/C4/2005/03, Final version September 2007, Ruprecht-Karls-Universität Heidelberg, <http://courtesa.eu/wp-content/uploads/2019/03/study_application_brussels_1_en.pdf>, pp. 66 and 277.
[74] Articles 45(1) and 46 of the Brussels I Regulation and of the Brussels I bis Regulation. See also Articles 37 and 47 of the Matrimonial Property Regulation and the Regulation on the Property Consequences of Registered Partnerships.

of enforcement.⁷⁵ Hence, lack of the *res iudicata* as a ground for refusal of declaration of enforceability of court settlements could be taken as an indication that the notion of 'court settlement' does not include any legal act or document having the *res iudicata* effect. Otherwise, the system would suffer from severe inconsistency – irreconcilability would be an obstacle for judgments which are not based on the parties' agreement, but would not be if parties have agreed as to the outcome of the proceedings and have made it part of the 'consent judgment'. Indeed, such interpretation reinforces the creation of the single judicial area in civil matters (in the EU or the part of it participating in the enhanced cooperation) in which the recognition and enforcement systems are intended to rule out the possibility that the rights and obligations of the parties which are final and enforceable in one Member State conflict with such rights and obligations in another Member State.

Assuming that the above interpretation is correct, no court settlement, as understood in the Croatian or Slovenian national laws, could be characterised as a court settlement within the meaning of Article 3(1)(e) of the Matrimonial Property Regulation and Article 3(1)(f) of the Regulation on the Property Consequences of Registered Partnerships. In the Croatian legal system, the court settlement pursuant to the national procedural law means the parties' agreement which is made in the form of the minutes of the court proceedings, signed by the parties whereby it becomes final, and enforceable, as the case may be.⁷⁶ Because no other proceedings may be carried out in the matter which previously ended by the court settlement within the meaning of the Croatian national law, it has been concluded that the procedural objection of *rei iudicaliter transactae* equals the procedural objection of *rei iudicatae* in Croatian law.⁷⁷ Similarly, Slovenian law provides that the court has to *proprio motu* decline the action wherever there is a previous court settlement in the matter pending before it – which embodies the principle *ne bis in idem*.⁷⁸ Therefore, the court settlement under the Slovenian national law is the *res transacta*, which has the same effect as the *res iudicata* and all the same applies to the court settlement

---

75   Article 59 in conjunction with Article 58(1) of the Brussels I Regulation and of the Brussels I bis Regulation. See also Article 60(3) of the Matrimonial Property Regulation and the Regulation on the Property Consequences of Registered Partnerships.

76   See Articles 321–324 of the Croatian Civil Procedure Act (*Zakon o parničnom postupku*), Službeni list SFRJ 4/77, 36/77, 6/80, 36/80, 43/82, 69/82, 58/84, 74/87, 57/89, 20/90, 27/90 and 35/91, and Narodne novine 53/91, 91/92, 58/93, 112/99, 88/01, 117/03, 88/05, 02/07, 84/08, 96/08, 123/08, 57/11, 148/11, 25/13, 89/14 and 70/19.

77   L. Vojković, 'Pravna priroda sudske nagodbe' ['Legal nature of the court settlement'], 40 *Zbornik Pravnog fakulteta Sveučilišta u Rijeci [Collection of Essays of the Faculty of Law of the University of Rijeka]* (2019), p. 957, 964.

78   Article 308 of the Civil Procedure Act (*Zakon o pravdnem postopku*), Uradni list RS, 73/07 – uradno prečiščeno besedilo, 45/08 – ZArbit, 45/08, 111/08 – odl. US, 57/09 – odl. US, 12/10 – odl. US, 50/10 – odl. US, 107/10 – odl. US, 75/12 – odl. US, 40/13 – odl. US, 92/13 – odl. US, 10/14 – odl. US, 48/15 – odl. US, 6/17 – odl. US, 10/17, 16/19 – ZNP-1 in 70/19 – odl. US).

as does to the final judgment.⁷⁹ Consequently, what Croatian and Slovenian legal systems consider 'court settlement' rendered by the respective country's court would be characterised as a 'judgment' or 'decision', rather than a 'court settlement' for the purpose of recognition and/or enforcement under the EU regulations in private international law. This having been said, judiciary whose national law does not know of 'court settlements' in the sense of the Twin Regulations, is still under duty to apply the Regulations to enforce 'court settlements' originating from other Member States.

3. EXTENDING THE EFFECTS OF AUTHENTIC INSTRUMENTS AND COURT SETTLEMENTS

The free movement of EU citizens is enhanced by their ability to directly rely on a single legal document in various Member States. Accordingly, the EU private international law shows a tendency of relaxing the formal procedures related to the use of the document in every Member State other than the Member State of origin. The more relaxed are the requirements for extending effects of the public legal acts and documents, the deeper is the mutual trust needed among the Member States.⁸⁰ Following the steps of the other EU regulations in the field of private international law, the Twin Regulations abolish all requirements for legalisation or other similar formality in respect of documents issued in a Member State in the context of the respective Regulation.⁸¹ The Twin Regulations further guarantee the 'acceptance' and the declaration of 'enforceability' in all participating Member States of authentic instruments in matters of matrimonial property and in matters of the property consequences of registered partnerships, respectively. They also guarantee simplified declaration of 'enforceability' of court settlements.

'Acceptance' and 'enforceability' relate to the effects of the authentic instruments and court settlements. Evidentiary and executory force of an authentic instrument⁸² is derived from the powers of the public authority

---

[79] Supreme Court of the Republic of Slovenia, II Ips 877/2009, 17.05.2012, SI:VSRS:2012:II. IPS.877.2009; N. BETETTO and A. GALIČ in L. UDE and A. GALIČ (eds.), *Pravdni postopek: Zakon s komentarjem, 3. Knjiga [Civil Proceedings: Act with Commentary, 3rd Book]*, Uradni list/GV Založba, Ljubljana 2009, p. 45.

[80] I. KUNDA, 'Međunarodnoprivatnopravni odnosi' ['Private International Law Relations'] in E. MIŠĆENIĆ (ed.), *Europsko privatno pravo: posebni dio [European Private Law: Special Part]*, Školska knjiga, Zagreb 2021, pp. 498–500.

[81] Article 61 of the Twin Regulations. Abolition of such requirements is also dealt with under the Hague Convention of 5 October 1961 Abolishing the Requirement of Legalisation for Foreign Public Documents, which instead introduced an *apostille*.

[82] J. FITCHEN, '"Recognition", Acceptance and Enforcement of Authentic Instruments in the Succession Regulation' (2012) 8 *Journal of Private International Law* 323, 327.

involved in its creation and the pertinent formal procedure prescribed by national law of the Member State of origin. While the probative force refers to the evidentiary potential that is given to the instrument in the Member State of origin, the executory force under the Member State of origin makes the instrument enforceable without the need for embarking on any additional court or administrative proceedings.[83] Likewise, the executory effects of the court settlement derive from the involvement of the courts in concluding or approving the parties' agreement on the matter in a pending dispute, and equally to the authentic instruments making them enforceable as such. However, for these effects to be extended outside the Member State of origin there has to be a private international law mechanism in place. Twin Regulations differentiate between two such mechanisms: 'acceptance' of authentic instruments, and 'declaration of enforceability' of authentic instruments and court settlements.

3.1. 'ACCEPTANCE' OF AUTHENTIC INSTRUMENTS

3.1.1. The Notion of 'Acceptance'

The notion of 'acceptance' was first introduced in the EU private international legislation by virtue of the Succession Regulation.[84] Echoing the earlier CJEU wording,[85] it presents the 'milestone' in the construction of the system of free circulation of authentic instruments.[86] It was replicated in the Twin Regulations continuing the trend towards simplified but restricted extension of legal effects stemming from the authentic instruments among the Member States.

Such innovative terminology is contained only in the title of Article 58 of the Twin Regulations, without being repeated in the text of the provisions itself. In the absence of any definition of the concept of 'acceptance' in the Twin Regulations, the phrasing of the provisions contained therein is the most relevant in understanding its meaning. The first sentence of Article 58(1) states that: 'An authentic instrument established in a Member State shall have the same evidentiary effects in another Member State as it has in the Member State of origin, or the most comparable effects, provided that this is not manifestly contrary to public policy (*ordre public*) in the Member State concerned.'

---

[83] P. WAUTELET, 'Article 58. Acceptation des actes authentiques' in A. BONOMI and P. WAUTELET (eds.), *Le droit européen des successions, Commentaire du règlement (UE) No 650/2012, du 4 juillet 2012*, 2nd ed., Bruylant, Brussels 2016, p. 1218.
[84] Article 58 of the Succession Regulation.
[85] See Case C-336/94, *Eftalia Dafeki*, EU:C:1997:579, para 19.
[86] P. WAUTELET, 'Article 58. Acceptation des actes authentiques' in A. BONOMI and P. WAUTELET (eds.), *Le droit européen des successions, Commentaire du règlement (UE) No 650/2012, du 4 juillet 2012*, 2nd ed., Bruylant, Brussels 2016, p. 1213.

Hence, 'acceptance' is directly related to the 'evidentiary effects' (or a probative force, as sometimes termed) of an authentic instrument. As such, the 'acceptance' refers precisely to the *instrumentum*, not the *negotium*.[87]

This understanding is consistent with the *traveaux preparatoire* in the course of adoption of parallel provision in the Succession Regulation, upon which the ones in the Twin Regulation were eventually modelled. Legislative history reveals that the concept of 'recognition' of authentic instruments received harsh criticism from an essentially doctrinal perspective because of the disorder it creates to the private international law structures.[88] There was a pressing concern that the use of the notion 'recognition' might entail recognition of the legal status without classical resort to the conflict of law rules.[89] The new approach is thus intended to differentiate the concept of 'acceptance' from the concept of 'recognition'.[90] Essentially, it is aimed at reducing the extent to which the effects of authentic instruments would be extended in other Member States.[91] Both leaning on the principle of mutual recognition as the underlying policy, the two mechanisms for the extension of the legal effects between Member States operate differently. Authentic instruments cannot have the same effects extended under Chapter V of the Twin Regulations as decisions can have when 'recognised' under Chapter IV of the Twin Regulations. Therefore, the new terminology should assure not only formal differentiation between the mechanisms of 'acceptance' and 'recognition' and documents they address, but also a functional one which is manifested in different the nature of the effects to be extended when relying on each of the mechanisms.

3.1.2. Extension of Evidentiary Effects

As described in Recital 58 of the Matrimonial Property Regulations and Recital 57 of the Regulation on Property Consequences of a Registered Partnership, the

---

[87] P. FRANZINA, 'Article 58. Acceptance of authentic instruments' in I. VIARENGO and P. FRANZINA (eds.), *The EU Regulations on the Property Regimes of International Couples: A Commentary*, Edward Elgar, Cheltenham 2020, pp. 438–439.

[88] See H.-P. MANSEL, 'Article 59. Acceptance of Authentic Instruments' in A.-L. CALVO CARAVACA, A. DAVÍ and H.-P. MANSEL (eds.), *The European Succession Regulation, A Commentary*, Cambridge University Press, Cambridge 2016, pp. 634–635, and abundant references therein.

[89] W.H. RECHBERGER, 'Cross-Border Enforcement of Public Documents' in V. RIJAVEC, K. DRNOVŠEK and C.H. VAN RHEE (eds.), *Cross-Border Enforcement in Europe: National and International Perspectives*, Intersentia, Cambridge 2020, p. 77.

[90] É. FONGARO, 'Les successions' in H. PÉROZ and É. FONGARO, *Droit international privé patrimonial de la famille*, 2nd ed., LexisNexis, Paris 2017, p. 321.

[91] R. GEIMER, '"Annahme" ausländischer öffentlicher Urkunden in Erbsachen gemäß Art. 59 EuErbVO', in A. DUTTA and S. HERRLER (eds.), *Die Europäische Erbrechtsverordnung*, C.H. Beck, München 2014, pp. 143–160.

authentic instrument must be accepted with the same evidentiary effects as in the Member State of origin, or, failing that, the most comparable effects. When determining the evidentiary effects of a given authentic instrument in another Member State or the most comparable effects, reference should be made to the nature and the scope of the evidentiary effects of the authentic instrument in the Member State of origin. The evidentiary effects which a given authentic instrument should produce in another Member State will therefore depend on the law of the Member State of origin. Clear reference to this law does not make the task any easier for the courts of the Member State of enforcement, given the variations in legal effects produced by the authentic instruments in different Member States.[92]

The extent of such variations was precisely the motivation for the EU legislators to include a specific provision for acceptance of the 'most comparable effects' as an alternative option where acceptance of the exact effects determined by the Member State of origin is not possible.[93] Such impossibility is logically not so severe as to trigger the operation of the *ordre public* clause.[94] Yet it is severe enough to constitute disruption to the procedural legal structures of the Member State of enforcement so that the adaptation technique[95] is called into assistance by the authority of the Member State of enforcement which is presented with the authentic instrument in question. As Franzina aptly puts, the most comparable effects are those which are 'functionally equivalent (to the largest possible extent) to the effects arising from the instrument under the law of the [Member] State of origin'.[96] To establish that it is necessary to understand the nature and scope of the evidentiary effects of an authentic instrument in the Member State of origin in comparison to the domestic effects. Indeed, the

---

[92] Although not on authentic instruments but on public documents certifying date of birth, the circumstances in *Eftalia Dafeki* show how significantly the probative value of the documents may vary between the Member States. See Case C-336/94, *Eftalia Dafeki* [1997] EU:C:1997:579, para. 12.

[93] P. WAUTELET, 'Article 58. Acceptation des actes authentiques' in A. BONOMI and P. WAUTELET (eds.), *Le droit européen des successions, Commentaire du règlement (UE) No 650/2012, du 4 juillet 2012*, 2nd ed., Bruylant, Brussels 2016, p. 1219. In the context of the Succession Regulations see J. FITCHEN, '"Recognition", Acceptance and Enforcement of Authentic Instruments in the Succession Regulation' (2012) 8 *Journal of Private International Law* 323, 356–357; H.-P. MANSEL, 'Article 59. Acceptance of Authentic Instruments' in A.-L. CALVO CARAVACA, A. DAVÍ and H.-P. MANSEL (eds.), *The European Succession Regulation, A Commentary*, Cambridge University Press, Cambridge 2016, pp. 652–653. For the opposing opinion see U. SIMON and M. BUSCHBAUM, 'Die neue EU-Erbrechtsverordnung Aufsatz' (2012) 62 *Neue Juristische Wochenschrift* 2393, 2397.

[94] On the *ordre public* clause see Section 3.1.5. of this chapter.

[95] This technique is employed in Article 29 of the Twin Regulations regarding the rights *in rem*. See Chapter 5 of this volume.

[96] P. FRANZINA, 'Article 58. Acceptance of authentic instruments' in I. VIARENGO and P. FRANZINA (eds.), *The EU Regulations on the Property Regimes of International Couples: A Commentary*, Edward Elgar, Cheltenham 2020, p. 440.

EU private international law is requiring the courts and other authorities to progressively develop their skills in comparative law methodology.

3.1.3. Optional Standardised Form

When a person wishes to rely on an authentic instrument in a Member State different from the Member State of origin, she or he may ask for the filled-in standardised from[97] contained in Annex II of the Implementing Regulations,[98] to be issued by the authority creating the instrument in question. In addition to stating essential information about the authentic instrument in question, such as the Member State of origin, the date of the instrument, the parties' names, the form enables the public authority to detail the legal effects deriving from the instrument, including the parties' declarations recorded in it, facts verified by the public authority, whether it may serve as basis for recording the right in the register of moveable or immoveable property and whether it was challenged.

Interestingly, the Twin Regulations use the word 'may ask' when addressing the use of the authentic instrument in a Member State other than the one of origin. This entails that the form is not mandatory and the authentic instrument may be relied on in that Member State even on its own merit (along with the certified translation, as the case may be). Regardless of the fact that the form is not mandatory, it may still be regarded as the advantageous means of communicating the essential information on the authentic instrument, in particular description of the evidentiary effects, to the authority in the Member State different from the one of origin.[99] This may be very useful, especially in situations where adaptation technique has to be applied to enable extension of the most comparable effects in the Member State of enforcement.

---

[97] The form must be established in accordance with the advisory procedure referred to in Art 67(2), which further points at Article 4 of the Regulation (EU) No 182/2011 of the European Parliament and of the Council of 16 February 2011 laying down the rules and general principles concerning mechanisms for control by Member States of the Commission's exercise of implementing powers [2011] OJ L 55, 28.2.2011.

[98] Commission Implementing Regulation (EU) 2018/1935 of 7 December 2018 establishing the forms referred to in Council Regulation (EU) 2016/1103 implementing enhanced cooperation in the area of jurisdiction, applicable law and the recognition and enforcement of decisions in matters of matrimonial property regimes, C/2018/8145 [2018] OJ L 314, 11.12.2018; Commission Implementing Regulation (EU) 2018/1990 of 11 December 2018 establishing the forms referred to in Council Regulation (EU) 2016/1104 implementing enhanced cooperation in the area of jurisdiction, applicable law and the recognition and enforcement of decisions in matters of the property consequences of registered partnerships, C/2018/8226 [2018] OJ L 320, 17.12.2018.

[99] P. BEAUMONT, J. FITCHEN and J. HOLLIDAY, The evidentiary effects of authentic acts in the Member States of the European Union, in the context of successions, European Parliament, Brussels 2016, <https://www.europarl.europa.eu/RegData/etudes/STUD/2016/556935/IPOL_STU(2016)556935_EN.pdf>, p. 43.

3.1.4. Challenges as Obstacles to 'Acceptance'

There are several different reasons why a foreign authentic instrument will not be accepted. The already mentioned challenges to the authenticity of the instrument and the challenges as to the substance of the recorded legal acts or legal relationships prevent acceptance if the challenge was successful. This will be decided by the competent authority in the Member State of origin (the matter of authenticity) or the court having jurisdiction pursuant to the Twin Regulations (the substance). As long as the challenge is pending before the competent authority, the authentic instrument in question cannot produce any evidentiary effect in any of the other Member States as regards the aspect which is being challenged.[100] If the instrument ends up being declared invalid and its acceptance refused, it can no longer produce any evidentiary effects.

3.1.5. Public Policy as the Ground for Refusal of 'Acceptance'

Acceptance, however, may be refused only on a single review ground – if it is manifestly contrary the public policy of the Member State of enforcement. This ground for refusal of acceptance is laid down in the first paragraph dealing with authentic instruments. According to the settled CJEU case law, public policy comprises the fundamental principles of a Member State and its legal order (including such international and European principles in that Member State), but the outer borders to this principles are defined by the EU legal system in order to confine the range of public policy to the narrow meaning relevant to the cases with international element.[101] Therefore, to find that an instrument is 'contrary to the public policy' and consequently refuse its acceptance, mere discrepancy between the two legal systems does not suffice; yet the authentic instrument needs to be utterly repugnant from the perspective of the fundamental principles of the Member State of enforcement. Furthermore, the contrariety of the authentic instrument in question to the public policy of the Member State of enforcement must be 'manifest'. This requirement means that the violation must be clear and obvious, hence there is no place for challenging an authentic instrument based on this ground in just any case.[102] For instance, the public policy clause may be triggered in situations in which the issuance of an authentic instrument in question was linked to a criminal offence, such as corruption,

---

[100] Article 58(2) and (3) of the Twin Regulations.
[101] See Case C-7/98 *Krombach*, EU:C:2000:164, paras. 22–23; Case C-38/98 *Renault*, EU:C:2000:225, paras. 27–28; Case C-302/13, *flyLAL-Lithuanian Airlines*, EU:C:2014:2319, para. 47. See further in I. KUNDA, 'Međunarodnoprivatnopravni odnosi' ['Private International Law Relations'] in E. MIŠĆENIĆ (ed.), *Europsko privatno pravo: posebni dio [European Private Law: Special Part]*, Školska knjiga, Zagreb 2021, pp. 546–548.
[102] More on public policy see in Chapter 6 of this volume.

fraud or coercion. However, these reasons should probably also be considered grounds to challenge the authentic instrument under the law of the Member State of origin and have it declared invalid, which would be in the interest of a party to it or a third party. If so, no evidentiary effects could flow from such in invalidated instrument in any of the Member States of potential enforcement.[103] However, if, despite such grave offences, the instrument is not invalidated in the member State of origin, the public policy clause might prove its utility.[104]

3.1.6. Incompatibility with Other Authentic Instruments, Court Settlements or Decisions

Although not explicitly mentioned in the Chapter V of the Twin Regulations, the situation in which the court or other authority of the Member State of enforcement is presented with an authentic instrument, court settlement or decision incompatible with the authentic instrument is partially addressed in the preamble, though in somewhat ambiguous manner.[105] In the CJEU case law, it is established that the irreconcilability exists where the decisions 'entail legal consequences that are mutually exclusive'.[106]

Conflict between multiple and incompatible authentic instruments may concern the respective evidentiary effects inherent in the instruments (*instrumentum*) or the legal act or legal relation contained in the instruments (*negotium*). The former is not to be expected frequently, whereas the latter may occur where the parties subsequently modify their previous dispositions.[107] Pursuant to Recital 63 of the Matrimonial Property Regulations and Recital 62 of the Regulation on Property Consequences of a Registered Partnership, the priority conflict between incompatible authentic instruments should be resolved by the authority to which they are presented in the Member State of enforcement taking into account the circumstances *in casu*. If it is not clear from those circumstances which authentic instrument, if any, should be given priority, the question should be determined by the courts having

---

[103] See Recital 62 of the Matrimonial Property Regulations and Recital 61 of the Regulation on Property Consequences of a Registered Partnership.
[104] Utility of the clause has been questioned in P. WAUTELET, 'Article 58. Acceptation des actes authentiques' in A. BONOMI and P. WAUTELET (eds.), *Le droit européen des successions, Commentaire du règlement (UE) No 650/2012, du 4 juillet 2012*, 2nd ed., Bruylant, Brussels 2016, pp. 1228–1229.
[105] For such account in relation to the parallel Recital in the Succession Regulation see H.-P. MANSEL, 'Article 59. Acceptance of Authentic Instruments' in A.-L. CALVO CARAVACA, A. DAVÍ and H.-P. MANSEL (eds.), *The European Succession Regulation, A Commentary*, Cambridge University Press, Cambridge 2016, p. 662.
[106] Case C-145/86 *Hoffman v Krieg*, EU:C:1988:61, para. 22.
[107] P. WAUTELET, 'Article 58. Acceptation des actes authentiques' in A. BONOMI and P. WAUTELET (eds.), *Le droit européen des successions, Commentaire du règlement (UE) No 650/2012, du 4 juillet 2012*, 2nd ed., Bruylant, Brussels 2016, p. 1232.

jurisdiction under the Twin Regulations or, where the question is raised as an incidental question in the course of proceedings, by the court seised of those proceedings.

In the event of incompatibility between an authentic instrument and a decision, the same recital provides that account should be taken of the grounds of non-recognition of decisions under the pertinent one of the Twin Regulations. This should be understood as a reference to the rules on priority between irreconcilable decisions under Article 37 of the Twin Regulations. If the conflict is between a foreign authentic instrument originating form a participating Member State and a domestic decision, the latter should take priority pursuant to subparagraph (c).[108] If the conflict is between a foreign authentic instrument originating from a participating Member State and an earlier decision given in another participating Member State, in a non-participating Member State or in a third State, the latter should also prevail pursuant to subparagraph (d) provided that the earlier decision fulfils the conditions necessary for its recognition in the Member State of enforcement (actually, recognition). These provisions do not address the incompatibility between domestic authentic instruments and foreign decisions from whatever country, which may be construed to mean that domestic authentic instruments enjoy priority unless the authority in the participating Member State in question decides otherwise, which would be entirely within its discretion as far as the Twin Regulations are concerned.

The Twin Regulations are completely silent as to the conflict between authentic instruments and court settlements. In a view of the nature of court settlements, the conflict could be resolved under the same principles as the incompatibility conflict between two authentic instruments.

3.2. 'DECLARATION OF ENFORCEABILITY' OF AUTHENTIC INSTRUMENTS AND COURT SETTLEMENTS

The provisions of Articles 59 and 60 of the Twin Regulations provide rules applicable to the 'declaration of enforceability' (*exequatur*) of authentic instruments and court settlements, respectively. In order for an authentic instrument or a court settlement originating in one participating Member State and enforceable in that state to be enforceable in another participating Member State, it must be declared as such in accordance with the procedure mentioned beforehand in the Twin Regulations in the context of recognition and

---

[108] It has been submitted that such outcome would in any case be logical and automatic. Ibid., p. 1233.

declaration of enforceability of decisions. Since Articles 59 and 60 are identical, their provisions are discussed together.

3.2.1. Enforceability in the Member State of Origin

An authentic instrument or a court settlement referred to in Articles 59 and 60 of the Twin Regulations have to carry within themselves the quality of enforceability under the law of the Member State wherefrom they originated. As per Wautelet, the act has to be enforceable *ex lege* and by its own nature.[109] Thus, as opposed to the evidentiary effects which concern the mechanism of acceptance of authentic instruments, it is the enforceability effect which is at stake here. In several Member States, especially those recognising notarial deeds, authentic instruments will posses this quality which is to be ascertained under the law of the Member State of origin. The court settlements also need to produce the executory effect to be captured by Article 60 of the Twin Regulations, this effect deriving from the law of the Member State of origin.

The quality of enforceability is attested in the standardised form issued by the court or competent authority of the Member State of origin.[110] It is intended, inter alia, to detail whether entire or only some obligations in the authentic instrument or court settlement bear the quality of enforceability.

3.2.2. Procedure for Declaring the Enforceability in the Member State of Enforcement

The procedure is regulated by the rules contained in Articles 44–57 of the Twin Regulations applied *mutatis mutandis* to the declaration of enforceability of an authentic instrument or a court settlement. The application procedure is generally governed by the law of the Member State of enforcement.[111] However, certain issues are fully or partially regulated by the unified procedural rules on the Twin Regulations which are only briefly addressed here as they are already elaborated above.[112]

The proceedings for declaration of the enforceability commences by submitting the 'application' by an 'interested party' pursuant to Article 59(1) of the Twin Regulations. The notion of 'interested party' includes not only parties

---

[109] P. WAUTELET, 'Article 59. Force exécutoire des actes authentiques' in A. BONOMI and P. WAUTELET (eds.), *Le droit européen des successions, Commentaire du règlement (UE) No 650/2012, du 4 juillet 2012*, 2nd ed., Bruylant, Brussels 2016, p. 1236; P. WAUTELET, 'Article 60. Force exécutoire des transactions judiciaires' in A. BONOMI and P. WAUTELET (eds.), p. 1251.
[110] Article 60(2) in conjunction with Article 45(3)(b) of the Twin Regulations.
[111] Article 45(1) of the Twin Regulations.
[112] See above Chapter 6 of this volume.

to the authentic instrument or court settlement, but also any other person that is affected by the relevant property regime and may have a legal interest in enforcing the authentic instrument or court settlement in question.[113] These can be spouses or registered partners or third parties whose rights depend on the matrimonial property regime or property regime of the registered partnership or dispositions made by the spouses or registered partners. For instance, the creditor of one of the parties having a direct interest in the legal act or legal relationship contained in the authentic instrument or the court settlement may submit an application for declaration of enforceability.[114] Article 45(2) of the Twin Regulations prevents the application of a common requirement in national procedural laws of the Member States for a party against whom the proceedings are commenced to have a postal address or an authorised representative in the Member State of enforcement. Instead, certain unified rules on the service of documents should facilitate cross-border communication between the court or competent authority and the applicant.[115]

The 'application' submitted before the court or competent authority in the Member State of enforcement has to be accompanied by: (i) a copy of the authentic instrument or the court settlement in question, which satisfies the conditions necessary to establish its authenticity; and (ii) the attestation issued by the court or competent authority of the Member State of origin using the standardised form.[116] The said form is set out in Annex II of the Implementing Regulations. If the mentioned attestation is not submitted along with the application, the court or competent authority has three options: it may set fixed time for its submission, accept an equivalent document, or give it up entirely. The latter will be done if the court or competent authority considers that already has sufficient information to decide on the application for *exequatur*.[117] Translation or transliteration of the authentic instrument or the court settlement in question is not mandatory under the Twin Regulations, but the court or competent authority dealing with an application for declaration

---

[113] P. FRANZINA, 'Article 59. Enforceability of authentic instruments' in I. VIARENGO and P. FRANZINA (eds.), *The EU Regulations on the Property Regimes of International Couples: A Commentary*, Edward Elgar, Cheltenham 2020, p. 449.

[114] P. WAUTELET, 'Article 60. Force exécutoire des transactions judiciaires' in A. BONOMI and P. WAUTELET (eds.), *Le droit européen des successions, Commentaire du règlement (UE) No 650/2012, du 4 juillet 2012*, 2nd ed., Bruylant, Brussels 2016, p. 1253.

[115] See Regulation (EC) No 1393/2007 of the European Parliament and of the Council of 13 November 2007 on the service in the Member States of judicial and extrajudicial documents in civil or commercial matters (service of documents), and repealing Council Regulation (EC) No 1348/2000 [2007] OJ L 324, 10.12.2007, which will be replaced as of 1 July 2022 by the Regulation (EU) 2020/1784 of the European Parliament and of the Council of 25 November 2020 on the service in the Member States of judicial and extrajudicial documents in civil or commercial matters (service of documents) (recast) [2020] OJ L 405, 2.12.2020.

[116] Article 45(3) of the Twin Regulations.

[117] Article 46(1) of the Twin Regulations.

of enforceability may request it from the applicant. Important to note is that, although the requested translation has to be an official translation, i.e. done by a person qualified to do translations,[118] this person need not be from the Member State of enforcement. It is equally acceptable if the translation is done by the person qualified in any Member State. Quite important in practical terms, this is yet another manifestation of the principle of mutual recognition.

An interested person may submit the application for a declaration of enforceability to the court or competent authority of the Member State of enforcement which has jurisdiction in accordance with Article 64 of the Twin Regulations. According to this provision, the Member States had to communicate to the Commission the information on their competent courts for this purpose. The list of competent courts can be found online on the European Judicial Atlas in Civil Matters, specifically its e-Justice Portal.[119] However, pursuant to Article 44(2) of the Twin Regulations, the local jurisdiction is determined by reference to the place of domicile of the party against whom enforcement is sought, or to the place of enforcement. To determine whether, for the purposes of the procedure for declaration of enforceability, a party is domiciled in the Member State of enforcement, the court seised shall apply the internal law of that Member State.[120] Just like in the Brussels I bis Regulation[121] and other EU private international law instruments, there is no autonomous definition of domicile of a natural person. Unlike the Brussels I Regulation, the Twin Regulations contain only a unilateral conflict rule pointing to the application of one law – *lex fori*. This is probably the result of the context in which the provisions operate. When jurisdiction is established for the declaration of enforceability in the Twin Regulations there is no need to determine domicile in any other Member State but the Member State of enforcement. The same, however, might be necessary when determining jurisdiction on the merits of the dispute under the Brussels I Regulation, in particular with regard to the personal scope of many of its provisions on jurisdiction which depends on the defendant being domiciled in a Member State.[122]

The authentic instrument or the court settlement in question shall be declared enforceable immediately on completion of the formalities set out in Article 45 of the Twin Regulation.[123] Just as an applicant may request a declaration of enforceability limited to parts of an authentic instrument or a court settlement, the court or competent authority may declare partial enforceability only in respect

---

[118] Article 46(2) of the Twin Regulations.
[119] See European Judicial Atlas in Civil Matters, e-Justice Portal, <https://e-justice.europa.eu> in particular <https://e-justice.europa.eu/559/EN/matters_of_matrimonial_property_regimes?CROATIA&member=1>.
[120] Article 43 of the Twin Regulations.
[121] See Article 62 of the Brussels I bis Regulation.
[122] See e.g. Articles 4 and 7 of the Brussels I bis Regulation.
[123] Article 47 of the Twin Regulations.

to one or more matters in the authentic instrument or the court settlement.[124] No review of the authentic instrument or the court settlement, otherwise applicable to decisions under Article 37 of the Twin Regulations, is permitted in these proceedings. Moreover, the court or competent authority carrying out the proceedings for declaration of enforceability is not permitted to modify the substance of the authentic instrument or the court settlement, either in full or in part.[125] Thus, it cannot refuse to declare the enforceability of the authentic instrument or the court settlement in question if the formal requirements are met and no violation of public policy is manifest. The party against whom enforcement is sought is not at this stage of the proceedings entitled to make any submissions on the application.[126] Provisional and protective measures on the basis of the authentic instrument or the court settlement in question can be sought, pursuant to Article 53 of the Twin Regulations, to protect the interest of a particular party, pending the decision on enforceability and/or the decision on the appeal challenging the declaration of enforceability.

3.2.3. Legal Remedies against the Declaration of Enforceability

Pursuant to Articles 49 or 50 of the Twin Regulations, the decision on the application for the declaration of enforceability may be appealed by either party before the court of the Member State of enforcement communicated to the Commission in accordance with Article 64 of the Twin Regulations.[127] As provided in Article 49(5) of the Twin Regulations, an appeal may be lodged only within 30 or 60 days of service thereof, depending on the addressee's domicile. The longer period of 60 days, calculated from the date of service, either on the party against whom enforcement is sought in person or at his or her residence, applies to situations in which that party is domiciled in a Member State other than that in which the declaration of enforceability was given. In all other situations, the shorter period of 30 days is applicable.

With the purpose of assuring the respect for the principle of *autdiatur et altera pars*, the appeal proceedings have to be carried out in accordance with the rules governing the procedure in contradictory matters. Moreover, the court has to act according to Article 16 of the Twin Regulations if the party against whom enforcement is sought fails to appear before the appellate court in proceedings

---

[124] Article 54 of the Twin Regulations.
[125] P. WAUTELET, 'Article 60. Force exécutoire des transactions judiciaires' in A. BONOMI and P. WAUTELET (eds.), *Le droit européen des successions, Commentaire du règlement (UE) No 650/2012, du 4 juillet 2012*, 2nd ed., Bruylant, Brussels 2016, p. 1254.
[126] Article 47 of the Twin Regulations.
[127] See European Judicial Atlas in Civil Matters, e-Justice Portal, <https://e-justice.europa.eu> in particular <https://e-justice.europa.eu/559/EN/matters_of_matrimonial_property_regimes?CROATIA&member=1>.

concerning an appeal brought by the applicant, regardless of where that party is domiciled.

Further recourse against the decision in the appeal proceedings is envisaged in Article 50 of the Twin Regulations, and refers strictly to the procedure communicated by the Member State of enforcement to the Commission in accordance with Article 64.[128] In that case, the court with which the appeal is lodged will only revoke the declaration of enforceability if the enforcement of the authentic instrument or the court settlement would be manifestly contrary to the public policy of the Member State of enforcement. This is set out in Article 59(3) of the Twin Regulations and refers to the concept already discussed in the context of acceptance of authentic instruments and recognition, enforceability and enforcement of decisions.[129]

If the declaration of enforceability is issued and the period to launch an appeal has expired without any appeal being submitted or if the appeal was rejected, the enforcement can begin, in accordance with the law of the Member State of enforcement.

4. CONCLUDING REMARKS

The approach to regulating the circulation of authentic instruments and court settlement adopted in the Twin Regulations does not entail radical changes when compared to the parallel systems established in other EU private international law regulations. By following the same structure and replicating the respective provisions of the Succession Regulation, the Twin Regulations do, however, belong to the cluster of regulations with modernised terminology and conceptualisation of the mechanisms for extending effects of authentic instruments and court settlements between the Member States.

So far these types of acts, namely, authentic instruments and court settlements, have taken only a minor share in the total number of acts circulating between the Member States. Perhaps with the increased party autonomy in choosing the applicable law to a matrimonial property matter or a matter of property consequences of the registered partnership,[130] the reliance of spouses and registered partners on their autonomy to regulate substantive aspects of their property relations will consequentially increase as well. Hence, the significance of these acts, especially in cross-border situations, might be expected to grow thus putting the respective provisions to test more than just occasionally.

---

[128] See European Judicial Atlas in Civil Matters, e-Justice Portal, <https://e-justice.europa.eu> in particular <https://e-justice.europa.eu/559/EN/matters_of_matrimonial_property_regimes?CROATIA&member=1>.
[129] See above Section 3.1.5. of this chapter, and Chapter 6 of this volume.
[130] See above Chapter 5 of this volume.

PART III
THE INTERSECTION BETWEEN THE TWIN REGULATIONS AND OTHER EU AND NATIONAL INSTRUMENTS

CHOOSING LAW AND JURISDICTION FOR MATRIMONIAL PROPERTY AND PROPERTY CONSEQUENCES OF REGISTERED PARTNERSHIPS: ASSOCIATED RISKS

Francesco Giacomo Viterbo and Roberto Garetto*

1. Introduction 192
2. Risks Associated With Timing and Context of Choice of Law and Jurisdiction: Preliminary Remarks 193
3. Risks Associated with Choice Made before or at Time of Conclusion of Marriage or Registered Partnership 195
4. Risks of a Delayed Choice Made During Marriage or Registered Partnership 199
5. Implicit or Tacit Choice of Applicable Law Admitted 202
6. The Context Surrounding the Choice of Law: Psychological Approach to Legal Issues 205
    6.1. Legal Professionals 206
    6.2. Is there a Weaker Party to be Protected? Who is It? 209
7. Risks Associated with Inadequate Legal Advice Prior to Agreement and Safeguards to Protect Weaker Party 212
8. Concluding Remarks 217

---

* Francesco Giacomo Viterbo, Associate Professor of private law at the University of Salento, Italy.
  Roberto Garetto, PhD, research fellow in private law at the Law School of the University of Camerino, Italy.
  Francesco Giacomo Viterbo is the author of Sections 1, 2, 3, 4, 5, 7 and 8 and Roberto Garetto is the author of Sections 6, 6.1. and 6.2 of this chapter.

1. INTRODUCTION

The Matrimonial Property Regulation[1] and the Regulation on the Property Consequences of Registered Partnerships[2] (the Twin Regulations) are in line with the growing trend to value private autonomy and freedom of contract as a connecting factor for the determination of the applicable law within EU cross-border families.[3] Adopting such regulations, the European Union has strengthened the choice-of-law options for spouses and partners with regard to the property consequences of marriage and registered partnerships. This possibility can be combined with the provision of choice-of-court mechanisms in order to achieve a concentration of jurisdiction and law, and thus simplify the legal framework of reference.[4] The parties can, in fact, not only choose the law

---

[1] Council Regulation (EU) 2016/1103 of 24 June 2016 implementing enhanced cooperation in the area of jurisdiction, applicable law and the recognition and enforcement of decisions in matters of matrimonial property regimes [2016] OJ L 183/1.

[2] Council Regulation (EU) 2016/1104 of 24 June 2016 implementing enhanced cooperation in the area of jurisdiction, applicable law and the recognition and enforcement of decisions in matters of the property consequences of registered partnerships [2016] OJ L 183/30.

[3] On the role of private autonomy in national family laws, see the national reports in J.M. Scherpe (ed.), *Marital Agreements and Private Autonomy in Comparative Perspective*, Hart Publishing, Oxford 2012. On the evolution of the role of private autonomy in private international family law in the Union, see J. Gray, *Party Autonomy in EU Private International Law. Choice of Court and Choice of Law in Family Matters and Succession*, Intersentia, Cambridge 2021, pp. 15–33; P. Kinsch, 'Les fondements de l'autonomie de la volonté en droit national et en droit européen' in A. Panet, H. Fulchiron, P. Wautelet (eds.), *L'autonomie de la volonté dans les relations familiales internationales*, Bruylant, Bruxelles 2017, pp. 17–22; D. Henrich, 'Zur Parteiautonomie im europäisierten internationalen Familienrecht' in A. Verbeke, J.M. Scherpe, C. Declerck, T. Helms, P. Senaeve (eds.), *Confronting the frontiers of family and succession law: liber amicorum Walter Pintens*, vol. 1, Intersentia, Antwerp 2012, pp. 701–714; P. Gannagé, 'La Pénétration de l'autonomie de la volonté dans le droit international privé de la famille' [1992] *Revue critique de droit international privé* 425, 425–439.

[4] Party autonomy is more limited with regard to the jurisdiction. The choice-of-court mechanism is not the main connecting factor as concentration of jurisdiction is seen as a priority. In accordance with Articles 4 and 5 of Twin Regulations, where a court of a Member State is seised in matters of the succession of a spouse pursuant to the Succession Regulation, or in order to rule on an application for divorce, legal separation or marriage annulment pursuant to the Brussels II a Regulation, the courts of that state shall have jurisdiction to rule on matters of the matrimonial property regime arising in connection with those applications, provided that, in certain cases, there is a specific consent of the parties to the concentration. Only if no court of a Member State has jurisdiction pursuant to Articles 4 or 5 or in cases other than those provided for in those Articles, the choice-of-court mechanism applies with a preference for the parallelism of *forum* and *ius* pursuant to Article 7. On the principle of concentration, which is the main criterion for determining jurisdiction, making the application of the choice-of-court mechanism residual, see L. Ruggeri in M.J. Cazorla González, M. Giobbi, J. Kramberger Škerl, L. Ruggeri (eds.), *Property Relations of Cross-Border Couples in the European Union*, Edizioni Scientifiche Italiane, Napoli 2020, p. 60; P. Bruno, *I regolamenti europei sui regimi patrimoniali dei coniugi e delle unioni registrate. Commento ai Regolamenti (UE) 24 giugno 2016, nn. 1103 e 1104 applicabili dal 29 gennaio 2019*, Giuffrè, Milano 2019, p. 102. See also Chapter 4 of this volume.

applicable to their property regime (*professio iuris*), but also attribute jurisdiction to the authority of the same state whose law is applicable.

Party autonomy is an important tool of EU private international family law. The parties are in a position to make an optimal choice that is best suited to their concrete situation; to adjust their conduct and foresee the associated legal consequences. This also leads to greater legal certainty, stability and predictability of solutions since the costs and delays arising from the need to identify the applicable law on the basis of objective connecting factors can be easily avoided.

The exercise of autonomy by couples in a cross-border context, however, is not without risk and uncertainty as to how and to what extent it can be conducted in practice, which may limit or jeopardise the above-mentioned benefits.

The purpose of this chapter is to analyse the main risks associated with both the timing and the specific context in which the agreement on *electio fori* and/or the choice of law applicable to the matrimonial property regime or the property consequences of registered partnerships is concluded.

2. RISKS ASSOCIATED WITH TIMING AND CONTEXT OF CHOICE OF LAW AND JURISDICTION: PRELIMINARY REMARKS

First, the timing of choice of law and choice of court agreements will be analysed. In fact, timing is very important as the timing of the choice may hold further implications in more than one respect.

First, Recital 45 of the Matrimonial Property Regulation and Recital 44 of the Regulation on the Property Consequences of a Registered Partnership specify that spouses and registered partners, respectively, are authorised to choose the law applicable to the property consequences of their relationship 'at any moment': the spouses, 'before the marriage, at the time of conclusion of the marriage or during the course of the marriage'; the partners, 'before the registration of the partnership, at the time of the registration of the partnership or during the course of the registered partnership'. Consistent with these provisions is the wording of Article 22(1) which speaks of 'spouses or future spouses' and 'partners and future partners'.[5]

The technique used by the European legislator in the Twin Regulations is very similar to that of the previous regulations on family matters. The spouses may agree to designate the law applicable to legal separation and divorce 'at any time, but at the latest by the time the court is seized', according to Article 5(1) and (2)

---

[5]   C. KOHLER, 'Choice of the Applicable Law' in P. FRANZINA and I. VIARENGO (eds.), *The EU Regulations on the Property Regimes of International Couples. A Commentary*, Edward Elgar, Cheltenham 2020, p. 201.

of the Rome III Regulation.[6] Article 8 of the Hague Protocol of 23 November 2007 on the Law Applicable to Maintenance Obligations provides that the maintenance creditor and debtor may '*at any time*' choose the law applicable to their relationship.[7]

When drafting the Twin Regulations, the European legislator primarily had couples in mind who at some point in their marriage or partnership changed their personal circumstances in an aspect which was relevant to the Regulations, i.e. by changing their citizenship or, more commonly, relocating their habitual residence to another state. In this perspective, the only way to give certainty to the regulation of such relationships is to take a snapshot of the situation of the couple at the time the agreement on *professio iuris* and *electio fori* is concluded.[8]

It follows from Articles 7(1) and 22(1) of the Twin Regulations that the point in time at which the agreement is concluded determines the object of the choice available to the couple, i.e. the range of laws (and courts) eligible for choice.[9] It follows from Article 23(2), (3) and (4) of the Twin Regulations that the point in time at which the agreement is concluded also determines the additional formal requirements for the validity of the agreement, where applicable.

> Consider a couple of Greek nationals who marry in Italy and transfer their habitual residence there. After a few years they move to Spain where they also acquire Spanish nationality, but a few years later they settle in Portugal. If they were to agree on the applicable law in the 'Italian period', the choice would be limited between Greek and Italian law, and in each case it would have to be verified that the agreement met the formal requirements of validity laid down by Italian law. If, on the other hand, they were to conclude the agreement in the 'Portuguese period', the range of options would no longer include Italian law (that is the applicable law until the parties make a choice), but Greek, Spanish and Portuguese law, and in each case it would have to

---

[6] A. Zanobetti, 'Divorzio all'europea. Il regolamento UE Rome III sulla legge applicabile allo scioglimento del matrimonio e alla separazione personale' [2012] *La nuova giurisprudenza civile commentata* 250, 255–257.

[7] Emphasis added. This provision allows the parties to choose the law applicable to the maintenance obligation at any time and even before a dispute arises: A. Bonomi, *Explanatory Report on the Hague Protocol of 23 November 2007 on the law applicable to maintenance obligations*, HCCH Publications, The Hague 2013, p. 53.

[8] In order to simplify the analysis that follows, the problems linked to whether the marriage or registered partnership is concluded before or after the entry into force of the Twin Regulations will be omitted.

[9] The Twin Regulations make it possible for spouses and registered partners to choose 'among the laws with which they have close links because of habitual residence or their nationality', according to Recital 45 of the Matrimonial Property Regulation and Recital 44 of the Regulation on the Property Consequences of a Registered Partnership. In addition, registered partners may choose 'the law of the state under whose law the registered partnership was created', pursuant to Article 22(1)(c) of the Regulation on the Property Consequences of a Registered Partnership.

be verified that the agreement met the formal requirements of validity laid down by Portuguese law.[10]

Another relevant factor to be taken into account is how the couple makes the choice of law and jurisdiction and, in particular, the circumstances under which the agreement is concluded.[11] In this respect, the Twin Regulations emphasise the formal requirements of the agreement, with far less emphasis on the context in which the parties make the decision.[12]

Nevertheless, some risks for the couple or for the weaker party of the couple may result from their factual approach to legal issues as well as from inadequate legal assistance by the legal professional (e.g. notary, lawyer) on whom the parties have relied. Some uncertainties concerning the conclusion of the agreement may arise from the question of whether the designation of the applicable law has to be explicit or may also be implicit. This could occur when the parties stipulate an agreement by which they organise their property regime after the marriage or registered partnership without an express choice of law.

Other risks can also be linked to the interactions among the current EU instruments on matrimonial property, registered partnerships, divorce, legal separation and maintenance obligations, all of which demand a greater margin of autonomy within family law.[13]

3. RISKS ASSOCIATED WITH CHOICE MADE BEFORE OR AT TIME OF CONCLUSION OF MARRIAGE OR REGISTERED PARTNERSHIP

The main advantage of the choice of applicable law as provided under Article 22 is to secure a stability and foreseeability with respect to the applicable law. If the parties have concluded upon such an agreement, the chosen law remains applicable despite any changes in their personal situations, and regardless of the authority seised in the event of a dispute. In particular, the change of the couple's habitual residence does not cause a change of the applicable law, unlike in the case of an absence of choice under Article 26 of the Twin Regulations.

---

[10] In addition, see Recital 47 of the Matrimonial Property Regulation according to which 'If, *at the time the agreement is concluded*, the spouses are habitually resident in different Member States which lay down different formal rules, compliance with the formal rules of one of these states should suffice. If, *at the time the agreement is concluded*, only one of the spouses is habitually resident in a Member State which lays down additional formal rules, those rules should be complied with' (emphasis added).
[11] On this issue, see below, Sections 5 and 7.
[12] On this issue, see below, Sections 6, 6.1 and 6.2.
[13] For more detail, see below, Section 7.

The possibility offered to the Member States bound by the Twin Regulations of imposing additional formal requirements for the agreement to be valid does, however, introduce an element of uncertainty into the choice-of-law mechanism. The validity of the agreement could be challenged long after its conclusion on the initiative of one of the spouses or partners who has an interest in the application of a different law.

Identifying the couple's habitual residence at the time of the choice is an operation that, in the case of cross-border couples, may prove to be the subject of conflicting assessments. The notion of 'habitual residence' has to be interpreted autonomously. It is a *factual situation* based on a 'genuine link' between the individual and the state and, in family relationships, it takes the form of the place where 'there are symptomatic indicators linked to the continuity of the couple's life or to the parties' intention to organise life together'.[14] However, its assessment must be made taking into account all of the aspects of the specific case, in the light of the particular context in which the criterion must operate.[15] Such a criterion is linked to a place which may change easily and quickly over time, giving rise to uncertainties in its application. In this instance, for the validity of the agreement, compliance with the formal rules of one of the states linked to the couple's life would suffice. This solution seems to be consistent with the principle of preservation of the act of private autonomy, which is a constant in European legislation.[16]

---

[14] Case C-279/93, *Finanzamt Köln-Altstadt v Schumacker*, ECLI:EU:C:1995:31; Case C-391/97, *Gschwind v Finanzamt Aachen-Außenstadt*, ECLI:EU:C:1999:409; Case C-87/99, *Patrik Zurstrassen v Administration des contributions directes*, ECLI:EU:C:2000:251. For more details on the concept of "habitual residence" in family relationships, see M. GIOBBI, in M.J. CAZORLA GONZÁLEZ, M. GIOBBI, J. KRAMBERGER ŠKERL, L. RUGGERI (eds.), *Property Relations of Cross-Border Couples in the European Union*, Edizioni Scientifiche Italiane, Napoli 2020, pp. 75–81.

[15] Case C-497/10 PPU, *B. Mercredi v R. Chaffe*, ECLI:EU:C:2010:829, point 47. For a broader analysis of case law, see A. LIMANTE, 'Establishing Habitual Residence of Adults under the Brussels IIa Regulation: Best Practices from National Case-Law' [2018] *Journal of Private International Law* 160–181. The adjective 'habitual' indicates the requirement of a certain permanence and stability and could therefore imply the condition of a certain passage of time in order to qualify a residence. However, the CJEU held that 11 years of residence of an Irish citizen in Germany, caused by medical necessity, was not sufficient for the previous habitual residence to be considered modified (Case C-255/13, *I c. Health Service Executive*, ECLI:EU:C:2014:1291). According to a different perspective, the adjective would primarily serve to prevent a mere occasional stay, even if prolonged in time, from being considered as 'residence'. This may not be true. A person who moves from a previous residence, which is abandoned, to a new one may immediately acquire habitual residence in the new place of habitation without the need for any lapse of time. What matters are the characteristics of the specific case, which must be assessed on a case-by-case basis, although it is undeniable that the duration of the stay may be a useful element in assessing habitual residence: A. ZANOBETTI, 'La residenza abituale nel diritto internazionale privato: spunti di riflessione' (2019) 2 *Liber Amicorum Angelo Davì. La vita giuridica internazionale nell'età della globalizzazione* 1361, 1399–1402.

[16] See L. RUGGERI, in M.J. CAZORLA GONZÁLEZ, M. GIOBBI, J. KRAMBERGER ŠKERL, L. RUGGERI (eds.), *Property Relations of Cross-Border Couples in the European Union*, Edizioni Scientifiche

Additionally, a choice of law and *forum* before or at the time of the marriage or registered partnership may have other drawbacks. If a long time passes after the conclusion of the agreement and a judicial procedure has to be initiated, the applicable law and the competent court are always identified by looking back at the past with the risk that at the time of filing the application, no spouse or partner has a concrete connection with that particular state anymore. If we consider the example above, the Greek couple could lose the connection to Italy during the Portuguese period. A possible solution to this problem, however, is provided by the Regulations themselves, where they specify that the couple may *at any time* change the applicable law, although such a change by the spouses or partners 'should not have retrospective effect unless they expressly so stipulate'.[17] Dynamic couples are thus given the opportunity to adapt the law applicable to the property consequences of their marriage or partnership to their changed life and current personal circumstances.[18]

Given that the parties are expressly allowed to choose applicable law before the conclusion of the marriage or registered partnership, the parties' autonomy might be hampered where the designated law is the law of a state that limits prenuptial agreements foreseeing division of property in case of divorce. On the other hand, if the parties designate the applicable law for the sole purpose of binding themselves to a prenuptial agreement permitted by that law, the entire agreement may not be valid under the *lex fori* because of its incompatibility with public policy (*ordre public*).

However, these risks seem to have been greatly mitigated in the EU.

In some Member States, the difficulties that emerged during the twentieth century in connection with the idea that agreements foreseeing consequences in case of separation or divorce were against public policy and void, seem to have been definitively overcome. A good example here is the case of the United Kingdom[19] where 'the courts have always adopted a more nuanced approach to

---

Italiane, Napoli 2020, p. 67. In accordance with a different opinion, it would be advisable, at the time of the agreement, to comply with any stricter formal requirements that may be laid down by the legal systems with which the spouses have significant points of contact in their lives, in order to avoid the agreement then running the risk of being considered invalid: A. ZANOBETTI, 'Divorzio all'europea. Il regolamento UE Rome III sulla legge applicabile allo scioglimento del matrimonio e alla separazione personale' [2012] *La nuova giurisprudenza civile commentata* 256.

[17] See Recital 46 of the Matrimonial Property Regulation and Recital 45 of the Regulation on the Property Consequences of a Registered Partnership.

[18] L. RADEMACHER, 'Changing the Past: Retroactive Choice of Law and the Protection of Third Parties in the European Regulations on Patrimonial Consequences of Marriage' (2018) 10(1) *Cuadernos de Derecho Transnacional* 7, 15.

[19] For more details, see N. LOWE, 'Prenuptial agreements. The Developing English Position' in A. VERBEKE, J.M. SCHERPE, C. DECLERCK, T. HELMS, P. SENAEVE (eds.), *Confronting the frontiers of family and succession law: liber amicorum Walter Pintens*, vol. 1, Intersentia, Antwerp 2012, pp. 867–885.

ante- and post-nuptial agreements', 'giving some and, in some circumstances, decisive weight to ante-nuptial agreements'.[20] Moreover, it may be noted that even in those Member States where domestic family law is still an obstacle to the admissibility of prenuptial agreements, the courts had held that such legal restrictions do not apply to agreements concluded by international couples. The case of Italy is emblematic, where the Court of Cassation affirmed the compatibility with international public policy of an agreement concluded between two US spouses residing in Italy who intended to regulate their mutual property relations in case of divorce.[21]

From a more general perspective, certain risks may be associated with an *optio legis* that enables parties to enter into agreements that are not permitted under the *lex fori*.[22] This question may be resolved by taking into account the recent decision of the Court of Justice of the European Union (CJEU) in the *JE v KF* case.[23] Applying the principle laid down in that judgment,

---

[20] See *Radmacher (Formerly Granatino) v Granatino* [2010] UKSC 42, [2010] 2 FLR 1900, point 62. In the context of common law jurisdictions to whom the institution of matrimonial property regime is unknown as such, the judge may take into account the provisions of a marriage contract concluded under foreign law, which, however, is not binding under English law.

[21] Cass. civ., 3 May 1984, n. 2682, in *Giurisprudenza italiana*, 1984, p. 370. For a recent analysis of this issue, see G. PERLINGIERI and G. ZARRA, *Ordine pubblico interno e internazionale tra caso concreto e sistema ordinamentale*, Edizioni Scientifiche Italiane, Napoli 2019. In Italy, the thesis that prenuptial agreements in contemplation of separation and divorce are void has been based on the interpretation of Article 160 of the Civil Code. However, the contrary opinion is prevailing in doctrine: see G. CHIAPPETTA, 'La "semplificazione" della crisi familiare: dall'autorità all'autonomia' in P. PERLINGIERI and S. GIOVA (eds.), *Comunioni di vita e familiari tra libertà, sussidiarietà e inderogabilità*, Edizioni Scientifiche Italiane, Napoli 2019, pp. 435 et seq.; T.V. RUSSO, 'I contratti prematrimoniali' in F.G. VITERBO and F. DELL'ANNA MISURALE (eds.), 'Nuove sfide del diritto di famiglia. Il ruolo dell'interprete' [2018] *Quaderni di 'Diritto delle successioni e della famiglia'* 193,193–222; G. OBERTO, 'Contratti prematrimoniali e accordi preventivi sulla crisi familiare' [2012] *Famiglia e diritto* 69, 69–103.

[22] Consider as an example Article 42 of the Croatian Family Act pursuant to which it is not permissible to choose foreign law as applicable to property relations by way of marriage contract. On such restriction to party autonomy see D. VRBLJANAC, 'The Matrimonial Property Regime Regulation: selected issues concerning applicable law. Working paper' in J. KRAMBERGER ŠKERL, L. RUGGERI and F.G. VITERBO (eds.), *Case studies and best practices analysis to enhance EU Family and Succession Law. Working Paper* (2019) 3 *Quaderni degli Annali della Facoltà Giuridica dell'Università di Camerino* 185, 192–196.

[23] Case C-249/19, *JE v KF*, ECLI:EU:C:2020:570, point 43, where the following principle is affirmed: 'in a situation such as that at issue in the main proceedings, in which the court having jurisdiction considers that the foreign law applicable pursuant to the provisions of Regulation Rome III permits an application for divorce only if that divorce has been preceded by a legal separation of three years, whereas the law of the forum does not lay down any procedural rules in relation to legal separation, that court must nevertheless, since it cannot itself declare such a separation, determine whether the substantive conditions laid down in the applicable foreign law are satisfied and make that finding in the context of the divorce proceedings before it'.

it may be held that, if the court having jurisdiction considers that the foreign law applicable pursuant to provisions of the Twin Regulations permits the conclusion of prenuptial agreements, whereas the *lex fori* does not provide for such an option, that court must nevertheless determine whether the substantive conditions laid down in the applicable foreign law are satisfied and make that finding in the context of the proceedings before it.

4. RISKS OF A DELAYED CHOICE MADE DURING MARRIAGE OR REGISTERED PARTNERSHIP

A choice of law made before or at the time of the conclusion of the marriage or registered partnership inherently has a prospective effect only. The matrimonial property regime (whether set by law or based on a particular party's agreement) starts with the marriage (registration of partnership).

If the law applicable to the matrimonial property regime or the property consequences of a registered partnership is *designated* by the couple during the course of the relationship, e.g. some years after the conclusion of the marriage or registered partnership, the choice of law agreed upon by the parties has the purpose to *change* the law applicable to their property relations. Indeed, until the conclusion of the agreement, property relationships are governed by the law designated under Article 26 of the Twin Regulations. The question is whether, in the period preceding the choice-of-law agreement, the entitlement to, for instance, purchases made by one of the spouses or partners should depend on the law applied at the time of the purchase, or whether the law designated *ex post* by the parties pursuant to Article 22 of the Twin Regulations takes precedence and applies retrospectively. In this respect, both Regulations state that a change of the applicable law 'shall have prospective effect only', unless the parties 'agree otherwise', pursuant to Article 22(2). This means that the 'new' law may also have retrospective effect provided that the parties 'expressly so stipulate'.[24] Furthermore, such a 'retroactive change of the applicable law' may not 'adversely affect the rights of third parties' deriving from the previous law (and property regime), pursuant to Article 22(3) of the Twin Regulations.[25]

---

[24] See Recital 46 of Regulation N. 1103 and Recital 45 of Regulation N. 1104.
[25] Changing the past may also come at the expense of third parties. On this topic, see D. MARTINY, 'The Effects of Marital Property Agreements in Respect of Third Parties' in A. VERBEKE, J.M. SCHERPE, C. DECLERCK, T. HELMS, P. SENAEVE (eds.), *Confronting the frontiers of family and succession law: liber amicorum Walter Pintens*, vol. 1, Intersentia, Antwerp 2012, pp. 903–927; L. RADEMACHER, 'Changing the past: retroactive choice of law and the protection of third parties in the european regulations on patrimonial consequences of marriages and registered partnerships' (2018) 10(1) *Cuadernos de Derecho Transnacional* 7–11.

It is necessary to focus on the two possible scenarios mentioned above. The first scenario arises when the parties expressly agree on a retroactive change of the applicable law. Naturally, this solution will not affect the property rights which were ended before the agreement was concluded. For instance, any and all property sold by the couple before the conclusion of the choice-of-law agreement remains subject to the law in force at the time of disposal, by virtue of the principle *tempus regit actum*.[26] On the other hand, property rights acquired by each spouse or partner during the term of the previous matrimonial property regime (e.g. property bought after the marriage but before the change of applicable law) will be subject to the application of the 'new' law chosen by the parties.

The second scenario arises when the parties agree to change the applicable law without stipulating the retroactive effect of the chosen law. In other words, the applicable law is set to apply only to the future.

One problem which arises in such a situation concerns the fragmentation of the laws governing the parties' property relationships. The law designated under Article 26 of the Twin Regulations – i.e. in most cases the law of the state of the 'first common habitual residence' after the marriage or 'the law of the state under whose law the registered partnership was created' – shall apply until the conclusion of the choice-of-law agreement. The law designated by the parties shall apply to their property relationships thereafter. However, most national family laws provide for rules, which necessitate the dissolution and liquidation of a property regime that ceases to govern a marriage or partnership. Such a liquidation typically will not lie in the spouses' or partners' interest and will be considered an undesirable complication.[27]

Another problem may arise if the parties had previously concluded a matrimonial property agreement or a partnership property agreement under the law of a state in which they did not have their 'first common habitual residence'.

> Consider the case of two Italian citizens who live in Germany and arrange their marriage in Italy where they sign an agreement opting for the 'separation of assets' regime in accordance with Article 215 et seq. of the Italian Civil Code. They continue to live in Germany for a number of years and finally decide to settle in Italy, where they enter into an agreement by which they choose Italian law without specifying its retrospective effect. The couple could think that, in accordance with their agreements, Italian law applies overall to their matrimonial property relationships. However, this is not necessarily the case.

---

[26] N. Cipriani, 'Rapporti patrimoniali tra coniugi, norme di conflitto e variabilità della legge applicabile' (2009) 1 *Rassegna di diritto civile* 19, 54.

[27] L. Rademacher, 'Changing the Past: Retroactive Choice of Law and the Protection of Third Parties in the European Regulations on Patrimonial Consequences of Marriage' (2018) 10(1) *Cuadernos de Derecho Transnacional* 7, 15.

The will of the parties is an important element in stabilising the appropriate regulation of their property relationships. Nevertheless, the question arises as to whether or not the earlier matrimonial property agreement concluded by the parties in Italy at the time of their marriage can be interpreted as an implicit choice-of-law agreement, with the result that Italian law also applies to their property relationships prior to their transfer to Italy. If not, the law of the first common habitual residence, that is to say German law, would apply to those relationships.

This question will be analysed in the next section. However, a hermeneutical solution aimed at strengthening the parties' autonomy might be the reason to interpret Article 22 of the Twin Regulations differently. Where this provision refers to the parties' freedom to 'change the applicable law', it might be interpreted as covering only the change of the law chosen by the parties on the basis of an earlier agreement, but not of the law applicable under Article 26 of the Twin Regulations. The notion of 'change of applicable law' would thus exclude the case of a *designation* of applicable law made later than the time at which the marriage or registered partnership is concluded. In such a case, the choice of applicable law would also have a *retrospective* effect, unless the parties agree otherwise.

The CJEU interpreting Article 4(3) of 2007 Hague Protocol on the Law Applicable to Maintenance Obligations,[28] recently stated that 'the risk of applying different laws in successive proceedings between the same parties appears to be inherent in the system of conflict-of-law rules'.[29] The same might be stated for the risk of applying different laws in the same proceedings between the same parties in the system of conflict of law rules laid down in the Twin Regulations. Nevertheless, these risks should be limited whenever a different interpretation of the relevant rules is possible in view of the rights to be protected. The problem is not only to avoid a fragmentation of the couple's property regime, but rather to prevent the risk that the choice of the law applicable to the property relations as a whole and at the time when the need for a settlement of interests arises will be brought forth.

---

[28] Hague Protocol of 23 November 2007 on the Law Applicable to Maintenance Obligations.
[29] Case C-214/17, *Alexander Mölk v Valentina Mölk*, ECLI:EU:C:2018:744. The Court stated that 'Article 4(3) of the Hague Protocol covers only a situation where the creditor indirectly chooses the law of the forum in the context of proceedings which he has initiated before the competent authority of the state where the debtor has his habitual residence and does not extend to subsequent proceedings initiated after the decision in the initial proceedings has acquired the force of *res judicata*'. This interpretation is open to criticism since, as the Portuguese Government argues, it leads to the paradox that competing applications in respect of a short period during which there has been no change in the habitual residence of the parties have to be examined under different legal systems. It should be emphasised that, in subsequent proceedings initiated by the debtor, the determination of the applicable law would have to be dependent on the initial choice of the law and *forum* made by the creditor under Article 4(3) of the Hague Protocol, in accordance with its objective of protecting the creditor, regarded as the weaker party in his dealings with the debtor.

5. IMPLICIT OR TACIT CHOICE OF APPLICABLE LAW ADMITTED

The parties may agree to designate or change the applicable law as long as the marriage or registered partnership lasts, ultimately in proceedings for divorce or dissolution of the partnership.[30] Nor can it be ruled out that agreement on the law applicable to the matrimonial property regime or the property consequences of the registered partnership may be part of the negotiation of the overall terms of the separation or divorce. Indeed, on the one hand, the parties might not be aware of this opportunity until the break-up of their relationship; on the other hand, the previous agreement might not reflect the parties' needs and circumstances at the time of divorce (or separation). In both scenarios, the parties will discuss possible solutions for such situations.

First, the concentration of jurisdiction takes priority. In accordance with Article 4, concentration of jurisdiction is foreseen in the event of death of one of the spouses. Article 5 of the Twin Regulations provides that where a court of a Member State is seised in order to rule on an application for divorce, legal separation or marriage annulment pursuant to the Brussels II bis Regulation, the courts of that state shall have jurisdiction to rule on matters of the matrimonial property regime or the property consequences of the registered partnership arising in connection with those applications. In addition, in certain cases, a specific agreement between the parties on the concentration will be required.[31]

A point which begs clarity concerns the situation in which the couple has previously concluded an agreement on the law applicable to separation and divorce in accordance with the provisions of the Rome III Regulation, but after the entry into force of the Twin Regulations has not concluded any further agreements. The question arises whether, in such a case, the law designated by the couple in contemplation of separation and divorce can also be considered applicable to the property consequences of the marriage or registered partnership. This means clarifying whether it can be assumed that the parties have made an implicit and, nonetheless, acceptable choice to this effect, even in the absence of their express request.

---

[30] C. KOHLER, 'Choice of the Applicable Law' in P. FRANZINA and I. VIARENGO (eds.), *The EU Regulations on the Property Regimes of International Couples. A Commentary*, Edward Elgar, Cheltenham 2020, p. 201 et seq.

[31] The cases referred to above are those set out in Article 5(2) of the Matrimonial Property Regulation. On the other hand, Article 5(1) of the Regulation on the Property Consequences of a Registered Partnership provides that 'Where a court of a Member State is seised to rule on the dissolution or annulment of a registered partnership, the courts of that state shall have jurisdiction to rule on the property consequences of the registered partnership arising in connection with that case of dissolution or annulment, *where the partners so agree*' (emphasis added).

It has been pointed out that the question of whether the designation of the applicable law has to be explicit or may also be implicit has to be given a uniform answer, on the basis of an 'autonomous interpretation' of the concept of 'agreement' under Article 22(1) of the Twin Regulations.[32] Thus, the choice of the applicable law should be 'expressly or clearly demonstrated by the terms of the contract *or* the circumstances of the case'.[33] However, some risks are associated with this view.

> To return to the case of the Italian couple who organise their marriage in Italy but are habitually resident in Germany, consider the following two scenarios:
>
> Scenario A
> At the time of the marriage, they concluded a marital agreement before an Italian notary designating the 'separation of assets' according to Article 215 et seq. of the Italian Civil Code as their matrimonial property regime. It may be argued that the choice of Italian law as the applicable law under Article 22(1) of the Matrimonial Property Regulation should be clearly demonstrated by the *terms of that agreement*.[34]
>
> Scenario B
> After the marriage, they concluded a choice-of-law agreement before a German notary designating German law as the law applicable to divorce and legal separation pursuant to Article 5(1) of the Rome III Regulation. Could these *circumstances* suffice to demonstrate that German law is the law the parties have chosen to apply to their relationships, implicitly including the matrimonial property regime?

In both examples, it should be noted that the 'terms of the agreement' and the 'circumstances' indicated in each scenario do not appear sufficient to answer the question of whether they amount to an implicit agreement on the choice of law applicable to the matrimonial property regime in accordance with Article 22(1) of the Matrimonial Property Regulation. The definition of what is a choice-of-law agreement under Article 22(1) is a point to be assessed on the basis of the criteria and requirements set out in Articles 22–24 and the relevant Recitals of the Twin Regulations, as well as those left to national law. In light of this approach, Recital 47 of the Matrimonial Property Regulation and Recital 46 of the Regulation on the Property Consequences of a Registered Partnership deserve special attention. These Recitals point out that the rules on

---

[32] C. KOHLER, 'Choice of the Applicable Law' in P. FRANZINA and I. VIARENGO (eds.), *The EU Regulations on the Property Regimes of International Couples. A Commentary*, Edward Elgar, Cheltenham 2020, p. 201 et seq.
[33] Ibid., p. 202. Emphasis added. The author justifies this interpretative solution with a reference to Article 3(1) of the Rome I Regulation, where the same issue arises. In his view, 'there is no plausible reason why a choice which is clearly demonstrated by the terms of an agreement between the parties or the circumstances which surround it should not be admitted under Article 22(1)'.
[34] Ibid.

the material and formal validity of a choice-of-law agreement laid down in the Twin Regulations are intended to facilitate the '*informed choice*'[35] of the spouses or partners and to ensure that they '*are aware of the implications of their choice*'.[36]

Having pointed that out, can one be sure that in the two examples given above the spouses made a genuinely informed choice of the law applicable to the matrimonial property regime? No, but this requirement is very unlikely to be met in scenario B, whereas it is only possible in scenario A. In both scenarios, the information that the parties received from the notary before or at the time they concluded the agreement has to be ascertained in the light of the concrete context surrounding their choice. The spouses should be properly informed by the notary not only of the possibility of choosing between German and Italian law, but also of the implications of this choice in view of the matrimonial property regimes under those laws. This information or advisory activity should be clear from the content of the agreement.

Thus, an implicit agreement by the couple on the law applicable to the matrimonial property regime or the property consequences of registered partnership can only be admitted if evidence is provided that the parties had the opportunity to make a genuinely informed choice about the range of options and their implications, on the basis of appropriate legal advice. Therefore, in scenario A, if this information was not provided to the parties, their marital property agreement cannot be interpreted as a choice-of-law agreement. It follows that if a few years later the parties choose to apply Italian law to their matrimonial property regime without an express agreement on its retrospective effect, German law will apply to their matrimonial property relations prior to the change of applicable law.

In view of these arguments and the fact that Article 23 of the Twin Regulations lays down specific rules on the formal validity of the agreement, as a rule the choice or change of applicable law may not be tacit.[37]

There is nothing stopping the spouse or partners from entering into a choice-of-law agreement governing their property relationships at the time the court is seised or before the court during the course of the proceeding.[38] However, such a procedural agreement on the choice of applicable law might

---

[35] This wording is used in both Recitals. Emphasis added.
[36] This wording is used in both Recitals. Emphasis added. It should be emphasised that these requirements are not laid down for the choice-of-court agreement.
[37] On this point see P. BRUNO, *I regolamenti europei sui regimi patrimoniali dei coniugi e delle unioni registrate. Commento ai Regolamenti (UE) 24 giugno 2016, nn. 1103 e 1104 applicabili dal 29 gennaio 2019*, Giuffrè, Milano 2019, p. 183; K. ZABRODINA, 'The law applicable to property regimes and agreements on the choice of court according to Regulations (EU) 1103 and 1104 of 2016' in J. KRAMBERGER ŠKERL, L. RUGGERI and F.G. VITERBO (eds.), *Case studies and best practices analysis to enhance EU Family and Succession Law. Working Paper* (2019) 3 *Quaderni degli Annali della Facoltà Giuridica dell'Università di Camerino* 199 et seq.
[38] Pursuant to Article 5(3) of the Rome III Regulation, the spouses may also designate the law applicable before the court in the course of the proceeding, 'if the law of the *forum*

not be tacitly concluded through both the claim brought forth by one spouse or partner before the court to invoke the application of the property regime provided for by that law and the lack of opposition by the other spouse or partner in the first defence. In such a case, it is up to the court to draw the parties' attention to the applicable law and examine whether they are informed of the implications of their choice, as required by the Twin Regulations.

The major role given to private autonomy makes it necessary to rigorously verify the presence of a clear and express agreement reached by the parties on the applicable law.[39]

6. THE CONTEXT SURROUNDING THE CHOICE OF LAW: PSYCHOLOGICAL APPROACH TO LEGAL ISSUES

While in other sectors, such as commerce, the approach to legal issues normally takes place on a level of deeper awareness, as far as the family is concerned, this is not always true.

A critical point can be identified at this level. Indeed, family law increasingly combines emotional aspects with the patrimonial approach that characterises other areas of law. When celebrating a marriage or establishing a registered partnership, the legal aspects related to the property relationships are often neglected by the couple that tends to focus more on the affective and relational dimension.[40] Only in a subsequent phase of dissolution of the marriage (or registered partnership) is the legal sphere significantly taken into account.[41]

Of course, the matrimonial property regime is also relevant when the marriage is going well (as well as the property consequences, in the event of registered partnerships). Property regime, indeed, may adversely affect

---

so provides'. It should be noted that this provision is not present in the Twin Regulations, but there is no reason to preclude the spouses from designating the law before the court in the course of the proceeding, regardless of what is provided for by the law of the *forum*.

[39] L. RUGGERI in M.J. CAZORLA GONZÁLEZ, M. GIOBBI, J. KRAMBERGER ŠKERL, L. RUGGERI (eds.), *Property Relations of Cross-Border Couples in the European Union*, Edizioni Scientifiche Italiane, Napoli 2020, p. 66. This is confirmed by the case law of the CJEU: see Case C-387/98, *Coreck Maritime GmbH c. Handelsveem BV and others*, ECLI:EU:C:2000:606, point 13; Case C-543/10, *Refcomp SpA c. Axa Corporate Solutions Assurance SA*, ECLI:EU:C:2013:62, points 27–28.

[40] J. WIGHTMAN, 'Intimate relationships, relational contract theory, and the reach of contract' (2000) *Feminist Legal Studies* 93, 112.

[41] K. BAKER, 'Property Rules Meet Feminist Needs: Respecting Autonomy by Valuing Connection' (1998) 59 *Ohio State Law Journal* 1523, 1578.

the rights of third parties (e.g. creditors of one of the spouses or registered partners).[42]

It must be taken into account that more often than not, partners tend not to be particularly vigilant even in cases where the negotiation of the property aspects of their relationship takes place. Psychologically, the spouses or partners are not supposed to realistically contemplate the risks of break up, nor consider the adversities that may occur in the couple's future.[43] Only in the event of death or divorce, the choice made with regard to the applicable law and the jurisdiction appears to be essential.

Regardless of the state of mind, when the couple opts for the choice of the law and/or jurisdiction, it is implicit that the choice made is in the interests of both the parties. Consideration should be given to the possibility that the agreement is aimed at pursuing personal convenience for only one of the parties. Sometimes the convenience can consist of particular purposes referable to a specific legal system.[44] At other times, the aim can be simply to reduce the costs related to possible future judgments.

There is, however, a real risk that one party will derive more advantage from the choice of law (and jurisdiction) to the detriment of the other party, and that the other party will not be aware of this.[45] The recourse to professionals such as consultants reduces this risk.

6.1. LEGAL PROFESSIONALS

Since the choice of law, requiring the support of legal professionals, involves costs, the parties will usually evaluate whether the benefits obtainable through the exercise of autonomy – in the specific case – justify the expense.[46]

---

[42] The particular creditor protection provided by the community regime is often controversial, mainly among scholars of common law. See A.B. CARROLL, 'The Superior Position of the Creditor in the Community Property Regime: Has the Community Become a Mere Creditor Collection Device' (2007) 47 *Santa Clara Law Review* 1, 2: 'Creditor protection may be a worthy societal goal, at least generally speaking. But the community regime has gone so far to provide such protection that it has significantly departed from its teleology'.

[43] G. LEVINGER, 'A Social Psychological Perspective on Marital Dissolution' (1976) 32 *Journal of Social Issues* 21, 37: 'A firmly committed spouse does not yearn for separation and may never even think of divorce.'

[44] See a case study in M.J. CAZORLA GONZÁLEZ, 'Ley aplicable al régimen económico matrimonial después de la disolución del matrimonio tras la entrada en vigor del Reglamento UE 2016/1104' (2019) 21 *Doctrina y Jurisprudencia* 87, 97–98.

[45] R. MONTINARO, 'Marital contracts and private ordering of marriage from the Italian family law perspective' (2017) 3 *The Italian Law Journal* 75, 86.

[46] L. WALKER, 'New (and old) Problems for Maintenance Creditors under the Maintenance Regulation' in P. BEAUMONT, M. DANOV, K. TRIMMINGS and B. YÜKSEL (eds.), *Cross-Border Litigation in Europe*, Hart Publishing, London 2017, p. 771.

Therefore, the parties will hardly be induced to the choice of the applicable law if they can obtain effects that are advantageous for them even in the absence of their choice. The structure of the Twin Regulations puts the possibility of choosing the law (Article 22) before the provision relating to the applicable law in the absence of the choice of the parties (Article 26). However, this logical succession does not correspond to the most recurrent situation. Mostly, the applicable law will be that deriving from the objective connection, and only if the predictable effects of the objective connection do not correspond to the expectations of the parties, will they opt for the choice of the applicable law.[47]

The choice of law also depends on the quality of information available to the couple. In ideal conditions, the couple should have precise and clear information on the legal aspects related to the property regime, yet this is generally not the case. The choice of the jurisdiction and of the applicable law can be potentially risky, without proper information deriving from a close examination of all related legal issues. This risk can be limited through highly qualified professional assistance, which of course can have a high cost. The role of the professionals that provide this assistance, however, is crucial.[48]

At the moment of the choice of the jurisdiction and/or the law, it is not known which points may arise that could lead to a dispute in the course of the marriage or registered partnership, and which issues would arise in case of divorce or dissolution of the partnership. Nor is it always clear which law will apply to the cross-border couple in case of a separation or if one of the parties dies. It is the specific function of legal professionals to create certainty out of uncertainty by predicting the possible disputes that might arise. They have to foresee the forum in which disputes will be settled, and the law applicable to those disputes, in the best interest of the parties. It is clear that the skills required of these professionals are tremendous. Furthermore, it is often not easy to find adequately trained professionals. In fact, professionals working in family law often do not have specific and advanced expertise in the field of private international law and comparative law.[49] In certain contexts, lawyers with proper skills in these sectors still need to be properly trained. In the absence of such training, a professional may be tempted to suggest the choice of law that is not advantageous for the couple itself, but is preferred by the lawyer due

---

[47] C. GONZALEZ BEILFUSS, 'Reflexiones en torno a la función de la autonomía de la voluntad conflictual en el derecho internacional privado de familia' (2020) 72 *Revista Española de Derecho Internacional* 101, 104.

[48] R.A. BRAND, *Transaction Planning Using Rules on Jurisdiction and the Recognition and Enforcement of Judgments*, Brill Nijhoff, Leiden 2014, p. 23.

[49] C. GONZALEZ BEILFUSS, 'Reflexiones en torno a la función de la autonomía de la voluntad conflictual en el derecho internacional privado de familia' (2020) 72 *Revista Española de Derecho Internacional* 105.

to the familiarity[50] that the parties and the professional have towards a given regulatory framework. In this sense, he or she could induce the clients to opt for the application of the *lex fori* even if less advantageous by itself, only because the professional approach is less complex.

Autonomy in choosing the applicable law and the jurisdiction is a tool to be used by the professionals to reduce (and sometimes eliminate) risks at the eventual break up of a relationship that involves a cross-border couple, both in case of marriage and registered partnership. Basically, the decision-making process[51] for the professionals considering issues of applicable law and the jurisdiction related to cross-border couples involves a set of three questions:

- What is the default rule of applicable law and jurisdiction?
- Could it be in the interest of the parties changing the default rule?
- Which applicable law and jurisdiction would serve the interests of the parties best?

Asking and answering these questions will allow the professional to determine how to reduce or eliminate risks otherwise placed on the parties by the default law and jurisdiction.

The decision-making process would require that the legal framework is formal and stable. This should allow legal professionals to make a precise diagnosis and take the necessary precautions. Without these requirements, it is in fact hard to foresee any anticipatory measures or to reduce potential risks. Family law, anyway, is simultaneously moving towards and away from such a connotation.[52]

In this context of potential instability within the relationship of the parties (and consequent unpredictability), the greatest risk that professionals must consider concerns the possibility of an escalation of the conflict between the parties. This escalation is particularly negative if we consider that the parties – even when in antagonistic positions – have been united by family relationships (e.g. the parental bond), that often persist. A certain legal predictability of the consequences of a break up makes it easier to reduce the risk of conflict.

---

[50] S. VOGENAJER, 'Regulatory Competition Through Choice of Contract Law and Choice of Forum in Europe: Theory and Evidence' (2013) 21 *European Review of Private Law* 13, 53: 'choices of law and forum are primarily driven by factors other than the substantive merits of the respective regimes' legal rules. By far the most important factor is the parties' familiarity with the chosen regime'.

[51] See in general, for private international law: R.A. BRAND, *Transaction Planning Using Rules on Jurisdiction and the Recognition and Enforcement of Judgments*, Brill Nijhoff, Leiden 2014, p. 24.

[52] R. AVIEL, 'A New Formalism for Family Law' (2014) 55 *William & Mary Law Review* 2003, 2006: 'Family law is simultaneously moving toward and away from formalist decision making'.

6.2. IS THERE A WEAKER PARTY TO BE PROTECTED? WHO IS IT?

In the sector of private law, relationships are traditionally gender blind. This is the result of the construction of a general concept of legal capacity and the creation of a single, universal subject of law.[53] Nevertheless, in the context of the family, the relevance of gender can still be noticed.[54] It should be borne in mind, in fact, that until a few years ago, marriage was characterised in a structural way with respect to gender.[55]

The principle of party autonomy in private international family law presumes that both parties have equal bargaining power and are equally informed. In this approach, such a principle reflects the idea of gender equality.

The judgment of the Spanish Supreme Court of 24 June 2015 is of great significance.[56] The case concerned a marriage agreement establishing separation of property. In the event of divorce, a guaranteed amount had to be paid monthly to the wife in the form of a life annuity. The Supreme Court did not see any waiver of rights (nor a waiver of the applicable law), as the agreement was not based on the need of either of the spouses or on the imbalance following the crisis of the marriage, as both the parties enjoyed a healthy economic condition. The subjection of one of the parties had not been imposed and there was no evidence that the agreement had been seriously detrimental to the husband. The Spanish Supreme Court alluded to the profound change in the current social and matrimonial model that demands a greater margin of autonomy within family law and considers the agreement not contrary to law, morality or public order, as it does not affect the equality of the spouses.

---

[53] A. GREAR, '"Sexing the Matrix": Embodiment, Disembodiment and the Law: Towards the Re-Gendering of Legal Personality' in J. JONES, A. GREAR, R.A, FENTON and K. STEVENSON (eds.), *Gender, Sexualities and Law*, Routledge, London 2011, p. 49.

[54] M.R. MARELLA, 'Gli accordi fra coniugi fra suggestioni comparatistiche e diritto interno' in G. FERRANDO (ed.), *Separazione e divorzio. Giurisprudenza sistematica civile e commerciale fondata da Bigiavi*, Utet, Torino 2003, p. 157.

[55] S.A. HILL, *Families: A Social Class Perspective*, SAGE, Los Angeles 2012, p. 9: 'Although defining marriage and enforcing marriage rules were often difficult, there was substantial agreement across cultures on one point: Men were to be the dominant partner in the marriage or the heads of their families, and wives were to be subservient and obedient to their husbands'. Similarly, K. BAKER, 'Property Rules Meet Feminist Needs: Respecting Autonomy by Valuing Connection' (1998) 59 *Ohio State Law Journal* 1525.

[56] Tribunal Supremo, 24 June 2015, Roj: STS 2828/2015 – ECLI: ES:TS:2015:2828. See A.M. PÉREZ VALLEJO, 'Waiver of economic benefits on premarital agreement with cross-border dimension' in J. KRAMBERGER ŠKERL, L. RUGGERI and F.G. VITERBO (eds.), *Case studies and best practices analysis to enhance EU Family and Succession Law. Working Paper* (2019) 3 *Quaderni degli Annali della Facoltà Giuridica dell'Università di Camerino* 154 et seq. More widely on the decision: ID. 'Notas sobre la aplicación del Reglamento (UE) 2016/1103 a los pactos prematrimoniales en previsión de la ruptura matrimonial' (2019) 21 *Revista Internacional de Doctrina y Jurisprudencia* 105, 115 et seq.

This poses, however, the question of effective protection of the weaker party. The issue is very broad in itself, since an imbalance is a common characteristic of many relationships between private parties, in particular because of the inequality in power and the different degree of knowledge available to the parties.[57] As a result, a wide list of subjects can be considered as the weaker party. It should also be pointed out that, in a comparative perspective, little attention is often paid to the need of considering the imbalance of power between the parties as an issue related to the fundamental rights of the person.[58]

It can no longer be said *a priori* that a woman has less negotiating power in the couple, nor that a man has more power just because he is a man. No doubt, women can be the stronger party in the relationship. This is, for example, the situation that gave rise to a 'landmark' case: *Radmacher (Formerly Granatino) v Granatino*.[59] A very wealthy German woman, Ms Radmacher, and a French man, Mr Granatino, entered into a pre-nuptial agreement that established that neither of the parties should have a claim against the separate property of the other party. Nine years after the wedding, the husband, who in the meantime had left a well-paid job to start a less lucrative academic career, claimed ancillary relief against the wife's assets. The court however rejected the claim and ruled that the pre-nuptial agreement was valid. In addition, it should be borne in mind that the taxonomic variety[60] of married or registered couples may also potentially impact issues related to gender roles: a couple can be composed of two women or two men. All of these considerations lead to the recognition that, in the family context, the situation of the weaker party must be identified on a case-by-case basis, without *a priori* stereotyping: both the wife and the husband can potentially be a weaker party.

Much more clarity in terms of balance of power exists in the relationship between a trader and a consumer or between an employer and an employee: a consumer and an employee, generally have less contractual power than their counterparties. This imbalance entails the risk that the choice of applicable law will be imposed by the stronger party, to the detriment of the weaker party. The same cannot be said with a similar certainty in the family sphere, especially in the light of the recent evolution of taxonomy in family law. Indeed, family

---

[57] O.O. CHEREDNYCHENKO, *Fundamental Rights, Contract Law and the Protection of the Weaker Party: A Comparative Analysis of the Constitutionalisation of Contract Law, With Emphasis on Risky Financial Transactions,* Sellier European Law Pub, München 2007, p. 14.

[58] Ibid.

[59] *Radmacher (Formerly Granatino) v Granatino* [2010] UKSC 42, [2010] 2 FLR 1900. On the question of the weaker spouse in the *Granatino* case, see J.M. SCHERPE, 'Fairness, Freedom and Foreign Elements – Marital Agreements in England and Wales after *Radmacher v Granatino*' (2011) 23 *Child and Family Law Quarterly* 513, 521 et seq.

[60] R. GARETTO in M.J. CAZORLA GONZÁLEZ, M. GIOBBI, J. KRAMBERGER ŠKERL and L. RUGGERI (eds.), *Property Relations of Cross-Border Couples in the European Union,* Edizioni Scientifiche Italiane, Napoli 2020, p. 87.

relationships are not as straightforward as commercial relationships. They are often characterised by inequality of bargaining power, but the inequalities may be different in relation to different issues. One may be in the stronger position financially but the other may be in the stronger position in relation to the children and to the home in which they live. One may care more about getting or preserving as much money as possible, while the other may care more about the living arrangements for the children. One may want to get out of the relationship as quickly as possible, while the other may be in no hurry to separate or divorce.

This requires a careful reflection on the notion of weakness itself, which is structurally related to the condition of vulnerability.[61] A definition of vulnerability that combines internal and external elements can be as follows: 'to be exposed to the possibility of harm while being substantially unable to protect oneself.'[62] Vulnerability does not constitute an intrinsic state of one party rather than the other, but concerns each member of the couple in a different way.[63] In certain cases, both members of the couple can be weak and/or vulnerable parties even simultaneously, depending on the circumstances of the specific case.

Parallel to vulnerability, it seems appropriate to also consider the situation of dependence. Everybody, starting from birth, is destined to be in a state of dependence in different phases of his or her existence. Vulnerability corresponds to the state of dependence which is concretely constituted and which is often not predictable in advance. These situations of dependence are relevant to the couple, and require different considerations depending on the circumstances of the specific case, since vulnerability has multiple facets. It can be related to economic, cultural, social and psychological aspects. It is true that, for example, the party of one sex (in heterosexual couples), the party whose nationality is related to certain geographical areas, or the younger party (in the case of a considerable age disparity in the couple) may frequently find themselves in a weaker economic position. However, the couple's dynamics may establish internal compensatory balances that refer to the other party's vulnerability. Factors linked, for example, to individual autonomy, to the psychological and relational sphere, and to health must indeed be taken into consideration. These factors may be relevant for the couple and create reciprocal states of dependency. Such situations may occur at any given stage in a relationship and may constantly evolve.[64]

---

[61] E. GILSON, *The Ethics of Vulnerability: A Feminist Analysis of Social Life and Practice*, Routledge, New York-London 2014, pp. 8–9.
[62] D. SCHROEDER and E. GEFENAS, 'Vulnerability: Too Vague and Too Broad?' (2009) 18 *Cambridge Quarterly of Healthcare Ethics* 113, 116.
[63] M.A. FINEMAN, 'Why Marriage?' (2001) 9 *Virginia Journal of Social Policy & the Law* 239, 242–243: 'marriage can also be seen as serving society by taking care of the dependency and vulnerability of some members of the marital family.'
[64] M.A. FINEMAN, 'Beyond Equality and Discrimination' (2020) 73 *SMU Law Review Forum* 51, 57.

When the question of divorce arises, vulnerability plays an important role. The parties may be tempted to lead their conduct on an emotional level, sometimes giving up what is due to them out of a sense of guilt, and at other times making demands on the basis of a feeling of revenge. This can determine the risk that one party attempts to prevaricate against the other, who is in a particularly vulnerable situation.

However, it is also possible that the parties remain on peaceful terms even if the relationship breaks up.[65] In this way the balance between situations of greater and lesser vulnerability of the parties will not be altered.

7. RISKS ASSOCIATED WITH INADEQUATE LEGAL ADVICE PRIOR TO AGREEMENT AND SAFEGUARDS TO PROTECT WEAKER PARTY

The overall context surrounding the choice of applicable law has to be taken into account. This implies the need to assess the range of options available to the couple in the light of certain recent trends in European family law.

First, despite the fact that maintenance obligations between spouses or partners should be excluded from the scope of the Twin Regulations in accordance with their Recital 22, there is a tendency in some Member States to strengthen both the rebalancing aim pursued by after-divorce allowance orders and the link between the property regime adopted during the marriage or registered partnership and the criteria for determining whether such an allowance is due and its amount.

In Spain, following the 2005 reform, the legislator has given the *pensión compensatoria* pursuant to Article 97 of the Civil Code, which is due to the spouse for whom the separation or divorce has led to an economic imbalance in relation to the other spouse's position, a rebalancing function.[66] Furthermore, the economic compensation provided by Article 1438 of the Spanish Civil Code forms part of the primary matrimonial property regime and is closely related to the duty of the spouses to contribute to fulfilling family needs; it is established exclusively for cases in which the matrimonial property regime is

---

[65] J. HERRING, 'Relational Autonomy and Family Law' in J. WALLBANK, S. CHOUDHRY and J. HERRING (eds.), *Rights, Gender and Family Law*, Routledge, Abingdon 2010, pp. 266–268.

[66] However, it is admitted that the *pensión compensatoria* 'is incorporated in a broad sense into the concept of maintenance obligation': on this point see A.M. PÉREZ VALLEJO, 'Waiver of economic benefits on premarital agreement with cross-border dimension' in J. KRAMBERGER ŠKERL, L. RUGGERI and F.G. VITERBO (eds.), *Case studies and best practices analysis to enhance EU Family and Succession Law. Working Paper* (2019) 3 Quaderni degli Annali della Facoltà Giuridica dell'Università di Camerino 151.

that of 'separation of assets'.[67] In Italy, a *revirement* in the case of law making after-divorce allowance composite in nature, namely both welfare-oriented and compensatory, is due to the judgement of the Court of Cassation of 11 July 2018.[68] Thus, after-divorce allowance can be ordered as an equitable compensation for the sacrifices made during the marriage by one spouse to meet family needs. Both the entitlement to after-divorce allowance and the evaluation of its amount are anchored to all the elements that are listed in Article 5(6) of the Italian law on divorce,[69] including the personal and financial contribution made by each spouse to the welfare of the family and the creation of personal and joint assets, as well as the income of both spouses. In both the Italian and Spanish systems, a compensatory allowance may be awarded to the spouse whose sacrifices during the marriage were much greater, allowing the other spouse to advance in their career and increase net income. The aim of rebalancing the differences in economic means between the parties is pursued by taking into account the property consequences of the marriage or registered partnership. This applies regardless of the fact that each individual can fully support himself or herself.[70]

In this context, the reason for the connection with the state of the creditor's habitual residence provided by the 2007 Hague Protocol may be lacking.[71] It is therefore likely that the CJEU will be asked whether in those cases the claim for a compensatory allowance after the divorce should fall within the notion of 'maintenance obligation' and thus within the scope of the Maintenance Regulation and the 2007 Hague Maintenance Protocol or rather within the notion of 'matrimonial property regime' or 'property consequences of a registered partnership'

---

[67] Article 1438 of the Spanish Civil Code seeks to mitigate the negative consequences that the regime of separation of property has on the spouse who has worked in the home. According to some authors, such compensation cannot be configured as alimony, so it would fall within the scope of the Matrimonial Property Regulation: ibid., p. 152.

[68] A *revirement* in the Italian case of law making after-divorce maintenance composite in nature, namely both welfare-oriented and compensatory, is due to Court of Cassation Joint Divisions, 11 July 2018, no. 18287, in *Giuisprudenza italiana*, 2018, pp. 1843–1852, with note of C. RIMINI, *Il nuovo assegno di divorzio: la funzione compensativa e perequativa*, ibid., pp. 1852–1861. For a brief description of the history of changes among judges and interpreters concerning the Italian law on after-divorce maintenance, see G. TERLIZZI, '"Ties that Bind": Maintenance Order After Divorce in Italy' (2018) 2 *The Italian Law Journal* 449, 449–476.

[69] The authors refer to the Italian law, no. 898 of 1 December 1970.

[70] In Italy, see Court of Cassation, 17 February 2021, no. 4224, in *Pluris online*.

[71] In these Spanish and Italian cases, the assignment of a compensatory allowance should be considered as a part of liquidation of the matrimonial property regime rather than as a maintenance obligation. In addition, the institution of the matrimonial property regime is unknown to the common law jurisdictions who have rules for the distribution of the spouses' property after the dissolution of the marriage. In this respect, see the hermeneutical criteria laid down by the CJEU in the case *Van den Boogaard v Laumen*: Case C-220/95, *Antonius van den Boogaard v Paula Laumen*, ECLI:EU:C:1997:91.

and thus within the scope of the Twin Regulations.[72] Apart from this interpretative issue, the European legislator has already emphasised the connection and coordination between these different matters pertaining to relations between spouses or partners, allowing the parties to make a 'dependent' choice of law, i.e. to absorb the law applicable to maintenance into the law applicable to the parties' property regime or to their separation or divorce, in accordance with Article 8(1)(c) and (d) of the Hague Maintenance Protocol.

It follows that it is up to the notary or the other legal professional assisting the parties in concluding the agreement on the law applicable to the property consequences of the marriage or registered partnership to point out the importance of coordination with the choice of the law applicable not only to separation and divorce but also to maintenance obligations.[73] In fact, the risk of legal uncertainty and fragmentation may arise if the parties do not conclude such a comprehensive choice-of-law agreement.[74] Unitary treatment of these matters would be convenient. Therefore, only adequate legal advice may ensure that the same law will govern all of them. It is possible to achieve coincidence of the applicable law through an agreement on the choice of the law of the common habitual residence or the nationality of one of the spouses or partners at the time of the designation, as provided for in all the relevant EU regulations.[75]

With agreeing on the choice of applicable law, the parties envisage the way in which their property relationships are to be treated under a range of possible laws and finally opt for the one that best serves their common interests.[76] Here again, proper legal advice is essential to enable the couple to make a choice

---

[72] On the issue of how the applicable law should be determined in those cases, see F.G. VITERBO, 'Claim for maintenance after divorce: Legal uncertainty regarding the determination of the applicable law' in J. KRAMBERGER ŠKERL, L. RUGGERI and F.G. VITERBO (eds.), *Case studies and best practices analysis to enhance EU Family and Succession Law. Working Paper* (2019) 3 Quaderni degli Annali della Facoltà Giuridica dell'Università di Camerino 171–183.

[73] On this point see A. BONOMI, 'The Interactions among the Future EU Instruments on Matrimonial Property, Registered Partnerships and Successions' (2011) 13 *Yearbook of Private International Law* 217, 217–231; B. CAMPUZANO DÍAZ, 'The Coordination of the EU Regulations on Divorce and Legal Separation with the Proposal on Matrimonial Property Regimes', ibid. 233, 233–253.

[74] The Twin Regulations do not contain a specific provision for the coordination of applicable laws, as they expressly provide for the determination of jurisdiction: D. DAMASCELLI, 'Applicable law, jurisdiction, and recognition of decisions in matters relating to property regimes of spouses and partners in European and Italian private international law' [2019] *Trusts & Trustees* 6, 6–16. Moreover, there is no coincidence between the criteria for identifying the applicable law in the absence of a choice by the parties: see I. VIARENGO, 'Effetti patrimoniali delle unioni civili transfrontaliere' (2018) 54 *Rivista di diritto internazionale privato e processuale* 33, 53–58.

[75] I. VIARENGO, 'Choice of law agreements upon property regimes, divorce and succession: stress-testing the new EU Regulations' [2016] *ERA Forum* 543, 543–554.

[76] This is an important function of the choice-of-law agreement: see F. SBORDONE, 'Potere di scelta della legge applicabile al contratto e funzione delle norme di diritto internazionale privato' [2006] *Il diritto civile oggi. Compiti scientifici e didattici del civilista* 211, 215–219.

that should be directed towards the most equitable law and property regime in relation to their option regarding the organisation of their matrimonial life or their registered partnership. This is particularly important, as there is a growing disparity between the Member States with regard to the mechanisms for protecting the weaker party. For example, in some states, the default regime is 'community of acquisitions' and, in the event of divorce, the law states that the weaker party is awarded periodic maintenance for an indefinite period or for an otherwise reasonable period. On the contrary, in other states, the default regime is 'separation of assets' and, in the event of divorce, the weaker party is awarded maintenance only in exceptional cases and for a fixed period.[77]

Some risks for the weaker party, which are linked to the above-mentioned, tend to give more space to private autonomy. The weaker party may be persuaded or forced to choose the applicable law providing for the lowest level of protection, as well as to reduce – or even renounce – maintenance after divorce (e.g. on the basis of an applicable law under which pre- or post-nuptial agreements are valid). This risk is made even more effective by the principle of 'universal application' under Article 20 of the Twin Regulations, pursuant to which the law of a third country may also apply.[78]

In order to avoid such abuses, the weaker party should always be informed about the laws that may be chosen and their favourable and unfavourable property consequences with a view to divorce. This requires that the legal advice given to the parties is fair and impartial. Effective protection of the weaker party can only be guaranteed in a context that always ensures the couple adequate and impartial information, in accordance with the Principles of European Family Law Regarding Property Relations between Spouses.[79] If such

---

[77] For an overview of family property regimes in Member States, see L. RUGGERI, I. KUNDA and S. WINKLER (eds.), *Family Property and Succession in EU Member States: National Reports on the Collected Data*, Rijeka 2019 <https://www.euro-family.eu/documenti/news/psefs_e_book_compressed.pdf>. In the states where divorced persons are able to find work easily and there are efficient income support measures, postmarital allowance recognition is exceptional. The principle of economic self-sufficiency is also laid down in Part II of the '*Principles of European Family Law Regarding Divorce and Maintenance between Former Spouses*' (Principle 2:2). On the contrary, in Member States where social welfare policies are lacking and inefficient, the right to maintenance becomes the main source of income/subsistence for the ex-spouse (or partner) who is economically weaker after the dissolution of the marriage relationship (or registered partnership).

[78] Article 20 states that: 'The law designated as applicable … shall be applied whether or not it is the law of a Member State.' However, it should be specified that the law of a third state chosen by the parties as applicable to their property relationships, in exceptional circumstances and in particular for reasons of public interest, may be disregarded by the courts of the Member States if the application of that law is manifestly incompatible with the public policy of the Member State concerned (see Article 31of the Twin Regulations).

[79] This set of Principles belongs to the *Principles of European Family Law* drafted by the Commission of European Family Law (CEFL). See the 'Principle 4:13 Obligations of a notary or other legal professional with comparable function', pursuant to which 'The notary or

information is lacking, this defect may in fact vitiate the consent given by one of the parties and the material validity of the choice-of-law agreement should be assessed under the hypothetical *lex causae*, i.e. the law which would govern the agreement pursuant to Article 22 of the Twin Regulations if it were valid.[80] Yet another safeguard for the protection of the weaker party is provided for in Article 24(2) of the Twin Regulations. In accordance with the latter, a spouse or partner, in order to establish that he or she did not consent to the choice-of-law agreement, may rely upon the law of the state in which he or she has his or her habitual residence at the time the court is seised. This is possible only if it appears from the circumstances that it would not be reasonable to determine the effect of his or her conduct in accordance with the law designated in the agreement.[81]

However, the Twin Regulations do not expressly provide for any limitation of the parties' autonomy as to the *consequences* of the choice-of-law agreement, in order to protect the weaker party. Instead, it would have been appropriate to include in the text of these Regulations a provision similar to that of Article 8(5) of the 2007 Hague Protocol, which states that: 'Unless at the time of the designation the parties were fully informed and aware of the consequences of their designation, *the law designated by the parties shall not apply where the application of that law would lead to manifestly unfair or unreasonable consequences for any of the parties*'.[82] Whether this kind of judicial review of content of the choice-of-law agreement may apply in cases which fall within the scope of the Twin Regulations is a matter of uncertainty.[83] Nevertheless, it is submitted that such limitations on parties' autonomy should apply on the basis of the hypothetical *lex causae* whenever this is the law of a Member State. The fairness principle and the principle of equality between spouses or partners

---

other legal professional with comparable function should a) give *impartial advice* to each spouse separately, b) ensure that each spouse understands the legal consequences of the marital property agreement, and c) ensure that both spouses freely consent to the agreement' (emphasis added). On this Principle see K. BOELE-WOELKI, F. FERRAND, C. GONZÁLES BEILFUSS, M. JÄNTERÄ-JAREBORG, N. LOWE, D. MARTINY, W. PINTENS, *Principles of European Family Law Regarding Property Relations between Spouses*, Intersentia, Cambridge 2013, pp. 126–129.

[80] In addition, if a spouse or partner opposes the validity of the agreement because he or she was in error about the consequences of the choice, the application of the rules of the *lex causae* on the relevance of an error or misrepresentation should take into consideration the objective pursued by the rules of the Twin Regulations on the material validity of the agreement: C. KOHLER, above 'Choice of the Applicable Law' in P. FRANZINA and I. VIARENGO (eds.), *The EU Regulations on the Property Regimes of International Couples. A Commentary*, Edward Elgar, Cheltenham 2020, p. 225.

[81] For more details on this provision, see C. KOHLER, ibid., pp. 229–231.

[82] Emphasis added.

[83] C. KOHLER, 'Choice of the Applicable Law' in P. FRANZINA and I. VIARENGO (eds.), *The EU Regulations on the Property Regimes of International Couples. A Commentary*, Edward Elgar, Cheltenham 2020, p. 227.

belong to the common core of European family law.⁸⁴ In addition, if a party's economic weakness is more pronounced because of, for instance, a health problem, the consequences of the choice-of-law agreement may be reviewed in light of the concrete circumstances and having regard to the principle of solidarity between the parties, even after the dissolution of the relationship, which is common to the Member States' constitutional values.

In this perspective, the validity of the choice-of-law agreement should at least be open to scrutiny by the competent court.

8. CONCLUDING REMARKS

The puzzle that emerges from this analysis is further complicated by the fact that European harmonisation is not geographically uniform. The Twin Regulations apply only to the Member States that participate in the enhanced cooperation.⁸⁵ Nevertheless, party autonomy must be fostered and promoted, not discouraged.

Choosing applicable law might be particularly important for cross-border couples changing their habitual residence during their marriage or partnership time. *When* and *how* the choice is made are essential aspects whose implications have been analysed in this chapter.

In accordance with the principles outlined by the CJEU, it is necessary to interpret Articles 22–24 of the Twin Regulations by taking into account not only the wording of those provisions, but also the context in which they occur and the objectives pursued by the rules of which they are part.⁸⁶ However, this approach requires further specification.

The risks associated with both the timing and the overall context of the choice of law, which have been highlighted in this chapter, may certainly lead the parties to enter into an agreement with uncertain and/or unfair property

---

[84] See the following CEFL Principles: 'Principle 4:2 Equality of the spouses'; 'Principle 4:12 Disclosure' which is an evident application of the fairness principle; 'Principle 4:13 Obligations of a notary or other legal professional with comparable function'; 'Principle 2:10 Maintenance agreement'. On this issue, see C. KOHLER, 'Choice of the Applicable Law' in P. FRANZINA and I. VIARENGO (eds.), *The EU Regulations on the Property Regimes of International Couples. A Commentary*, Edward Elgar, Cheltenham 2020, p. 228: where the agreement leads to manifest unfair consequences for the weaker party, the review of the choice-of-law agreement would be based on Article 22 of the Twin Regulations as interpreted in the light of the Charter of Fundamental Rights and the European Convention of Human Rights; in this view, 'the yardstick for a review of the content of the agreement is to be found in the autonomous concept [of choice-of-law agreement] in Article 22 and not in national law.'

[85] On the enhanced cooperation and its impact on party autonomy under Matrimonial Property Regulation, see A. LIMANTE and N. POGORELČNIK VOGRINC, 'Party Autonomy in the Context of Jurisdictional and Choice of Law Rules of Matrimonial Property Regulation' (2020) 13 *Baltic Journal of Law & Politics* 135, 140 et seq.

[86] See Case C-214/17, *Alexander Mölk v Valentina Mölk*, ECLI:EU:C:2018:744, point 27; Case C-184/14, *A v B*, ECLI:EU:C:2015:479, point 32.

consequences, to their detriment or that of the weaker party. However, if these risks are adequately taken into account, the legal professional will guide the couple towards an optimal choice of applicable law and the property regime governing their marriage or registered partnership.

Matrimonial property questions mostly come together with divorce, maintenance and parental responsibilities. If the interplay of related EU instruments is taken into account by the legal professional, this will ensure both the certainty and concentration of jurisdiction and applicable law to the parties' past, present and future relationships, irrespective of changes in their individual and joint lives. To this end, adequate legal advice must be provided to the parties. This means that the parties must be provided with correct, complete and impartial information, in simple and understandable language, and highlighting the favourable and unfavourable consequences of each possible choice for both the couple and each party. If necessary, adequate balancing measures should be envisaged to protect the weaker party.

It follows that there is not exclusively a problem of formal validity of the choice-of-law and/or choice-of-court agreement. It is also necessary that the agreement is concluded in compliance with the principle of fairness and the values of equal dignity of the parties, social equity and solidarity. These values indeed form the basis of both European family law and the EU Charter of Fundamental Rights, as well as of the 'law' of each Member State. The normative relevance of these principles and values could be seen as a threat to legal certainty. However, 'if the interpreter … refuses to employ legal principles, then he will not find a solution which is the best fit for the specific features of the actual case, since the "law" is a broader experience than the mere application of rules.'[87]

---

[87] P. PERLINGIERI, 'Legal Principles and Values' (2017) 3 *The Italian Law Journal* 125, 125–147.

PROPERTY RELATIONS OF CROSS-BORDER SAME-SEX COUPLES IN THE EU

Filip Dougan*

1. Introduction 219
2. The Issue of Same-Sex Couples – One of the Major Reasons for
   a Lengthy Path to the Adoption of the Twin Regulations.............. 221
3. Material and Personal Scope of Application........................ 223
   3.1. Registered Partnership....................................... 223
   3.2. The Notion of Marriage and the Characterisation of Same-Sex
        Marriages... 225
4. Alternative Jurisdiction 232
5. Party Autonomy – A Possible Solution to Uncertainty?............... 234
   5.1. Choice-of-Court Agreements................................... 234
   5.2. Choice-of-Law Agreements 239
6. Recognition and Enforcement 240
7. Concluding Remarks 243

1. INTRODUCTION

Over the last three decades, significant progress has been achieved in granting and protecting the rights of same-sex couples in Europe. From such milestones as the adoption of the Danish Act on Registered Partnership in 1989, which for the first time allowed for the formalisation of same-sex partnerships[1] and the amendment of Article 30 of the Dutch Civil Code, which in 2001 for the first time opened marriage to same-sex couples,[2] more and more countries

---

*   Filip Dougan, BA, MA, Teaching and Research Assistant at the Department of Civil Law, University of Ljubljana, Slovenia.
[1] I. Lund-Andersen, 'Northern Europe: Same-sex Relationships and Family Law' in K. Boele-Woelki and A. Fuchs (eds.), *Same-sex Relationships and Beyond*, Intersentia, Cambridge 2017, p. 5.
[2] F. W. J. M. Schols and T. F. H. Reijnen, 'The Netherlands' in L. Ruggeri, I. Kunda, S. Winkler (eds.), *Family Property and Succession in EU Member States: National Reports on the Collected Data*, University of Rijeka, Faculty of Law, Rijeka 2019, p. 487.

around the world and in particular within the European Union (the EU) started introducing legislation that legally recognises same-sex relationships and, accordingly, the rights (including property rights) arising out of such relationships. On the other hand, it can be observed that these advancements also faced an increased concern in some Member States which consider that granting more rights to same-sex couples or even allowing them to marry might undermine the 'traditional values' relating to family and partnership relations. Latvia, Hungary, Croatia and Slovakia event went so far as to enact a constitutional ban on same-sex marriages.[3]

These divergent views on the legal recognition of same-sex couples and their rights result in notable differences in national family law approaches in EU Member States. This is obvious not only when it comes to the recognition of same-sex relationships, but also regarding the regulation of their property rights. In this regard, EU Member States could roughly be divided into three groups. The first group of thirteen Member States[4] recognises same-sex marriage; the second group consisting of eight Member States,[5] does not allow same-sex couples to marry, but allow them to enter into a registered partnership;[6] the third group consists of six Member States[7] where neither marriage nor registered partnership is allowed for same-sex couples.[8] Depending on the group to which the country belongs to, its position with regard to same-sex couples differs. While the first group grants the most extensive rights to such couples, their situation in the third group (countries refusing to legally recognise same-sex couples) is much less protected.

Vast differences in national law inevitably pose great challenges to the harmonisation of private international law among the Member States. This was also evident within the process of the adoption of the Matrimonial Property Regulation and the Regulation on the Property Consequences of Registered

---

[3] S. Kraljić, 'Same-sex partnerships in Eastern Europe' in K. Boele-Woelki and A. Fuchs (eds.), *Same-sex Relationships and Beyond*, Intersentia, Cambridge 2017, pp. 61–62.
[4] Austria (2019), Belgium (2003), Denmark (2012), Finland (2017), France (2013), Germany (2017), Ireland (2015), Luxemburg (2015), Malta (2017), the Netherlands (2001), Portugal (2010), Spain, (2005) and Sweden (2009).
[5] Croatia (2014), Cyprus (2015), Czechia (2006), Estonia (2016), Greece (2015), Hungary (2009), Italy, (2016) and Slovenia (2006).
[6] It should be noted that national legislation of those Member States often refer to such registered partnerships with various terms such as civil union, civil partnership, life partnership, cohabitation agreement, etc. For the purpose of this chapter, however, the term registered partnership is used intentionally as it reflects the terminology of the Regulation on Property Consequences of a Registered Partnership. It should also be noted that the rights deriving from such relationships vary significantly between these Member States.
[7] Bulgaria, Latvia, Lithuania, Poland, Slovakia and Romania.
[8] See, inter alia, L. Ruggeri, I. Kunda, S. Winkler (eds.), *Family Property and Succession in EU Member States: National Reports on the Collected Data*, University of Rijeka, Faculty of Law, Rijeka 2019.

Partnerships (the Twin Regulations). Although one of the main aims of the Twin Regulations was to achieve a higher level of legal certainty for cross-border couples regarding their property relations,[9] same-sex cross-border couples still face a substantial amount of unpredictability. It can be observed that their legal certainty was often sacrificed in order to achieve unanimity and to address the concerns of the Member States, which feared that adoption of the Regulations would force them to recognise same-sex unions unknown in their legal systems.[10] This chapter will therefore attempt to present some of the challenges that such couples face concerning their property relations under the Twin Regulations. It will also explore the possibilities which may mitigate their uncertain legal position, identify questions that remain open and propose solutions in order to ensure same-sex cross-border couples a greater level of legal predictability.

2. THE ISSUE OF SAME-SEX COUPLES – ONE OF THE MAJOR REASONS FOR A LENGTHY PATH TO THE ADOPTION OF THE TWIN REGULATIONS

More than 17 years have passed since the initial idea of a European instrument regulating private international law aspects of the matrimonial property regimes and the adoption of the Twin Regulations. The legislative process demonstrates that this long period may be attributed in part to the issues concerning the recognition of same-sex relationships.[11] At the same time a closer look at the *travaux préparatoires* may also provide a better understanding of the reasons for the treatment of same-sex cross-border couples under the Twin Regulations and the challenges that they face.

The need for harmonisation of private international law in the area of property relations of couples was first stressed in the 1998 Vienna Action Plan[12] and the Programme of Measures for Implementation of the Principle of Mutual Recognition of Decisions in Civil Commercial Matters,[13] adopted in the year 2000. While the former referred solely to matrimonial property regimes, the latter also proposed the introduction of legal instruments concerning 'property

---

[9] Recital 15 of the Twin Regulations.
[10] A. WYSOCKA-BAR, 'Enhanced Cooperation in Property Matters in the EU and Non-Participating Member States' (2019) 20 *ERA Forum* 187, 192.
[11] For more detail analysis on the process leading to adoption of the Twin Regulations and the challenges faced see Chapter 2 of this volume.
[12] Council and Commission Action Plan of 3 December 1998 on how best to implement the provisions of the Treaty of Amsterdam on the creation of an area of freedom, security and justice [1999] OJ C 19/1.
[13] Draft programme of measures for implementation of the principle of mutual recognition of decisions in civil and commercial matters [2001] OJ C 12/1.

consequences of the separation of unmarried couples'. Neither, however, made any reference to same-sex couples. This changed in 2006, when the European Commission published a Green Paper on matters of matrimonial property regimes[14] and launched a 'wide ranging consultation' on the subject. Despite omitting an explicit mention of same-sex couples, the Green Paper pointed out that Member States increasingly provide for registered partnerships and the European Commission thus extended the consultation also to the property consequences of such unions.

When the European Commission presented the proposals for the Twin Regulations[15] – dealing separately with matrimonial property regimes and the property consequences of registered partners – it quickly became clear that reaching a consensus would be an onerous task. It should be noted that the EU tried to exercise its competence based on Article 81(3) of the Treaty on the Functioning of the European Union (TFEU),[16] requiring a unanimous decision of the Member States in the Council. Upon introducing the proposals, several Eastern European Member States expressed concerns that the adoption of the Twin Regulations would force their courts to recognise property consequences stemming from same-sex marriages and registered partnerships, which would consequently extend the legal effects of such relationships to their territory.[17] During the Council meeting in December 2015, it finally became clear that a consensus could not be reached due to the opposition of Hungary and Poland.[18] Several Member States, therefore, expressed their wish to establish enhanced cooperation in this field. Their proposal was authorised by the Council[19] and the Twin Regulations were adopted on 24 June 2016. As a result, the Twin Regulations are applicable in only 18 participating Member States,[20] while the

---

[14] Green Paper on conflict of laws in matters concerning matrimonial property regimes, including the question of jurisdiction and mutual recognition, COM(2006) 400 final.

[15] Proposal for a Council Regulation on jurisdiction, applicable law and the recognition and enforcement of decisions in matters of matrimonial property regimes, COM/2011/126 final and Proposal for a Council Regulation on jurisdiction, applicable law and the recognition and enforcement of decisions regarding the property consequences of registered partnerships, COM/2011/127 final.

[16] Consolidated version of the Treaty on the Functioning of the European Union [2012] OJ C 326/47.

[17] A. WYSOCKA-BAR, 'Enhanced Cooperation in Property Matters in the EU and Non-Participating Member States' (2019) 20 ERA Forum 187, pp. 193–194.

[18] Outcome of the Council Meeting, Brussels, 3 and 4 December 2015 <https://www.consilium.europa.eu/ media/23027/st14937en15_v5.pdf>; A. MARINI, 'Poland and Hungary Blocked EU' [2015] Euinside <http://www.euinside.eu/en/news/poland-and-hungary-blocked-eu-on-matrimonial-property-regimes>.

[19] Council Decision (EU) 2016/954 of 9 June 2016 authorising enhanced cooperation in the area of jurisdiction, applicable law and the recognition and enforcement of decisions on the property regimes of international couples, covering both matters of matrimonial property regimes and the property consequences of registered partnerships [2016] OJ L 159/16.

[20] Austria, Belgium, Bulgaria, Croatia, Cyprus, the Czech Republic, Finland, France, Germany, Greece, Italy, Luxembourg, Malta, the Netherlands, Portugal, Slovenia, Spain and Sweden.

remaining Member States continue to apply their domestic private international law rules.

3. MATERIAL AND PERSONAL SCOPE OF APPLICATION

The central issue, which may significantly influence cross-border same-sex couples, is the question of whether or not the Twin Regulations can be applied by the competent court when deciding on their property relations and if so, which of the two Regulations will be applied.

While the territorial and temporal scope of application, as well as the contents of the Twin Regulations mirror each other closely (see Chapter 3 of this volume), the most important distinction occurs in relation to their material and personal scope of application. Pursuant to Article 1, the Matrimonial Property Regulation applies to 'matrimonial property regimes' and the Regulation on the Property Consequences of Registered Partnerships applies to 'property consequences of registered partnerships'. Both expressions are defined within Article 3 of each regulation respectively. The former represents 'a set of rules concerning the property relations between spouses and in their relations with third parties, as a result of marriage or its dissolution'; and the latter establishes 'the set of rules concerning the property relationships of the partners, between themselves and in their relations with third parties, as a result of the legal relationship created by the registrations of the partnership or its dissolution'.

At first glance, it seems that these definitions draw a clear line between their scope of application. The Matrimonial Property Regulation shall apply to property relations of spouses and the Regulation on the Property Consequences of Registered Partnerships shall apply to property relations of registered partners. However, a closer look reveals that this distinction remains relatively unclear when it comes to same-sex couples. To address these issues, the notions 'marriage' and 'registered partnership' need to be examined more closely.

3.1. REGISTERED PARTNERSHIP

The Regulation on the Property Consequences of Registered Partnerships includes an autonomous definition of a registered partnership in Article 3(1)(a). It defines registered partnership as a 'regime governing the shared life of two people which is provided for in law, the registration of which is mandatory under that law and which fulfils the legal formalities required by that law for its creation'. This, in fact, was the first time that an EU instrument in the field of private international law provided a definition of a registered partnership.[21] However, it should be noted that such a definition was established solely for the purpose of the Regulation on the Property Consequences of Registered Partnerships and the actual substance of the concept of registered partnership remains defined in the national laws of the Member States (Recital 17 of Regulation on the Property Consequences of Registered Partnerships).

From the wording of Article 3(1)(a) three main conclusions can be drawn. First, the definition omits any reference to the gender of partners as a condition to fall under the notion of registered partnership. The personal scope of application thus extends not only to opposite-sex registered partnerships, but also to same-sex registered partnerships.[22] This conclusion is further corroborated by the *travaux préparatoires* of the Regulation on the Property Consequences of Registered Partnerships, where it can be observed that it was in fact one of the aims of its adoption to address property consequences of registered partnerships, which are open to same-sex couples.[23] Secondly, the definition clearly stipulates that registration of a partnership is mandatory to fall within the scope of the Regulation on the Property Consequences of Registered Partnerships. Recital 16 further explains that a distinction should be drawn between couples whose union is institutionally sanctioned by the registration of their partnership with a public authority and couples in *de facto* cohabitation. Therefore *de facto* unions of either same-sex or opposite-sex clearly fall beyond the scope of application.[24] Their property relations will thus be regulated by domestic rules of private international law.[25] Finally, it can be observed, as was noted by some commentators on the Twin Regulations, that in accordance with the definition, spouses clearly do not fall under the scope of application of the Regulation on the Property Consequences of Registered Partnerships.[26] Although such a conclusion would follow from the wording and the structure of both Regulations, nevertheless, in some Member States same-sex spouses might nonetheless be treated as registered partners, as will be explained below.

---

[21] C. RUDOLF, 'European Property Regimes Regulations – Choice of Law and the Applicable Law in the Absence of Choice by the parties' (2019) 11 *LeXonomica* 127, p. 133.

[22] R. HAUSMANN, *Internationales und Europäisches Familienrecht*, C. H. Bech, München 2018, p. 980; M. ANDRAE, *Internationales Familienrecht*, Nomos, Baden-Baden 2019, p. 243; A. RODRIGUEZ BENOT, 'Article 3' in P. FRANZINA and I. VIARENGO, *The EU Regulations on the Property Regimes of International Couples: A Commentary*, Edward Elgar, Cheltenham 2020, p. 38.

[23] See, inter alia, Green Paper, COM(2006) 400 final, p. 10.

[24] For property relations of cross-border de facto couples, see Chapter 10 of this volume.

[25] Special provisions on *de facto* union can be found in Article 41 of Slovenian Private International Law and Procedure Act and in Article 40 of Croatian Private International Law Act.

[26] RODRIGUEZ BENOT, 'Article 3' in P. FRANZINA and I. VIARENGO, *The EU Regulations on the Property Regimes of International Couples: A Commentary*, Edward Elgar, Cheltenham 2020, p. 35; M. ANDRAE, *Internationales Familienrecht*, Nomos, Baden-Baden 2019, p. 241.

3.2. THE NOTION OF MARRIAGE AND THE CHARACTERISATION OF SAME-SEX MARRIAGES

Unlike the Regulation on the Property Consequences of Registered Partnerships, the Matrimonial Property Regulation does not define marriage as the necessary basis for the existence of matrimonial property regimes. Instead, some light is shed on the matter in Recital 17, which states that marriage is defined by the *national law of Member States*. An autonomous European definition of marriage was thus avoided in the Matrimonial Property Regulation. It has to be noted that this approach was taken intentionally due to divergent views of the Member States towards same-sex marriages.[27] It was intended that by omitting an autonomous definition of marriage, unanimity among the Member States, particularly those that limit marriage to opposite sex spouses, would be easier to achieve. At the same time, this also enables the non-participating Member States, which do not allow same-sex marriages, to join the enhanced cooperation at a later date.[28]

While reasons for this 'pragmatic' approach may be understandable considering the difficulties that appeared in the process of adoption of the Twin Regulations, the lack of an autonomous definition severely hinders legal certainty and legal security of same-sex couples. The reference to the national law of Member States in Recital 17 means that each participating Member State may interpret the notion of marriage differently. Consequently, the delimitation between the personal scope of application of Twin Regulations is not regulated autonomously.[29] In practice, this results in the fact that some Member States will apply the Matrimonial Property Regulation when deciding on the property relations of same-sex spouses, while the others might apply the Regulation on the Property Consequences of Registered Partnerships instead.

Uncertainty also stems from the vagueness of Recital 17. It is unclear which national law of Member States Recital 17 is pointing to. Several interpretations are possible. The predominant view in scientific literature seems to be that reference to national law means the law of the state whose courts are seised with the matter (*lex fori*).[30] However, even with this interpretation, the question remains whether the competent court should characterise same-sex marriage

---

[27] A. Dutta, 'Beyond Husband and Wife – New Couple Regimes and the European Property Regulations' (2017/2018) 19 *Yearbook of Private International Law* 145, 148.

[28] M. Andrae, *Internationales Familienrecht*, Nomos, Baden-Baden 2019, p. 243.

[29] R. Hausmann, *Internationales und Europäisches Familienrecht*, C. H. Bech, München 2018, p. 980.

[30] A. Dutta, 'Beyond Husband and Wife – New Couple Regimes and the European Property Regulations' (2017/2018) 19 *Yearbook of Private International Law* 145, 149; I. Kunda 'Novi međunarodnoprivatnopravni okvir imovine bračnih i registriranih partnera u Europskoj uniji: polje primjene i nadležnost' (2019) 3 *Hrvatska pravna revija* 27, 29.

in accordance with its substantive law or in accordance with its conflict of laws rules.[31]

The legal position of same-sex couples is most certain in 11 participating Member States where such couples are allowed to marry.[32] It is widely accepted that these states should characterise same-sex marriage simply as marriage and apply the Matrimonial Property Regulation.[33] The characterisation in accordance with the *lex fori* should not represent particular problems to the application of Matrimonial Property Regulation, as these Member States equalise same-sex marriages with traditional marriages between the spouses of the opposite sex.

On the other hand, the legal situation is less certain when the competence to decide on the matrimonial property regime of same-sex spouses lies with the courts of seven participating Member States whose law does not envisage same-sex marriage.[34] If the reference to national law in Recital 17 is interpreted as a reference to substantive (national) law of the Member State whose courts were seised, the competent court might have to conclude that same-sex spouses do not fall within the scope of application of the Matrimonial Property Regulation. If the court reaches such a conclusion, it is commonly proposed that it should 'downgrade' same-sex marriage into registered partnership and apply the Regulation on the Property Consequences of Registered Partnerships.[35]

However, as previously mentioned, another interpretation is possible. Instead of characterising same-sex marriage in accordance with the substantive law of the Member State whose courts were seised, the competent court could also refer to its national conflict of laws rules. This option again leads to several possibilities. The court could either characterise the same-sex marriage in accordance with *lex causae* applicable under domestic conflict rules or it could examine whether the relationship between the same-sex couple may be recognised in any form.[36]

---

[31] C. RUDOLF, 'European Property Regimes Regulations – Choice of Law and the Applicable Law in the Absence of Choice by the parties' (2019) 11 *LeXonomica* 127, 134–135; S. MARINO, 'Strengthening the European Civil Judicial Cooperation: the patrimonial effects of family relationships' (2017) 9 *Cuadernos de Derecho Transnacional* 265, 267.

[32] Austria, Belgium, Finland, France, Germany, Luxembourg, Malta, the Netherlands, Portugal Spain and Sweden.

[33] R. HAUSMANN, *Internationales und Europäisches Familienrecht*, C. H. Bech, München 2018, p. 980; S. MARINO, 'Strengthening the European Civil Judicial Cooperation: the patrimonial effects of family relationships' (2017) 9 *Cuadernos de Derecho Transnacional* 265, 268.

[34] Bulgaria, Croatia, Cyprus, Czech Republic, Greece, Italy and Slovenia.

[35] See R. HAUSMANN, *Internationales und Europäisches Familienrecht*, C. H. Bech, München 201, p. 980; S. MARINO, 'Strengthening the European Civil Judicial Cooperation: the patrimonial effects of family relationships' (2017) 9 *Cuadernos de Derecho Transnacional* 265, 268; A. BONOMI, 'Fragen des Allgemeinen Teils: Qualifikation, Vorfrage, Renvoi und ordre public' in A. DUTTA and J. WEBER (eds.), *Die Europäischen Güterrechtsverordnungen*, C. H. Beck, Munich 2017, pp. 133–134.

[36] A. DUTTA, 'Beyond Husband and Wife – New Couple Regimes and the European Property Regulations' (2017/2018) 19 *Yearbook of Private International Law* 145, 152.

According to scientific literature, this solution is preferable to the approach where the competent court relies solely on the definition in its substantive law.[37] By approaching characterisation of same-sex marriages in this way, the application of the Matrimonial Property Regulation is not entirely excluded in the Member States that do not regulate such marriages in their substantive law as will be demonstrated below. This approach may therefore also be preferable to same-sex spouses since it leaves the possibility that their marriage will not be 'downgraded'.

Nonetheless, even with this understanding of Recital 17, the 'downgrading' of same-sex marriage cannot be completely avoided. Domestic private international law in some participating Member States anticipated the above-mentioned problems with the characterisation of same-sex marriages and tried to resolve this issue in advance. In Italy, Article 32-bis of the Law no. 218 of 31 May 1995 (Legge 31 maggio 1995, n. 218)[38] stipulates that marriage contracted abroad by Italian citizens with a person of the same-sex produces the effects of a registered partnership (*unione civile*) as regulated by Italian law. This provision was included in order to prevent Italian citizens from concluding same-sex marriages abroad, thus circumventing Italian law, which only envisages same-sex registered partnerships.[39] By the decision of the Italian Supreme court[40] this 'downgrading' appears not only in situations where marriage was concluded abroad by two Italian citizens, but also in cases of mixed same-sex marriages between an Italian citizen and a foreigner.[41] This indicates that when dealing with property relations of cross-border same-sex spouses where at least one spouse is Italian, the courts in Italy will have to apply the Regulation on the Property Consequences of Registered Partnerships.

An even more restrictive approach can be observed in Croatia. Article 32(2) of the Croatian Private International Law Act (*Zakon o međunardonom privatnom pravu*, ZMPP)[42] stipulates that same-sex marriages celebrated abroad shall be recognised as civil unions (under the condition that marriage was concluded in accordance with the law of the state, where the marriage was celebrated). Unlike the situation in Italy, this provision leads to the conclusion that all same-sex

---

[37] A. BONOMI, 'Fragen des Allgemeinen Teils: Qualifikation, Vorfrage, Renvoi und ordre public' in A. DUTTA and J. WEBER (eds.), *Die Europäischen Güterrechtsverordnungen*, C. H. Beck, Munich 2017, p. 132; A. DUTTA, 'Beyond Husband and Wife – New Couple Regimes and the European Property Regulations' (2017/2018) 19 *Yearbook of Private International Law* 145, 152–153.

[38] GU n.128 del 03-06-1995 – Suppl. Ordinario n. 68.

[39] M. WINKLER, 'A Case with peculiarities: Mixed Same-Sex Marriages Before the Supreme Court' (2018) 4 *The Italian Law Journal* 273, 281.

[40] Corte di Cassazione n 11696/2018 of 14 May 2018.

[41] See also M. WINKLER, 'A Case with peculiarities: Mixed Same-Sex Marriages Before the Supreme Court' (2018) 4 *The Italian Law Journal* 273, 284–286.

[42] NN 101/17.

marriages (not only those that can be considered as circumventing national law) will be 'downgraded' and treated as registered partnerships.

It is important to note that this issue is far from being solely theoretical. The 'downgrading' of same-sex marriage may have important implications on the property regime between the spouses. In order to demonstrate these practical consequences, an example is provided below.

> Peter (a German citizen) and Michael (a Danish citizen) concluded marriage in Germany on 1 February 2019. At the time of marriage, they both worked in Austria where they had their habitual residence at the time and after getting married. On 1 February 2020, the spouses moved to Alternative 1: Germany, Alternative 2: Croatia; Alternative 3: Slovenia, where the courts were seised on the 1 June 2021 to decide on their matrimonial property (divorce proceedings were not initiated). Spouses concluded neither a choice-of-court nor choice-of-law agreement.[43]

In order to demonstrate how moving to a different country affects the outcome of the case, the example provides three alternatives. However, it should be noted first that in all three alternatives (and regardless of which of the two Regulations shall be applicable) the international jurisdiction will be governed by the same connecting factor. Considering that proceedings on matrimonial property were not initiated in connection with application for divorce, legal separation or marriage annulment, nor in connection with succession proceedings after a spouse, the jurisdiction will lie with the courts of the Member State in whose territory the spouses/partners are habitually resident at the time the court is seised (Article 6(1)(1) of the Matrimonial Property Regulation and the Regulation on the Property Consequences of Registered Partnerships).[44] Thus depending on the alternative, the jurisdiction in the present case will lie with the courts of Germany, Croatia or Slovenia.

In Alternative 1, the German courts will apply the Matrimonial Property Regulation (Germany takes part in enhanced cooperation) in order to decide on the property relations of Peter and Michael. At first glance, the conclusion that the Matrimonial Property Regulation is applicable may be reached by noting that German substantive law opened the institution of marriage to

---

[43] Since the marriage between Peter and Michael was concluded on 1 February 2019 and the courts were seised on 1 June 2021, the Twin Regulations can be applied as a whole. It should nonetheless be noted that pursuant to Article 69(3), Chapter III, which contains conflict-of-law provisions, is only applicable to spouses who marry or who specify the applicable matrimonial property regime on or after 29 January 2019. Had the spouses concluded their marriage prior to that date, the courts would need to apply domestic conflict rules. See Chapter 3 of this volume concerning the temporal scope of application of the Twin Regulations.

[44] See Chapter 4 of this volume in regard to international jurisdiction under the Twin Regulations.

same-sex spouses.[45] However, if one follows the argument that reference to national law in Recital 17 also includes domestic private international law, provisions of the German Introductory Act to the Civil code (*Einführungsgesetz zum Bürgerlichen Gesetzbuche*, EGBGB)[46] need to be examined as well. From its provisions, it can be observed that the German legislator anticipated problems with characterisation of same-sex marriage. Article 17.b(4) of EGBGB thus explicitly stipulates that property consequences of marriage between same-sex spouses (or spouses where at least one does not identify with female or male sex) should be determined in accordance with the applicable law under Matrimonial Property Regulation.[47] The applicable law in the present case will therefore be determined in accordance with Article 26(1)(a) of the Matrimonial Property Regulation. This will be Austrian law, as this is the law of the state of the spouses' first common habitual residence after the conclusion of marriage. This conclusion will likely fulfil the legitimate expectations of the spouses. The Matrimonial Property Regulation and consequent Austrian law is thus applicable whether the spouses remained in Austria or moved to Germany. In other words, their move to Germany would not influence the applicable law to their matrimonial property regime.

On the other hand, Alternative 2 may prove less satisfactory to the expectations of Peter and Michael. The Croatian Constitution[48] and the Family Act[49] limit marriage to opposite-sex couples only. Same-sex partners may instead conclude a civil union.[50] As mentioned above, the Croatian legislator also anticipated problems regarding the characterisation of same-sex marriage and dealt with this matter in Article 32(2) of ZMPP, which states that same-sex marriages celebrated abroad shall be recognised as civil unions. Pursuant to Article 40(3) of ZMPP the law applicable to property consequences of civil unions shall be determined in accordance with the Regulation on the Property Consequences of Registered Partnerships. This leads us to the conclusion that Croatian courts will most likely 'downgrade' the marriage of Peter and Michael and treat it as a registered partnership. The applicable law to their property regime will thus be determined pursuant to Article 26(1) of the Regulation on the Property Consequences of Registered Partnerships, which points to the law of the state under whose law the registered partnership was created. In the

---

[45] A. DUTTA, 'Beyond Husband and Wife – New Couple Regimes and the European Property Regulations' (2017/2018) 19 *Yearbook of Private International Law* 145, 152.
[46] Einführungsgesetz zum Bürgerlichen Gesetzbuche in der Fassung der Bekanntmachung vom 21. September 1994 (BGBl. I S. 2494; 1997 I S. 1061), das zuletzt durch Artikel 2 des Gesetzes vom 4. Mai 2021 (BGBl. I S. 882) geändert worden ist.
[47] See also M. ANDRAE, *Internationales Familienrecht*, Nomos, Baden-Baden 2019, p. 241.
[48] Ustav Republike Hrvatske, NN 56/90,135/97, 08/98, 113/00, 124/00, 28/01, 41/01, 55/01, 76/10, 85/10, 05/14; Article 62(2).
[49] Obiteljski zakon, NN 103/15, 98/19, Article 12.
[50] Zakon o životnom partnerstvu osoba istog spola, NN 92/14, 98/19.

present case, this is German law. From Alternative 2, it can be observed that the spouses' relocation to Croatia caused the change of the applicable law to their property regime. This, however, might not be in line with the expectations of the couple. Instead of applying the Austrian matrimonial property regime of separation of property (*Gütertrennung*),[51] the spouses would fall under the German regime of property of accrued gains (*Zugewinngemeinschaft*).[52] If the spouses had instead moved to a participating Member State where same-sex marriages are recognised and treated simply as marriage, such change of the applicable law would not have happened (as can be seen from Alternative 1).

Unlike in Germany and Croatia, the Slovenian legislator (Alternative 3) did not envisage any provision in the domestic private international law, which would address the characterisation or recognition of same-sex marriages. To determine which of the Twin Regulations shall be applicable, the courts will have to interpret Recital 17. If the court holds that the reference to 'national law' in Recital 17 is to be understood as a reference to the substantive law of the Member State whose courts were seised, it will reject the application of the Matrimonial Property Regulation. Similarly to Croatia, Slovenian law does not envisage same-sex marriages.[53] Instead, it enables same-sex couples to conclude a civil union.[54] In this case, the court could 'downgrade' the same-sex marriage into a registered partnership and apply the Regulation on the Property Consequences of Registered Partnerships. On the other hand, if the reference to national law is understood as a reference to a definition or concept of marriage under the domestic private international law, a view that is also supported by the author of this chapter, the Slovenian court might still come to the conclusion that such marriage can be characterised as marriage and thus apply the Matrimonial Property Regulation.

Slovenian Private International Law and Procedure Act (*Zakon o mednarodnem zasebnem pravu in postopku*, ZMZPP)[55] does not include any explicit provisions regulating the recognition of a foreign marriage (or even same-sex marriage). In Article 34 it stipulates that the requirements for the conclusion of marriage shall be governed for each person by the law of the state of their nationality at the time of conclusion of a marriage. The form

---

[51] Allgemeine bürgerliches Gesetzbuch, Article 1237; see also T. PERTOT, 'Austria' in L. RUGGERI, I. KUNDA, S. WINKLER (eds.), *Family Property and Succession in EU Member States: National Reports on the Collected Data*, University of Rijeka, Faculty of Law, Rijeka 2019, p. 7.

[52] Lebenspartnershaftgesetz, Article 6; Bürgerliche Gesetzbuch, Article 1363; see also T. PERTOT, 'Germany' in L. RUGGERI, I. KUNDA, S. WINKLER (eds.), *Family Property and Succession in EU Member States: National Reports on the Collected Data*, University of Rijeka, Faculty of Law, Rijeka 2019, p. 267.

[53] Družinski zakonik, Official Gazette of Republic of Slovenia, no. 15/17, 21/18 – ZNOrg, 22/19, 67/19 – ZMatR-C in 200/20 – ZOOMTVI), Article 3.

[54] Zakon o partnerski zvezi, Official Gazette of Republic of Slovenia, no. 33/16, Article 2.

[55] Uradni list RS, št. 56/99, 45/08 – ZArbit in 31/21 – odl. US.

of conclusion, on the other hand, is governed by the law of the state where the marriage was celebrated (Article 35 of ZMZPP). Although the available databases of court practice show that the Slovenian courts have yet to pronounce their views on the recognition of same-sex marriages, it can be argued that the marriage in question can be recognised. The above-mentioned provisions of ZMZPP are gender neutral. It is also unlikely that the courts would hold that such recognition would be contrary to Slovenian public policy.[56] Furthermore, it can be observed that our spouses, who are citizens of Germany and Denmark, where same-sex marriages are possible, fulfil the requirements under the law of their nationality. Based on these considerations, the marriage in question could be categorised as marriage for the purpose of matrimonial property regime proceedings.

The interpretation of Recital 17 by Slovenian courts will be decisive for answering the question regarding which of the Twin Regulations shall be applied. This decision will, as already demonstrated above, also influence the applicable law in the present case. In the case of 'downgrading' the same-sex marriage the courts will apply German law as this is the law of the state under whose law the registered partnership was created (Article 26(1) of the Regulation on the Property Consequences of Registered Partnerships). On the other hand, if they treat the same-sex marriage as marriage, the applicable law will be Austrian law as the law of the state of the spouses' first common habitual residence after the conclusion of marriage (Article 26(1)(a) of the Matrimonial Property Regulation).

The example demonstrates how the lack of an autonomous definition of marriage and, consequently, the lack of an autonomous delimitation between the Twin Regulations impacts same-sex spouses. Considering that providing legal certainty and a degree of predictability was one of the central goals of the twin Regulations,[57] it can be concluded that these goals were reached only in part. As demonstrated above, a move to another participating Member State may cause a change of applicable law to the matrimonial property regime of same-sex spouses. This is contrary to the aims expressed in Recital 46 of the Matrimonial Property Regulation and may also thwart the freedom of

---

[56] Slovenian Civil union act stipulates that a civil union produces the same effects as marriage in all legal fields (apart from adoption and fertilisation with biomedical assistance). The property consequences of a (same-sex) civil union are thus identical to marriage. Furthermore, when interpreting the concept of public policy, the Slovenian Supreme Court already ruled that recognition of a foreign decision allowing for the adoption of a child by same-sex spouses is not contrary to Slovenian public policy (Decision II Ips 462/2009, 28. 1. 2010). Although this decision was rendered in different factual circumstances, it nonetheless indicates the Supreme Court's view of the limitations to the interpretation of public policy.

[57] See, inter alia, Recitals no. 15, 43, 46 and 72 of the Matrimonial Property Regulation and Recitals no. 15, 42, 45 and 70 of the Regulation on the Property Consequences of Registered Partnerships.

movement, another goal of the Twin Regulations. Lastly, the unequal treatment of same-sex spouses, caused by the lack of an autonomous definition of marriage, could also be seen as contrary to the principle of non-discrimination enshrined in Article 21 of the Charter of Fundamental Rights of the European Union (the Charter).[58]

To mitigate these problems and to ensure a harmonised application of Twin Regulations, another approach was suggested by Dutta. Instead of characterising same-sex marriage in accordance with the *lex fori*, reference to the national law of Member States in Recital 17 may also be interpreted as a reference to the law of the Member State, where marriage was concluded (*lex loci celebrationis*).[59] This approach can improve the legal predictability for same-sex spouses. In other words, it would enable those participating Member States, whose national law does not allow same-sex marriages, to nonetheless apply the Matrimonial Property Regulation. Thus, a more uniform delimitation between the scopes of application of Twin Regulations could still be achieved. However, this interpretation – although potentially desirable to same-sex spouses – is less likely.[60] Recital 17 mentions the national law of Member States. Had the spouses concluded marriage in a non-participating Member State or a third state, such characterisation would not be possible. It is also unlikely that the Member State, where attempts to resolve the problem of characterisation were already made in their conflict of laws rules, would resort to this approach.

4. ALTERNATIVE JURISDICTION

Omitting a definition of marriage was not the only attempt to address the concerns of 'conservative' Member States. In Article 9, the Matrimonial Property Regulation provides for 'Alternative jurisdiction'. This provision, which is considered by some to be the most original in the Regulation,[61] allows the court that has jurisdiction pursuant to Articles 4, 6, 7, or 8 to exceptionally decline jurisdiction if it holds that under its private international law, the marriage in question is not recognised for the purposes of matrimonial property regime

---

[58] Pursuant to Article 51 of the Charter, the courts of the Member States are bound by its provisions when applying EU law. C 326/391, 26. 10. 2012.

[59] A. DUTTA, 'Beyond Husband and Wife – New Couple Regimes and the European Property Regulations' (2017/2018) 19 *Yearbook of Private International Law* 145, 149.

[60] See also I. KUNDA, 'Novi međunarodnoprivatnopravni okvir imovine bračnih i registriranih partnera u Europskoj uniji: polje primjene i nadležnost' (2019) 3 *Hrvatska pravna revija* 27, 29.

[61] P. FRANZINA, 'Article 9: Alternative Jurisdiction' in P. FRANZINA and I. VIARENGO, *The EU Regulations on the Property Regimes of International Couples: A Commentary*, Edward Elgar, Cheltenham 2020, p. 104; S. MARINO, 'Strengthening the European Civil Judicial Cooperation: the patrimonial effects of family relationships' (2017) 9 *Cuadernos de Derecho Transnacional* 265, 276.

proceedings. Courts that wished to decline jurisdiction must do so without undue delay.

As indicated above, this provision responds to divergent ways in which the Member States regulate same-sex partnerships and attempts to reassure those Member States that limit marriage to opposite-sex couples, that they will not be forced to recognise forms of partnerships unknown to their legal system and potentially contrary to their public policy.[62] Parallels are often drawn between Article 9 of the Matrimonial Property Regulation and Article 13 of the Rome III Regulation.[63,64] The latter stipulates, inter alia, that the courts of participating Member States are not obliged to pronounce divorce by virtue of Rome III Regulation if their law does not deem the marriage in question valid for the purposes of divorce proceedings. Although Article 9 relates to international jurisdiction and Article 13 to applicable law, it can be observed that they both serve a similar purpose and were included to facilitate unanimity among the Member States.

If the courts of a participating Member State avail themselves of the possibility under Article 9 of the Matrimonial Property Regulation and decline the jurisdiction, the spouses could bring their case before the courts of other participating Member States. Article 9(2) offers them several possibilities. They may either designate the competent courts by concluding a choice-of-court agreement pursuant to Article 7, or they may seise the courts of other participating Member State pursuant to Article 6 (Jurisdiction in other cases) or Article 8 (Jurisdiction based on the appearance of the defendant). They may also seise the courts of the Member State, where the marriage was concluded.

It is argued that Article 9 carries important practical consequences for same-sex spouses as it avoids the risk that a court – when deciding on the merits of the case – would pronounce that their marriage produced no matrimonial property consequences.[65] Such a decision on the merits would produce *res iudicata* effects and could hinder the possibility of spouses reaching a decision on their matrimonial property in other Member States.[66] The refusal to hear the case as regulated in Article 9 would thus be preferable for the spouses.

---

[62] P. FRANZINA, 'Article 9: Alternative Jurisdiction' in P. FRANZINA and I. VIARENGO, *The EU Regulations on the Property Regimes of International Couples: A Commentary*, Edward Elgar, Cheltenham 2020, pp. 104–105.

[63] Council Regulation (EU) No. 1259/2010 of 20 December 2010 implementing enhanced cooperation in the area of the law applicable to divorce and legal separation [2010] OJ L 343/10.

[64] P. FRANZINA, 'Article 9: Alternative Jurisdiction' in P. FRANZINA and I. VIARENGO, *The EU Regulations on the Property Regimes of International Couples: A Commentary*, Edward Elgar, Cheltenham 2020, p. 105.

[65] S. MARINO, 'Strengthening the European Civil Judicial Cooperation: the patrimonial effects of family relationships' (2017) 9 *Cuadernos de Derecho Transnacional* 265, 276.

[66] Ibid.

The inclusion of Article 9, however, raises another question. If references to national law in Recital 17 were indeed to be understood as a reference to the substantive law of the forum, then Article 9 would bear little practical value.[67] Those Member States that limit marriage to spouses of the opposite sex would refuse to characterise same-sex marriage as marriage and would therefore reject the application of the Matrimonial Property Regulation (and its Article 9). This further corroborates the view that Recital 17 should be understood as a reference to the definition of marriage under private international law of the forum.

5. PARTY AUTONOMY – A POSSIBLE SOLUTION TO UNCERTAINTY?

With the aim of increasing legal predictability and legal security of cross-border couples, the Twin Regulations enable them to exercise party autonomy.[68] Both spouses and registered partners may conclude choice-of-court and choice-of-law agreements. This solution may seem particularly attractive to same-sex spouses who wish to avoid some of the uncertainty stemming from divergent acceptance of same-sex marriages between the Member States. While the conclusion of such agreements may in certain circumstances prove helpful, a closer examination shows that system of party autonomy established in Twin Regulations comes with several limitations, and party autonomy should therefore be exercised with caution and with awareness of potential problems.

5.1. CHOICE-OF-COURT AGREEMENTS

In accordance with Article 7 of the Twin Regulations, if the application of Articles 4 and 5 and consequent concentration of jurisdiction is not possible,[69] spouses and partners may agree that courts of the chosen Member State shall have exclusive jurisdiction to decide on their property relations. Such choice-of-court agreements may be concluded before or after the marriage was celebrated

---

[67] See also P. FRANZINA, 'Article 9: Alternative Jurisdiction' in P. FRANZINA and I. VIARENGO, *The EU Regulations on the Property Regimes of International Couples: A Commentary*, Edward Elgar, Cheltenham 2020, pp. 105–106. See also A. DUTTA, 'Beyond Husband and Wife – New Couple Regimes and the European Property Regulations' (2017/2018) 19 *Yearbook of Private International Law* 145, 151; M. ANDRAE, *Internationales Familienrecht*, Nomos, Baden-Baden 2019, p. 285.

[68] See Recitals no. 36, 45 and 46 of the Matrimonial Property Regulation and Recitals no. 37, 44 and 45 of the Regulation on the Property Consequences of Registered Partnerships.

[69] See Chapter 4 of this volume for questions relating to international jurisdiction.

(or the partnership was registered).[70] They may either form part of a broader marital agreement or be connected to a choice-of-law agreement or even be concluded separately.[71]

Conclusion of a choice-of-court agreement seems to be a useful tool, especially for same-sex spouses. First, by designating the competent courts, same-sex spouses may avoid the jurisdiction of the courts in a Member State where their marriage is likely to be 'downgraded' into a registered partnership. Secondly, this may also avoid the possibility that the competent court would refuse the application of a provision of the designated law by relying on its public policy as stipulated in Article 31 of the Twin Regulations.

Under the Twin Regulations, spouses or registered partners may only choose courts of the 18 participating Member States.[72] Pursuant to Article 7 of the Matrimonial Property Regulation, spouses are further limited to four possibilities. They may choose the courts of the Member State whose law is applicable pursuant to a choice-of-law agreement (Article 22 of the Matrimonial Property Regulation) or the courts of the Member State whose law is applicable either pursuant to Article 26(1)(a) or Article 26(1)(b), namely the courts of the Member States of the spouses' first common habitual residence after the conclusion of marriage or of the spouses' common nationality at the time of conclusion of marriage. Finally, the spouses may also choose the courts of the Member States of the conclusion of their marriage. As Recital 37 explains, the latter is the Member State before whose authorities the marriage is concluded. For same-sex spouses, the possibility to choose the courts of the Member State of the conclusion of marriage is of particular importance as it reassures them that a decision on their matrimonial property regime will be made by a court that will recognise their marriage. Registered partners, on the other hand, may only choose between two possibilities. They may either agree on the exclusive jurisdiction of the courts of the Member State whose law is applicable pursuant to a choice-of-law agreement (Article 22 of the Regulation on the Property Consequences of Registered Partnerships) or the courts of the Member State under whose law the registered partnership was created.[73]

---

[70] M. ANDRAE, *Internationales Familienrecht*, Nomos, Baden-Baden 2019, p. 275.
[71] Ibid., p. 276.
[72] Generally, spouses may also choose courts of non-participating Member States or third states. However, such agreements will be governed by the national Private international law of the chosen state and not the Twin Regulations.
[73] Article 7 of Regulation on the Property Consequences of Registered Partnerships also stipulates that registered partners may choose the court of the Member State whose law is applicable under Article 26(1). Pursuant to Article 26(1) these are the courts of the Member State under whose law the registered partnership was created. This connecting factor thus appears twice in Article 7.

In concluding a choice-of-court agreement, spouses and registered partners must also observe the requirements for formal validity, which are stipulated in Article 7(2) of the Twin Regulations. Their agreement must be 'expressed in writing, dated and signed by the parties'. Communications by electronic means which provide a durable record of the agreement are also deemed equivalent to the written form. While the formal validity is expressly regulated in Twins Regulation, no provision concerning substantive validity is included. This should therefore be ascertained in accordance with the law of the Member State, whose courts were chosen.[74]

It is important to note that Article 7(1) states that parties may determine which courts shall have exclusive jurisdiction. The term 'parties' needs to be interpreted autonomously[75] and it may – in addition to the spouses or registered partners – also include third parties such as creditors of the couple. However, such third parties will only be bound by the choice-of-law agreement concluded between the spouses if they also agree to it.[76] Same-sex spouses that concluded a choice-of-court agreement wishing to avoid the possibility of having their marriage 'downgraded' may still incur that risk if the third person, who is not bound by their agreement, seises the court of a Member State where same-sex marriages are not recognised.

Further unpredictability stems from the fact that pursuant to Article 7 of the Matrimonial Property Regulation, a choice-of-court agreement is only possible 'in cases which are covered by Article 6' (Jurisdiction in other cases). This means that spouses are not able to derogate from jurisdiction under Article 4 (Jurisdiction in the event of death of one of the spouses) and Article 5 (Jurisdiction in cases of divorce, legal separation or marriage annulment). These two articles aim to achieve concentration between related proceedings and thus grant jurisdiction to decide on the matters of matrimonial property regimes to the courts of the participating Member States, which were seised in matters concerning succession and divorce, legal separation or marriage annulment. In practice, matters of matrimonial property regime most commonly arise either in connection with the death of one of the spouses or in connection with the divorce. Therefore, it can be expected that jurisdiction under the Matrimonial Property Regulation will usually be determined based on these two articles. Article 6, on the other hand, will most probably be applied less frequently and will present the basis for jurisdiction in other cases such as in disputes between

---

[74] P. FRANZINA and I. VIARENGO, 'Article 7' in P. FRANZINA and I. VIARENGO, *The EU Regulations on the Property Regimes of International Couples: A Commentary*, Edward Elgar, Cheltenham 2020, p. 90; M. ANDRAE, *Internationales Familienrecht*, Nomos, Baden-Baden 2019, p. 278.

[75] U. BERGQUIST, D. DAMASCELLI, R. FRIMSTON, P. LAGARDE and B. REINHARTZ, *The EU Regulations on Matrimonial and Patrimonial Property*, Oxford University Press, Oxford 2019, p. 63.

[76] M. ANDRAE, *Internationales Familienrecht*, Nomos, Baden-Baden 2019, p. 276.

the spouses, whether certain property belongs to spouses' common property or forms parts of one spouse's separates property.[77] To see how this applies in practice, let us consider the following example:

> Maria (a Spanish citizen) and Judith (an Austrian citizen) concluded marriage on 15 March 2019 in Spain, where they lived at the time and where they continued to live and work. On 15 March 2019, the spouses also concluded a choice-of-court agreement pursuant to Article 7 of the Matrimonial Property Regulation conferring exclusive jurisdiction to decide on their matrimonial property regime to Spanish courts. In March 2020 both spouses moved to Slovenia, where Maria died on 30 May 2021. Following her death, a disagreement arose between Judith and Maria's mother regarding the shares of the spouses' apartment in Ljubljana.

The example first raises the questions concerning international jurisdiction and applicable law in the matter of succession. Both issues are regulated in the Succession Regulation.[78] In the present case, the jurisdiction will lie with Slovenian courts, which will have to apply Slovenian law as Slovenia is the Member State in which the deceased had her habitual residence at the time of death (Articles 4 and 21 of the Succession Regulation). However, in the context of succession, a connected question concerning matrimonial property has arisen. Under Article 4 of the Twin Regulations, the court of a participating Member State, which was seised in matters of a succession of a spouse or a registered partner pursuant to the Succession Regulation, shall also have jurisdiction to rule on the matters of the matrimonial property regime (or matters of property consequences of registered partnership) arising in connection with that succession case. Thus, despite the choice-of-court agreement between the spouses, Slovenian courts will also have the jurisdiction to decide on the dispute concerning the shares on the spouses' matrimonial property. The fact that a choice-of-court agreement was concluded will not exclude the jurisdiction of Slovenian courts as it will be based on Article 4. Furthermore, it can also be observed that the parties involved in the matrimonial property dispute will be Judith and Maria's mother, who did not participate in the prorogation of jurisdiction. As jurisdiction lies with Slovenian courts, they will have to determine whether to apply the Matrimonial Property Regulation or to 'downgrade' the marriage and apply the Regulation on the Property Consequences of Registered Partnerships. The choice-of court-agreement thus failed to provide additional legal certainty to same-sex spouses.

---

[77] P. FRANZINA and I. VIARENGO, 'Article 7' in P. FRANZINA and I. VIARENGO, *The EU Regulations on the Property Regimes of International Couples: A Commentary*, Edward Elgar, Cheltenham 2020, p. 79.

[78] Regulation (EU) No 650/2012 of the European Parliament and of the Council of 4 July 2012 on jurisdiction, applicable law, recognition and enforcement of decisions and acceptance and enforcement of authentic instruments in matters of succession and on the creation of a European Certificate of Succession, L 201/107, 27. 7. 2012.

On the other hand, Article 5 of the Matrimonial Property Regulation will be less relevant to same-sex spouses. It stipulates that a court of a Member State, which was seised to rule on the application for divorce, legal separation or marriage annulment pursuant to the Brussels II bis Regulation[79] shall also have jurisdiction to rule on matters of the matrimonial property regime arising in connection with that application. As it is commonly accepted that the Brussels II bis Regulation excludes same-sex marriages from its scope of application,[80] it is thus unlikely that matters of matrimonial property regime of same-sex spouses could arise in connection with an application under the Brussels II a Regulation.

Another issue may arise in connection with the choice-of-court agreements. As can be seen above, the Matrimonial Property Regulation offers spouses a broader set of options in comparison to those offered to registered partners by the Regulation on the Property Consequences of Registered Partnerships. Spouses may thus also choose the courts of the Member State of their first common habitual residence after the conclusion of marriage or the courts of the Member State of their common nationality at the time of the conclusion of marriage – two options, which are not available to registered partners. It is possible to imagine a case (although probably unlikely in practice), where same-sex spouses would conclude a choice-of-court agreement, that would be valid pursuant to the Matrimonial Property Regulation, but not pursuant to the Regulation on the Property Consequences of Registered Partnerships. If one of the spouses later decided to disregard the agreement and seised a court of a Member State which 'downgrades' same-sex marriages and consequently applies the Regulation on the Property Consequences of Registered Partnerships to their property relations, the question could arise whether such an agreement will be accepted as valid by that court. In other words, will the court that was seised declare that it has no jurisdiction due to the prorogation, or will it hold that agreement as invalid? This problem somewhat resembles another issue, which was pointed out in scientific literature. Namely, the application of *lis pendens* rule where in relation to the same marriage courts of one Member State would be seised pursuant to the Matrimonial Property Regulation and the courts of another Member State pursuant to the Regulation on the Property Consequences of Registered Partnerships.[81] At the moment, the solution to this question remains opened.

---

[79] Council Regulation (EC) No 2201/2003 of 27 November 2003 concerning jurisdiction and the recognition and enforcement of judgments in matrimonial matters and the matters of parental responsibility, repealing Regulation (EC) No 1347/2000, L 338/1, 23. 12. 2003.

[80] T. RAUSCHER, 'Brüssel IIa-VO' in T. RAUSCHER (ed.), *Europäisches Zivilprozess- und Kollisionsrecht EuZPR/EuIPR, Band IV*, Otto Schmidt, Cologne 2015, p. 47; R. HAUSMANN, *Internationales und Europäisches Familienrecht*, C. H. Bech, München 2018, p. 980.

[81] A. DUTTA, 'Beyond Husband and Wife – New Couple Regimes and the European Property Regulations' (2017/2018) 19 *Yearbook of Private International Law* 145, 150.

5.2. CHOICE-OF-LAW AGREEMENTS

In addition to choice-of-court agreements, Twin Regulations also enable spouses and registered partners to conclude choice-of-law agreements. Thus, they may designate the law, which will apply to all assets that form their matrimonial property or property consequences of their registered partnership, regardless of where these assets are located (Article 21 of Twin Regulations). Spouses and registered partners may avail themselves of this possibility even before their relationship was formalised (Article 22 of the Twin Regulations).

This possibility may prove particularly beneficial for same-sex spouses. Due to divergences in the domestic family law regulation of same-sex marriage, they are faced with the possibility that Article 26 of the Matrimonial Property Regulation (Applicable law in the absence of choice by the parties) will point to the law which does not allow the conclusion of same-sex marriage and consequently does not regulate any property consequences of such marriages. This may occur, inter alia, when spouses established their first common habitual residence after the conclusion of marriage in such a state. On the one hand, it can be argued that the competent court could nonetheless apply the law of such a state since provisions concerning matrimonial property regimes are usually gender neutral.[82] However, to avoid any risk, same-sex spouses may also conclude a choice-of-law agreement in which they designate as applicable the law of a state which opened marriage to couples of same-sex and envisages property consequences of such marriages. The possibility that the applicable law will not regulate property consequences of registered partnerships was, on the other hand, predicted in the Regulation on the Property Consequences of Registered Partnerships. Within this regulation, Article 26, therefore, points to the law of the state under whose law the registered partnership was created since this law will also regulate the property consequences of such partnerships.

Due to the principle of universal application in Article 20 of Twin Regulations, couples may designate as applicable either the law of a participating Member State or of any other state. However, in choosing the applicable law, couples also face several limitations. Spouses may designate as applicable either the law of the state where both or one of them is habitually resident at the time the agreement is concluded or the law of the state of the nationality of either spouse at the time of conclusion of the agreement. It is nonetheless advisable that same-sex spouses choose the law of the state which allows same-sex couples to marry and envisages the property consequences of such marriages. Registered partners on the other hand are limited by the requirement that the designated law needs to attach property consequences to the institution of the registered partnership. This approach is needed, since,

---

[82] Ibid., 153; M. ANDRAE, *Internationales Familienrecht*, Nomos, Baden-Baden 2019, p. 242.

unlike marriage, only certain states regulate registered partnerships. If this condition is fulfilled, registered partners may choose between three options. First, they may designate as applicable the law of the state where both or one of them is habitually resident at the time the agreement is concluded. Secondly, they may choose the law of nationality of either partner at the time the agreement is concluded or thirdly they may opt for the law of the state under whose law the registered partnership was created.

Spouses and registered partners who concluded a choice-of-law agreement, nonetheless, need to be wary of some limitations to the effects of such agreements. Since the law, designated by the couple, also governs the effects of the matrimonial property regime (or property consequences of registered partnership) on a legal relationship between a spouse (or partner) and third parties (Article 27(f) of the Twin Regulations), special protection is envisaged for the third parties. By virtue of Article 28 of the Twin Regulations, the designated law may not be invoked against the third party unless the third party knew or should have known of that law. Furthermore, any retroactive effects of a choice-of-law agreement (if the couple decides that the agreement should produce retroactive effects) may not adversely affect the third parties (Article 22(3) of the Twin Regulations).

6. RECOGNITION AND ENFORCEMENT

Once a court has ruled on the property relations of a same-sex couple, the recognition and enforcement of such a decision in a foreign state may present itself as the final uncertainty the couple will face. The central issue arising in relation to same-sex couples is the possibility that a court will reject the recognition and enforcement of a foreign decision by invoking reasons of public policy (*ordre public*). The legislative process of the Twin Regulations demonstrates that this issue was particularly problematic for some (more conservative) Member States. As noted earlier, their reservations were based particularly on the fear that under the Twin Regulations their courts will have to recognise and enforce decisions on property relations of same-sex couples, which would consequently extend the effects of such relationships also to their territory.[83]

The provisions in Chapter IV of the Twin Regulations, relating to recognition and enforcement, will be applied only when a decision was rendered in one participating Member State and its recognition and enforcement is sought in another participating Member State. It can be observed that provisions in Chapter IV resemble and follow the system of recognition and enforcement in other EU instruments such as in the aforementioned Brussels II bis Regulation

---

[83] A. WYSOCKA-BAR, 'Enhanced Cooperation in Property Matters in the EU and Non-Participating Member States' (2019) 20 *ERA Forum* 187, 193–194.

and the Succession Regulation as well as in the Brussels I Regulation[84] and the Maintenance Regulation.[85] This is particularly important as the court practice of the Court of Justice of the European Union (CJEU) regarding these regulations can be used when interpreting the Chapter IV of the Twin Regulations.[86]

Pursuant to Article 36 of the Twin Regulations, a foreign decision can be recognised without any special procedure (*ipso iure* recognition). Alternatively, a decision may also be recognised in a special procedure or considered incidentally (as a preliminary question). On the other hand, a foreign decision can be enforced in another Member State only if it has been (on the application of any interested party) declared enforceable by the courts of that state (Article 42 of Twin Regulations). The grounds for a refusal of recognition and enforcement are listed in Article 37, which includes the four 'classical' grounds also found in other EU instruments in the field of private international law. Inter alia, the recognition and enforcement of a foreign decision may also be refused if this would be manifestly contrary to the public policy of the Member State where recognition is sought (Article 37(1)(a)). This leads to the question of whether the recognition and enforcement of a decision can be refused on the ground of public policy solely because the court of origin has ruled on property relations of same-sex spouses. This question will be discussed in the example below:

> Louis (a Belgian citizen) and Mark (a Dutch citizen) concluded marriage in April 2019 in Belgium and settled in Brussels. Upon marriage, the spouses concluded a marital agreement and opted for the regime of separation of property. After a divorce was pronounced in Belgium in April 2021, Mark also succeeded with the claim for compensation on the basis of spouses' property regime and he seeks the declaration of enforceability in Bulgaria, where Louis has previously purchased a holiday villa on the coast of the Black Sea.

In the present case, a court in Bulgaria will first need to determine which of the Twin Regulations should be applied in the proceeding of enforcement. It should be noted that Bulgarian law does not envisage same-sex marriages (the Bulgarian constitution explicitly limits marriage to spouses of the opposite sex) nor same-sex registered partnerships.[87] Due to the above-mentioned lack of

---

[84] Council Regulation (EC) No 44/2001 of 22 December 2000 on jurisdiction and the recognition and enforcement of judgments in civil and commercial matters [2001] OJ 12/1.

[85] Council Regulation (EC) No 4/2009 of 18 December 2008 on jurisdiction, applicable law, recognition and enforcement of decisions and cooperation in matters relating to maintenance obligations [2009] OJ L 7/1.

[86] U. BERGQUIST, D. DAMASCELLI, R. FRIMSTON, P. LAGARDE and B. REINHARTZ, *The EU Regulations on Matrimonial and Patrimonial Property*, Oxford University Press, Oxford 2019, pp. 140–141.

[87] D. SARBINOVA, 'Bulgaria' in L. RUGGERI, I. KUNDA, S. WINKLER (eds.), *Family Property and Succession in EU Member States: National Reports on the Collected Data*, University of Rijeka, Faculty of Law Rijeka, 2019, p. 52.

an autonomous delimitation between their personal scope of application, it is thus possible that the Bulgarian court will apply the Regulation on the Property Consequences of Registered Partnerships, although the Belgian judgment was rendered pursuant to the Matrimonial Property Regulation.[88] This, however, is of no practical consequence for the spouses, since the provisions on recognition and enforcement are identical in both regulations. It should also be observed that the Bulgarian court cannot decline jurisdiction pursuant to Article 9, since this is only possible when a court is seised pursuant to Articles 4, 6, 7, and 8.[89]

A more pressing matter for the spouse would be if the Bulgarian court (on the appeal of the other spouse) would regard that the enforcement of such a judgement is manifestly contrary to its public policy. On this note, several considerations need to be taken into account. Although the public policy is a concept which is defined differently in every participating Member State, national courts should nonetheless consider the jurisprudence of the CJEU, which has continually drawn limits to its application.[90] This jurisprudence shows that all grounds for refusal should be interpreted strictly as they represent an obstacle to the free movement of judgments.[91] A particular caution should be exercised in regard to the public policy clause, which should only be invoked in exceptional cases.[92] The recourse to public policy clause should therefore only be possible where the recognition and enforcement of a foreign decision would be manifestly contrary to the fundamental values of the state, where recognition and enforcement are sought and would cause intolerable legal effects in that legal order.[93]

Furthermore, the court where the recognition and enforcement is sought also needs to consider the restrictions stipulated in Article 38 of the Twin Regulations. According to its wording, all grounds for refusal shall be applied in 'observance of the fundamental rights and principles recognised in the Charter,

---

[88] Cf. M. ANDRAE, *Internationales Familienrecht*, Nomos, Baden-Baden 2019, p. 241.

[89] See also M. GEBAUER, 'Article 38: Fundamental rights' in P. FRANZINA and I. VIARENGO, *The EU Regulations on the Property Regimes of International Couples: A Commentary*, Edward Elgar, Cheltenham 2020, pp. 358–359.

[90] U. BERGQUIST, D. DAMASCELLI, R. FRIMSTON, P. LAGARDE and B. REINHARTZ, *The EU Regulations on Matrimonial and Patrimonial Property*, Oxford University Press, Oxford 2019, p. 152.

[91] Case C-414/92, *Solo Kleinmotoren GmbH v Emilio Boch*, ECLI:EU:C:1994:221; see also N. POGORELČNIK VOGRINC, 'Refusal of Recognition and Enforcement' in M. CAZORLA GONZALEZ, M. GIOBBI, J. KRAMBERGER ŠKERL, L. RUGERRI and S. WINKLER (eds.), *Property relations of cross border couples in the European Union*, Edizioni Scientifiche Italiane, Naples 2020, p. 148.

[92] Case C-7/98, *Dieter Krombach v André Bamberski*, ECLI:EU:C:2000:164; Case C-145/86, *Horst Ludwig Martin Hoffmann v Adelheid Krieg*, ECLI:EU:C:1988:61.

[93] J. KRAMBERGER ŠKERL, '(Ne)razumevanje pridržka javnega reda in posvojitev s strain istospolnih partnerjev' (2010) no. 29–30 *Pravna praksa* 26, 26. See also Case C-507/15, *Agro Foreign Trade & Agency Ltd v Petersime NV*, ECLI:EU:C:2017:129.

in particular in Article 21 thereof on the principle of non-discrimination'. This is the first time that any EU instrument in the field of private international law would include such provision. Previously, such references to the Charter were only made in the preambles[94] or omitted altogether.[95] This move from the preamble to the normative part can be understood as intended to strengthen the importance of the observance of fundamental rights.[96] It can also be seen as trying to strengthen the free movement of judgments among participating Member States.

Although the limits to the interpretation of public policy exception will need to be established by the courts of the participating Member States (and potentially by the CJEU), the above considerations and, in particular, the inclusion of Article 38, referencing the principle of non-discrimination, indicate that a refusal to recognise or enforce a foreign decision solely on the fact that it rules on property relations of same-sex couples may not be possible. Article 38 thus represents a welcome novelty in the EU private international law and provides an important safeguard in relation to same-sex couples.

7. CONCLUDING REMARKS

The adoption of the Twin Regulations demonstrated how difficult it is for the EU to find unanimity in the field of European family law and how contentious same-sex relationships remain in a number of Member States. In searching for the smallest common denominator, legal certainty of same-sex couples (and in particular same-sex spouses) was often sacrificed for the sake of unanimity. With this, an important opportunity was missed, and the same-sex spouses will continue to face a lack of predictability offered to the 'traditional' opposite sex spouses.

It is particularly regrettable (even if understandable) that an autonomous European definition of marriage was avoided in the Twin Regulations. In relation to same-sex couples, this omission can be seen as the central issue causing this lack of predictability. As this chapter demonstrates, such treatment of same-sex couples may not only contradict the principle of non-discrimination enshrined in Article 21 of the Charter, but may also hinder the free movement of same-sex couples within the EU.

Although the development of court practice in participating Member States and by the CJEU can be expected to produce more clarity regarding the

---

[94] See, inter alia, Recital no. 81 of the Regulation 650/2012 and Recital no. 33 of the Regulation 2201/2003.
[95] See for example the Regulation 4/2009.
[96] A. Wysocka-Bar, 'Enhanced Cooperation in Property Matters in the EU and Non-Participating Member States' (2019) 20 *ERA* Forum 187, 193.

material and personal scope of application of the Twin Regulations, the fact remains that the treatment of same-sex spouses will continue to depend on the national understanding of the notion of marriage: a problem, which most likely can only be overcome in the future by an increased social and legal acceptance of same-sex relationships in the Member States and a consequent readiness for consensus.

DE FACTO COUPLES

Between National Solutions and European Trends

Sandra Winkler*

1. Introduction 245
2. *De Facto* Couples: European Legal Systems in Comparison. 248
   - 2.1. Croatia and Slovenia 248
     - 2.1.1. Croatia 250
     - 2.1.2. Slovenia. 253
   - 2.2. Italy... 254
   - 2.3. Spain 257
   - 2.4. Lithuania 258
   - 2.5. Similarities and Differences between Compared Legal Systems... 259
3. *De Facto* Couples in European Family Law......................... 260
   - 3.1. The Role of Fundamental Human Rights in the Europeanisation of Family Law 261
   - 3.2. Regulations' Scope of Application: Exclusion of *De Facto* Couples 264
4. Concluding Remarks 267

1. INTRODUCTION

National legislation of EU Member States differs greatly in the heterogeneity of legal solutions adopted in many areas of family law. European law takes into great consideration families, especially cross-border, and defines an ever-greater number of transnational aspects.[1] In this respect, the so-called Twin Regulations, which deal with the property regimes of spouses and registered partners, have recently been adopted. However, the scope of application of the

---

* Sandra Winkler, Assistant Professor at the Chair of Family Law of the Faculty of Law, University of Rijeka, Croatia.
[1] P. Bruno, *Le controversie familiari nell'Unione Europea. Regole, fattispecie, risposte*, Giuffrè, Milano 2018.

two Regulations is not analysed in this chapter.² Instead, attention is paid to a matter excluded from the scope of the Twin Regulations, focusing specifically on the regulation of property relationships of cross-borders *de facto* couples.

An attempt to reconstruct the reasons that have led the European legislator to exclude *de facto* couples from the list of family formations whose property profiles are dealt with by the Twin Regulations, particularly in terms of conflict and procedural rules, is attempted later.³ It is first important to start from a comparative analysis of the legal rules governing *de facto* couples in various European legal systems. Combining the trends of migration and movement of persons within (and outside) EU borders and constant social changes, leads to the conclusion that it is necessary to compare foreign legal systems by reflecting on how (and whether) cross-border *de facto* couples find legal protection.⁴

Historically, people's necessity to live in communities has always been noted. The tightest community is commonly defined as family, which represents the primary society in which individuals recognise the place and the refuge to fulfil the most basic needs in their lives, usually described as intimacy in interpersonal relationships.⁵ However, it is not simple to classify all the unions that express this intimate need, particularly from a comparative legal perspective.⁶

Generally, families can take the form of marriage, registered partnerships, and *de facto* unions.⁷ Considering that these forms of family life can be either between persons of different sexes or between persons of the same sex, the different interpretations of the idea of family communities and their different legal protection in each national system across the European Union can easily be envisaged. Article 8 of the European Convention on Human Rights (ECHR) clearly protects the right to private and family life of every person.

---

[2] See for details P. BRUNO, *I regolamenti europei sui regimi patrimoniali dei coniugi e delle unioni registrate, Commento ai Regolamenti (UE) 24 giugno 2016, nn. 1103 e 1104 applicabili dal 29 gennaio 2019*, Giuffrè Francis Lefebvre, Milano 2019; A. DUTTA; J. WEBER, *Die Europäischen Güterrechtsverordnungen*, Beck, München 2017.

[3] For more about national laws and European trends see S. WINKLER, 'Imovinski odnosi u obitelji: nacionalna pravna rješenja i europski trendovi' (2019) X(1) *Godišnjak Akademije pravnih znanosti Hrvatske* 447–467.

[4] See more at <https://ec.europa.eu/eurostat/documents/3217494/7089681/KS-04-15-567-EN-N.pdf>.

[5] The term 'natural society' ('società naturale') is, for example, used in the Italian Constitution in Article 29. See C. M. BIANCA, *La Famiglia*, 2.1., *Diritto civile*, 5th ed., Giuffrè, Milano 2014, pp. 2 et seq.

[6] J. M. SCHERPE, 'The legal status of cohabitants – Requirements for legal recognition' in K. BOELE-WOELKI (ed.), *Common Core and Better Law in European family Law*, Intersentia, Antwerp 2005, pp. 283 et seq.; B. VERSCHRAEGEN, 'The right to private life and family life, the right to marry and to found a family, and the prohibition of discrimination' in K. BOELE-WOELKI, A. FUCHS (eds.), *Legal Recognition of Same-Sex Couples in Europe*, Intersentia, Antwerp 2003, pp. 194 et seq.

[7] See R. GARETTO, 'The Impact of Multicultural Issues on the Notion of "Family Member"' (2019) LXXIX *Zbornik znanstvenih razprav* 7 et seq.

Nevertheless, it must be remembered that the same Convention also emphasises that each country retains its own autonomy in legally regulating family formations capable of protecting this fundamental human right.[8]

A very significant question arises at this point. Does protecting the right to family life mean that all the different family formations must be treated in the same way, or does it mean that each different family formation must be offered the basis on which family life can be protected while respecting the structural diversity of the various family communities?

A comparative analysis of these phenomena is of great help in understanding the extent of this question.[9] More precisely, the diversity of types of family formations inevitably varies depending on how widely the concept of family is interpreted.[10] Differences in the approach are apparent.[11] In fact, some legal systems recognise the legal significance of all the legal formations mentioned above, whether composed of opposite-sex or same-sex couples.[12] In contrast, other systems grant protection only to marriage and family formations characterised by precise formalities regarding when they came into existence or when they ended.[13] Here, one should further differentiate between legal systems that recognise such rights for all couples, for heterosexual couples only, or limit registration to same-sex couples. In essence, there are legal systems that recognise *de facto* unions as having limited legal relevance, presumably considering that their essence lies precisely in their existence outside of a certain legal framework.

Proving the existence of these *de facto* unions is considered complex given that it can vary from law to law. Sometimes these informal unions are not

---

[8] Convention for the Protection of Human Rights and Fundamental Freedoms, Article 8(2), which states 'There shall be no interference by a public authority with the exercise of this right except such as is in accordance with the law and is necessary in a democratic society in the interests of national security, public safety or the economic well-being of the country, for the prevention of disorder or crime, for the protection of health or morals, or for the protection of the rights and freedoms of others'.

[9] I. CURRY-SUMNER, *All's well that ends registered?, The substantive and private international law aspects of non-marital registered relationships in Europe*, Intersentia, Antwerp 2005.

[10] S. PATTI, 'Modelli di famiglia e convivenza' in S. PATTI, M. G. CUBEDDU (eds.), *Introduzione al diritto della famiglia in Europa*, Giuffrè, Milano 2008, p. 116.

[11] D. HENRICH, 'Rechtsregeln fuer nichteheliches Zusammenleben – Zusammenfassung' in I. KROPPENBERG, D. SCHWAB, D. HENRICH, P. GOTTWALD, A. SPICKHOFF (eds.), *Rechtsregeln für nichteheliches Zusammenleben*, Gieseking, Bielefeld 2009, pp. 329 et seq.

[12] Many efforts have been made to rebuild a taxonomic framework of existing family formations in the EU. See 'Report on Collecting Data Methodological and Taxonomical Analysis', Roberto Garetto (ed.), 2019, available at <https://www.euro-family.eu/documenti/news/psefs_report_data_2019.pdf>.

[13] With regard to registered partnerships see *amplius* I. SCHWENZER, 'Convergence and divergence in the law on same-sex partnerships' in M. ANTOKOLSKAIA (ed.), *Convergence and Divergence of Family Law in Europe*, Intersentia, Antwerp 2007, pp. 45 et seq.; M. BOGDAN, 'Registered Partnerships and EC Law' in K. BOELE-WOELKI, A. FUCHS (eds.), *Legal Recognition of Same-Sex Couples in Europe*, Intersentia, Antwerp 2003, pp. 171 et seq.

identified as requiring protection. Regardless of these issues, the fact remains that even the European legislator has left *de facto* couples outside the scope of the Twin Regulations.

In the comparative examination which is carried out below, it will not be possible to consider all legal systems.[14] Therefore, only selected European legal systems considered interesting for the legal solutions they offer (or do not offer) are dealt with.

2. *DE FACTO* COUPLES: EUROPEAN LEGAL SYSTEMS IN COMPARISON

An explicit theoretical definition of *de facto* unions can be rarely found in legal systems, including the laws of the countries examined in this chapter. An eminent Croatian scholar – the importance of his observation goes beyond national borders – noted that from the perspective of the theory of law, there is no reason for a single definition of *de facto* unions since not all conceivable structures of family life in the society can be reduced to a single model.[15]

As already mentioned, the complex phenomenon of *de facto* couples and the heterogeneity of social contexts have led to different solutions in family law when regulating these unions in each single European legal system. In Europe, only a small number of states do not regulate unions other than marriage of persons of different sex. Indeed, most legal systems recognise the legal protection for family formations other than marriage, favouring the registration of such unions, which may be composed of persons of the same or different sex.

The solutions Croatia, Slovenia, Italy, Spain and Lithuania have adopted in the field of *de facto* couples will be analysed to present different approaches and solutions that the countries adopt.

2.1. CROATIA AND SLOVENIA

In these legal systems particular attention is paid to socio-cultural phenomena, which are at the foundation of changes within family law.[16] This has been the

---

[14] For an accurate report for every single EU's Member State see L. RUGGERI, I. KUNDA, S. WINKLER (eds.), *Family Property and Succession in EU Member States National Reports on the Collected Data*, Sveučilište u Rijeci, Pravni fakultet, Rijeka 2019, available at <https://www.euro-family.eu/documenti/news/psefs_e_book_compressed.pdf>.

[15] See M. ALINČIĆ, 'Promjene u propisima o braku i drugim životnim zajednicama' in D. HRABAR (ed.), *Hrestomatija hrvatskoga obiteljskoga prava*, Pravni fakultet Sveučilišta u Zagrebu, Zagreb 2010, p. 78.

[16] A detailed reconstruction of the influence that these currents of thought had in general in the former socialist countries can also be found in M. MLADENOVIĆ, C. JESSEL-HOLST,

case both in the past, under the influence of conceptual orientations that were to some extent in Croatia and Slovenia different from those of western part of Europe, and today, under the influence of current European trends. As social ties represent clear evidence of changing customs, *de facto* unions cannot but play a role in the central interest of those dealing with these issues.[17]

Croatia and Slovenia stand out for their choices related to the regulations of *de facto* and registered unions but, above all, for the significant evolution that the regulation of *de facto* unions has undergone and is still undergoing.[18] *De facto* cohabitation between a man and a woman has been recognised in these two states for several decades.[19] Moreover, although it was implemented later than that for heterosexual cohabitation, both in Croatia and Slovenia, homosexual unions also are legally recognised.

Even though during the comparison, differences in the approach often emerged, in the end, one conclusion can be reached that is common to both legal systems: both Croatian and Slovenian law reveal that the countries continue to give preference to the institution of marriage, which is frequently taken as a model in regulating *de facto* unions. It is true that both states regulate heterosexual cohabitation; however, it is equally true that the regulation is limited since these are alternative unions to marriage. Only opposite-sex couples can get married if they prefer since, in both legal systems, only persons of different sexes may marry. Both states also regulate same-sex partnerships and recognise the need to provide greater legal protection for those who cannot currently marry, and it is no coincidence that for homosexual couples more detailed rules are set than those applied for heterosexual partnerships.[20]

 'The Family in post-socialist countries' in A. CHLOROS, M. RHEINSTEIN, M. A. GLENDON (eds.), *International Encyclopedia of Comparative Law*, vol. IV, *Persons and Family*, Mohr Siebeck, Martinus Nijhoff Publishers, Tübingen, Leiden, Boston 2007, pp. 3 et seq.

[17] Moreover, it is well known that the legal systems under consideration (Croatian and Slovenian) have paid particular attention to the comparative study of foreign laws; this has allowed an easy circulation of different legal models and the acceptance of foreign solutions (also from non-European legal systems). In this respect see K. ZUPANČIČ, 'Izvenzakonska skupnost v primerjalnem pravu' (1987) *Pravnik* 147 et seq.

[18] See S. WINKLER, 'Le unioni di fatto nell'Europa centro-orientale: esperienze a confronto' in G. GABRIELLI, S. PATTI, A. ZACCARIA, F. PADOVINI, M.G. CUBEDDU WIEDEMANN, S. TROIANO (eds.), *Famiglia e Successioni, II, Liber amicorum per Dieter Henrich*, Giappichelli, Torino 2012, pp. 122 et seq.

[19] It is necessary to take a step back into the common, less recent legal history of these countries. See D. HRABAR, 'Legal Status of Cohabitants in Croatia' in J. M. SCHERPE, N. YASSARI (eds.), *Die Rechtsstellung nichtehelicher Lebensgemeinschaften*, Max Planck Institut für ausländisches und internationales Privatrecht, Mohr Siebeck, Tübingen 2005, pp. 399 et seq.

[20] See S. WINKLER, 'Le unioni di fatto nell'Europa centro-orientale: esperienze a confronto' in G. GABRIELLI, S. PATTI, A. ZACCARIA, F. PADOVINI, M.G. CUBEDDU WIEDEMANN, S. TROIANO (eds.), *Famiglia e Successioni, II, Liber amicorum per Dieter Henrich*, Giappichelli, Torino 2012, p. 134.

2.1.1. Croatia

In Croatian family law, there is no expressed theoretic definition of *de facto* unions. In this regard, in the Croatian doctrine, it is pointed out that there is no reason for such a concept to exist, as all unions cannot be reduced to a single definition.[21] However, *de facto* unions can be formed by couples of different sexes and couples of the same sex.

Despite the lack of a definition, it is possible to indirectly reconstruct it by analysing the constitutive elements that characterise these couples.[22] To start with heterosexual couples, these factual unions, usually named 'extramarital cohabitation' (*izvanbračne zajednice*), are regulated under Article 11 of the Croatian Family Act.[23] According to the Croatian family law, extramarital cohabitation is generally defined as the life community between a woman and a man, both unmarried, which lasts at least three years or less when a mutual child is born or if it continues with marriage. Such a union starts and ends in a completely informal manner.

Although these *de facto* unions between persons of different sexes have been legally regulated for decades,[24] their prerequisites have been changed over the years.[25] The newest Family Act (2015), largely based on the Family Act (2003), in its Article 11 offers an exhaustive list of prerequisites (unmarried heterosexual couple, cohabitation lasting at least three years or less when a mutual child is born or if it continues with marriage) that the interpreter has to evaluate to recognise whether or not a factual union is recognised in the Croatian legal system.

Due to the absence of any kind of formality of such a cohabitation, it might be complicated to apply the criteria mentioned above. This is especially true

---

[21] See D. HRABAR, 'Die vermögensrechtliche Beziehungen zwischen Ehegatten und nichtehelichen Partnern im kroatischen Recht' (1999) *Eheliche Gemeinschaft und Vermögen im europäischen Vergleich* 143 et seq.

[22] M. BUKOVAC PUVAČA, I. KUNDA, S. WINKLER, D. VRBLJANAC, 'Croatia' in L. RUGGERI, I. KUNDA, S. WINKLER (eds.), *Family Property and Succession in EU Member States, National Reports on the Collected Data*, Sveučilište u Rijeci, Pravni fakultet, Rijeka 2019, pp. 68–92, available at <https://www.euro-family.eu/documenti/news/psefs_e_book_compressed.pdf>.

[23] Obiteljski zakon, Narodne novine, No. 103/15, 98/19 and 47/20.

[24] Zakon o braku i porodičnim odnosima, Narodne novine, No. 11/1978, 27/1978, 45/1989 and 59/1990. In the 1970s, the legislator did not offer any definition to specify which cohabitations were worth being protected and which were not. More precisely, Article 12 of the Marriage and Family Relations Act establishes that the obligation of mutual maintenance and some other rights and duties following from the property law arise from the extramarital union between a woman and a man. Except for the mentioned gender diversity of the partners, there was no mention of the duration of the relationship, or of the status of the partners, or of the existence of their own children born during the relationship

[25] Obiteljski zakon, Narodne novine, No. 162/1998; Obiteljski zakon, Narodne novine, No. 116/03, 17/04, 136/04, 107/07, 57/11, 61/11, 25/13, 05/15; Obiteljski zakon, Narodne novine, No. 75/2014, 83/2014 and 05/2015; Obiteljski zakon, Narodne novine, No. 103/15, 98/19 and 47/20.

for the requirement that a cohabitation should last for three years because it is hard to determine the precise beginning or the precise termination of a *de facto* union. It can be said that the legislator provides an exhaustive definition but that in the absence of any formal constraint, it is destined to remain extremely vague, i.e. subject to various court interpretations.[26] Confusion is further increased by the fact that, in addition to the definition contained in the Family Act, several definitions of factual unions are contained in various special laws; definitions that often collide and enable different qualifications of the same union.[27] The reason for the *de facto* unions of persons of different sexes to be included in various laws is that they are granted numerous rights by the legislator. Article 11 of the Family Act only lays down those rights that concern family law, while other laws regulate legal consequences in the sphere of labour, pension, fiscal, succession rights, etc. Therefore, although this normative technique is the subject of criticism in the doctrine, these laws often also dictate the qualification of these *de facto* formations (although they do not do the same for others, such as marriage).[28] The property relationships of *de facto* heterosexual couples are regulated in the Family Act only, so the problem noted above does not arise here. These property consequences are regulated in Article 11(2) of the Family Act. Furthermore, they are regulated in a very clear manner: by referring *in toto* to the rules governing matrimonial property regimes.[29]

The Croatian legal system also regulates same-sex unions.[30] However, the legislator chose to regulate such unions by a law other than the Family Act.[31]

Previously, *de facto* homosexual couples were regulated under the Act on Same-Sex Unions (2003),[32] while from 2014, the new Same-Sex Life Partnership Act has been in force, which introduced the possibility to register

---

[26] For a detailed overview, see N. Lucić, *Izvanbračna zajednica i pravna sigurnost*, Narodne novine, Zagreb 2020.

[27] D. Hrabar, 'Izvanbračna zajednica – neka otvorena pitanja' (2010) 2 *Hrvatska Pravna Revija* 43 et seq.

[28] M. Bukovac-Puvača, S. Winkler, 'Nasljednopravni učinci izvanbračnih zajednica i neformalnih životnih partnerstava' (2021) IX(9) *Zbornik radova, Deveti međunarodni naučni skup Dani porodičnog prava* 129–154.

[29] In this regard see A. Korać Graovac, 'Imovinski odnosi' in M. Alinčić, D. Hrabar, D. Jakovac-Lozić, A- Korać Graovac (eds.), *Obiteljsko pravo*, Narodne novine, Zagreb 2007, pp. 495–533; V. Belaj, 'Stjecanje imovine (vlasništva) u bračnoj i izvanbračnoj zajednici' (2005) 26(1) *Zbornik Pravnog fakulteta Sveučilišta u Rijeci* 346.

[30] While, for an extensive reconstruction of de facto same-sex unions before the 2003 Croatian Act came into force, see N. Hlača, 'Zajednica života osoba istog spola' (1992) 42(4) *Zbornik Pravnog Fakulteta u Zagrebu* 447 et seq.

[31] Cf. R. Pacia, S. Winkler, 'Invisible Minorities within Extramarital Unions – Comparison of Different Solutions Provided by the Family Laws' in N. Bodiroga-Vukobrat, G.G. Sander, S. Barić (eds.), *Unsichtbare Minderheiten. Invisible Minorities*, Verlag dr. Kovač, Hamburg 2013, pp. 57–93.

[32] Zakon o istospolnim zajednicama, Narodne novine, No. 116/2003.

a life partnership between same-sex couples.[33] More precisely, the relevant legislation recognises two types of same-sex unions: those subject to registration and those entirely informal. The latter appears to be similar to *de facto* unions formed by persons of different sexes. However, there are some interesting distinctions concerning the requirements that the legislator lays down regarding the existence of *de facto* unions of the same-sex persons. Article 3 of the Same-Sex Life Partnership Act (2014) establishes that:

> the informal life partnership is a union of two persons of the same sex, which have not registered their partnership in front of a registrar, which has been lasting for at least three years and which meets the requirements for valid registration of a life partnership from the outset.

The first difference compared to *de facto* heterosexual unions is that the recognition of a *de facto* homosexual union is subject to the fulfilment of the requirements for registration validity. These requirements are: (i) the partners have to be of age (adults); (ii) the partners have to be in full possession of their faculties or if they are incapable of acting with regard to actions relating to their personal status, the approval of their guardian is received; (iii) they have not registered a partnership with another partner or entered into marriage and (iv) they are not relatives by blood or by adoption. It is evident that some of the mentioned requisites have been clearly put together to follow some of the marital impediments.

Although there are these differences in the requirements for homosexual *de facto* unions compared to heterosexual ones, what they have in common is the absence of formality. Hence, with regard to *de facto* homosexual couples the same problem of proving their existence arises. Finally, concerning their legal consequences – under Article 4 of the Same-Sex Life Partnership Act (2014), similarly to what the legislator establishes in the Family Act – these consequences are similar to those provided for registered partners of the same sex. For legal consequences not provided in the Same-Sex Life Partnership Act itself, other special laws are referenced. The existence of a double track is evident, where the two formal family formations (marriage for persons of different sexes and registration for persons of the same sex) are juxtaposed with the two informal versions of these relationships, which, despite their vagueness, if recognised, give rise to important legal consequences. As far as this is concerned, these are property consequences that find no protection at the supranational level, despite the fact of a high number of *de facto* couples in Europe.

---

[33] Zakon o životnom partnerstvu osoba istog spola, Narodne novine, No. 92/2014.

2.1.2. Slovenia

Unlike Croatian law, Slovenian law has not undergone many and frequent reforms of family law. From the 1970s to 2019, the same law remained in force, namely the Marriage and Family Relations Act.[34] The new Family Code came into force on 15 April 2019.[35] It should be noted that the recent reform of Slovenian family law has not led to any significant changes in the rule defining extramarital unions in Slovenian law. Under Article 4 of the new Family Code, it is stated that:

> an extramarital union is a long-term living arrangement between a man and a woman who are not married and for whom there are no grounds for the marriage to be invalid. Such a union shall have the same legal consequences under this Code concerning them as if they had contracted a marriage; in other areas of law, such a union shall have legal consequences if the law so provides.[36]

Unlike the solution envisaged in Croatian law, here, the definition is composed differently. Indeed, it is defined as a life union between an unmarried woman and an unmarried man, although other elements are different. The Slovenian Family Code (2019) does not refer to a specific period, nor can this period be shortened in the presence of other conditions such as the birth of a child.[37] Furthermore, the Slovenian legislator clearly underlines that the validity of such a union is subject to the absence of any matrimonial impediment. Thus, it is observable that the Slovenian legislator has shaped the regulation of an extramarital partnership between a man and a woman by clearly drawing inspiration from the institution of marriage.[38] As in Croatian law, the absolute absence of any formality characterises both the beginning and the end of the *de facto* relationship, creating the same problems in proving their existence.[39]

---

[34] Zakon o zakonski zvezi in družinskih razmerjih, OJ SRS, No. 15/76 with further changes. K. ZUPANČIČ, *Družinsko pravo*, Uradni list Republike Slovenije, Ljubljana 1999, p. 97.

[35] Družinski zakonik, OJ RS, No. 15/2017 with further changes. On the family law reform, see the introductory remarks of K. ZUPANČIČ, B. NOVAK, V. ŽNIDARŠIČ SKUBIC, M. KONČINA-PETERNEL, *Reforma družinskega prava*, Uradni list, Ljubljana 2009, pp. 17 et seq.

[36] For an accurate analysis of the Article 4, see B. NOVAK (ed.), *Komentar Družinskega zakonika*, Uradni list RS, Ljubljana 2019.

[37] Ibid., p. 44.

[38] See S. WINKLER, 'Le unioni di fatto nell'Europa centro-orientale: esperienze a confronto' in G. GABRIELLI, S. PATTI, A. ZACCARIA, F. PADOVINI, M.G. CUBEDDU WIEDEMANN, S. TROIANO (eds.), *Famiglia e Successioni, II, Liber amicorum per Dieter Henrich*, Giappichelli, Torino 2012, p. 132.

[39] Part of the Slovene doctrine criticises the new family law reform project precisely because it does not provide for the registration of de facto heterosexual partnerships. In this regard see B. ZADRAVEC, 'Pomanjkljivosti Družinskega zakonika' (25.02.2010) 29/930, *Pravna Praksa*

On the other hand, proof of their existence is essential for recognising the legal consequences of such *de facto* unions. Here, too, as previously observed, the legislator has opted for a full reference to the legal rules of marriage for all legal consequences (including patrimonial ones) arising from such *de facto* relationships.[40]

The Slovenian legal system regulates same-sex unions as well. The legal recognition of same-sex unions was introduced for the first time in a distinct act: the Act on the Registration of Same-Sex Unions (*Zakon o registraciji istospolne partnerske skupnosti*) of 2005.[41] This Act was replaced in 2016 by the Civil Union Act (*Zakon o partnerski zvezi*), which entered into force in 2017.[42] Similarly to the provisions of Croatian law, the Slovenian regulations envisage two different formations composed of same-sex couples: 'formal' and 'informal' civil union. This means that the law permits the registration of such a union; however, it also recognises the legal effects for *de facto* couples (not registered). The 'informal' union is qualified as a lasting life community between persons of the same sex who have not registered their union if there are no grounds for the invalidity of their union. The legal rules governing marriage 'apply *mutatis mutandis* to civil unions',[43] which is true for the 'formal' and 'informal' ones. As to the legal consequences arising from a *de facto* civil union and in the case of a registered civil union, they are therefore identical with regards to the property consequences arising from the marriage.[44]

2.2. ITALY

In Italian law, the term *de facto* family (*famiglia di fatto*) is used for those unions which, despite not being formalised, have a structure similar to family based on marriage.[45] Before 2016, the Italian legal order did not provide either

---

8, 11 et seq.; V. ŽNIDARŠIČ SKUBIC, 'Zunajzakonska skupnost – nekateri (aktualni) problemi' (2007) XXXII (1) *Podjetje in delo* 205 et seq.

[40] See B. NOVAK, *Komentar Družinskega zakonika*, Uradni list RS, Ljubljana 2019, p. 45.

[41] Zakon o registraciji istospolne partnerske skupnosti, Uradni List RS n. 65/2005. In literature see B. NOVAK, 'Slowenien hat die gleichgeschlechtlichen Partnerschaften rechtlich geregelt' (2006) *FamRZ* 600.

[42] Zakon o partnerski zvezi, Uradni list RS, No. 33/16.

[43] See F. DOUGAN, 'Slovenia' in L. RUGGERI, I. KUNDA, S. WINKLER (eds.), *Family Property and Succession in EU Member States, National Reports on the Collected Data*, Sveučilište u Rijeci, Pravni fakultet, Rijeka 2019, p. 593 available at <https://www.euro-family.eu/documenti/news/psefs_e_book_compressed.pdf>.

[44] Ibid., p. 594.

[45] V. BONANNO, 'Patrimonial regimes and de facto cohabitation in European and Italian law' in J. KRAMBERGER ŠKERL, L. RUGGERI, F. G. VITERBO (eds.), *Case studies and best practices analysis to enhance EU family and succession law. Working paper*, (2019) 3 *Quaderni degli Annali della Facoltà Giuridica dell'Università di Camerino* 19–30.

specific legislation or a legal definition of such unions.⁴⁶ However, a number of legal provisions defining individual legal aspects arising from mentioned 'life situations' increased notably in the last years before the reform in Italian family law.⁴⁷ It can be concluded that the resistance to regulate *de facto* unions of persons of different sex was overcome. Similarly, the time has proved ripe for the legal recognition of same-sex couples' registration. Indeed, Act No. 76 of 20 May 2016 introduced the civil union into the Italian legal system and, at the same time, regulated cohabitation. After enacting this Act of 2016, the Italian law recognises two different *de facto* unions (in the sense of cohabitation), depending on whether they arose before or after 2016.⁴⁸ The distinction between couples before and after enacting the Act of 2016 is relevant because *de facto* couples may have different protection depending on the time of their creation. It must be noted that prior to 2016, there was no specific legislation regulating such unions. Consequently, no legal regulation regarding criteria for the existence and legal consequences of such unions was determined.⁴⁹

As to unmarried heterosexual couples, there are two constitutive elements of these unions. The first one is of an objective character and is represented by a stable cohabitation of partners. The second element has a subjective basis characterised by the *affectio maritalis*, i.e. mutual participation of a partner in the other partner's life, expressing affection, solidarity, and financial support. Before 2016, it seemed possible to extend the notion of the *de facto* couple to those cohabitations where one or both partners were not unmarried. This was a consequence of a past rule of Italian family law, which implied that years'-long

---

[46] For a reconstruction of the rules on de facto unions in Italian law before 2016 see R. Mazzariol, *Convivenze di fatto e autonomia privata: il contratto di convivenza*, Jovene editore, Napoli 2018. Also see M.G. Cubeddu Wiedemann, 'Rechtsregeln für nichteheliches Zusammenleben in Italien' in I. Kroppenberg, D. Schwab, D. Henrich, P. Gottwald, A. Spickhoff (eds.), *Rechtsregeln für nichteheliches Zusammenleben, Beitrage zum europäischen Familienrecht*, Gieseking, Bielefeld 2009, pp. 119 et seq. Recently R. Garetto, M. Giobbi, A. Magni, T. Pertot, E. Sgubin, M. V. Maccari, 'Italy' in L. Ruggeri, I. Kunda, S. Winkler (eds.), *Family Property and Succession in EU Member States, National Reports on the Collected Data*, Sveučilište u Rijeci, Pravni fakultet, Rijeka 2019, pp. 356–390, available at <https://www.euro-family.eu/documenti/news/psefs_e_book_compressed.pdf>.

[47] About different family unions see more in G. Perlingieri, 'Interferenze tra unione civile e matrimonio. Pluralismo familiare e unitarietà dei valori normativi' (2018) 1 *Rassegna di diritto civile* 101.

[48] R. Garetto, M. Giobbi, A. Magni, T. Pertot, E. Sgubin, M. V. Maccari, 'Italy' in L. Ruggeri, I. Kunda, S. Winkler (eds.), *Family Property and Succession in EU Member States, National Reports on the Collected Data*, Sveučilište u Rijeci, Pravni fakultet, Rijeka 2019, p. 361.

[49] Nevertheless, a great effort was carried out by case law, which, together with isolated legal solutions that protected certain aspects of such unions, provided some fragmented form of legal framework. In this regard, see R. Pacia, S. Winkler, R. Pacia, S. Winkler, 'Invisible Minorities within Extramarital Unions – Comparison of Different Solutions Provided by the Family Laws' in N. Bodiroga-Vukobrat, G.G. Sander, S. Barić (eds.), *Unsichtbare Minderheiten. Invisible Minorities*, Verlag dr. Kovač, Hamburg 2013, pp. 63–83.

separation between two spouses was necessary before the divorce. Separated spouses were still married; they were legally compelled to wait for the expiration of separation to be legally divorced, while, emotionally, they considered the matrimonial union already terminated. After 2016, the notion in Article 1 of the Act of 2016 clearly states that one of the necessary requirements for such a union to exist is the free status of the persons involved.

In the absence of the communion of life that expresses the *animus* typical of married life (*affectio maritalis*), *de facto* unions – although denoted by an affective dimension and reciprocal solidarity – cannot be recognised as family formations protected under family law.[50] Obviously, these relationships are always characterised by the absence of any formality: they start and end outside any formal framework.

As to the legal consequences regarding unmarried heterosexual couples that came into existence after 2016, they can conclude a cohabitation contract to regulate their property relations.[51] *A contrario*, it means that if they do not conclude such a contract, there is no precise legal framework that would regulate their patrimonial assets.[52]

Same-sex couples are also regulated in the Italian legal system since the 2016 reform. The new legislation introduced the possibility for homosexual couples to register their union. In addition, the legal regulation of *de facto* couples includes heterosexual and homosexual couples alike. A form of registered same-sex couple (*unione civile*) has the same personal and patrimonial rights as those prescribed for a marital relationship, even if in this case, there is no duty of marital fidelity. Thus, under Article 13 of Act No. 76 of 2016, the property regime of the civil union of same-sex couples follows the same rules as those applicable to marriage. Indeed, the community of assets is the applicable legal regime unless the parties agree otherwise. If additional rules are needed, reference is made to the provisions of the Civil Code related to the community of assets, the separation of the assets, the conventional community of property, and the patrimonial fund.[53] What differs from the Slovenian and Croatian

---

[50] It could be the case of unions with significant mutual financial or religious support, particularly among the elderly.

[51] See L. RUGGERI, S. WINKLER, 'Neka pitanja o imovinskim odnosima bračnih drugova u hrvatskom i talijanskom obiteljskom pravu' (2019) 40(1) *Zbornik Pravnog fakulteta Sveučilišta u Rijeci* 167–200.

[52] See R. PACIA, S. WINKLER, 'Invisible Minorities within Extramarital Unions – Comparison of Different Solutions Provided by the Family Laws' in N. BODIROGA-VUKOBRAT, G.G. SANDER, S. BARIĆ (eds.), *Unsichtbare Minderheiten. Invisible Minorities*, Verlag dr. Kovač, Hamburg 2013, p. 78.

[53] R. GARETTO, M. GIOBBI, A. MAGNI, T. PERTOT, E. SGUBIN, M. V. MACCARI, 'Italy' in L. RUGGERI, I. KUNDA, S. WINKLER (eds.), *Family Property and Succession in EU Member States, National Reports on the Collected Data*, Sveučilište u Rijeci, Pravni fakultet, Rijeka 2019, pp. 365–370.

systems analysed above is that in Italy *de facto* couples are not treated the same as marriage or civil unions.

2.3. SPAIN

The legal framework that Spanish law provides for *de facto* couples composed of persons of the same or opposite sex is extremely articulate and complex.[54] It includes a combination of different civil law rules within the Spanish legal system depending on whether the Civil Code is applied as the primary source or whether special rules may represent a distinct and prevailing legal source over the national one.[55] Similarly to what has been observed so far, Spain also essentially recognises three family formations: marriage between persons of different sexes or between persons of the same sex; registered (formalised) partnerships between persons of the same or opposite sex; and *de facto* unions between persons of the same and opposite sex. It would be impossible to reconstruct the very complicated Spanish system, whose peculiarity becomes evident when compared with others. Suffice it to say that all family formations listed are present, if not in all, then in at least in some territories.

In particular, as for the *de facto* unions, the absence of a general, common provision needs to be highlighted. In other words, there is no one unique definition of *de facto* unions on the level of national legislation. As in the past in the Italian legal system (before the Act of 2016), the qualification of *de facto* couples virtually depends on the effort of case law and doctrine. Thus, the definition of a union revolves around the character of stability, which tends to represent proof of communion of life by the sharing of interests, intimate needs and a common life project.

It is very interesting to note that in the case of such *de facto* unions which are entirely informal in their nature, it is in the first place up to the partners to protect their interests (especially their assets) through special agreements. If they do not do so, the judicial authorities will decide on property consequences

---

[54] For an accurate analysis see A. M. PÉREZ VALLEJO, M. J. CAZORLA GONZÁLEZ, 'Spain' in L. RUGGERI, I. KUNDA, S. WINKLER (eds.), *Family Property and Succession in EU Member States, National Reports on the Collected Data*, Sveučilište u Rijeci, Pravni fakultet, Rijeka 2019, pp. 616 et seq., available at <https://www.euro-family.eu/documenti/news/psefs_e_book_compressed.pdf>.

[55] See C. GONZÁLEZ BEILFUSS, 'Property relationship between spouses – SPAIN' <http://ceflonline.net/property-relations-reports-by-jurisdiction/> p. 2. The author in her report offers a very clear and precise introductory note: 'Since Spanish law is a non-unified legal system, there is no uniform Spanish law regarding the property relationship between spouses. This report deals only with the rules of the misleadingly entitled "Derecho civil común," which coexist with the rules of the so-called "Derechos civiles forales" (Catalonia, the Balearic Islands, Aragon, Navarre, the Basque Country and Galicia).' In addition, she highlights, 'which law applies to a given couple is a conflict of law issue …)'.

on a case-by-case basis. On this point, the Spanish Supreme Court is very clear in stressing that such *de facto* unions are not to be equated with marriage.[56]

In this sense, a difference may be seen from what has been observed above in other legal systems, where the tendency is to equate family formations, creating 'duplication'. The interpretation found in Spanish case law is interesting and acceptable since it avoids the existence of family formations that are comparable in terms of the legal effects they produce, even though their legal nature is unquestionably different. Therefore, it is not even easy to state what the legal consequences of *de facto* unions are. This is especially true when considering the various property regimes existing in the Spanish legal system since they vary from act to act. It is up to the judge to identify both the existence of a *de facto* union and its potential legal consequences.

2.4. LITHUANIA

Basically, the Lithuanian legal system does not regulate any other form of family life apart from marriage between a man and a woman;[57] even though, to be more precise, in addition to marriage, the Lithuanian Civil Code recognises one more type of union – registered partnership. This can only be a union between opposite-sex couples.[58] The property relations of a registered opposite-sex couple is regulated under Articles 3.229-3.235 of the Lithuanian Civil Code. The conditions stated by the Lithuanian Civil Code for the coming into existence of a registered partnership are very similar to those for marriage. The partners have to be of full age, possess full legal capacity, be of opposite sex and not married and they cannot be blood related. Thus, similar to other countries already compared, the registration of a partnership between persons of the opposite sex is allowed only between adults, which means that the registration of a partnership between minors is not permitted. Moreover, a partnership has

---

[56] See A. M. Pérez Vallejo, M. J. Cazorla González, 'Spain' in L. Ruggeri, I. Kunda, S. Winkler (eds.), *Family Property and Succession in EU Member States, National Reports on the Collected Data*, Sveučilište u Rijeci, Pravni fakultet, Rijeka 2019, p. 617. The authors expressly refer to Sentencia del Pleno 611/2005, de 12 septiembre de 2005 (Tol 725211), 'As the Supreme Court (SC) reiterated in its ruling of 12 September 2005: "the de facto union is an institution that has nothing to do with marriage, even though both are part of family law"'.

[57] See A. Limante, T. Chochrin, 'Lithuania' in L. Ruggeri, I. Kunda, S. Winkler (eds.), *Family Property and Succession in EU Member States, National Reports on the Collected Data*, Sveučilište u Rijeci, Pravni fakultet, Rijeka 2019, pp. 408–426, available at <https://www.euro-family.eu/documenti/news/psefs_e_book_compressed.pdf>.

[58] In this regard see G. Sagatys, 'The Concept of Family in Lithuanian Law' (2010) 1 *Jurisprudencija Mokslo darbų žurnalas* 184, available at <https://ojs.mruni.eu/ojs/jurisprudence/article/view/1094/1047>.

to be verified: for instance, the partners must have lived together for at least one year.[59]

However, partnerships cannot be registered in practice for the time being because of a lack of implementing laws.[60] *De facto* couples are not expressly regulated by law but find protection in case law. In this regard, it is interesting to recall the jurisprudence of the Supreme Court of Lithuania, which highlights that, in the case of couples conducting a lifestyle similar to that of a married couple, their property relations are seen as a 'joint venture agreement'.[61]

As for same-sex couples, Lithuanian family law does not give legal recognition to any communion of life between persons of the same sex, thus belonging to the minority group of European legal systems that do not grant legal protection to same-sex couples.[62]

2.5. SIMILARITIES AND DIFFERENCES BETWEEN COMPARED LEGAL SYSTEMS

Although Spanish and Lithuanian law differ substantially in their approach to the recognition (or non-recognition) of same-sex unions, they have in common the way they treat *de facto* couples. In other words, by distinguishing them from marriage or registered partnerships, Lithuania and Spain recognise a factual characteristic that distinguishes *de facto* couples from other family formations, leaving them outside the legal framework.

---

[59] See I. MICHAILOVIENE, 'Informal relationships – LITHUANIA', pp. 1–36 <http://ceflonline.net/informal-relationships-reports-by-jurisdiction/>. Indeed, quoting, 'Although the Lithuanian Civil Code has been in force … (from 2001 onwards) norms regulating relations between cohabitants are still lacking, because no special law has been adopted since such inconsistency and the lack of legal clarity obviously influence legal disputes within society and the different approaches within the case law. The above-mentioned provisions of the Lithuanian Civil Code (Art. 3.229-3.235) have not been applied in practice; however, they have not been abolished either …'.

[60] Ibid., pp. 1–3. As to the patrimonial consequences, the Author pinpoints, 'bearing in mind that Art. 3.229-3.235 of the Lithuanian Civil Code are not applied in practice, the courts usually rely on general provisions while considering material disputes between non-married individuals, such as the provisions of Book IV, "Material Law", of the Lithuanian Civil Code on the division of joint-partial property between co-owners as well as the provisions of Book VI, "Law of Obligations", of the Lithuanian Civil Code regarding an agreement on joint activities (a partnership) in creating joint-partial property'.

[61] A. LIMANTE, T. CHOCHRIN, 'Lithuania' in L. RUGGERI, I. KUNDA, S. WINKLER (eds.), *Family Property and Succession in EU Member States, National Reports on the Collected Data*, Sveučilište u Rijeci, Pravni fakultet, Rijeka 2019, p. 418. One of the most recent decisions the authors refer to is the Supreme Court ruling of 28 March 2011, No. 3K-3-1343.

[62] See G. SAGATYS, 'The Concept of Family in Lithuanian Law' (2010) 1 *Jurisprudencija Mokslo darbų žurnalas* 184, 193–194, available at <https://ojs.mruni.eu/ojs/jurisprudence/article/view/1094/1047>.

The same approach (not regulating *de facto* couples) was applied in the past in Italian law, which, with the 2016 legislation, radically changed the pre-existing legal framework. This was done, on the one hand, by defining *de facto* heterosexual couples and, on the other, introducing a 'double track' regulation of these unions: couples arising before the entry into force will have certain legal effects; those after the entry into force will have others. However, a significant step forward has been taken when compared to minority countries that do not recognise the legal protection for same-sex partnerships.[63] Italy is halfway there, more in line with Croatia and Slovenia, which, by laying down very similar rules, offer a degree of legal protection to all family formations, whether heterosexual or homosexual couples, and even go further in equating the legal effects of *de facto* unions with formal ones. This certainly affords broad protection, but it raises the question of why the intrinsic diversity of the legal nature of these family formations is completely flattened out with regard to legal consequences.

3. *DE FACTO* COUPLES IN EUROPEAN FAMILY LAW

Family law in the EU is not harmonised at the level of substantive rules. Nonetheless, both under the influence of fundamental rights and EU secondary legislation, family law is undergoing a process of Europeanisation that does not leave even substantive law untouched. Such indirect harmonisation happens even though the European legislator is not competent to lay down rules on the substantive level, which remains the exclusive prerogative of Member States.[64] Substantive law solutions are explored above from a comparative point of view to discover the differences and similarities that are useful for an adequate understanding and interpretation of single legal institutes of family law.[65]

---

[63] See: R. GARETTO (ed.), *Report on Collecting Data Methodological and Taxonomical Analysis*, 2019 available at <https://www.euro-family.eu/documenti/news/psefs_report_data_2019.pdf>. In the publication all information regarding the recognition of the different family formations in each EU Member State can be found.

[64] Family law, which for a long time remained in the background, is undergoing a significant process of harmonisation at European level. In recent years, the efforts of legal science in this respect are being rapidly stepped up. *Ex plurimis*: M. ANTOKOLSKAIA, *Harmonisation of Family Law in Europe: A Historical Perspective, A Tale of two Millennia*, Intersentia, Antwerp 2006; M. T. MEULDERS-KLEIN, 'Towards a uniform European family law? A political approach. General conclusions' in M. ANTOKOLSKAIA (ed.), *Convergence and Divergence of Family Law in Europe*, Intersentia, Antwerp 2007, pp. 271 et seq.; S. PATTI, M. G. CUBEDDU (eds.), *Introduzione al diritto della famiglia in Europa*, Giuffrè, Milano 2008; K. BOELE-WOELKI, 'What comparative family law should entail' in K. BOELE-WOELKI (ed.), *Debates on Family Law around the Globe at the Dawn of the 21st Century*, Intersentia, Antwerp 2009, pp. 3 et seq.

[65] D. HENRICH, 'Entwicklungen des Familienrechts in Ost un West' (2010) 5 *FamRZ*, p. 333 et seq.

This is useful in order to provide the best possible protection, especially at the supranational level for family situations with elements of a cross-border nature.[66]

The increasing number of families composed of persons of different nationalities or living in countries other than that of their nationality creates the need to develop common rules in the field of family law. New families are born, then end, leaving many legal questions unresolved. This is why the European legislator has made significant progress in harmonising the rules of private international law.[67] However, although these solutions offer a more homogeneous framework, by identifying common rules for the identification of the applicable (national) law, a certain diversity between national laws persists at the substantive level. The national substantive laws are much less involved in the Europeanisation process. Thus, the starting point for any attempt to analyse and reconstruct the phenomenon of the Europeanisation of family law is the comparison of different European legal systems. In fact, in order to assess the advantages and disadvantages of the Europeanisation of family law, one must first get to know the individual European family legal systems and understand how and to what extent they differ,[68] which was discussed in the first part of the chapter.

3.1. THE ROLE OF FUNDAMENTAL HUMAN RIGHTS IN THE EUROPEANISATION OF FAMILY LAW

At this point, a premise should be made. The term 'European family law' is frequently used in literature.[69] Often, however, the delineations of what this

---

[66] With regard to property regimes see M. J. CAZORLA GONZÁLEZ, M. GIOBBI, J. KRAMBERGER ŠKERL, L. RUGGERI, S. WINKLER (eds.), *Property Relations of Cross-Border Couples in the European Union*, Edizioni Scientifiche Italiane, Napoli 2020, available at <https://www.euro-family.eu/documenti/news/esi_en_psefsbook.pdf>.

[67] F.D. BUSNELLI, M.C. VITUCCI, 'Frantumi europei di famiglia' (2013) I *Rivista di diritto civile*, 777 et seq.

[68] There is a very important (soft law) source in the process of Europeanisation of family law that does not come from Brussels: the Principles on European Family Law (PEFL) drawn up by the Commission on European Family Law (CEFL). This Commission is made up of legal experts from many European countries who have been meeting in Utrecht since 2001 to study family law in European countries with a view to finding common solutions. The results of the research conducted by the CEFL, like those conducted by other groups of scholars in other areas of private law, converge in 'principles' which are the expression of current trends in family law in Europe. Individual national legislators, although in no way bound by these principles, take them into account; some recent reforms of family law in individual national legal systems have been influenced by them. For an in-depth analysis of the work of the Commission on European Family Law, see the official website <www.ceflonline.net>, where the questionnaires, the individual national reports and the resulting Principles relating to the individual topics dealt with so far can be found in full and in several languages.

[69] K. BOELE-WOELKI, 'Obiteljsko pravo u Europi: prošlost, sadašnjost, budućnost' in I. KUNDA (ed.), *Obitelj i djeca: europska očekivanja i nacionalna stvarnost*, Pravni fakultet u Rijeci, Hrvatska udruga za poredbeno pravo, Rijeka 2014, pp. 17–28.

term covers are unclear. There are two different levels: European family law 'in the broad sense' and European family law 'in the narrow sense'.

European family law in the broad sense consists of a body of rules resulting from the work of three separate organisations: the Council of Europe, the Hague Conference on Private International Law, and the European Union.[70] On the other hand, when we speak of European family law in the narrow sense, we refer to the new legislative and jurisprudential rules that the European Union has only recently begun to lay down. Indeed, the way the European institutions proceed is very fragmentary and cautious. Fragmentary because often only some specific aspects of the matter are regulated in the absence of a more general regulatory framework. Cautious because, in view of the exclusive competence of national legislatures to legislate on substantive aspects of family law, the European legislature is careful not to overstep these boundaries.[71]

It is, therefore, necessary to start by analysing the role that fundamental human rights have played in the development of family law and, in particular, in the slow emergence of European family law.[72]

Starting with a broad perspective, within the ECHR, a role of primary importance in this process has Article 8 guaranteeing the right to private and family life, as well as Article 14 prohibiting any form of discrimination. The European Court of Human Rights (ECtHR) case law suggests clearly that the concept of private and family life is very comprehensive. In particular, under Article 8(1) of the ECHR, a family does not consist exclusively of a man-woman cell from which a marital relationship results.[73] Contrary to this, a form of family may also be found in a different form of an emotional relationship. Indeed, the ECtHR recognises an affective relationship of persons also living in a *de facto* form of the family if such cohabitation is a union sufficiently stable to make it possible to identify the *animus* and *corpus*. These distinguish different life unions and give origin to a family project. Furthermore, in applying the principles of non-discrimination referred to in Article 14 of the ECHR, the ECtHR said that

---

[70] See I. MAJSTOROVIĆ, 'Obiteljsko pravo kao različitost u jedinstvu: Europska unija i Hrvatska' in A. KORAĆ GRAOVAC, I. MAJSTOROVIĆ (eds.), *Europsko obiteljsko pravo*, Narodne novine, Zagreb 2013, pp. 1–24. I. ŠIMOVIĆ, I. ĆURIĆ, 'Europska unija i obiteljsko pravo. Međunarodnoprivatnopravni, procesnopravni i materijalnopravni aspekti' (2015) 22(2) *Ljetopis socijalnog rada* 163–189.

[71] See more in S. WINKLER, 'Il diritto di famiglia', in G.A. BENACCHIO, F. CASUCCI (eds.), *Temi e Istituti di Diritto Privato dell'Unione Europea*, Giappichelli, Torino 2017, pp. 293 et seq.

[72] For a detailed analysis of the regulation of same-sex partnerships in the light of fundamental human rights, see A. KORAĆ GRAOVAC, 'Ljudska prava i pravno uređenje istospolnih zajednica u domaćem zakonodavstvu' in D. HRABAR (ed.), *Hrestomatija hrvatskoga obiteljskog prava*, Pravni fakultet Sveučilišta u Zagrebu, Zagreb 2010, pp. 235 et seq.

[73] See G. SAGATYS, 'The Concept of Family in Lithuanian Law' (2010) 1 *Jurisprudencija Mokslo darbų žurnalas* 184, 187, available at <https://ojs.mruni.eu/ojs/jurisprudence/article/view/1094/1047>.

each state of the European Council should take reasonable measures in order to avoid discrimination against same-sex couples, i.e. take reasonable measures proportional to the aim that represents a balance between public and private interest.[74]

Similarly, reference should be made to Article 7 and Article 9 of the Charter of Fundamental Rights of the European Union.[75] In particular, the Charter, in addition to recognising the right to respect for private and family life (Article 7), prohibits any form of discrimination based, inter alia, on sexual orientation (Article 21). Moreover, the Charter's Article 9 provides for the right to marry and the right to found a family. More precisely, it provides that 'the right to marry and the right to found a family shall be guaranteed in accordance with the national laws governing the exercise of these rights'. As to the mentioned Article 9, two facts should be pointed out: the lack of reference to the spouses' sex and the need to distinguish the right to marriage from the right to found a family. In other words, the Charter of Fundamental Rights, when it comes to the notion of family, refers to the legal tradition and culture of every single country. This means that the concept of family (and also its scope) can vary substantially. In addition, it can be concluded, as far as the topic here is concerned, that there is no obligation for the national legislator to recognise cohabitations that cannot be linked with the family concept of that specific country.

Due to the systematic coordination of the European Charter and the ECHR, which was made possible by the Lisbon Treaty, the correspondence of these legal sources has occurred regarding the fundamental rights of the person in family legal relationships to achieve equality of terms and to address the importance of both. Social, cultural and legal diversities of national solutions under family law lead to the conclusion that it is up to the legislator to decide whether or not to regulate *de facto* unions.

It is interesting to dwell for a moment on the case law of the Court of Justice whose judgments are applied directly to the internal legal systems. The CJEU judges have, until recently, made statements only about issues relating to the rights to freedom of movement and social rights of workers (and their family members) and the ban on discrimination based on gender or sexual orientation, but always in the context of individuals' social and labour rights. However, a sign of change comes from the recent ruling in the *Coman* case.[76] The case concerned

---

[74] Recently see the decision of the ECtHR of the 14 December 2017, in the case *Orlandi and others v Italy*, Application No. 26431/12.

[75] Charter of Fundamental Rights of the European Union, OJ C 202/389, 7.6.2016. In the literature see A. KORAĆ GRAOVAC, 'Povelja o temeljnim pravima Europske unije i obiteljsko pravo' in A. KORAĆ GRAOVAC, I. MAJSTOROVIĆ (eds.), *Europsko obiteljsko pravo*, Narodne novine, Zagreb 2013, pp. 25–51.

[76] Case C-673/16, Relu Adrian Coman and Others *v* Inspectoratul General pentru Imigrări and Ministerul Afacerilor Interne, EU:C:2018:385. See in the literature M. Ní SHUILLEABHAIN,

recognition of same-sex marriage (for the purpose of migration law), and not *de facto* unions, but it is very significant in the context of the Europeanisation of family law. This judgment made it clear that the question of personal status, as well as the legal consequences arising from a family relationship, is a matter of national law and that EU law does not interfere in this area. More precisely, it emphasises that the Member States decide independently whether or not to regulate a given community of life (in this case, same-sex marriage). However, the judgement also points out, and this is very significant, that the rights granted to certain individuals by EU law cannot be restricted by national law.

Leaving aside the case law and looking in a broader sense, it can be concluded that although there is no common European normative framework in the field of family law, supranational tendencies have an impact on individual national systems, which are encouraged to rethink their rules.[77] This rethinking must not result in a distortion of each individual country's tradition and legal culture, which is reflected, in particular, in family law. However, it represents the normal course of evolution of things in a much more mobile and integrated society, which, also in law, is inevitably impacted by the consequences of the profound cultural and sociological changes that have occurred in recent decades. Family law, more than any other law, reflects these great changes.

3.2. REGULATIONS' SCOPE OF APPLICATION: EXCLUSION OF *DE FACTO* COUPLES

It has already been noticed that even if the Twin Regulations are not intended to approximate the substantive rules on family law, nevertheless, their importance is central for the process of Europeanisation of family law. They do not only lay down common procedural and conflict of law rules but also have the merit of motivating the comparison of the different national family law systems, in particular, with regard to the questions they deal with. Indeed, the recent Matrimonial Property Regulation and the Regulation on the Property Consequences of a Registered Partnership offer a regulatory framework,

---

'Cross-Border (Non-)Recognition of Marriage and Registered Partnership: Free Movement and EU Private International Law' in J.M. SCHERPE, E. BARGELLI (eds.), *The Interaction between Family Law, Succession Law and Private International Law, Adapting to change*, Intersentia, Cambridge 2021, p. 16.

[77] Great comparative analyses have been carried out, especially in the last 20 years. In this respect, the reader should consult the numerous studies conducted by the Commission on European Family Law. See more at <https://ceflonline.net/>. As to the rights of *de facto* couples see K. BOELE-WOELKI, F. FERRAND, C. GONZALEZ BEILFUSS, M. JÄNTERÄ-JAREBORG, N. LOWE, D. MARTINY, V. TODOROVA, *Principles of European Family Law Regarding Property, Maintenance and Succession Rights of Couples in* de facto *Unions*, Intersentia, Cambridge 2019.

resulting from the enhanced cooperation of a relevant number of EU Member States in the area of jurisdiction, applicable law, recognition and enforcement of decisions on matrimonial property regimes and the property consequences of registered partnerships, respectively.[78]

However, apart from the difficulties arising from the heterogeneity of the rules on family property regimes laid down in the individual states, a central issue was the question as to which family units would be regulated in the future regulations, i.e. whether the legislator should regulate only the relationships between spouses or also those arising in other forms of family such as registered partnerships and *de facto* partnerships.

In the end, the legislator opted to regulate relations between spouses (in one regulation) and between registered partners (in another regulation).

Given the colourful legal framework described above with regard to only a few legal systems, it should be borne in mind that there can be many combinations (same-sex, different-sex or both) of registered and/or *de facto* couples consisting of persons of different sexes or of the same sex. Moreover, some systems registered partnerships are open to all types, other countries legally recognise only partnerships of same-sex couples, while others reserve the institution of partnership only to opposite-sex couples. No wonder that in 2015 this led to the abandonment of the idea of issuing binding regulations for all European legal systems. Eighteen EU countries have, therefore, opted to use enhanced cooperation.[79] This led to the adoption of the Twin Regulations.

These Regulations, which entered into force on 29 January 2019, do not touch upon substantive law. Thus, in Recital 17 of the Matrimonial Property Regulation, it is expressly stated that there is no definition of marriage, referring for this purpose to individual national laws. Similarly, Recital 17 of the Regulation on the Property Consequences of a Registered Partnership clarifies that:

> 'Registered partnership' should be defined here solely for the purpose of this Regulation. The actual substance of the concept should remain defined in the national laws of the Member States. Nothing in this Regulation should oblige a Member State whose law does not have the institution of registered partnership to provide for it in its national law.[80]

---

[78] P. LAGARDE, 'Règlements 2016/1103 et 1104 du 24 juin 2016 sur les régimes matrimoniaux et sur le régime patrimonial des partenariats enregistrés' (2016) *Rivista di diritto internazionale privato e processuale* 680 et seq.

[79] Thus, Austria, Belgium, Bulgaria, Cyprus, Croatia, Finland, France, Germany, Greece, Italy, Luxembourg, Malta, the Netherlands, Portugal, the Czech Republic, Slovenia, Spain and Sweden have expressed a desire to establish enhanced cooperation in the field of property regimes of international couples.

[80] See A. R. BENOT, 'Article 3 Definitions' in I. VIARENGO, P. FRANZINA (eds.), *The EU Regulations on the Property Regimes of International Couples, A Commentary*, Edward Elgar, Cheltenham 2020, p. 35.

One thing is certain, however: *de facto* couples are excluded from the scope of both Regulations.[81] Between the Twin Regulations, it would seem more logical to add *de facto* couples to the content of the Regulation on the Property Consequences of a Registered Partnership. The latter, however, clearly states the exclusion of such family formations from the list of cross-border couples who find legal protection in this source of EU secondary law. In particular, Article 1(1) of the Regulation on the Property Consequences of a Registered Partnership expressly states that 'this Regulation shall apply to matters of the property consequences of registered partnerships'. In order to better understand this provision, the article should be read in conjunction with Recital 16. Moreover, Article 3(1)(a) of the Regulation on the Property Consequences of a Registered Partnership should be taken into consideration:

> registered partnership means the regime governing the shared life of two people which is provided for in law, the registration of which is mandatory under that law and which fulfils the legal formalities required by that law for its creation.

If the relevant provisions are put together, it is clear that European legislation (specifically, the Regulation on the Property Consequences of a Registered Partnership) merely regulates certain issues concerning the property consequences of registered couples, leaving the individual national legal systems a wide scope for interpretation. It has already been said that a registered partnership can mean many things, or *rectius* can offer legal protection to couples composed in different ways, but all united by a formal requirement: registration.[82] On the contrary, by stressing the great diversity of national rules on *de facto* unions', the European legislator chose not to include them. One of its

---

[81] See Recital 16 of the Regulation on the Property Consequences of a Registered Partnership, which states; 'The way in which forms of union other than marriage are provided for in the Member States' legislation differs from one State to another, and a distinction should be drawn between couples whose union is institutionally sanctioned by the registration of their partnership with a public authority and couples in de facto cohabitation. While some Member States do make provision for such de facto unions, they should be considered separately from registered partnerships, which have an official character that makes it possible to take account of their specific features and lay down rules on the subject in Union legislation. In order to ensure the smooth functioning of the internal market, barriers to the free movement of people who have entered into a registered partnership need to be eliminated, particularly those creating difficulties for such couples in the administration and division of their property. In order to achieve those objectives, this Regulation should bring together provisions on the jurisdiction, applicable law, recognition or, as the case may be, acceptance, enforceability and enforcement of decisions, authentic instruments and court settlements'.

[82] A. R. BENOT, 'Article 1 Scope' in I. VIARENGO, P. FRANZINA (eds.), *The EU Regulations on the Property Regimes of International Couples, A Commentary*, Edward Elgar, Cheltenham 2020, p. 20.

consequences of this is that the legal position of cross-border *de facto* couples is very different from that of cross-border couples whose property relations are ruled by the Twin Regulations (i.e. married or registered couples). Indeed, these couples are invisible and without legal protection at the European level. This being invisible on the supranational level creates quite a few problems.[83] We can fully accept the position of those who do not recognise the need to legally protect such family formations or those who believe that the recognition of couples to whom European legislation is applicable in the absence of any formal prerequisites becomes highly complex and uncertain. However, it must also be borne in mind that in many legal systems, family law reserves more than one legal consequence for the multitude of informal unions. Take, for example, *de facto* unions of persons of different sexes in Croatian law. Under Croatian law, *de facto* unions are practically equivalent to marriage in terms of the legal effects of their property. However, if there is an element of transnationality, such unions become unregulated. Their property effects are, in the presence of cross-border elements, left to the individual rules of private international law laid down by each state, with the consequent amplification of potential situations that prejudice the free movement of persons.

4. CONCLUDING REMARKS

The European legal landscape varies to such an extent that uniform characteristics that are able to create the lowest common denominator referring to *de facto* unions do not yet exist. The most critical point emerging from the comparison of national laws is the need for legal recognition in all the European countries. Currently, some systems decided to regulate only *de facto* unions composed of opposite-sex couples, others only same-sex unions, while a third regulate both. Without clear legal regulation, persons who live in such unions could be considered invisible.

It should also be noted that there are often weaknesses behind the protection established in the single national order, especially regarding a citizen's movement and the recognition of one's familial status. The adoption of the Twin Regulations certainly represents a step forward. However, it is a timid and uncertain step that once again shows the limits of the unavoidably fragmented approach of

---

[83] See R. Pacia, S. Winkler, 'Invisible Minorities within Extramarital Unions – Comparison of Different Solutions Provided by the Family Laws' in N. Bodiroga-Vukobrat, G.G. Sander, S. Barić (eds.), *Unsichtbare Minderheiten. Invisible Minorities*, Verlag dr. Kovač, Hamburg 2013, p. 65. T. Kruger, 'Partners limping across borders' in I. Kunda (ed.), *Obitelj i djeca: europska očekivanja i nacionalna stvarnost*, Pravni fakultet u Rijeci, Hrvatska udruga za poredbeno pravo, Rijeka 2014, pp. 185 et seq.

the European legislator in the field of family law. *De facto* couples are tangible proof of how complex it is to study and apply family law in the EU. Nonetheless, their position should be taken into account since the number of couples living in unregistered partnerships is certainly not negligible among cross-border couples.

PROPERTY REGIMES AND LAND REGISTERS FOR CROSS-BORDER COUPLES

Lucia RUGGERI and Manuela GIOBBI*

1. Land Registers in Europe: A Fragmented Regulatory Framework 269
2. Autonomy of the will and Protection of Third Parties: A Difficult Combination 273
3. The Arduous, but Necessary, Dialogue between *Lex Causae* and *Lex Registri* 276
4. The Principle of Unity and the Protection of the Third Party 279
5. Law Applicable to the Property Regime and Knowledge Held by Third Parties 282
6. Recording of Rights *in Rem* and the Scope of the Twin Regulations 285
7. Disclosure of Assets and Effects in Respect of Third Parties 287
8. Adaptability of Rights *in Rem* 289
9. Concluding Remarks 291

1. LAND REGISTERS IN EUROPE: A FRAGMENTED REGULATORY FRAMEWORK

The Twin Regulations on property regimes and the property consequences of cross-border couples exclude from their scope of application matters of real estate and property disclosure (Article 1(2) of the Twin Regulations). This exclusion is not new. The Succession Regulation also excludes from its scope questions relating to the recording in a register of a right in immovable or movable property (Article 1(2) sub l). It is the law of the Member State in

---

* Lucia Ruggeri, Full Professor of civil law at the Faculty of Law, the University of Camerino, Italy.
Manuela Giobbi, PhD, research fellow in private law at the Law School of the University of Camerino, Italy.
Lucia Ruggeri is the author of Sections 1, 2, 3, 4 and Manuela Giobbi is the author of Sections 5, 6, 7, 8, 9 of this chapter.

which the register is kept or where the immovable property is located that determines the legal conditions and recording procedures.

In this context, land registers constitute an area still strongly characterised by legislative fragmentation.[1] Its harmonisation at the European level is difficult due to the high degree of different national approaches that characterises the rights and obligations regarding real estate property. This can be seen in the field of guarantees, as well as with regard to the nature and content of institutions, such as timeshare, tenure, trust, etc.

Based on this situation, the exclusion made by EU regulations in the field of family and succession law is an almost mandatory choice the aim of which is to provide legal certainty, while the reference to national law in fact avoids the difficulty in determining the applicable legislation. The function of transparency is so important that any uncertainty would probably lead to conflicts in fundamental areas such as the knowledge of acts or facts of relevant importance by third parties. In some countries, a couple's bond determines the appearance of peculiar legal relationships of a patrimonial content. As a consequence, not only does the relevant act or fact that is to be registered need to be disclosed, but also the specific personal situation of the person, related to such an act or fact.

Such a fragmentation does not make the life of couples who live in countries other than those of origin, or who are composed of people of different nationalities, any easier. Each state attributes the keeping of registers to different ministries and organises registration in various ways by centralising, decentralising, separating or aggregating in a single register information related to the matrimonial regime or registered partnership and information related to property or real estate guarantees.

For this reason, dialogue between land registries initiated by the European Land Information Service (EULIS)[2] project and continued with the Land Registers Interconnections (LRI)[3] project is to be considered a complementary tool to the European policies laid out in the Twin Regulations. Freedom of movement laid out in Article 21 Treaty on the Functioning of the European Union (TFEU) may also become effective and be encouraged through a different organisation of the land registers aimed at making them easily accessible and intelligible.

---

[1] Significantly, it highlights that each property regime has an internal logic with its own rules on the subject of deeds of purchase, disposal and disclosure. E. CALÒ, 'Variazioni sulla *professio iuris* nei regimi patrimoniali delle famiglie' (2017) 6 *Rivista del Notariato* 1093.

[2] The project (initiated in 2006) has enabled the integration of the registers of the following countries: Ireland (Property Registration Authority), Lithuania (Valstybės įmonė Registrų centras – State Enterprise Centre of Registers), Netherlands (Kadaster), Austria (Bundesministerium für Justiz) and Spain (Colegio de Registradores de la Propiedad, Mercantiles y de Bienes Muebles de España).

[3] The goal of this project is to create a single access point through an e-justice portal, a description of which can be found at <https://dg-justice-portal-demo.eurodyn.com/ejusticeportal/content_land_registers_interconnection_lri-36276-en.do>

Accessibility to the different land registers would be easier for citizens and companies, as long as technological interoperability is accompanied by careful clarification of the legal terminology in order to better understand the similarities or differences that the institutions attribute to the term 'land'. In common law systems, this word has a broad meaning including not only the land but also every immovable property and every type of right exercised over this property.[4] Such a broad term, which can also be found in the Italian legal system (Article 813 of the Italian Civil Code),[5] makes interoperability difficult. The European legislative choice is justified also by the fact that states have over time developed measures that identify specific regulatory regimes for certain goods or rights.[6] For example, one just needs to consider the concept of ownership and the difficulties in making distinctions among different models such as long leasehold.[7] There are also systems such as the German or Anglo-Saxon ones[8] in which the recording of the sale of real estate has the constitutive effect[9] of law, unlike personal based systems, such as the Italian one, in which a transcription mainly is of a declarative function.[10]

Harmonisation conducted by the EU through regulatory instruments that involve only some Member States (as do the Twin Regulations) aggravates the problem. The set of third states in the matters of registration of family property regimes is, in fact, composed not only of traditional third countries but also of all those EU Member States that have not adhered to the enhanced cooperation procedure that led to the adoption of the Matrimonial Property Regulation and the Regulation on the Property Consequences of Registered Partnerships. The couple's choice to formalise a living communion in the form of marriage or registered partnership through a registration procedure that has not been harmonised is combined with the non-harmonised regulations of registration

---

[4] V.I. FERRARI, *Land Law nell'Era Digitale*, Cedam, Padova 2013, pp 4–7.

[5] Article 813 of the Italian Civil Code reads: 'Unless otherwise stated by the law, the provisions concerning immovable property also apply to rights *in rem* concerning immovable property and related actions; the provisions concerning movable property apply to all other rights'.

[6] S. GARDNER and E. MACKENZIE, *An Introduction to Land Law*, 4th ed., Hart Publishing, Oxford 2015, p. 7.

[7] V.M.P. THOMPSON and M. GEORGE, *Modern Land Law*, Oxford University Press, Oxford 2017, p. 245.

[8] M.D. PANFORTI, 'Torrens title', *Digesto delle Discipline Privatistiche*, Utet, Torino 2000, Agg. I, p. 715. Sulle origini germaniche del sistema Torrens v, fra gli altri, A. ESPOSITO, 'Ulrich Hubbe's Role in the Creation of the Torrens System of Land Registration in South Australia' (2003) 24(2) *Adelaide Law Review* 263–304, HeinOnline.

[9] For example, in England and Wales, disclosure has assumed a constitutive value following the Land Registration Act 2002. V.I. FERRARI, *Land Law nell'Era Digitale*, Cedam, Padova 2013, pp. 185–186.

[10] In some Italian regions (Trentino Alto-Adige and Friuli Venezia Giulia) there is a system of real estate advertising of German origin called 'intavolazione'. This type of transcription has constitutive effects. See F. PADOVINI, 'voce "trascrizione"' in Noviss. Dig. It., app. VII, Torino, 1987, p. 800 et seq.

of the financial consequences deriving from different family models. From this perspective, the exclusion of the matter of disclosure from the European legislation is only a temporary solution to a problem that still remains: no harmonisation of the field of family property consequences can work well unless it is possible also to achieve harmonisation of the rules regarding the registration of family models and the property consequences of the chosen models. Even where the legislator preferred not to introduce specific property regimes deriving from marriage the property discipline could be influenced by the presence of a marriage. Reference can be made to English jurisprudence regarding the assignment of a family home. In a country that attributes an exemplary constitutive value to land registers, this position was held in the case of *Grant v Edwards*.[11] In this case, a married woman who was not the owner of the house obtained recognition of community ownership of the property. This was made based on an assessment of the behaviour of the parties and of the specific circumstances from which it emerged that it was contrary to good faith to assign the formal title of the property to the husband alone.

Interference among family situations, ownership structures and different systems on registration of property deeds are such[12] that is necessary to harmonise registration systems among the various states. This process, prefigured by the EU since the adoption of the Green Paper on Mortgage Credit,[13] has not yet taken place. The discussion of this issue with reference to the European framework introduced by the Twin Regulations can only take note of it.

The current legislation regarding family property regimes has its effects well beyond the couple itself. It may concern everyone whenever rights *in rem* are involved, while these have *erga omnes* effect in the legislative tradition of many states. Therefore, a close connection exists between a property regime, ownership or joint ownership of a property, registration rules and the protection of third parties who, for example, have a claim against one of the couple. The Twin Regulations expressly excluded from their scope 'any recording in a register of rights in immoveable or moveable property, including the legal requirements for such recording, and the effects of recording or failing to record such rights in a register' (Article 1(2)(h). But this exclusion made by the Twin

---

[11] *Grant v Edwards* [1986] 3 WLR 114 Court of Appeal.
[12] The varied taxonomy of couples, which can no longer be reduced to the scheme of heterosexual marriage, has led to referrals to property regimes 'derived from sexual choices'. For the use of the term 'sexual property law', G.L. GRETTON and A.J.M. STEVENS, *Property, Trusts and Succession*, Bloomsbury, London 2017, p. 112. More generally on this topic see W. PINTENS, 'Matrimonial Property Law in Europe' in K. BOELE-WOELKI, J. MILES and J. M. SCHERPE (eds.), *The Future of Family Property in Europe*, Intersentia, Antwerp 2011, pp. 19–46; K. BOELE-WOELKI, F. FERRAND, C. GONZÁLEZ-BEILFUSS, M. JÄNTERÄ-JAREBORG, N. LOWE, D. MARTINY and W. PINTENS, *Principles of European Family Law Regarding Property Relations Between Spouses*, Intersentia, Antwerp 2013, pp. 1–420.
[13] COM(2005) 0327 final.

Regulations is not conclusive. It specifically does not eliminate the need to study the interference between the law applicable to the property relationship and the *lex registri*, verifying the impact on the position of the third party who, for various reasons, came into contact with only one or both of the couple.

2. AUTONOMY OF THE WILL AND PROTECTION OF THIRD PARTIES: A DIFFICULT COMBINATION

The applicable law identified based on the Twin Regulations determines the effects of the property regime between spouses or partners of the registered partnership and the legal relationships between a spouse or a partner[14] and third parties. The law identified by the spouses during or prior to the marriage or registered partnership constitutes the *lex causae*. It governs not only the property relationships of the couple, but, as highlighted in Recital 18 of the Matrimonial Property Regulation, it includes also relationships between an individual spouse and third parties. Such a third party might be a creditor of a single or both spouses or partners, whereas a relationship may derive from a contract, from an unlawful fact, or from any other act or fact that may give rise to the mandatory relationship.

The law applicable to matrimonial property regimes or the property consequences of a registered partnership is the expression of a couple's negotiating freedom, which, by the expressly stated provision of Article 22 of the Twin Regulations, could also be changed with retroactive effect. The position of the third party is safeguarded by preventing the *ius variandi* exercised by the couple and therefore adversely affecting the third party on whom the law originally applied to the property regime will continue to have effect.[15]

There are many possible scenarios when concluding an agreement on the choice of law. Couples can identify the applicable law prior to formalising their union, or they can await the conclusion of the marriage or registered partnership to choose the law, they can stay with the first chosen law, or can later change it, even retroactively, or else make a choice of law that will have effect from a specific date. The choice of the applicable law, thus conceived, caters to the needs of the couple who is, based on the concrete situation, able to identify which law of which state can best govern the relationship. However, this is less satisfactory for third parties who enter into contact with the couple.

---

[14] A typographical error is noted in Article 27 point *f* of the Regulation on the Property Consequences of Registered Partnerships (Italian translation) where instead of a partner it reads 'spouse' ('coniuge').

[15] There is a wide debate on the possible retroactivity of the *ius variandi*. V.L. RADEMACHER, 'Changing the Past: Retroactive Choice of Law and the Protection of Third Parties in the European Regulations on Patrimonial Consequences of Marriages and Registered Partnerships' (2018) 10 *Cuadernos de Derecho Transnacional* 1, 10.

The Twin Regulations were adopted on the basis of Article 81(3) of the TFEU as family law instruments with transnational implications. However, it is certain that whenever an individual member of a couple or both of them enter into contracts or assume obligations, the legal activity interacts with family law. Although the exclusion of disclosure on the one hand respects the traditions of each individual state and constitutes the leitmotif of European legislation in family and succession matters, on the other hand it prevents an adequate level of protection to third parties.

The Twin Regulations have intervened in an area that not even international conventions were able to regulate. In 1905[16] a convention was drawn up regarding the effects of marriage, which was overturned by the two world wars. In 1978, another convention[17] specifically regulated property regimes between spouses; however, it too was unsuccessful as it was ratified only by France, Luxembourg and the Netherlands. From this point of view, the adoption of the Twin Regulations is of great success on the path taken by the EU aimed at simplifying the life of cross-border couples.

The adoption of what is known as the autonomy of the will,[18] the basis of any rule that introduces the freedom to choose the applicable law, means, when it comes to family matters, sacrificing the needs of third parties. Family relationships are not exclusively personal, but inevitably also include a patrimonial character. The home is a place where the right to private and family life is exercised; however, at the same time it constitutes an asset regulated by the rules of real estate law. In order to manage their life, the couple necessarily establishes different contractual relationships. A wish of spending together their free time most likely includes travelling and rental contracts for holiday homes. For this reason, in some countries, marriage or the conclusion of a registered partnership also has consequences on the property regime of the members of the couple. Such consequences inevitably reverberate on relations with third parties who establish qualified relations with the members of the couple. The effects of the autonomy of the couple will therefore unravel beyond the couple itself and therefore implies a reversal from the traditional

---

[16] This refers to the Hague Convention of 17 July 1905 on matrimonial property. The text can be consulted at <https://www.hcch.net/en/instruments/the-old-conventions/1905-effects-of-marriage-convention>.

[17] This refers to the Hague Convention of 14 March 1978 on the Law Applicable to Matrimonial Property Regimes.

[18] The adoption of the criterion of the autonomy of the will to identify the applicable law in contexts characterised by internationality dates back to a famous French case (see Cass. civ., 5 December 1905, *American Trading Company v Quebec Steamship Company Limited*), but it also constitutes a tradition dating back to English culture (see *Girnar v Meyer* (1796), 2 Hy. Bl. 603). On this subject, see M. Giuliano and P. Lagarde, 'Relazione sulla Convenzione relativa alla legge applicabile alle obbligazioni contrattuali', *Comunicazione al Consiglio* in GUCE 31 October 1980, C 282, p. 16.

principle according to which an agreement has effect only between the parties that stipulate it. The choice of a living communion sealed by a formal marriage or a registered partnership, in the case of cross-border couples, determines the possibility of choosing the law applicable to the relationship with inevitable consequences on third parties. Article 27, point f of the Twin Regulations, therefore, reaffirms the effectiveness of a principle consolidated in private international law. However, it is characterised by greater difficulty in implementation. In fact, the third party is burdened by knowing the law chosen by the parties or the choice temporarily affecting the couple's relationships whenever the couple has exercised the *ius variandi* granted to it by Article 22, paragraphs 2 and 3 of both regulations.

The scope of the chosen law is very broad, concerning not only the matters listed by Article 27 of the Twin Regulations, but also additional aspects that the parties wish to assign to the chosen law or that fall within the scope of the law as an effect determined by the specifically applicable national law.[19] The impact of Article 27 on third parties is even more interesting considering that this provision did not feature in the original proposal of the regulations.[20] Each state has its own approach to the property consequences of marriage or registered partnerships. As a consequence of that, many matters referred to in Article 27 of both regulations would, without this specific regulatory intervention, have been governed by the *lex fori* rather than by the law chosen by the parties. However, a provision as it is, enables the possibility of expanding matters that are subject to the chosen law, which reduces the impact of the possible application of the *lex fori*. The consequences of the *lex causae* in areas that are extremely relevant for those who come into contact with the couple is very problematic. On the one hand, this excludes the possibility for the Regulations to govern aspects such as the nature of rights *in rem* or issues regarding the registration of titles on movable or immovable property, while on the other hand, the instrument of choice of applicable law allows for the resolution of many issues by the lex causae with the consequent exclusion of the effect of the *lex fori* that would have been operating by default in matters excluded from the scope of the Twin Regulations. On the other hand, through the instrument of choice of applicable law, many issues are resolved by the *lex causae* with the consequent exclusion of the effect of the *lex fori* which would have been operating by default in matters excluded from the scope of the regulations.

---

[19] J.M. CARRUTHERS, 'Article 27' in I. VIARENGO and P. FRANZINA (eds.), *The EU Regulations on the Property Regimes of International Couples. A Commentary*, Edward Elgar 2020, p. 262.

[20] COM (2011) 126 final. The introduction of specific details regarding the scope of application of the autonomy of the will is the subject of ongoing debate. See, among others, O. LANDO, 'Contracts' in K. LIPSTEIN (ed.), *Private International Law*, in *International Encyclopedia of Comparative Law*, vol. III, Brill, Leiden 1977, pp. 106–125.

For issues regarding rights *in rem*, the *lex fori* will be in effect. The judge will also be able to identify a corresponding right *in rem* in his or her own legal system which can produce the effects that the parties would have liked to produce by using a right *in rem* from another legal system, but which did not exist in the legal system of the judge.[21]

Any question regarding the recording in a register pertains to the *lex registri*, which does not necessarily coincide with the *lex fori*: when the property is real estate, questions regarding the recording of the property fall within the field of application of the place where the immovable property is located (*lex rei sitae*). The registry system was considered as excluded from harmonisation with the aim to safeguard the exclusive competence of states to better organise the requirements for the registration of an asset in a specific register. The *lex registri*, which, in the case of real estate, coincides with the *lex rei sitae*, determines the conditions of registration, but also allows for the identification of the authorities in charge of verifying the documents that are necessary for the registration.

3. THE ARDUOUS, BUT NECESSARY, DIALOGUE BETWEEN *LEX CAUSAE* AND *LEX REGISTRI*

It is not easy to untangle this complex regulatory framework. On one hand, it must be understood how far the *lex causae* can affect specific areas of the *lex registri*, and, on the other hand, it must be verified how the knowledge of third parties is modulated. The latter is necessary for the enforceability of the effects of acts done by the couple regarding movable and immovable property that must be subject to registration.

The *lex causae* allows for the identification of the nature of the property, which in some countries may be legally classified as a personal asset or communal property. This circumstance impacts a third-party creditor who will be able to count on property guarantees whose content and conditions will be established by the *lex causae*. The European regulatory framework regarding family property regimes makes it necessary to analyse the level of protection granted to third parties who come into contact with the couple. The exclusion of the matter of the property registers from the scope of the regulations does not exclude this matter from an analysis regarding the specific situation of the third party. The latter ends up being influenced by the *lex causae* under relevant conditions, such as the knowledge that the third party may have about the family property regime.

---

[21] See P. Bruno, *I regolamenti europei sui regimi patrimoniali dei coniugi e delle unioni registrate*, Giuffrè, Milano 2019, pp. 62–63.

The disclosure systems of property regimes are different in different states or are completely absent in some of them. For example, in Austria,[22] Croatia,[23] Ireland, Slovakia or Luxembourg, no form of disclosure is provided for family property regimes. Cyprus is also different given that it has introduced the principle of 'property independence' both for marriages[24] and for civil partnerships:[25] the marriage or the civil union do not affect the property independence of the spouses or of the partners.[26] Poland also lacks specific registers where it is possible to obtain information on property regimes from the Central Register of Entrepreneurial Activities,[27] as does Sweden, where the registration of spouses' and partners' agreements is handled exclusively for tax purposes.[28]

In some states, such as Italy, disclosure takes place through the civil registry records. When the *lex causae* is Italian law, an interested third party can identify whether the special regime of legal communion is in effect or if there are matrimonial agreements, or, again, a property fund.[29] The nature of the asset and its regime is regulated by the *lex causae* and, on this basis, a third party will be able to establish which rights and powers he or she can exercise, or may not exercise, on a particular asset.

However, where a state considers forms of disclosure of family property regimes, it is necessary to verify for what purpose such a disclosure is provided. In Italy, the civil registry allows for two different forms of disclosure. With regard to the personal *status* (e.g. records of marriage, finalised divorce), the civil register provides disclosure in the form of notification, that is, it constitutes a burden whose non-fulfilment can give rise to sanctions, but does not produce invalidity. In the event of failure to record, the burden of providing proof that the third party had knowledge of the situation of which he or she had not been given notice rests on one of the couple in question. If, on the contrary, the recording has taken place, the third party cannot invoke a lack of knowledge of that particular situation.

The recording of marriage agreements in the civil registry is, on the other hand, a disclosure with only declarative effects, the omission of which renders the act impossible to invoke against third parties. Precisely regarding property

---

[22] See T. PERTOT, 'Austria' in L. RUGGERI, I. KUNDA and S. WINKLER (eds.), *Family Property and Succession in EU Member States. National Reports on the Collected Data*, Rijeka Faculty of Law, Rijeka 2019, p. 9.
[23] See M. BUKOVAC PUVAČA, 'Croatia' in L. RUGGERI, I. KUNDA and S. WINKLER (eds.), ibid., p. 77.
[24] See L. 232/1991, Sezione 13.
[25] See L. 184(I)/2015, Sezione 33.
[26] See A. Plevri, 'Cyprus' in L. RUGGERI, I. KUNDA and S. WINKLER (eds.), *Family Property and Succession in EU Member States. National Reports on the Collected Data*, Rijeka Faculty of Law, Rijeka 2019, p. 102.
[27] See M. WĄSIC, 'Poland' in L. RUGGERI, I. KUNDA and S. WINKLER (eds.), ibid, p. 513.
[28] See S. THORSLUND, 'Sweden', L. RUGGERI, I. KUNDA and S. WINKLER (eds.), ibid., p. 663.
[29] In Italy, the disclosure is not mandatory but only if the act has been transcribed can this act be opposed to a third party.

regimes or the property consequences of registered partnerships, many states opt for a disclosure with declarative effects only. In addition to Italy, also Belgium,[30] Finland, Portugal and Spain[31] expressly subordinate the possibility to invoke the effects of the marriage and/or partnership against third parties to the recording of marriage or various types of partnership agreements in civil registers and to the recording of marriage agreements in registers of the various types of relationships. This allows for a possibility that the effects of the marriage and/or partnerships can be invoked against third parties.[32] In Czech law, the position of the third party is subject to specific protection since the marriage agreement may not infringe the rights of the third party unless the third party has consented in the agreement.[33]

In Denmark, the separation regime when chosen by the couple needs to be disclosed by publication in the Official Gazette of Denmark (*Statstidende*)[34] so as to allow it to be invoked against third-party creditors. In Estonia and Romania, there are specific registers devoted to matrimonial property regimes, the management of which is assigned to the Chamber of Notaries. Their aim is to enable the existence of the property regime to be invoked against third parties, which provides for an increased level of protection of the interests of third parties and of legal certainty.[35]

In France, although there is no specific register for property regimes, third-party creditors obtain information of the changes that have occurred in a couple's property regime by means of a notice published in specialised journals. The so-called Pact Civil de Solidarité (PACS) is entered in the civil registry with an aim of making its existence known to third parties. The enforceability of the property ownership regime is, however, subject to the transcription of the purchase deeds in public land registers.[36]

---

[30] The *lex causae* can, by virtue of the principle of universality, also be that of a state that has not adhered to the enhanced procedure, thus making relevant an investigation that also includes a state such as Bulgaria.

[31] In Spain, the registration of marriage agreements occurs in the national Civil Register. The regulation of the systems of disclosure of registered partnerships, on the other hand, does not have a national character and is an expression of the regulatory power of the local authorities. See A.M. Pérez Vallejio, 'Spain' in L. Ruggeri, I. Kunda and S. Winkler (eds.), *Family Property and Succession in EU Member States. National Reports on the Collected Data*, Rijeka Faculty of Law, Rijeka 2019, p. 624.

[32] See Article 1395 §2 Code Civil.

[33] Based on Article 719 of the Civil Code, no legal effect can be produced by an agreement that has not involved the third party for the profiles of his or her concern.

[34] See L. Nielsen, *Study on Matrimonial Property Regimes and the Property of Unmarried Couples in Private International Law and Internal Law*, Europäische Kommission/Generaldirektion Justiz und Inneres, Brussels 2003, pp. 1–78.

[35] See S. Liin, 'Estonia' in L. Ruggeri, I. Kunda and S. Winkler (eds.), *Family Property and Succession in EU Member States. National Reports on the Collected Data*, Rijeka Faculty of Law, Rijeka 2019, p. 193. Per la Romania v. G. Russo, 'Romania' in L. Ruggeri, I. Kunda and S. Winkler (eds.), 'ibid', p. 556.

[36] See <http://www.coupleseurope.eu/en/france/topics>.

The recording of the property regime chosen by the couple, even though not required for the deed to be valid, is a condition of it being invoked against third parties in German law. The formation of the register at the *Amtsgericht* allows for the knowledge that makes the couple's property situation be applied against the third party.[37] Additionally, publication of the registration in journals specialised in legal notices is also provided.

In Greece, a register kept at the Court of First Instance situated in Athens collects all the agreements concerning the property regimes of couples. Hungary has a specific national register of agreements concerning property relations of couples joined in marriage or registered partnership. The registration, therefore, certifies the existence of the agreements and enables them being applied against third parties. Lithuania, Netherlands, and Slovenia[38] also keep a specific register of marriage agreements: failure to record the agreements in the register makes them impossible to be applied against third parties, unless they otherwise had knowledge of them.[39]

On the contrary, Malta does not have a specific register dedicated to marriage agreements; however, these agreements must be entered into the Public Register kept at the Ministry of Justice. Such a form of registration fulfils the function of notification for third parties, who are thus presumed to possess legal knowledge of this fact.[40]

As can be concluded, the innate dialogue between *lex causae* and *lex registri* stresses the need for a case-by-case evaluation of the third party's position: the relationship between the third party and the couple is, in fact, tendentiously governed by the *lex causae*, but the system of disclosure remains anchored to the not always necessarily coincident *lex registry*. As a consequence, the autonomy of the couple's will ends up by adding to the burdens and obligations of the third party regarding the rules specifically applicable to his or her relationship.

4. THE PRINCIPLE OF UNITY AND THE PROTECTION OF THE THIRD PARTY

It follows from the complex regulatory framework that the *lex causae* chosen by the spouses or partners governs all property relationships, including those

---

[37] See T. Pertot, 'Germany' in L. Ruggeri, I. Kunda and S. Winkler (eds.), *Family Property and Succession in EU Member States. National Reports on the Collected Data*, Rijeka Faculty of Law, Rijeka 2019, p. 268.
[38] See F. Dougan, 'Slovenia', in L. Ruggeri, I. Kunda and S. Winkler (eds.), ibid., p. 595.
[39] See A. Limante, 'Lithuania' in L. Ruggeri, I. Kunda and S. Winkler (eds.), ibid., p. 416. Per l'Olanda v. F.W.JM Schols and T.F.H. Reijnen, 'The Netherlands' in L. Ruggeri, I. Kunda and S. Winkler (eds.), ibid., p. 493.
[40] See M.V. Maccari, 'Malta' in L. Ruggeri, I. Kunda and S. Winkler (eds.), ibid., p. 468.

regarding real estate. Real estate law does not foresee any exception to the principle of unity introduced by Article 21 of the Twin Regulations. This article therefore applies to all family property relations with international elements. The undifferentiated application of the applicable law limits the negotiating autonomy of the couple who are not able to identify a different law for assets that are located in countries other than the one whose law governs all their property relations. However, the technique of *dépeçage*[41] constitutes an important management tool capable of adapting the choice of applicable law to the needs and peculiarities of a specific case. By combining adherence to the principle of unity with the application of the *lex registri*, it turns out that it is impossible to outline a common and general framework of the various regimes of disclosure of the property belonging to couples joined in marriage or civil unions.

The first difficulty is the non-existence of a single category of third parties: they can only be identified by referring to the *lex causae* that does not necessarily coincide with the *lex registri* as the law applicable to the property. In general, it can be assumed that a third party is either a creditor the position of who derives from an obligation that is not necessarily only contractual, or a person with other protected interests towards the couple. Such a third person can therefore make respective patrimonial claims.

The identification of the third party and his or her powers in relation to the couple's property can be derived from Article 28 of the Twin Regulations, which provide for different scenarios with different regulatory solutions.

Only if the third party has an effective knowledge of the law applicable to the property regime is this law invocable against the third party. The possibility of invoking this law determines that whatever the geographic location of the property, the law applicable to the relationship between the couple and the third party will be the one chosen by the couple or the one identified using Article 26 of either of the Twin Regulations. As can be understood, subjective conditions, such as a habitual residence or common citizenship, ultimately take the relationship between the third party and the couple back to a regulatory field that can be very different from that of the *lex registri*. In this regard, the European legislator strikes a good balance between legislative automatism and third-party protection when in Article 26(3) of the Twin Regulations the penultimate subparagraph establishes the split between the *lex causae* and the

---

[41] The technique of dépeçage is a concept within the field of conflict of laws whereby different issues within a single case are governed by the laws of different Countries. See 8 W. L M REESE, 'Dépeçage: A Common Phenomenon in Choice-of-law' (1973) 73 Colum L Rev at 58; C. G. STEVENSON, 'Dépeçage: Embracing Complexity to Solve Choice-of-Law Issues' (2003–2004) 37 Ind L Rev 303, 309. An example of dépeçage could be find in the Rome Convention on the Law Applicable to the Contractual Obligations, Art 3(1): 'A contract shall be governed by the law chosen by the parties. The choice must be expressed or demonstrated with reasonable certainty by the terms of the contract or the circumstances of the case. By their choice the parties can select the law applicable to the whole or a part only of the contract.'

law applicable to the relationship between the third party and the couple. In fact, if one of the couple on the basis of Article 26(3) has asked the judicial authority to decide on the basis of a law other than the one provided for in Article 26(1), the law thus identified cannot regulate relations with the third party, but can be effective exclusively to regulate the property relations of the couple. In such case, a law of the state in which the spouses or partners have had a common habitual residence for a significant period and longer than the period of their life spent in the first common habitual residence, applies.

Reason guides the identification of the law applicable to relations with third parties. The *lex causae* binds the third party even in mere awareness of the applicable law, since actual knowledge is not required, but simply the possibility, through the exercise of due diligence, to identify the law that the parties or the legislator itself identifies as applicable to the property regime (Article 28, paragraph 1 of both regulations). The *lex causae* cannot bind the third party if it was not possible to acquire knowledge of it or whenever the law has been applied using exceptional criteria and in the exclusive interest of the spouses (Article 26, paragraph 3, penultimate subparagraph).[42]

The mitigation of the risk of legal uncertainty adds a further value pursued by the European legislator to strike a better balance between the protection of the couple's interests and those of related third parties. In fact, where the *lex causae* governs the agreement between a couple and a third party, or where a spouse or partner resides in the same state as the third party, the presumption of knowledge is in effect.[43] Due to the silence of the law, it is possible to debate the extent of the presumption which, in the opinion of the author, seems to be considered *iuris et de iure*, in order to minimise conflict in such a complex regulatory system, and to favour legal certainty.[44] The presumption of knowledge introduced by Article 28 of the Twin Regulations regarding immovable property deserves attention: if, in fact, the *lex causae* coincides with the law of the state in which these assets are located, the third party has no excuse regarding his or her lack of knowledge of the applicable law. Based on the

---

[42] Following Article 26 'The application of the law of the other State shall not adversely affect the rights of third parties deriving from the law applicable pursuant to point (a) of paragraph 1'. The third party cannot be affected by the lex causae if the judicial authority 'by way of exception and upon application by either spouse', decide that the law of a state other than the state whose law is applicable pursuant to point (a) of paragraph 1 shall govern the matrimonial property regime. This exceptional application occurs when the applicant demonstrates that: (a) the spouses had their last common habitual residence in that other state for a significantly longer period of time than in the state designated pursuant to point (a) of paragraph 1; and (b) both spouses had relied on the law of that other state in arranging or planning their property relations.

[43] See Article 28 of the Twin Regulations.

[44] The presumptions are also relevant in the context of the successions. With regard to the third's party presumption of good faith, see I. Riva, *Certificato successorio europeo. Tutele e vicende acquisitive*, ESI, Napoli 2017, pp. 161–166.

principle of unity of applicable legislation, the application of a law that coincides with the law of the place where the immovable property is located cannot be a surprise: in such a case, the third-party benefits from the coincidence between the *lex causae* and the *lex registri*, which cannot be seen in other cases.

The complex and articulated system of interference between the *lex causae* and the *lex registri* is specified by Article 28(2), point *b*. As can be seen, in some states the property regime of the spouses or the property consequences of registered partnerships benefit from specific registration tools or specific disclosure systems. If one of the spouses or partners has fulfilled the recording obligation required by the law of the state in which the property is located, then in this case, too, the *lex causae* cannot but coincide with the *lex registri*. If the recording has taken place by following the law of the state whose law is applicable to the transaction between a spouse or a partner and the third party, or the law of the state where the contracting spouse and the third party have their habitual residence, the third party cannot object the legal presumption of knowledge of the applicable law.

Article 28 of both regulations constitutes an indispensable point of reference for understanding which law is applicable to the relationship between a spouse or a partner and third party whenever the *lex causae* is not effective. The lack of alignment between the law applicable to the couple's property relations and the law applicable to the third party is resolved by considering the presence or absence of immovable property. If such a property exists, the third party benefits from the application of the law of the state in which the property is located, with the consequent application of the *lex registri*. If, on the contrary, there is no immovable property, the applicable law is the one that applies to the transaction between a spouse or a partner and the third party.

Article 28 of the Twin Regulations is a peculiarity that deserves to be analysed. A discrepancy exists between what is established with regard to legal knowledge and what is established in the matter of the law applicable to the third party in the case where the *lex causae* cannot be applied. In the first case, the legislator only mentions immovable property, and in the second, the legislator also refers to 'registered assets or rights'. The different drafting of the text can be overcome by systematic interpretation. It is clear that where the ownership of an asset or a right must be registered in order to be known and made invocable, the third party is given the possibility to gain knowledge of the existence of property rights on that particular asset or on the ownership of that particular right.

5. LAW APPLICABLE TO THE PROPERTY REGIME AND KNOWLEDGE HELD BY THIRD PARTIES

The Twin Regulations determine that the property regime of a cross-border couple is governed by a predictable law that governs all the assets, independent of their nature or different places in which they are located.⁴⁵ However, this also entails a continuous comparison between the different regulatory systems.⁴⁶ The main problems encountered by couples in the management of family property concern the identification of ownership of the assets, the legitimacy of one of the spouses to dispose of an asset belonging to the family, the methods of registration of the assets and the consequent invocability against third parties.

The property consequences deriving from the regime chosen by the spouses or partners reflect their rights and obligations within the family organisation. However, they are also relevant in regard to the disclosure required for the effects *erga omnes* of the ownership of the assets or of the rights derived from them.⁴⁷ Depending on whether the property regime is attributable to the joining or the separation of the assets, the condition of third parties who exercise rights against the couple or against only one of the partners on the basis of reliance on the apparent legal situation may also vary.

It must be taken into account that the applicable rules not only refer to the administration of the property regime, but also affect the credit or debt situations of each spouse or partner.⁴⁸ Therefore, particular importance is attached to the correct identification of the ownership of assets acquired by the couple and of their property regime.

In some, mainly common law systems, the spouses' assets generally tend to remain separate, without prejudice to any different judicial decision.⁴⁹

---

[45] Council Regulation (EU) 2016/1103 [2016] OJ L183/1; Council Regulation (EU) 2016/1104 [2016] OJ L183/30; L. Ruggeri, 'I Regolamenti europei sui regimi patrimoniali e il loro impatto sui profili personali e patrimoniali delle coppie *cross-border*' in S. Landini (eds.), *EU Regulations 650/2012, 1103 and 1104/2016: Cross-border Families, International Successions, Mediation Issues and New Financial Assets*, ESI, Napoli 2020, pp. 118–130.

[46] P. Bruno, 'I regolamenti UE n. 1103/16 e 1104/16 sui regimi patrimoniali della famiglia: struttura, àmbito di applicazione, competenza giurisdizionale, riconoscimento ed esecuzione delle decisioni' in <www.distretto.torino.giustizia.it>.

[47] P. Bruno, *I regolamenti europei sui regimi patrimoniali dei coniugi e delle unioni registrate*, Giuffrè, Milano 2019, p. 185.

[48] N. Cipriani, 'Rapporti patrimoniali tra coniugi, norme di conflitto e variabilità della legge applicabile' (2019) 1 *Rassegna di diritto civile*, 27, 29; M.J. Cazorla González, 'Matrimonial Property Regimes after the Dissolution by Divorce: Connections and Variables that Determine the Applicable Law' in J. Kramberger Škerl, L. Ruggeri, F.G. Viterbo (eds.), *Case Studies and Best Practices Analysis to Enhance EU Family and Succession Law. Working Paper*, in *Quaderni degli Annali della facoltà giuridica dell'Università di Camerino* 3, Università di Camerino, Camerino 2019, pp. 40–48, available at <https://afg.unicam.it/node/111> and also at <https://www.euro-family.eu/news-126-case_studies_and_best_practices_analysis_to_enhance_eu_family_and_succession_law_working_paper>; L. Ruggeri, 'Property and cross-border couples from the perspective of European regulation' (2021) *Actualidad Jurídica Iberoamericana*, 15, pp. 252–274.

[49] G. Oberto, 'La comunione coniugale nei suoi profili di diritto comparato, internazionale ed europeo' (2008) *Il diritto di famiglia e delle persone* 369. See also K. Boele-Woelki, F. Ferrand, C. Gonzales Beilfuss, M. Jänterä-Jareborg, N. Lowe, D. Martiny and W. Pintens, *Principles of European Family Law Regarding Property Relations Between Spouses*, Cambridge 2013, p. 11; G. Oberto, 'Il divorzio in Europa' (2021) 1 *Famiglia e diritto* 112.

These common law systems do not include the concept of matrimonial property regime. As a consequence, these (common law) systems do not by themselves include the concept of a matrimonial regime, so that the decision on the allocation of the assets or part of the ownership shares is delegated to the judge, even regardless of the formal ownership. The judge bases the judgment on the criteria of reasonableness and fairness,[50] but also through an assessment of the economic and personal contribution that each spouse has made to the family organisation. Civil law systems mostly provide the communion of the assets purchased by the couple after the marriage.[51] Thus, in the event that a couple identifies the Italian law as the law applicable to their property regime, the assets purchased individually by the partners will constitute common assets if the separation of the property regime has not been chosen. This is different in the other Member States. In Austria, for example, it is generally expected that the purchase of assets by one of the spouses remains his or her exclusive property, or, alternatively, if purchased jointly, the assets enter into ordinary co-ownership. Therefore, depending on the applicable law, an agreement signed by one or both of the spouses or partners with a third party determines different effects.

As indicated by Recital 52 of the Matrimonial Property, and Recital 51 of the Regulation on Property Consequences of a Registered Partnership, the law determined as the law applicable by the couple should include the effects of the property regime of the spouses or partners on a legal relationship between a spouse and third parties. However, the effects of the law chosen by the partners or spouses can be invoked against a third party only if the latter has knowledge pursuant to Article 27, point *f* of the Twin Regulations. Therefore, it is necessary to assess whether third parties have the actual possibility or know with certainty the effects or legal consequences that the applicable law asserts on the couple's property regime and thus rely on this.

If the choice of law of spouses or registered partners can be changed at any time, the position of the third party must also be taken into account. It is necessary that the change of the chosen law can be invoked against third parties only where the formalities required for the recording in the appropriate registers have been correctly respected.

In this regard, notwithstanding Article 27, point *f* of the Twin Regulations, their Article 28(1) provides for uninvocability against third parties, in the event of a dispute, of the law applicable to the property regime of the spouses or partners, unless the third party knew or, in the exercise of due diligence, should

---

[50] G. PERLINGIERI, 'Sul criterio di ragionevolezza' in C. PERLINGIERI and L. RUGGERI (eds.), *L'incidenza della dottrina sulla giurisprudenza nel diritto dei contratti*, ESI, Napoli 2016, pp. 29–71.

[51] The following states can be included among those that provide for the communion of assets: Belgium, France, Italy, Luxembourg, Portugal, Spain, Poland, the Slovak Republic, the Czech Republic, Hungary, Romania and Bulgaria.

have known of that law.[52] In such a case, as determined in Article 28(3), where the applicable law cannot be invoked by a spouse against a third party by virtue of Article 28(1), the effects of the matrimonial property regime with respect to the third party are governed by the law of the state applicable to the transaction and, in the cases relating to immovable property, by the law of the place where it is located or where the assets or rights are registered.

Therefore, it seems that it is necessary to adopt harmonised rules that can clarify the modalities in which any third party can have knowledge of the law chosen by the couple to regulate the property regime and thus be aware of the legal relationships that he or she intends to put in place.

With regard to the legal relationship, due diligence is presumed for the parties, which consists of the burden of fulfilling the disclosure provided for by the applicable law for the purpose of making it known to third parties, so as to avoid them inadvertently being subjected to rules other than those relied on.

6. RECORDING OF RIGHTS *IN REM* AND THE SCOPE OF THE TWIN REGULATIONS

According to what is indicated in Recital 27 of the Twin Regulations, the requirements relating to the recording in a register of a right on movable or immovable property are excluded from the scope of application of the Twin Regulations. Therefore, each Member State is required to determine the legal conditions and procedures for registration in its own land registers, as well as to indicate the authorities responsible for verifying the requirements and the necessary documentation.

Recital 28 of the Twin Regulations furthermore specifies that the effects of the recording of a right in a register are excluded from the rules of the Twin Regulations. They mandate the law of the Member State in which the register is kept to establish whether the recording is declaratory or constitutive in effect. Furthermore, Article 1(2) of the Twin Regulations expressly exclude from their scope of application the 'nature of rights in rem' point *g* and 'any recording in a register of rights in the immovable or moveable property, including the legal requirements for such recording, and the effects of recording or failing to record such rights in a register' (point *h*).

It is the task of the interpreter to identify the specific register to which the Twin Regulations are referred. This activity must be conducted by analysing

---

[52] On this issue, see A. ZANOBETTI, 'Il regime patrimoniale della famiglia nel diritto internazionale privato' in F. ANELLI and M. SESTA (eds.), *Regime patrimoniale della famiglia*, in *Trattato di diritto di famiglia* diretto da P. ZATTI, vol. III, 2nd ed., Milano 2011, p. 43; A. CLERICI, 'Art. 30', in F. POCAR (eds.) *Commentario del nuovo diritto internazionale privato*, Cedam, Padova 1996, p. 142.

domestic regulation because there is no specific definition of 'register' at the EU regulation level. On the base of the *lex registri* it will be possible to understand which type of 'register' can carry out the disclosure function for the property regime of the spouses or partners. For example, if the *lex registri* is the Italian law,[53] the disclosure is carried out by two different registers with different functions and effects: the land register and the civil registry. Immovable property must be registered in the land register.[54] In the civil registry the marriage or registered partnership and the property regime chosen by the spouses or partners must be recorded.[55] Consequently, it is always necessary to consult the land register to know the ownership of real estate property and the civil registry to know which property regime has been chosen by the spouses or partners. The complex Italian disclosure system is not present in other European countries which, for example, do not include a specific recording for the family property regime and which provide different systems of real estate disclosure.[56]

In order to ensure the certainty of legal transactions and the *erga omnes* effect of the acquisition of a right on movable or immovable property, reference must, therefore, be made to the registration provided for in the law of the relevant Member State. At the same time, the property regime chosen by the couple, or the property effects in registered partnerships must be taken into account. Thus, in the event where a transaction has been carried out according to Italian law, or the property is located in Italy, or one of the parties has Italian residence, the recording of the property regime resulting from the formalities carried out on the basis of Italian law can be invoked against any third party, even if the law chosen by the couple is that of a different Member State or that of a third state. In this regard, points *a* and *b* of Article 28(2) of the Twin Regulations establish a presumption of knowledge by the third party,[57] where the parties have fulfilled their recording and disclosure obligations.

As noted before, in Italian law the civil registry gives disclosure to the property regime chosen by spouses or partners, while the land register gives disclosure to the recording of immovable property. The Italian law regulates real

---

[53] On the Italian law, the property recording system or to the recording property regime of the spouses or partners, it is necessary to take account of the plurality of the registers.

[54] In Italy, the complex system of real estate disclosure is achieved by recording real estate property in the land register held by the 'Agenzia delle Entrate'. The register is public and may be consulted by any person who so requests. On this issue, see P. PERLINGIERI, *Manuale di diritto civile*, ESI, Napoli, 2021, pp. 843–854.

[55] Marriages, registered partnerships and the property regime chosen by spouses or partners shall be recorded in the civil registry. The recording is mandatory. The register is present in every Italian municipality.

[56] On this point, see above Section 3.

[57] E. CALÒ, 'Variazioni sulla *professio iuris* nei regimi patrimoniali delle famiglie' (2017) 6 *Rivista del Notariato* 1093, 1097. On this issue see A. BONOMI and P. WANTELET, *Le droit européen des relations patrimoniales de couple. Commentaire des Réglements (UE) 2016/1103 et 2016/1044*, Bruylant, 2021, pp. 843–883.

estate disclosure through two different systems.[58] The deed system is in force on nearly the entire Italian territory, while the title system is still currently operating in Friuli Venezia Giulia and in a few other northern provinces, including Trento and Bolzano.[59] A consequence of land registers is a disclosure of constitutive, translational and extinguishing contracts of ownership and other rights *in rem* over immovable property. Declarative disclosure is, therefore, in the function of attributing legal knowledge to a fact of which, as a consequence, no one can plead ignorance.

Invocablity against third parties and anyone who claims title to the property is limited to cases in which the formalities required for disclosure in those registers have been properly carried out. For example, the establishment of the property fund, if it relates to real estate, also needs to be transcribed (Article 2647 Civil Code), despite the fact that an apostille on the marriage deed is required for it to be invocable against third-party creditors. More generally, the land register constitutes a system aimed at making a specific case known and invocable against anyone and, consequently, also at addressing the needs of protecting third parties.

As far as the Italian legal system is concerned, the rules provided for marriage are applicable to registered partnerships introduced by law no. 76/2016, the so-called Cirinnà law, which provides for a general extension of the legislative provisions in family matters.[60]

7. DISCLOSURE OF ASSETS AND EFFECTS IN RESPECT OF THIRD PARTIES

In order to provide information as complete as possible, the family property regime is mentioned in the system of recording the property in the 'transcription note',[61] but without this being able to constitute a means of integrating the apostille on the marriage certificate, but only a declarative disclosure provided for in Article 162 of the Italian Civil Code. In this case, the disclosure of property regimes assumes the mere function of information disclosure. This type of disclosure has been the object of examination by the most recent jurisprudence.

---

[58] The recording in the Italian land register is further distinct in deed system and title system.
[59] The deed system so-called 'trascrizione' has declarative effect. Other system so-called 'intavolazione' has constitutive effects. The system of Real Estate Registers can be found at <https://e-justice.europa.eu/content_land_registers_in_member_states-109-it>.
[60] On civil partnerships, see G. PERLINGIERI, 'Interferenze tra unione civile e matrimonio. Pluralismo familiare e unitarietà dei valori normativi' (2018) 1 *Rassegna di diritto civile* 102.
[61] The 'transcription note' so-called 'nota di trascrizione' is a document describing the asset to be recorded. It is a document required for assisting recording.

In the case No. 376/2021,[62] R.C. requested from the bankruptcy authorities of her spouse, P.T., from whom she had legally separated, the exclusive ownership of a property purchased after the separation, but before the opening of the bankruptcy procedure. The failure to mention the change of the property regime following the separation in the transcription note had, in fact, prevented third parties from gaining knowledge of it. As ruled by the Supreme Court, the property purchased by one of the spouses after the legal separation does not constitute communal property. The event of the separation itself causes a dissolution of the legal community. For the purpose of the effects of the dissolution of the communion deriving from the separation of the spouses being invocable against third parties, the recording in the land registers must be considered necessary and sufficient. Such a recording must correspond to the change of the property separation regime, regardless of the apostille on the act of separation on the marriage certificate. This is necessary because the deed system of disclosure is more accessible for consultation, albeit burdensome, than that on the marriage certificate on the civil registry. Therefore, the court notes that despite the dissolution of the legal community between the spouses, this cannot be invoked against third parties of good faith who have relied on the results of consulting the land registers, which did not indicate the separation of the assets resulting from the personal separation. The personal purchase of the property could, for example, not be invoked against the third party.

In this way, the court protects the formal content visible to third parties through access to land registers rather than the actual content of the title of ownership, which has indeed been transcribed, but is difficult to consult.

It follows that, even though reference must be made to the disclosure provided for in the civil registry to produce *erga omnes* effects of property regimes, along with the recording deed system, it has increased the degree of reliability regarding third parties and the social function of property.[63]

Similarly, as with the registers for the recording of the property regime of spouses or the property effects of registered partnerships, the systems of transcription of real estate or the registration of mortgages are not regulated in the same way within each Member State. Each of them has a system of recording of immovable and movable property inspired by completely different logics and mechanisms.

Just as an example, according to the Portuguese legislation, the recording of immovable property regulated in the *Registo Predial* has a declaratory effect. It can be invoked against third parties if it has been executed. As a result, such a disclosure represents a burden for the buyer. Recording in the register leads to the presumption that the right belongs to the person indicated as the owner.

---

[62] Cass. civ., 13 January 2021, n. 376, in *DeJure*.
[63] G. PETRELLI, 'L'autenticità del titolo della trascrizione nell'evoluzione storica e nel diritto comparato' (2007) *Rivista di diritto civile* 609.

Another different system is the French one, where several registration offices for recording property exist, which do not have a coordinated data retrieval mechanism. Additionally, they are difficult to consult since third parties cannot access them freely.

The lack of homogeneity of property recording systems among the Member States seems to require greater uniformity of rules. The goal is for the disclosure system to effectively ensure the invocability of the property regime of cross-border couples and the related applicable law against third parties.

8. ADAPTABILITY OF RIGHTS *IN REM*

With regard to the system of disclosure of couple's property and property regimes, the rules introduced by the Twin Regulations do not appear to be fully adjusted to the composition of the different regulatory solutions in various Member States. A harmonised disclosure mechanism could facilitate the acquisition of legal knowledge about the ownership of property purchased by the couple and the consequent effects with regard to third parties. The law chosen to govern the property regime also influences the debt liabilities of spouses and partners, and consequently, it will also affect relationships with possible third-party creditors. In fact, the Twin Regulations determine in their Article 27, point *c*, that they govern also the responsibility of one spouse or partner for liabilities and debts of the other spouse or partner.

The change in the law applicable to the property regime and property consequences of a marriage or registered partnership can, however, result in the transfer of the property from one category to another. If this extends or limits the rights of one or both spouses or partners to dispose of the property, important adverse effects can impact third parties who had relied on such a regime[64] if an adequate degree of knowledge of the change made has not been ensured.

If a conflict arises between the law applicable to the property regime by the partners or spouses and that of the state in which a right of a third party may be invoked, Article 29 of the Twin Regulations allows for the 'adaptation of rights *in rem*'. Therefore, although rights *in rem* are not included in the scope of application of the Twin Regulations, their Recital 24 determines that the creation or a transfer of a right in immovable or movable property should be allowed, as provided for in the law applicable to the property consequences of

---

[64] See L. RADEMACHER, 'Changing the Past: Retroactive Choice of Law and the Protection of Third Parties in the European Regulations on Patrimonial Consequences of Marriages and Registered Partnerships' (2018) 10 *Cuadernos de Derecho Transnacional* 1, 7–18. More generally, see W. PINTENS, 'Matrimonial Property Law in Europe' in K. BOELE-WOELKI and J.M. SHERPE (eds.), *The Future of Family Property in Europe*, Intersentia, Antwerp 2011, pp. 19–46; D. MARTINY, 'European Family Law' in J. BASEDOW, K.J. HOPT and R. ZIMMERMANN (eds.), *The Max Planck Encyclopaedia of European Private Law I*, Oxford 2012, p. 595.

the spouses or the matrimonial property regime. Such a right, however, should not affect the limited number of rights *in rem* known in the national law of each Member State. Additionally, a Member State should not be required to recognise a right *in rem* relating to property located in that Member State if this right is not known in its legal system.

A recent decision rendered by the Court of Justice of the European Union (CJEU)[65] seems relevant in this regard. In the case *Kubicka* (C-218/16), a Polish citizen residing in Germany was denied by the German legal system a request for the recognition of the material effects of a legacy 'by vindication', which is allowed by Polish law for which the testator had opted in conformity with Article 22(1) of the Succession Regulation. The denial was based on the fact that the object of a legacy was a right *in rem* in an immovable property situated in Germany, which does not provide for the establishment of a legacy having a direct material effect.

The CJEU emphasised that for reasons of legal certainty, the chosen law should govern the succession as a whole, that is to say, all of the property forming part of the estate, irrespective of the nature of the assets and regardless of whether the assets are located in another Member State or in a third State. The CJEU also noted that the legacy 'by vindication' provided for by Polish law, and a legacy 'by damnation' provided for by German law, constitute methods of transfer of ownership of an asset, and as also highlighted by the Advocate General, a right *in rem* that is recognised in both of the legal systems concerned. The testator's will was essentially to transmit a right *in rem* on immovable property located in German territory by means of a legacy 'by vindication'. Therefore, the CJEU held that the case did not concern the method of the transfer of rights *in rem*, but only the content of rights *in rem*, and therefore the right had to be recognised.[66]

Article 29 of the Twin Regulations introduce the possibility of the adaptation of rights *in rem*. Specifically, if a person invokes a right *in rem* on the basis of the law applicable to the property regime, and the law of the Member State in which the right is invoked does not provide for the same right, it is possible to adapt it to the closest equivalent right under the law of that state. However, such adaptation must be made taking into account the aims and the interests pursued by the specific right and its effects.

Therefore, it seems that to perform a correct analysis of the law and to carry out the consequent adaptation, an investigation must be conducted not only in

---

[65] Case C-218/16 *Aleksandra Kubicka*, ECLI: EU:C:2017:387.
[66] See P. Bruno, *I regolamenti europei sui regimi patrimoniali dei coniugi e delle unioni registrate*, Giuffrè, Milano 2019, pp. 220–221; D. Damascelli, 'Applicable Law, Jurisdiction, and Recognition of Decision in Matters Relating to Property Regimes of Spouses and Partners in European and Italian Private International Law' (2019) 1 *Trusts & Trustee*, 6, 16; C. Consolo, 'Profili processuali del Reg. UE 650/2012 sulle successioni transnazionali: il coordinamento tra le giurisdizioni' (2018) 1 *Rivista di diritto civile* 18.

general terms. A specific case must be examined and an adequate protection of the interests underlying that particular process has to be pursued.[67] Such a process fits into the more general principle of serving in the best possible way the interests of the spouses or partners, as well as third parties. Such an examination is of a positive value if the exercise of the rights proves to be adequate for the realisation of the actual interests of the parties and for the compliance of the law with the applicable regulatory provisions.[68]

9. CONCLUDING REMARKS

Although the Twin Regulations have harmonised the rules governing the matrimonial property regime and the property consequences of registered partnerships, there are still many differences in the property recording system and disclosure of the assets in the Member States. Therefore, it would have been useful to provide for a simplification of legal terms in the Twin Regulations, and to implement a coordinated system that would have made it easier to access the different land registers in the Member States. This provision could certainly encourage third parties to become aware of the property regime chosen by the spouses or partners, and thus increase the level of protection of the interests of their spouses, partners and third parties. Thus, it seems necessary to harmonise the property recording system and disclosure of the assets, and these aspects should be the subject of further regulatory action by the European Union.

In conclusion, if the uniformity introduced by Article 21 of the Twin Regulations delineates predictable rules for the purposes of certainty, it should still favour the provision of uniform and functional models of disclosure for the correct identification of the adopted property models and of the consequent effects.

---

[67] On this point, cf. P. PERLINGIERI, 'Fonti e interpretazione', vol. II, *Il diritto civile nella legalità costituzionale secondo il sistema italo-europeo delle fonti*, 4th ed., ESI, Napoli 2020, p. 379.

[68] M. LIBERTINI, 'Le nuove declinazioni del principio di effettività' (2018) 4 *Europa e diritto privato*, 1071.

SUCCESSION REGULATION, MATRIMONIAL PROPERTY AGREEMENTS AND INCONSISTENCIES AMONG EUROPEAN PRIVATE INTERNATIONAL LAW RULES

Stefano DEPLANO*

1. Introduction 293
2. Understanding of 'Agreement as to Succession' and its Relation to National Instruments... 297
3. Problems Linked to Agreements on Succession of Several Persons 300
4. Limitations on Party Autonomy under Article 25 Succession Regulation 304
5. Challenges in Applying Succession Regulation and Twin Regulations in Parallel 307
6. Concluding Remarks 311

1. INTRODUCTION

Since the mid-19th century, legal scholars have suggested the introduction of uniform rules on conflict of laws in matters of succession.[1] Nonetheless, it took more than a century for legally binding provisions to finally come into force.

Since the Second World War, there has been a gradual convergence of private international law in areas where the segmentation of domestic rules was an obstacle to the integration.[2] Focusing on the law of succession, this process

---

*   Stefano Deplano, PhD, Associate Professor in civil law at University of Campania 'Luigi Vanvitelli' of Naples.
[1] V. SCIALOJA, 'Sistema del diritto romano attuale' in Federico Carlo di Savigny '*Traduzione dall'originale tedesco*', vol. 8, Unione Tipografico-Editrice, Turin 1898, pp. 115–129.
[2] J. BONELL, 'Comparazione giuridica e unificazione del diritto' in VV. AA. (eds.), *Diritto privato comparato. Istituti e problemi*, 4th ed., Laterza, Rome-Bari 2011, p. 3 et seq. also for further bibliographical references.

has spread across a number of initiatives such as the Hague Conference on Private International Law[3] and the research carried out by the *Institut de droit international*[4] and the *Groupe européen de droit international privé*.[5]

At the legislative level, a specific mention should be made of the Convention of 5 October 1961 on the Conflict of Laws Relating to the Form of Testamentary Dispositions,[6] and the Hague Convention of 1 August 1989 on the Law Applicable to Succession to the Estates of Deceased Persons.[7] Although the latter has never entered into force, it has been an important point of reference for a number of national legislators and, above all, in the drafting of the European conflict of law rules on succession,[8] i.e. the Succession Regulation (also known as the Brussels IV Regulation[9]).

The approval process for this piece of legislation was marked by considerable difficulties. These were primarily due to the different legal traditions of the Member States, particularly deep-rooted in the area of succession law.[10] It is therefore not surprising that the dialogue between theoretical and practical jurists engaged in this harmonisation exercise was especially difficult.[11]

---

[3] E. RABEL, 'The Conflict of Laws: A Comparative Study' [1958] *Michigan Legal Studies Series* 250 et seq. and H. LEWALD, 'Questions de droit international des successions. Recueil de recours' (1925) 9 The Hague 5.

[4] H. WEHBERG (ed.), *Résolutions de l'Institut de droit international (1873–1956)*, Basel 1957, p. 40.

[5] See 'The Proposal for a Convention concerning jurisdiction and the enforcement of judgments in family and succession matters of 1993': <www.gedip-egpil.eu/documents/gedip-documents-3pe.html>. See also E. JAYME, 'Entwurf eines EG- Familienund Erbrechtsübereinkommens' [1994] 14 *Praxis des Internationalen Privat-und Verfahrensrechts*, 67.

[6] F. MAJOROS, *Les conventions internationales en matière de droit privé. Abrégé théoretique et traité pratique*, vol. 2, Pedone, Paris 1976, p. 395.

[7] P. LAGARDE, 'La nouvelle convention de La Haye sur la loi applicable aux successions (1989)' 78 *Revue critique de droit international privé* 249; H. VAN LOON, 'The Hague Convention on the Law Applicable to Succession to the Estates of Deceased Persons' [1989] *Hague Yearbook of International Law* 48; A. BORRÁS, 'La convention de la Haye de 1989 sur la loi applicable aux successions à cause de mort et l'Espagne' in A. BORRÁS, A. BUCHER, T. STRUYCKEN, M. VERWILGHEN (eds.), *E Pluribus Unum. Liber Amicorum Georges A.L. Droz*, Martinus Nijhoff Publishers, The Hague-Boston-London 1996, p. 7. Analyses the reasons for Hague Convention's lack of success T. PERTOT, 'European Certificate of Succession' in M.J. CAZORLA GONZÁLEZ, M. GIOBBI, J. KRAMBERGER ŠKERL, L. RUGGERI and S. WINKLER (eds.), *Property relations of cross border couples in the European Union*, ESI, Naples, 2020, p. 124 et seq.

[8] On this point, see M. PAZDAN and M. ZACHARIASIEWICZ, 'Highlights and Pitfalls of the EU Succession Regulation' (2020) 26 Problemy Prawa Prywatnego Międzynarodowego 127.

[9] The Succession Regulation entered into force on 16.08.2012 and applies to successions opened on or after 17.08.2015.

[10] A. DAVÌ, 'Introduction' in A.L. CALVO CARAVACA, A. DAVÌ and H.P. MANSEL (eds.), *The EU Succession Regulation: A Commentary*, Cambridge University Press, Cambridge 2016, p. 1 et seq; M. PFEIFFER, 'Legal certainty and predictability in international succession law' (2016) 12 *Journal of Private International Law* 566–570.

[11] J. HARRIS, 'The proposed EU regulation on succession and wills: prospects and challenges' (2008) 22 *Trust Law International* 181; E. LEIN, 'A further step towards a European Code of Private International Law: The Commission proposal for a Regulation on succession' (2009)

Except for Denmark and Ireland,[12] the Succession Regulation applies in all EU countries. This Regulation is important for a number of reasons.

First, the Succession Regulation has brought about a 'revolution'[13] in the legal systems of several EU Member States. This is because the European regulation – thanks to a choice widely approved in legal scholarship[14] – has adopted the so-called monist system (already present in German and Austrian conflict of laws rules), aimed at applying a single conflict of laws rule to all of the assets making up an estate and thus achieving a unitary succession.[15] Secondly, Article 21 of the Succession Regulation has established 'habitual residence'[16] as a criterion for identifying both the applicable law and jurisdiction in matters of succession. Consequently, states that used the nationality of the deceased as

---

11 *Yearbook of Private International Law* 107; A. BONOMI and C. SCHMID (eds.), *Successions internationales. Réflexions autour du futur règlement européen et son impact pour la Suisse*, Genève, 2010; MAX PLANCK INSTITUTE, 'Comments on the European Commission's Proposal for a Regulation of the European Parliament and of the Council on jurisdiction, applicable law, recognition and enforcement of decisions and authentic instruments in matters of succession and the creation of a European Certificate of Succession' (2010) 74 *Rabels Zeitschrift für ausländisches und internationales Privatrecht* 522.

12 In accordance with Articles 1 and 2 of the Protocol No. 21 on the position of the United Kingdom concerning the area of freedom, security and justice, annexed to the Treaty on European Union and to the Treaty on the Functioning of the European Union, this former Member State decided not to take part in the adoption of the regulation and not to be subject to its application.

13 P. LAGARDE, 'Les principes de base du nouveau règlement européen sur les successions' (2012) 101 *Revue critique de droit international privé* 691: 'Ce règlement ... constitue pour le droit français actuel une veritable revolution'; C. KOHLER, L'autonomie de la volonté en droit international privé: un principe universel entre libéralisme et étatisme [2013] *Recueil des Cours* 359, 463: 'Il constitue un veritable tournant copernicien pour la matière'.

14 A. DUTTA, 'Succession and Wills in the Conflict of Laws on the Eve of Europeanisation' (2009) 73 *Rabels Zeitschrift für ausländisches und internationales Privatrecht* 555; A. BONOMI, 'Choice of-Law Aspects of the Future EC Regulation in Matters of Succession-A First Glance at the Commission's Proposal' in K. BOELE-WOELKI, T. EINHORN, D. GIRSBERGER and S. SYMONIDES (eds.), *Convergence and Divergence in Private International Law*, Liber Amicorum Kurt Siehr, Eleven International Publishing, The Hague-Zurich 2010, p. 162; M. ZAŁUCKI, 'Attempts to harmonize the inheritance law in Europe: past, present, and future' (2018) 103 *Iowa Law Review* 2330.

15 For a general perspective see A. DAVÌ, 'Introduction' in A.L. CALVO CARAVACA, A. DAVÌ and H.P. MANSEL (eds.), *The EU Succession Regulation: A Commentary*, Cambridge University Press, Cambridge 2016, p. 3 et seq.; A. BONOMI, 'Succession' in J. BASEDOW, G. RÜHL, F. FERRARI, P.A. DE MIGUEL ASENSIO (eds.), *Encyclopedia of private international law*, Edward Elgar, Cheltenham 2017, p. 1683 et seq.

16 On this point, see M. BOGDAN, 'The EC Treaty and the Use of Nationality and Habitual Residence as Connecting Factors in International Family Law' in M. PERTEGÁS, G. STRAETMANS and F. SWENNEN (eds.), *International Family Law for the European Union*, Intersentia, Antwerp 2007, pp. 314–316. See also J. PIRRUNG, 'Hague Conference on PIL' in J. BASEDOW, K.J. HOPT and R. ZIMMERMANN (eds.), *The Max Planck Encyclopedia of European Private Law*, vol. I, Oxford University Press, Oxford 2012, pp. 818–819; W. PINTENS, 'Public Policy in Succession Matters' in *Liber Amicorum Kohler*, Gieseking Verlag, Bielefeld 2018, p. 395.

the main connecting factor (for example Italy and Germany)[17] experience an important shift to a brand-new paradigm.[18] Thirdly, the number of preliminary rulings[19] and the Court of Justice of the European Union (CJEU) case law[20] concerning the Succession Regulation is constantly growing. Lastly, the Succession Regulation has led to significant developments within national legal systems.[21]

This chapter intends to focus on a problematic issue: the law applicable to agreements between cross-border spouses or registered partners relating to succession of the estate of a deceased spouse or registered partner. The analysis begins (Section 2) with an examination of the broad definition of 'agreement as to succession' set out in the Succession Regulation. Secondly, it focuses on some critical aspects of the Succession Regulation that seem likely to complicate the succession planning of cross-border couples. Although Recital 7 of the Succession Regulation establishes that one of the primary purposes of the regulation is that 'citizens must be able to organise their succession in advance', and its Recital 38 specifies that '[the Succession Regulation] should enable citizens to organise their succession in advance by choosing the law applicable to their succession', there are numerous rules that do not appear to be in line with this aim. These issues are highlighted in Sections 3 and 4. Particular attention is devoted (Section 5) to agreements between cross-border spouses or registered partners in order to plan their succession. Lastly (Section 6), some concluding remarks are offered on the process of European integration achieved through the private international law (PIL) and the role of the courts in a unitary and complex legal system.

---

[17] Italian PIL, for instance, used nationality as the main connecting factor (Article 46, Law no. 218 of 31 May 1995). The same happened under German PIL (Art. 25 I Einführungsgesetz BGB). See A. BONOMI, 'Testamentary Freedom or Forced Heirship? Balancing Party Autonomy and the protection of Family Members' in M. ANDERSON and E. ARROYO I AMAYUELAS (eds.), *The Law of Succession: Testamentary Freedom: European Perspectives*, Europa Law Publishing, Groningen/Amsterdam 2011, p. 30.

[18] M. PAZDAN and M. ZACHARIASIEWICZ, 'Highlights and Pitfalls of the EU Succession Regulation' (2020) 26 *Problemy Prawa Prywatnego Międzynarodowego* 127.

[19] Recent requests for preliminary questions include: C-277/20 (see, in detail, note 38 below); C-301/20 (validity and effectiveness of a certificate of succession); C-387/20 (whether the admissibility of a choice of law under the Regulation prevails over a bilateral agreement between a Member State and a non-member which does not envisage choice in succession matters).

[20] For example, C-218/16 Kubicka, ECLI:EU:C:2017:755; C-558/16 Mahnkopf, ECLI:EU:C:2018:138 (see below n. 83); C-20/17 Oberle, ECLI:EU:C:2018:485; C-658/17 WB, ECLI:EU:C:2019:444; C-102/18 Brisch, ECLI:EU:C:2019:34; C-80/19 E.E., ECLI:EU:C:2020:569.

[21] A. SANDERS, 'EU Formalities for Matrimonial Property Agreements and Their Effects on German Family Law' in J.M. SCHERPE and E. BARGELLI (eds.), *The Interaction between Family Law, Succession Law and Private International Law. Adapting to change*, Intersentia, Cambridge 2021, p. 79 et seq.; E. GOOSENS, 'The Impact of the European Certificate of Succession on National Law. A Trojan Horse or Much Ado about Nothing' in J.M. SCHERPE and E. BARGELLI (eds.), ibid., p. 157 et seq.

2. UNDERSTANDING OF 'AGREEMENT AS TO SUCCESSION' AND ITS RELATION TO NATIONAL INSTRUMENTS

With the wording similar to that of Article 8 of the 1989 Hague Convention, Article 3(1)(b) of the Succession Regulation defines agreement as to succession as an 'agreement, including an agreement resulting from mutual wills, which, with or without consideration, creates, modifies or terminates rights to the future estate or estates of one or more persons party to the agreement'.[22] Agreements as to succession are usually contracts. The purpose of such a rule is, therefore, to exclude them from the application of the Rome I Regulation.[23] Secondly, the definition is completely independent of the corresponding definitions established in national laws,[24] tending to be much broader. This is a fundamental observation for the purposes of this chapter: the aforementioned Article can be applied to a large number of legal institutions, including those traditionally excluded from the area of succession law, such as trusts and, above all, agreements concerning matrimonial property relations.[25]

First of all, it is not clear whether the provisions of Chapter III of the Succession Regulation are applicable to both agreements whereby the testator arranges his or her own succession while still alive and testamentary succession agreements (whereby a person has inheritance rights arising from a succession that is not yet in probate) as well as succession rejection agreements[26] (negotiated between living persons, whereby an individual renounces the rights that will arise from a future estate).[27]

---

[22] M. WELLER, 'Article 1' in A.L. CALVO CARAVACO, A. DAVÌ and H.P. MANSEL (eds.), *The EU Succession Regulation: A Commentary*, Cambridge University Press, Cambridge 2016, pp. 76 et seq.

[23] This is noted by G. BIAGIONI, 'Article 1' in P. FRANZINA and F. SALERNO (eds.), *Commentario al Regolamento n. 593/2008 del Parlamento europeo e del Consiglio del 17 giugno 2008 sulla legge applicabile alle obbligazioni contrattuali ('Roma I')*, Nuove leggi civili commentate, Padua 2009, p. 568, arguing that succession agreements are governed by the lex successionis.

[24] A. KÖHLER, 'Agreements as to Succession Under the New European Private International Law' [2005] *Revija za evropsko parvo* 25–30; L.E. PERRIELLO, 'Succession agreements and public policy within EU Regulation 650/2012' in S. LANDINI (ed.), *Insights and proposals related to the application of the European Succession Regulation 650/2012*, ESI, Naples 2019, p. 375; A. DUTTA, 'Article 3' in *Münchener Kommentar zum Bürgerlichen Gesetzbuch*, vol. 12, 8th ed., Beck, Munich 2020, no. 9 et seq.

[25] See below, Section 5 of this chapter.

[26] For the Italian legal system see C. GANGI, *La successione testamentaria nel vigente diritto italiano*, Giuffré, Milan 1964, p. 40 et seq.; M.V. DE GIORGI, *I patti sulle successioni future*, Jovene, Naples 1976, p. 60 et seq.; G. GROSSO and A. BURDESE, 'Le successioni. Parte generale' in G. VASSALLI (ed.) *Trattato di diritto civile*, vol. XII, UTET, Turin 1977, p. 92 et seq.; L. FERRI, 'Successioni in generale – Artt. 456–511' in A. SCIALOJA and G. BRANCA (eds.), *Commentario al codice civile*, Zanichelli, Bologna-Rome, 1980, p. 95 et seq.; M.V. DE GIORGI, *Patto successorio*, in Enc. dir., XXXII, Giuffré, Milan 1982, p. 533 et seq.

[27] For Belgium see B. DELAHAYE and F. TAINMONT, *Le rapport des donations à la lumière de la réforme du droit successoral. L'option, la condition, le terme et la substitution: effets civils et*

A literal interpretation of Article 3(1)(b) of the Succession Regulation certainly makes the regulation applicable to agreements whereby the testator arranges his or her own succession while still alive. On the other hand, several authors assume that the aforementioned Article does not necessarily apply to testamentary succession agreements and succession rejection agreements[28] because in these cases the person whose succession is problematic is not a party to the contract. Consequently, there is a widespread view that testamentary succession agreements and succession rejection agreements, if concluded in the presence of a foreign element, should be governed by the *lex contractus* (and not by the *lex successionis*).[29] This argument is worthy of acceptance but with one clarification:[30] if, in the specific case, the person whose estate is at issue is a party to the agreement as to succession, the Succession Regulation must apply. This is because the (testamentary succession or the succession rejection) agreement is, in concrete, part of the estate planning of the deceased.

Italian legal scholarship has also recently pointed out that the rules applicable to an agreement as to succession cannot disregard the concrete purpose that the agreement actually serves:[31] it is always necessary to ascertain whether the agreement concerning an estate has the effect of creating, modifying or extinguishing rights to a future estate of a person who is 'party to the contract' as stated by Article 3(1) Succession Regulation. This is not the case, for instance, in a bilateral succession rejection agreement where, for example, one brother promises the other brother to renounce his father's future inheritance. Consequently, in addition to the wording of the Succession Regulation, courts

---

fiscaux sur l'organisation et la transmission d'un patrimoine, Limal, Anthemis 2017, p. 367. For France see below Sections 3 and 4 of this chapter, and G. Raoul-Cormeil, 'La persistence de la prohibition des pactes successoraux' [2012] *Les Petites Affiches* 25 et seq.

[28] With reference to the German legal system A. Dutta, 'Article 3' in *Münchener Kommentar zum Bürgerlichen Gesetzbuch*, vol. 12, 8th ed., Beck, Munich 2020, no. 9 et seq.

[29] J. Rodriguez Rodrigo, 'Article 25' in A.L. Calvo Caravaco, A. Davì and H.P. Mansel (eds.), *The EU Succession Regulation: A Commentary*, Cambridge University Press, Cambridge 2016, p. 382 et seq. advocating for the application of the lex contractus; A. Fusaro, 'Linee evolutive del diritto successorio europeo' [2014] *Giustizia civile* 510–538. In the opposite direction P. Kindler, 'La legge applicabile ai patti successori nel Regolamento UE 650/2012' [2017] *Rivista diritto internazionale privato e processuale* 17 considers that the broad wording of Art. 3(1)(b) implies that it also applies to succession rejection agreements.

[30] As highlighted, among others, by L. Perriello, 'Succession agreements and public policy within EU Regulation 650/2012' in S. Landini (ed.), *Insights and proposals related to the application of the European Succession Regulation 650/2012*, ESI, Naples 2019, p. 377.

[31] V. Barba, *I patti successori e il divieto di disposizione della delazione*, ESI, Naples, 2015, p. 32 et seq. is critical of the legal scholarship that tends to standardise the scope of agreements as to succession. See also F. Magliulo, 'Il divieto del patto successorio istitutivo nella pratica negoziale' [1992] *Rivista del notariato* 1418 et seq.; C. Caccavale, 'Il divieto dei patti successori' in P. Rescigno (ed.), *Successioni e donazioni*, vol. 1, CEDAM, Padua 1994, p. 25 et seq.; C. Caccavale, 'Patti successori: il sottile confine tra nullità e validità negoziale' [1995] *Notariato* 552 et seq.

must always refer to the concrete purpose a specific agreement is intended to achieve (so-called functionally oriented interpretation).[32]

Following this perspective, the opinion considering that contracts to make (or not to make) a will are also subject to Article 3(1)(b) of the Succession Regulation may be considered worthy of support.[33] These contracts are widespread in common law systems.[34] They do not confer direct succession rights but require the party whose estate is involved (not) to make one or more dispositions relating to their property after death. Although they are not covered by the literal provision of Article 3(1)(b) of the Succession Regulation, a functionally oriented interpretation leads to the last-mentioned rule being applied to this proposition as well.[35]

A further problem relates to the hermeneutical relationship between Articles 3(1)(b) and 1(2)(g) of the Succession Regulation. The latter provision excludes 'property rights, interests and assets created or transferred otherwise than by succession, for instance by way of gifts ...' from the scope of the regulation. Some specific questions arise in the case of *mortis causa* gifts:[36] scholars have emphasised that this category of acts deserves to be equated to agreements as to succession.[37] This is an argument that deserves to be endorsed

---

[32] Emphasising functions rather than structures in succession law is the idea of P. PERLINGIERI, 'La funzione sociale del diritto successorio' [2009] *Rassegna di diritto civile* 121–131, pointing out that structure is not an a priori, but a post with regard to the effects of the act; accordingly, it cannot be determined in advance, but only by taking into account the interests pursued by party autonomy.

[33] A. DAVÌ and A. ZANOBETTI, *Il nuovo diritto internazionale privato europeo delle successioni*, Giappichelli, Turin 2014, p. 68.

[34] See R. KERRIDGE, *Parry and Kerridge: The Law of Succession*, 13th ed, Sweet & Maxwell, London 2016, pp. 110 et seq.

[35] In favour of including such instruments within the scope of Article 25 of the Succession Regulation: C. DÖBREINER, *Das internationale Erbrecht nach der EU-Erbrechtsverordnung (Teil II), Mitteilungen des Bayerischen Notarvereins 2013*, Munich 2014, p. 439; A. DAVÌ and A. ZANOBETTI, *Il nuovo diritto internazionale privato europeo delle successioni*, Giappichelli, Turin 2014, p. 106; A. BONOMI in A. BONOMI and P. WAUTELET, *Le droit européen des successions*, 2nd ed, Bruylant, Brussels 2016, pp. 157 et seq. For the opposite point of view: C.F. NORDMEIER, 'Erbverträge und nachlassbezogene Rechtsgeschäfte in der EuErb-VO-eine Begriffsklärung' [2013] *Zeitschrift für Erbrecht und Vermögensnachfolge* 123.

[36] For Italian case law see, Cass., 29 luglio 1971, n. 2404, in Giustizia civile, 1971, I, p. 1536; Cass., 16 febbraio 1995, n. 1683, ibid., 1995, I, p. 1501; Cass., 9 maggio 2000, n. 5870, in Rivista del notariato, 2001, p. 227; Cass., 19 novembre 2009, n. 24450, in Nuova giurisprudenza civile commentata, 2010, 5, I, p. 560 et seq.

[37] H. DÖRNER, 'EuErbVO: Die Verordnung zum Internationalen Erb- und Erbverfahrensrecht ist in Kraft!' [2012] *Zeitschrift für Erbrecht und Vermögensnachfolge* 508; A. DUTTA, 'Das neue internationale Erbrecht der Europäischen Union – Eine erste Lektüre der Erbrechtsverordnung' [2013] *Zeitschrift für das gesamte Familienrecht* 5–10; P. LAGARDE, 'Les principes de base du nouveau règlement européen sur les successions' (2012) 101 *Revue critique de droit international privé* 691, 717.

since these categories of acts – again, on the functional level – pursue the same objective as agreements as to succession: estate planning.[38]

A functionally oriented interpretation also leads to the view that the *donation-partage* or *partage d'ascendant, l'institution contractuelle, la donation de biens à venir,* and the so-called *patto di famiglia* (the former typical of the French legal system, the latter Italian[39]) despite having the typical features of an agreement without consideration should be governed by the Succession Regulation if, without any doubt, they serve to implement estate planning.[40]

3. PROBLEMS LINKED TO AGREEMENTS ON SUCCESSION OF SEVERAL PERSONS

As shown in the previous section, the above-mentioned definition of a succession agreement cuts across several areas within national legal systems. In addition to the problem of definitions, it is also necessary to analyse in detail the rules applicable to agreements containing international elements. These rules are laid down in Article 25 of the Succession Regulation, which makes a distinction on the basis of whether the agreement is meant to regulate the succession of one or more persons.

This chapter focuses on the agreements on succession of several persons in order to highlight how certain choices adopted by the Succession Regulation may hinder the succession planning of those habitually resident in the EU Member States.[41]

---

[38] The matter was referred for a preliminary ruling by the Oberster Gerichtshof (Austria) on 24 June 2020 – Case C-277/20. The Austrian Court requested a decision as to whether donation mortis causa constitutes an agreement as to succession and whether Regulation applies to choices of applicable law made before 17.08.2015.

[39] P. Kindler, 'La legge applicabile ai patti successori nel regolamento UE nr 650/2012' [2017] *Rivista diritto internazionale privato e processuale* 17–18; F. Vismara, 'Patti successori nel regolamento (UE) n. 650/2012 e patti di famiglia: un'interferenza possibile?' [2014] *Rivista di diritto internazionale privato e processuale* 813. For the opposite point of view, D. Damascelli, 'Le pacte de famille' in A. Bonomi and M. Steiner (eds.) *Les pactes successoraux en droit comparé et en droit international privé,* Libraire Droz, Genève 2008, p. 626.

[40] P. Lagarde, 'Les principes de base du nouveau règlement européen sur les successions' in U. Bergquist, D. Damascelli, R. Frimston, P. Lagarde, F. Odersky and B. Reinhartz (eds.), *EU Regulation on succession and wills. Commentary,* Ottoschmidt, Köln 2015, p. 148; C.F. Nordmeier, 'Die französische institution contractuelle im Internationalen Erbrecht: International-privatrechtliche und sachrechtliche Fragen aus deutscher und europäischer Perspektive' (2014) 34 *Praxis des Internationalen Privat- und Verfahrensrechts* 424–425; S. Frank, D. Bureau and H.M. Watt, *Droit international privé,* vol. 2, Presses Universitaires de France Paris 2017, p. 316; M. Revillard, *Droit international privé et européen: pratique notariale,* Defrenois, Paris 2018, p. 661.

[41] See, on this point, Recital 38 of the Succession Regulation Analyses the relationship between the Succession Regulation and third country legal systems J. Basedow, '"Member States"

As set out in Article 25(2) of the Succession Regulation, an agreement as to succession regarding the inheritance of several persons is admissible only if all of the laws which, under this regulation, would have governed the succession of all those involved if they had died on the day the agreement was concluded. As regards its substantive validity and binding effects between the parties, the agreement as to succession will be governed by the law with which it has the closest connection. The law that will govern the succession will therefore regulate aspects such as:[42] the capacity to make or receive dispositions of property upon death; the admissibility of representation; the interpretation of the disposition; and questions relating to the consent or intention of the person making the disposition.[43]

This is a significant problem in practical terms because the rules relating to limitations to the power of disposal arising from compliance with mandatory national rules may not be fully known at the time when the agreement as to succession is concluded. The greater the distance between the date on which the agreement was concluded and the date on which the succession was opened, the graver the problem becomes. This aspect represents a first and incisive problem with regard to certainty in inheritance planning. As already stated, when entering into their agreement, the parties can have no definite certainty as to the existence of any limitations: these depend on a future law that cannot be determined at the time and is susceptible to unpredictable changes.[44] This uncertainty about which law to apply is totally unsatisfactory, especially in the light of the aim of 'mak[ing] it easier for succession rights acquired as a result of an agreement as to succession to be accepted' as stated in Recital 49 of the Succession Regulation.

One element that increases uncertainty in estate planning are the rules on the so-called '*hereditary reserve*'. Several Member States' legal systems (such as Italy's and France's) limit the autonomy of the deceased by reserving a portion of the estate to certain categories of heirs, called 'mandatory heirs' (*eredi necessari* in Italy, *héritiers réservataires* in France). In presence of these heirs, the succession is divided in two parts: the 'available portion' can freely be given to anyone, the 'reserved portion', on the other hand, belongs to 'mandatory heirs'. It is clear that the rules adopted by the European legislator are not intended to conflict with

---

and "Third States" in the Succession Regulation' (2020) 26 *Problemy Prawa Prywatnego Międzynarodowego* 15 et seq.

[42] D. DAMASCELLI, *Diritto internazionale privato delle successioni a causa di morte*, Giuffré, Milan 2013, p. 96.

[43] In relation to the application of an interpretative rule belonging to the law of the state of Illinois v. Amtsgericht Hamburg-Wandsbeck, 17.05.2018 [2018] *Zeitschrift für Das Gesamte Familienrecht* 1274 et seq. with a critical comment by Ludwig.

[44] A. DAVÌ and A. ZANOBETTI, *Il nuovo diritto internazionale privato europeo delle successioni*, Giappichelli, Turin 2014, p. 68.

national rules protecting the hereditary reserve.[45] This is not a revolutionary position: the Succession Regulation does not deviate from either the 1989 Hague Convention or national conflict laws,[46] which, in any event, respect the rights of that particular category of heirs.[47]

This approach appears to be reflected from a further perspective: the Commission's original proposal – Article 18(4), corresponding to Article 25 of the Succession Regulation – excluded the party involved in the agreement as to succession from the protection conferred on them by the *lex successionis* at the time.[48] The purpose of the rule was to prevent the law applicable to the succession from limiting the validity of the agreement as to succession. This provision, however, was deleted from the final text of the regulation. As confirmed by Recital 50 of the Succession Regulation, a party to an agreement of succession may therefore claim – even at the cost of breaking the general rule *nemo potest venire contra factum proprium*[49] – that 'the binding effects of … an agreement as between the parties, should be without prejudice to the rights of any person who, under the law applicable to the succession, has a right to a reserved share or another right of which he cannot be deprived by the person whose estate is involved'.

It would appear that policy option adopted by Succession Regulation seeks to ensure 'overprotection' of the 'mandatory heirs', in line with the legal traditions of some Member States.[50] This appears questionable because it is likely to constitute a further obstacle to effective succession planning. It should also be

---

[45] For French legal system see Rapport sur la réserve héréditaire published in December 2019 and available at <http://www.presse.justice.gouv.fr/art_pix/2019.12.20%20Rapport%20reserve%20hereditaire.pdf>. For Italian legal system, see M.C. Tatarano, 'La successione necessaria', G. Perlingieri and R. Calvo (eds.), *Diritto delle successioni e delle donazioni*, ESI, Napoli 2015, p. 485 et seq.

[46] On this specific point see A. Davì, 'Rifessioni sul futuro diritto internazionale privato europeo delle successioni' [2005] *Rivista di diritto internazionale* 324 et seq.

[47] A. Bucher, 'Successions' in A. Bucher (ed.), *Commentaire romand. Loi sur le droit international privé. Convention de Lugano*, Helbing Lichtenhahn, Bâle 2011, p. 816. On the contrary H. Kuhn, *Der Renvoi im internationalen Erbrecht der Schweiz*, Schulthess Polygraphischer, Zürich 1998, p. 58 et seq.; A. Heini, 'Art. 90' in M. Müller-Chen and C. Widmer-Lüchirger (eds.), *Zürcher Kommentar zum IPRG*, 2nd ed., Schultess, Zürich-Basel-Genf 2004, p. 1067.

[48] A. Bonomi, 'Successions internationales: conflits de lois et de juridictions' [2010] *Recueil des cours* 350, p. 253.

[49] See L. Isola, *Venire contra factum proprium. Herkun und Grundlagen eines sprichwörtlichen Rechtsprinzips*, Peter Lang Publishing, Frankfurt am Main 2017, p. 10 et seq.

[50] During the discussions concerning the preparatory work on the Succession Regulation, the French Senate adopted a resolution. It considered the principle of the réserve héréditaire as 'a legal translation of a true moral duty' and 'an essential rule of French law', L. Rass-Masson, 'The impact of European Private International Law and the Réserve héréditaire in France' in J.M. Scherpe and E. Bargelli (eds.), *The Interaction between Family Law, Succession Law and Private International Law. Adapting to change*, Intersentia, Cambridge 2021, p. 201.

noted that the courts of those countries that guarantee a reserved portion of the estate have also reconsidered their traditional positions.[51]

This is, for example, the case of the French Supreme Court. Even before the Succession Regulation came into force, there had already been two similar cases:[52] two French citizens who had been living in California for many years had bequeathed all their estate to their spouses. They had intentionally left no part of their estate to their sons, as permitted under the law of California, which does not recognise the hereditary reserve.

The sons of the deceased initiated proceedings to obtain their share of the forced heirship portion. In the end, they appealed to the French *Cour de Cassation*. To support their claim, they relied on the so-called 'right to collect' (*droit de prélèvement*),[53] whereby French heirs who have been deprived of their share in the deceased person's assets located abroad, have the right to collect an amount equal to any share of the deceased person's assets located in France.

The French Supreme Court dismissed this argument. In particular, it affirmed that the law of California (the last place of residence of the deceased) was applicable to the succession of the estate and further specified that, pursuant to the foreign law designated by the conflict of law rule, the exclusion of the forced heirship portion was not, in itself, contrary to French international public order policy.[54]

In a subsequent decision, the same court also reiterated that the legal basis of the 'hereditary reserve' cannot be found in French international public policy.[55]

Overcoming a long tradition to the contrary,[56] Italian legal scholarship and case law have come to similar conclusions.

---

[51] A. BONOMI, 'Quelle protection pour les héritiers réservataires sous l'empire du futur réglement européen' in *Droit international privé. Travaux du Comité français de droit international privé 2008–2010*, Pedone, Paris 2011, p. 272.

[52] Cass., 27 Septembre 2017, nos. 16-13.151 and 16-17.198, Dalloz 2017, p. 2185. See A. BOICHÉ, 'La réserve héréditaire n'est pas d'ordre public international' [2017] *L'Actualité juridique: Famille*, 595 et seq.; L. USUNIER, 'La reserve héréditaire n'est pas d'ordre public international' [2017] *Revue trimestrielle de droit commercial* 833 et seq.; H. FULCHIRON, 'Ordre public successoral et réserve héréditaire: réflexions sur les notions de précarité et de besoin' [2017] *Recueil Dalloz* 2310 et seq.

[53] The French Constitutional Council declared this law unconstitutional in 2011: Cons. const., 5 August 2011, No. 2011-159, see H. GAUDEMET-TALLON, 'Panorama de droit international privé' [2012] *Recueil Dalloz* 1228.

[54] See H. FULCHIRON, 'Ordre public successoral et réserve héréditaire: réflexions sur les notions de précarité et de besoin' [2017] *Recueil Dalloz* 2310 et seq. and A. BOICHÉ, 'Succession de Johnny Hallyday: le droit international privé saisi par l'actualité people' [2018] *L'Actualité juridique: Famille* 138.

[55] Cass. 4 July 2018, N° 17.16.-515 and 17-16.522 [2018] in *Juris-Classeur périodique*, édition notariale 2018, p. 1313, note E. Fongaro. See also L. RASS-MASSON, 'Cour de cassation: Ordre public und Pflichtteilsrecht in Frankreich' [2019] *Zeitschrift für Europäisches Privatrecht* 823.

[56] P. GALLO, 'Successioni in diritto comparato. Aggiornamento' in *Digesto disciplina privatistiche*, Sezione civile, Turin 2011, p. 851 et seq.

It has been authoritatively stated that the rules protecting *eredi necessari*, even if mandatory, do not implement inviolable human rights or other fundamental principles within the Italian legal system.[57] This is because the reserved portion is not, per se, functional to the protection of the human person (Article 2 of the Italian Constitution) but, on the contrary, it can even be harmful in relation to other principles whose protection is recognised and guaranteed by the Constitution (such as the protection of work, enterprise and savings, Articles 1, 4, 43, 47 of the Italian Constitution), as recognised by the Italian legislator with the introduction of the 'patto di famiglia' in 2006 (Articles 768 bis et seq. of the Italian Civil Code).[58] Consequently, at least with reference to the Italian legal system, it would appear correct to say that rules protecting hereditary reserve do not, in themselves, run contrary to international public policy[59] except for some circumstances in which the solidarity-based reasons behind hereditary reserve are impaired. A similar conclusion was also reached by the Spanish[60] and Italian[61] Supreme Courts.

4. LIMITATIONS ON PARTY AUTONOMY UNDER ARTICLE 25 SUCCESSION REGULATION

The European legislator's intention not to clash with national provisions protecting hereditary reserve is not the only limitation the Succession Regulation places on the effectiveness of contractual succession planning.

---

[57] G. PERLINGIERI and G. ZARRA, *Ordine pubblico interno e internazionale tra caso concreto e sistema ordinamentale*, ESI, Naples 2019, p. 183.

[58] G. PERLINGIERI and G. ZARRA, ibid., p. 184. The 2006 law introducing 'patto di famiglia' aims to protect enterprise (Article 43 Italian Constitution) and employees (Articles 1 and 4 Italian Constitution) during the generational changeover. The legislator intended to avoid the division of the enterprise between several *eredi necessari* at the time of his death. The 'patto di famiglia' is an agreement by which the deceased transfers, without consideration, the enterprise to a single erede necessario who undertakes to 'compensate' the other heirs by paying the value of their reserved portions. The reserved portion of the heirs who do not get the enterprise is therefore not paid by the deceased.

[59] A. DAVÍ and A. ZANOBETTI, *Il nuovo diritto internazionale privato europeo delle successioni*, Giappichelli, Turin 2014, p. 175. See also W. PINTENS, 'Public Policy in Succession Matters' in *Liber Amicorum Kohler*, Gieseking Verlag, Bielefeld 2018, p. 395 et seq.

[60] See Tribunal Supremo, 15 Noviembre 1996, Lowenthal, in Revista Española de Derecho Internacional, 1997, p. 264; Tribunal Supremo, 21 Mayo 1999, Denney, ibid., 1999, p. 756.

[61] See Cass., 24 Giugno 1996, n. 5832, in Giustizia civile, 1997, I, p. 1668 concerning the succession of an Italian citizen (naturalised Canadian) whose forced heirs were Italian citizens, and Cass., 30 Giugno 2014, n. 14811, with commentary by E. Calò, 'La vedova non è piú allegra: la mancanza di reciprocità con Cuba preclude lo status di legittimario' [2015] *Diritto successioni famiglia* 567 et seq., which held that forced heirship is not covered by the Constitution, and the legislator could well reform it, or even cancel it anytime. The case concerned a Cuban citizen trying to recover the reserved portion from her Italian husband's estate; the Court ruled that the claimant had not satisfied the principle of reciprocity, given that Cuban law does not make provision for forced heirship.

The rule laid down in Article 25(2) of the Succession Regulation appears to be particularly restrictive in terms of private autonomy. As pointed out, it provides that an agreement as to succession relating to several persons is valid only if admissible by all of the laws which, under this regulation, would have governed the succession of all those involved if they had died on the day the agreement was concluded. Furthermore, the agreement will be governed by the law with which it has the closest connection. In contrast, Article 18(2) of the Commission's proposal was inspired by a more liberal policy towards the admissibility of agreements as to succession concluded by several persons: it would have been valid and admissible if provided for by the law of the (single) state in which one of the parties had its habitual residence.[62] However, it has been authoritatively stated that not all Member States whose legal tradition is fundamentally opposed to the admissibility of agreements as to succession would have been prepared to accept the solution proposed by the Commission.[63]

The idea that the aforementioned states are so radically opposed to agreements as to succession, however, needs to be tempered. It is true that there are still many countries that prohibit agreements whereby the testator arranges his or her own succession while still alive: France, Belgium, Luxembourg (Article 1130, para. 2, of the Civil Code), Netherlands (Article 4.4, para. 2 of the NBW), Portugal (Article 2028, para. 2, of the Civil Code), Greece (Article 368 of the Civil Code), Spain (although derogations are provided for at regional level),[64] and Italy (Article 458 of the Civil Code). A closer look, however, shows that this prohibition is by no means without exceptions.

In France, for example, case law has ruled in favour of the admissibility of agreements as to succession.[65] The French legislator also passed Law no. 2006-728 of 23 June 2006 in order to widen the space reserved for private autonomy and speed up estate settlement.[66] In its current wording, the French Civil

---

[62] Article 18(2) of the Proposal for a Regulation of the European Parliament and of the Council on jurisdiction, applicable law, recognition and enforcement of decisions and authentic instruments in matters of succession and the creation of a European Certificate of Succession (SEC (2009) 410) (SEC (2009) 411): 'An agreement concerning the succession of several persons shall be valid in substantive terms only if this validity is accepted by the law which, pursuant to Article 16, would have applied to the succession of one of the persons whose succession is involved in the event of death on the day on which the agreement was concluded'.

[63] A. DAVÍ and A. ZANOBETTI, *Il nuovo diritto internazionale privato europeo delle successioni*, Giappichelli, Turin 2014, p. 178.

[64] MARTINEZ M., 'Les pactes successoraux dans les droits régionaux d' Espagne' in A. BONOMI, M. STEINER (eds.), *Les pactes successoraux en droit comparé et en droit international privé*, Librairie Droz, Genève 2008, p. 107 et seq.

[65] With reference to France, see Cass., 30 May 1985, in J Dalloz, 1986, p. 65 et seq.; Cour d'appel Aix-en-Provence, 16 October 2003, in *Revue critique droit international privé*, 2004, p. 589 et seq.

[66] PH. MALAURIE, 'Examen critique du projet de loi portant réforme des successions et des libéralités' [2005] *Defrenois* 38298; D. VIGNEAU, 'Le règlement de la succession. Observation

Code maintains the general rule prohibiting agreements on future successions (Articles 722, 791, 943, 1389, 1600, 1837). At the same time, nonetheless, it establishes a regime of exceptions for the (not so few) cases provided for by law.[67] Nowadays there are many examples of typical agreements as to succession, such as the *clause commerciale*[68] and the *donation partage*.[69] Legal scholarship, indeed, questions whether the prohibition has not, in substance, been completely lost.[70]

Even the most authoritative Italian legal scholarship has held, moreover, that an agreement as to succession settlement admitted on the basis of a foreign law chosen pursuant to Article 25(2) of the Succession Regulation may be deemed admissible and valid. According to this perspective, the entry into force of the Succession Regulation means that the validity and effectiveness of the agreement as to succession should not be measured against abstract domestic prohibitions which, by themselves, cannot prevent their application.[71]

Practical application problems arising from Article 25(2) may be mitigated by the provisions of Article 25(3) of the Succession Regulation.[72] The difference between both is clear. It has been described as a real 'internal contradiction' in the Succession Regulation, as was the case in relation between Articles 10 and 11 of the Hague Convention.[73]

On closer inspection, however, even Article 25(3) may not be helpful in estate planning. It does not prevent a split between the law applicable to the succession

---

sur le projet de loi portant réforme des successions et des libéralités' [2006] *Juris-Classeur périodique*, édition notariale 1144; A.M. Leroyer, 'Reforme des successions et des libéralités. Loi n. 2006-728 of 23 June 2006' [2006] *Revue trimestrelle droit civil* 613.

[67] A. Braun, 'Towards a Greater Autonomy for Testators and Heirs: Some Reflections on Recent Reforms in France, Belgium and Italy' [2012] *Zeitschrift für Erbrecht und Vermögensnachfolge* 461 et seq.

[68] F. Xavier Testu, 'Pactes sur succession future exceptionnellement autorisés' in M. Grimaldi (ed.), *Droit patrimonial de la famille*, Dalloz, Paris 2009, p. 395 et seq.

[69] A.M. Leroyer, 'Reforme des successions et des libéralités. Loi n. 2006-728 of 23 June 2006' [2006] *Revue trimestrelle droit civil* 613.

[70] N. Baillon-Wirtz, 'Que reste-t-il de la prohibition des pactes sur succession future?' [2006] *Droit de la Famille* 8 et seq.

[71] G. Perlingieri and G. Zarra, *Ordine pubblico interno e internazionale tra caso concreto e sistema ordinamentale*, ESI, Naples 2019, p. 198. On this topic, with reference to the Italian legal system, see also C. Caccavale, 'Contratto e successioni' in V. Roppo (ed.), *Trattato dei contratti*, vol. VI, Giuffré, Milan 2006, p. 403 et seq. and V. Putortí, 'Il divieto dei patti successori alla luce del Regolamento UE 650/2012' [2016] *Diritto successioni famiglia* 845 et seq.; V. Barba, *I patti successori e il divieto di disposizione della delazione*, ESI, Naples, 2015, p. 10 et seq.

[72] The German Bundesgerichtshof applies this provision to an agreement as to succession concluded before the entry into force of the Succession Regulation, see BGH, 10.07.2019, IV ZB 22/18, Zeitschrift für Das Gesamte Familienrecht 2019, p. 1561, commented by Von Bar.

[73] A. Daví and A. Zanobetti, *Il nuovo diritto internazionale privato europeo delle successioni*, Giappichelli, Turin 2014, p. 183.

(under Articles 21 and 22 of the Succession Regulation) and the law governing the agreement as to succession. Moreover, its application risks breaching the principle of unity of succession. All that remains is to hope, as stated above, that 'parties will exercise this autonomy wisely'.[74]

5. CHALLENGES IN APPLYING SUCCESSION REGULATION AND TWIN REGULATIONS IN PARALLEL

Within this context, identifying the law applicable to a cross-border married or registered couple who wishes to organise their succession planning appears somewhat problematic. This is a very sensitive issue, as qualification implies a systematic interpretation involving the Matrimonial Property Regulation and the Regulation on the Property Consequences of Registered Partnerships (the Twin Regulations), currently applied in 18 Member States.[75]

Articles 22 of the Twin Regulation allow spouses and partners to choose the law of the state where at least one of them is resident or the law of the nationality of one of them, or else, for registered partners, the law of the state under whose law the registered partnership was created. Therefore, depending on the nature of the agreement, the role of party autonomy could be relevant to a greater or lesser degree:[76] the limited leeway granted by the law governing similar agreements as to succession[77] clearly shows the distinction with regard to 'couple-related' property agreements, for which the possibility to choose the applicable law under the EU regulations is wider.[78]

A very significant problem concerns agreements between spouses or partners regarding, or having an effect on, their inheritance planning. Should the Succession Regulation or, alternatively, the Twin Regulations apply and, consequently, which law will be applicable?

Many cases risk falling into this 'grey area' due to the described problems of coordination between the regulations. This is the case, for example, of 'contracts

---

[74] M. PAZDAN and M. ZACHARIASIEWICZ, 'Highlights and Pitfalls of the EU Succession Regulation' (2020) 26 *Problemy Prawa Prywatnego Międzynarodowego* 127, 134.

[75] Nine Member States are still outside enhanced cooperation. Regarding these states, see A. WYSOCKA-BAR, 'Enhanced cooperation in property matters in the EU and non-participating Member States' (2019) 20 *ERA Forum* 187 et seq.

[76] P.R. WAUTELET, 'What's Wrong with Article 22? The Unsolved Mysteries of Choice of Law for Matrimonial Property' [2018] available at <https://ssrn.com/abstract=3266879>.

[77] See above Sections 3 and 4 of this chapter.

[78] See E. BERGAMINI, 'Agreements between spouses and partners, and agreements as to successions' in S. LANDINI (ed.), *EU Regulations 650/2012, 1103 and 1104/2016: cross-border families, international successions, mediation issues and new financial assets*, ESI, Naples 2020, p. 106.

of inheritance' with *post mortem* effects (the German *Erbvertrag*,[79] Article 2264 of the *Bürgerliches Gesetzbuch* and the Austrian succession agreement under Sections 1249 et seq. of the *Allgemeines Bürgerliches Gesetzbuch*) and the *Berliner Testament* under Article 2265 of the BGB. According to these provisions, spouses and partners are set up as mutual heirs. They also establish that the entire inheritance after the death of the last one to die must go to the children of the couple. Similar examples in the French legal system are the *liberalités-partages* and the *clause commerciale*.[80]

Theoretically, the dividing line between the Succession Regulation and the Twin Regulations is very clear. Indeed, while Article 1(2)(d) of the Succession Regulation excludes matrimonial property from its substantive scope, Article 1(2)(d) of the Twin Regulations leaves out successions. The above examples, however, show that, in concrete terms, drawing the boundaries between the two instruments largely depends on the exact meaning of 'succession' on the one hand, and 'matrimonial property regime', on the other.[81]

The practical issue arising from this lack of coordination is that the law applicable under Article 22 of the Twin Regulations may differ from that applicable to a given succession under the Succession Regulation. Two different laws will govern matrimonial property and succession whenever, at the time of death of one of the spouses or partners, he or she had his or her habitual residence in a country other than that of the first habitual residence after the marriage. This mostly happens where a cross-border couple has changed its common habitual residence during marriage or partnership. This would clearly be an additional obstacle to inheritance planning for couples.[82]

The Court of Justice of the European Union (CJEU) addressed this issue in the *Mankopf* case,[83] a dispute regarding the German *Zugewinngemeinschaft*.[84]

---

[79] E.A. AMAYUELAS, *The Law of succession. Testamentary Freedom*, Groningen, European Law Publishing 2011, p. 165 et seq. and H. BROX and W. WALKER, *Erbrecht*, 28th ed., Beck, Vahlen, 2018, p. 10 et seq.

[80] See above, Sections 3 and 4 of this chapter.

[81] As noted by A. BONOMI, 'The Interaction Among the Future EU Instruments on Matrimonial Property, Registered Partnerships and Successions' (2011) 13 *Yearbook Private International Law* 219 et seq.

[82] A. BONOMI, 'The Regulation on Matrimonial Property and Its Operation in Succession Cases – Its Interaction with the Succession Regulation and Its Impact on Non-participating Member States' (2020) 26 *Problemy Prawa Prywatnego Międzynarodowego* 85.

[83] C-558/16 Mahnkopf, ECLI:EU:C:2018:138 in which the court ruled that a provision such as Article 1371(1) of the BGB 'which prescribes, on the death of one of the spouses, a fixed allocation of the accrued gains by increasing the surviving spouse's share of the estate falls within the scope of that regulation'. J. WEBER, 'Ein Klassiker neu aufgelegt: Die Qualifikation des §1371 BGB unter dem Regime der Europäischen Erbrechtsverordnung' (2018) *Neue Juristische Wochenschrift* 1357.

[84] See I. BARRIÈRE BROUSSE, 'Conflit de lois' (2018) 4 *Journal du droit international* 1218 et seq. For a critical evaluation of the case, see J. VON HEIN, 'The CJEU settles the issue

Mr Mahnkopf was married to Mrs Mahnkopf. They were German nationals habitually residents in Berlin. Mr Mahnkopf died on 29 August 2015 having made no disposition of property upon his death: the sole heirs were his wife and their only son. Mr and Mrs Mahnkopf had not entered into a marriage contract. Consequently, they were subject to the statutory property regime of community of accrued gains. The estate included a half share in the co-ownership of a property in Sweden.

Mrs Mahnkopf's half share of the estate resulted from the application of Article 1931(1) of the BGB under which the surviving spouse's share on intestacy, which was one quarter, was increased by an additional quarter when both spouses were subject to the matrimonial property regime of community of accrued gains. The widow applied for a European Certificate of Succession in Germany in order to register an estate in Sweden.[85] The notary submitted Mrs Mahnkopf's application to the local court. The latter rejected the application on the grounds that the share allocated to the deceased's spouse was based (as regards one quarter of the deceased's estate) on a regime governing succession and (as regards another quarter of his estate) on the matrimonial property regime provided for in Article 1371(1) of the BGB. In its view, the rule under which the other quarter was allocated, which relates to a matrimonial property regime and not a succession regime, does not fall within the scope of the Succession Regulation. In this case, the question arose as to whether the scope of application of the Succession Regulation also includes provisions on matrimonial property regimes that result in an increase in the share of one spouse or partner following the death of the other spouse or partner.

The CJEU did not analyse whether this provision is of a matrimonial or succession nature in German law, which is a tangled question much debated in German private law theory.[86] Rather, the Court made an objective and function-oriented analysis of the question. It pointed out that the statutory provision did not deal with the distribution of property between spouses or partners but operated once the distribution had taken place, and only after death. Consequently, it stated that 'for the purposes of the Regulation', Article 1371(1) of the BGB is applicable with regard to succession.

---

of characterising the surviving spouse's share of the estate in the context of the Succession Regulation' [2018] available at <conflictoflaws.net>.

[85] For an evaluation of the correlation between family relationships and the ECS, see D. DAMASCELLI, 'Brevi note sull'efficacia probatoria del certificato successorio europeo riguardante un soggetto coniugato o legato da unione non matrimoniale' [2017] *Rivista di diritto internazionale processuale* 67 et seq.

[86] See T. JÄGER, 'Der neue Güterstand der Wahl-Zugewinngemeinschaft. Inhalt und seine ersten Folgen für die Gesetzgebung und Beratungspraxis' [2010] *Deutsche Notar-Zeitschrift* 804 et seq. and W. PINTENS, 'Ehegüterstände in Europa' in Lipp-Schumann-Veit (ed.), *Die Zugewinngemeinschaft. Ein europäisches Modell?*, Universitätsverlag Göttingen, Göttingen 2009, p. 23.

According to the CJEU interpretation,[87] national rules come under 'succession' when 'they deploy their effect in the case of succession' and 'determine the rights of the surviving spouse in the relationship with the other heirs'.[88] It should be pointed out that, given the diversity of national legal traditions, the yardstick used by the CJEU is, again, the function of the concrete act.[89] It is precisely this rule of interpretation that should be used to overcome the antinomy described above. The CJEU does not engage in analysis of the basis of either the will of the parties nor national legal traditions. On the contrary, it qualifies concrete cases in relation to the objective purpose of the agreements between spouses or partners.

It is on this basis that the antinomy should be resolved: if an agreement between spouses and partners deploys its effect in matters of succession and determines the rights of the surviving spouse in relation to the other heirs, it should be governed by Article 25 of the Succession Regulation.

Such reasoning may be also applied in similar cases. Despite its nature as an agreement between spouses, for example, the *clause commerciale* should be characterised – 'for the purposes of the Regulation' – as dispositions upon death (and more specifically as agreements as to succession, within the meaning of Article 3(1)(b) of the Succession Regulation). Consequently, even though this is an institution traditionally linked to the matrimonial property regime, the conflict rule would not fall under Article 22 of the Twin Regulations.

The same solution may be analysed in the similar above described cases if, functionally speaking, they produce the effects seen in *Mankopf*, an example being the French 'donations between spouses' (*institution contractuelle*).[90]

The problem of interpretation would have been overcome if the Succession Regulation had allowed the law of the habitual residence of one of the parties involved to be used as the law applicable to the agreement. In this way, the difficulties in distinguishing the different kinds of agreements would have become less significant: 'it would have been possible for couples to make a choice of law valid under both [Twins Regulations and Succession] Regulations that could cover all kinds of reciprocal agreements were they to be considered as related to succession or to matrimonial/partnership properties'.[91]

---

[87] And, in a similar sense, also the CJEU case, C-218/16, Kubicka, ECLI:EU:C:2017:755. On this point see W. Bańczyk, 'The efficiency of the foreign legacy "by vindication" in a state not recognising it and the borders of succession law, based on Regulation (EU) No 650/2012' [2020] *Zeitschrift für europäisches Privatrecht* 710–728.
[88] Case C-558/16 Mahnkopf, ECLI:EU:C:2018:138, para 40.
[89] On the complexity and functional unity of the current legal system see P. Perlingieri, *Il diritto civile nella legalità costituzionale secondo il sistema italo-europeo delle fonti*, vol. 2, 4th ed., ESI, Naples 2020, p. 59 et seq.
[90] See D. Damascelli, *Diritto internazionale privato delle successioni a causa di morte*, Giuffré, Milan 2013, p. 93 et seq.
[91] E. Bergamini, 'Agreements between spouses and partners, and agreements as to successions' in S. Landini (ed.), *EU Regulations 650/2012, 1103 and 1104/2016: cross-border families,*

On the level of practical application, however, there remains the problem of the guidance to be given to cross-border couples who wish to plan their succession, directly or otherwise. Legal scholars have rightly pointed out that coordination between Article 22 of the Twins Regulations and Articles 3 and 25 of the Succession Regulations can be achieved by the spouses or registered partners through the choice of the applicable law.[92] In particular, should they change their habitual residence, they can submit their matrimonial property relationship to the law of their new habitual residence. This choice will be useful if it will be the law applicable to their succession. If they agree that their choice has a retroactive effect, just one law may apply to all of these issues.[93]

6. CONCLUDING REMARKS

It is clear that the development of the law regarding recognition of the legal effects of relationships is very dynamic, both at the substantive and the PIL level. Over the last decade, the map of Europe has been changing constantly and is still shifting at high speed.[94]

The Europeanisation of the conflict rules seems to have loosened the traditional links that PIL rules had with national laws and, in particular, with nationality.[95] At the same time, however, this fragmentation does not seem to have broken the link with substantive law.[96]

Unlike other areas, where harmonisation has been immediate and direct (e.g. consumer law), the Europeanisation of conflict rules has consolidated and enhanced dialogue between courts,[97] an essential prerequisite for the creation of future European private law.[98] In this context, PIL requires national legal

---

[92] *international successions, mediation issues and new financial assets*, ESI, Naples 2020, p. 107.
A. BONOMI, 'The Regulation on Matrimonial Property and Its Operation in Succession Cases – Its Interaction with the Succession Regulation and Its Impact on Non-participating Member States' (2020) 26 *Problemy Prawa Prywatnego Międzynarodowego* 85, 86.
[93] A. BONOMI, ibid., p. 85.
[94] W. SCHRAMA, 'Empowering private autonomy as a means to navigate the patchwork of EU Regulations' in J.M. SCHERPE and E. BARGELLI (eds.), *The Interaction between Family Law, Succession Law and Private International Law. Adapting to change*, Intersentia, Cambridge 2021, p. 55.
[95] M. PERTEGAS SENDERS and M.C. BOGDAN, *Concise Introduction to EU Private International Law*, 4th ed., Groeningen, Europa Law Publishing, 2019, p. 13 et seq.
[96] See J. BASEDOW, 'The Communitarisation of Private International Law' (2009) 73 *Rabels Zeitschrift für ausländisches und internationales Privatrecht* 455 et seq.
[97] See D. ACHILLE, 'Lex successionis e compatibilità con gli ordinamenti degli Stati membri nel Reg. UE n. 650/2012' [2018] *Nuova giurisprudenza civile commentata* 697 et seq.
[98] A. GAMBARO and R. SACCO, 'Sistemi giuridici comparati' in R. SACCO (ed.), *Trattato di diritto comparato*, UTET, Turin 2008, p. 27 et seq. See also S. DEPLANO, 'Verso un codice europeo dei contratti?' [2010] *Rivista giuridica Molise e Sannio* 105 et seq.

scholars and national professionals to take into account the legal systems of other Member States[99] in order to develop an area of freedom, security and justice in which the free movement of all persons is ensured.[100]

This is a very welcome result, especially in relation to a legal area with a strong traditional component such as the family and inheritance.[101] However, the importance of PIL as a driver of the European integration process risks being severely curtailed by inconsistent provisions of EU legislation.[102] A central role in overcoming these inconsistencies, perhaps inevitable in view of the complexity of the legislation, is played by national legal theories and the CJEU, which is assuming an increasingly central role in the process of interpretation.[103] Further contribution by the CJEU would be welcome in order to facilitate and harmonise the application of PIL regulations in the EU Member States.[104]

---

[99] For an example in family law area see M.J. CAZORLA GONZÁLEZ, M. GIOBBI, J. KRAMBERGER ŠKERL, L. RUGGERI and S. WINKLER (eds.), *Property relations of cross border couples in the European Union*, ESI, Naples, 2020, p. 14 et seq.

[100] P. BENVENUTI, 'Il diritto internazionale privato' in C. CASTRONOVO and S. MAZZAMUTO (eds.), *Manuale di diritto internazionale privato*, vol. 1, Giuffré, Milan 2007, p. 125 et seq., stating that private international law makes it possible to relativise, by way of integration, the fact that each system of private law belongs to an original state legal order.

[101] C. CONSOLO and F. GODIO, 'Profili processuali del Reg. UE n. 650/2012 sulle successioni transnazionali: il coordinamento tra giurisdizioni' [2018] *Rivista di diritto civile* 18 et seq.

[102] V. HEINZE, 'The European Succession Regulation 650, 2012. An Overview' in G. ALPA (ed.) *I nuovi confini del diritto privato europeo (New borders of European private law)*, Giuffré, Milan 2016, p. 45: EU private international law was not enacted as an all-encompassing codification, but rather proceeds in steps, each related to a specific substantive area.

[103] On the role of the CJEU in the unification process, in particular of European private law, see I. KLAUER, *Die Europäisierung des Privatrechts*, Baden Baden, Nomos 1998; J. SMITS, *The making of European Private Law. Towards a Ius Commune Europaeum as a Mixed Legal System*, Intersentia, Antwerp, 2002, p. 19 et seq. and C. TWIGG-FLESNER, *The Europeanisation of Contract Law. Current controversies in law*, 2nd ed., London-New York, Taylor & Francis, 2013.

[104] On the relationship between national and international courts in the current legal system see P. FEMIA, 'Decisori non gerarchizzabili, riserve testuali, guerra tra Corti. Con un (lungo) intermezzo spagnolo' in V. RIZZO and L. RUGGERI (eds.), *Il controllo di legittimità costituzionale e comunitaria come tecnica di difesa*, ESI, Naples 2010, pp. 85–270.

MISCELLANEOUS THOUGHTS ON EUROPE, ITS PEOPLE AND MIGRATION

Nenad HLAČA*

1. European History of Migration 313
2. Current Migration Challenges for the European Union 314
3. Conceptualising European Identity against the Background
   of Migration 319
4. Migration and Cross-Border Families 321

1. EUROPEAN HISTORY OF MIGRATION

From the very beginnings, migration is the constant state of humans.[1] Since the early stage when predecessors of homo sapiens were populating the world until modern times which have seen waves of migrants, migration never stopped. While the motives in prehistoric times were search of a better climate, natural resources and food growing conditions, in the modern times migrations are driven by industrialisation, politics or labour/market considerations. Whatever the case may be humans are in a constant search for better conditions, Europe not being an exception. It is actually continuous migrations that created both Europe and what we refer to as a 'Western' civilisation.

Interestingly, the etymology of the word 'Europe' has been discussed vividly by historical linguists aided by anthropologists, archaeologists, genetic historians, demographic historians, ethnohistorians, literature and art historians, philologists, etc. However, there are multiplicity of theories ranging from the Ancient Greek origin (Εὐρώπη, Eurṓpē), meaning 'wide gazing' and related to the name of the mythic Phoenician princess abducted by the great

---

*   Nenad Hlača, PhD, Professor at the University of Rijeka, Faculty of Law, Croatia.
[1] Recognised also by the EU institutions. See e.g. European Commission, Communication from the Commission on a New Pact on Migration and Asylum, Brussels, 23.9.2020, COM(2020) 609 final.

god Zeus to ancient the Sumerian and Semitic root of the word 'Ereb' (עֶרֶב, eh'-reb), meaning 'darkness' or 'descent' from the perspective of the region's western location in relation to middle East. This could lead to the conclusion that it meant the 'land where the sun sets'. Some of the many meanings of the word 'Ereb' in Semitic languages include also desert, nomad, nomadic, merchant, moving around. Hence, etymologically, Europe is also the last, final step of migrations from the east towards the west. Opposite to the land of the rising sun, Europe is the land of *ereb* – evening and sunset: the end of the day, or one might also say the end of migration flows.

Migration is influenced by a combination of economic, environmental, political and social factors: either in a migrant's country of origin (push factors) or in the country of destination (pull factors). Historically, the relative economic prosperity and political stability of the EU are thought to have exerted a considerable pull effect on immigrants.[2] Although it may seem to some that we are now faced with the unprecedented migrations, it is a matter of fact that migrations are the core of the identity of Europeans. Throughout history, Europe has been attractive to many, including warrior migrations of first the Celtic people and later on the Barbarian tribes as well as the colonial and post-colonial migrations to some European countries.

Europe seen as the immigrants' destination is, of course, only one side of the coin which we are looking at in present times. Just as Europe was inviting millions to come and inhabit it, constantly throughout human history millions emigrated from Europe. On the other hand it should be noted that emigrations from Europe have occurred from the times of Ancient Greeks who created many colonies on the Mediterranean, to the Middle Ages when millions of Europeans relocated to the Americas following their discovery in 1492 and to the Americas and Australia and New Zealand especially in the nineteenth and twentieth centuries.

2. CURRENT MIGRATION CHALLENGES FOR THE EUROPEAN UNION

Migration policies within the EU have been increasingly concerned with attracting a particular migrant profile, often in an attempt to alleviate specific skills shortages.[3] Besides policies to encourage labour recruitment, immigration policy is often focused on two additional areas: preventing unauthorised

---

[2] E. BALABANOVA, A. BLACH, 'Sending and receiving. The ethical framing of intra-EU migration in the European press' (2010) 25(4) *European Journal of Communication* 382–397.

[3] R. ORŁOWSKA, 'Immigration in the European Union in the Second Decade of the 21st Century: Problem or Solution?' (2011) 10(1) *Folia Oeconomica Stetinensia* available at <https://sciendo.com/article/10.2478/v10031-011-0015-0>.

migration and the illegal employment of migrants who are not permitted to work, as well as promoting the integration of immigrants into society. Significant resources have been mobilised to fight people smuggling and trafficking networks in the EU.

Migration numbers in the EU are remarkably high. According to Eurostat,[4] on 1 January 2020, 23 million people (5.1%) of the 447.3 million people living in the EU were non-EU citizens. A total of 4.2 million people immigrated to one of the EU Member States during 2019, while 2.7 million emigrants were reported to have left an EU Member State. However, these total figures do not represent the migration flows to/from the EU as a whole since they also include flows between the different EU Member States. In 2019, there were an estimated 2.7 million immigrants to the EU from non-EU countries, and approximately 1.2 million people emigrated from the EU to a country outside the EU. In addition, 1.4 million people previously residing in one EU Member State migrated to another EU Member State.

Germany reported the largest total number of immigrants (886.3 thousand) in 2019, followed by Spain (750.5 thousand), France (385.6 thousand) and Italy (332.8 thousand). Germany also reported the highest number of emigrants in 2019 (576.3 thousand), followed by France (299.1 thousand), Spain (296.2 thousand) and Romania (233.7 thousand). A total of 22 of the EU Member States reported more immigration than emigration in 2019. However, in Bulgaria, Croatia, Latvia, Denmark and Romania, the number of emigrants outnumbered the number of immigrants.

Information on citizenship has often been used for research on immigrants with a foreign background. However, since citizenship can change over the lifetime of a person, it is also useful to analyse information regarding the country of birth. The relative share of native-born immigrants within the total number of immigrants was highest in Bulgaria (59% of all immigrants), followed by Romania (49%) and Lithuania (46%). By contrast, Luxembourg and Spain reported relatively low shares of native-born immigrants, 5% or less of all immigration in 2019.

An analysis by the previous residence reveals that Luxembourg reported the largest share of immigrants coming from another EU Member State (91% of its total number of immigrants in 2019), followed by Austria (63%) and Slovakia (60%); relatively low shares were reported by Spain as well as Slovenia (both 16%). Regarding the sex distribution of immigrants to EU Member States in 2019, there were slightly more men than women (54% compared with 46%). The EU Member State reporting the highest share of male immigrants was

---

[4] See Eurostat data available at <https://ec.europa.eu/eurostat/statisticsexplained/index.php/Migration_and_migrant_population_statistics#column-one Migration> and migrant population statistics – data extracted in March 2021>.

Croatia (77%); by contrast, the highest share of female immigrants was reported in Cyprus (53%). Half of the immigrants were aged under 29. Immigrants into EU Member States in 2019 were, on average, much younger than the total population already resident in the country of destination. On 1 January 2020, the median age of the total population of the EU stood at 43.9 years, while it was 29.2 years for immigrants in 2019.

The number of people residing in the EU with citizenship of a non-member country on 1 January 2020 was 23 million, representing 5.1% of the EU population. In addition, 13.5 million persons were living in one EU Member State on 1 January 2020 with citizenship of another EU Member State. In absolute terms, the largest numbers of non-nationals living in the EU Member States on 1 January 2020 were found in Germany (10.4 million persons), Spain (5.2 million), France (5.1 million) and Italy (5.0 million). Non-nationals in these four EU Member States collectively represented 71% of the total number of non-nationals living in all EU Member States together, while the same four EU Member States had a 58% share of the EU's population.

On 1 January 2020, Belgium, Ireland, Luxembourg, Austria and Slovakia were the EU Member States where non-nationals living in those states were mainly citizens of another EU Member State. This means that in most EU Member States, the majority of non-nationals were citizens of non-EU countries. In Latvia and Estonia, the proportion of citizens from non-member countries is considerable due to the high number of non-citizens, mainly former Soviet Union citizens, who are permanently resident in these countries but have not acquired any other citizenship.

In relative terms, the EU Member State with the highest share of non-nationals was Luxembourg, as non-nationals accounted for 47% of its total population. A high proportion of foreign citizens (more than 10% of the resident population) was also observed in Malta, Cyprus, Austria, Estonia, Latvia, Ireland, Germany, Belgium and Spain. In contrast, non-nationals represented less than 1% of the population in Poland (0.9%) and in Romania (0.7%). The relative share of foreign-born within the total population was highest in Luxembourg (48% of the resident population), followed by Malta (23%) and Cyprus (22%). By contrast, Poland reported the lowest share of foreign-born, only 2% of its total population, on 1 January 2020, followed by Bulgaria (2.7%), Slovakia (3.6%) and Romania (3.7%).

Romanian, Polish, Italian and Portuguese citizens were the four biggest groups of EU citizens living in other EU Member States in 2020. An analysis of the age structure of the population indicates that, for the EU as a whole, the foreign population was younger than the national population. The distribution of foreigners by age, compared to nationals, shows a more significant proportion of relatively young working-age adults. On 1 January 2020, the median age of the national population in the EU was 45 years, while the median age of non-nationals living in the EU was 36 years. As evident from these figures, though limited to 2019 only, the EU simultaneously faces two types of migrations: internal and external. Citizens of EU Member States have the freedom to travel and freedom of movement within the EU's internal borders. These intra-EU migrations have impacted the Member States' economies and societies, of both the dominantly immigrant and dominantly emigrant Member States. With nearly every enlargement wave there were accompanying migration trajectories. The same is true for Brexit: in the attempt to neutralise the post-Brexit decrease in the EU-immigration, the UK government seems to have adjusted the non-EU immigration policy.[5] As a result, European societies are at present, and will also be in the future, increasingly diverse. The EU is actually supporting the intra-EU migration phenomenon by the variety of its policies and instruments in addition to the cornerstone freedom of movement guaranteed by the Founding Treaties. Some of these instruments are treated in this volume and they are aimed at consolidating Member State rules for the benefit of the EU citizens and persons residing in EU whenever their family property has cross-border implications.[6]

Mention of the external migration instantly recalls to the minds of many Europeans the pictures of numerous migrants from third counties, who came to the European Union in huge waves staring in 2015 and causing a severe 'migration crises'. It was in fact a desperate response to the need to juvenilise the workforce which was created by the negative demographic trends in the EU. Member States are indeed demographically old, some experiencing a strong decline in population. The predictions for the future are also very pessimistic unless the Member States put sufficient efforts into devising a holistic and efficient migration policy.[7]

Despite the positive impact on the host Member State economy, sometimes migrations are perceived to threaten the host nation's identity and culture. While the EU takes steps to coordinate intensive migration policies of the European Union,[8] such attempts seem to have limited effect. Member States still largely differ in many respects which are relevant to the development of the migration processes. They are at different degrees of economic development; they have different levels of multiculturalism in their societies; their national immigration policies and regulatory framework differ; some have many settled migrants from previous stages of migration while others

---

[5] J. PORTES, 'Immigration and the UK economy after Brexit', IZA DP No. 14425, May 2021, available at <http://ftp.iza.org/dp14425.pdf>.

[6] See Section 4 of this chapter.

[7] See e.g. G. ZBIŃKOWSKI, 'Migrant Crisis in the EU and it's Demographic Context Directions of Poland's Migration Policy After 2018' (2019) 373(4) *Przegląd Zachodni* 91–106; M. JERIĆ, 'Contemporary Emigration of Croats: What is the Future of the Republic of Croatia?' (2019) 9(2) *Oeconomica Jadertina* 21–31.

[8] See Timeline – European Union Migration Policy, available at <https://www.consilium.europa.eu/en/policies/eu-migration-policy/migration-timeline/>.

have a small immigrant population. These and other circumstances attribute to the attractiveness of a particular Member State over other Member States for migrants, asylum seekers and refugees. For these reasons, only several Member States tend to be desired immigrant destinations; whereas the others, usually less prosperous Member States, cannot keep their own population within, let alone the immigrants.

These migration waves intensified the ideological tensions between the value of universal humanism and nation-centred utilitarianism. The crisis also harshly affected the solidarity among European Union Member States and led to many institutional and legislative attempts to reform the system, most notably the New Pact on Migration and Asylum, announced by the European Commission in September 2020. The Pact is intended to create a genuine and comprehensive system to coordinate Member States actions in immigration policies. It has been described as a as a three-floor building in which all levels must be equally stable and reliable. The first floor is the external dimension, aimed at developing relations with some 25 countries of origin and to affect the transit of migrants and asylum seekers so that they do not have the need to leave. The second floor relates to the management of the EU external borders, which would be a common and shared responsibility, not only of those Member States of the first entry. It would involve strengthening Frontex, the European Border and Coast Guard Agency, obligatory screening procedures and effective return mechanisms. The third floor would form a new system in which mechanisms of solidarity and burden sharing would be key factors in achieving the efficiency of the overall system.[9] It remains to be seen with what success this Plan will be realised especially in a view of its very ambitious schedule.

Whatever their origin, another EU Member State or a third country, immigrants take part in the more or less intense acculturation process. The more different the social and cultural setting in the country of origin is, the more difficult and longer lasting is the acculturation process. As a multidimensional development, this process entails adoption of new values and changing of old habits, to eventually result in the formation of new identities. Changes in the social status of migrants may take different forms, from marginalisation and stigmatisation to assimilation and full integration in the host society and culture.[10] Unless migrants adopt the complex public and political reality of the

---

[9] Margaritis Schinas, European Commission Vice-President, 'Check against delivery', Speech by Vice-President Schinas on the New Pact on Migration and Asylum, Brussels, 23 September 2020, available at <https://ec.europa.eu/commission/presscorner/detail/en/SPEECH_20_1736>; Margaritis Schinas, European Commission Vice-President, Keynote speech at the Webinar on the New Pact, organised by the King's College of London and the British Institute of International and Comparative Law, on 22 April 2021.

[10] A. NYLUND, 'Review of "Discursive constructions of identity in European politics"' by R. C. M. Mole (ed.), Basingstoke and New York: Palgrave Macmillan, 2007 in (2009) 38(5) *Language in Society* 642–643.

new host country, they cannot be functionally integrated into their new habitat. Sometimes schools, religious associations, cultural or even sports clubs in which a homeland majority prevails offer an important feeling of security and help to overcome the turbulent period of adaptation. However, if immigrants remain thus isolated, even many years later, those from the first generation of migrants remain divided citizens.[11] Realising the severity of the threats to the internal functioning not only of the Member States, but also of the EU as a whole, the Council of the European Union, made recommendations concerning the integration of third-country nationals legally residing in the EU.[12] This came in addition to the earlier European Commission's communications entitled 'Action Plan on the integration of third-country nationals'[13] and 'New Skills Agenda for Europe'[14] as well as several acts by the European Parliament.[15]

3. CONCEPTUALISING EUROPEAN IDENTITY AGAINST THE BACKGROUND OF MIGRATION

The foremost question posed by many scholars is: What is European identity? In the words of a citizen of the EU, the questions might read: What makes me European? The answer to this question is important from an individual perspective, but it also impacts Member States' policies and the policies of the EU as a supranational organisation. This question, for instance, also emerges in the course of the debate on the degree of sovereignty which the Member States transfer to the EU. While part of the European societies is pro-European Union, some insist that if a clearly-felt national identity is eclipsed too quickly

---

[11] L. ACKERS, P. DWYER, 'Fixed laws, fluid lives: the citizenship status of post-retirement migrants in the European Union' (2004) 24(3) *Ageing & Society* 451–475.

[12] Council of the European Union, Conclusions of the Council and the Representatives of the Governments of the Member States on the integration of third-country nationals legally residing in the EU, Brussels, 9 December 2016, (OR. en), 15312/16, available at <https://data.consilium.europa.eu/doc/document/ST-15312-2016-INIT/en/pdf>.

[13] European Commission, Communication 'Action Plan on the integration of third-country nationals', Brussels, 7.6.2016, COM(2016) 377 final, available at <https://ec.europa.eu/home-affairs/sites/default/files/what-we-do/policies/european-agenda-migration/proposal-implementation-package/docs/20160607/communication_action_plan_integration_third-country_nationals_en.pdf>.

[14] European Commission, Communication, 'A New Skills Agenda for Europe. Working together to strengthen human capital, employability and competitiveness', Brussels, 10.6.2016, COM(2016) 381 final, available at <https://eur-lex.europa.eu/legal-content/EN/TXT/?uri=CELEX:52016DC0381>.

[15] See Opinion of the European Economic and Social Committee on Integration of refugees in the EU, the European Parliament Resolution of 5 July 2016 on refugees: 'Social inclusion and integration into the labour market, and the Opinion of the Committee of Regions', Commission for Citizenship, Governance, Institutional and External Affairs 'Action plan on the integration of third-country nationals'.

by a European identity (sometimes also called a pan-European identity, often perceived as distant or even fanciful), negative consequences can be expected.

So, what exactly is meant by 'being European'? In one of his speeches, a European *par excellence*, Václav Havel, the former President of the Czech Republic, remarked in 2000:

> I was so obviously and naturally European that I did not even think about it. And I am sure that applies to the majority of Europeans. They are profoundly European, but they are not even aware of it, they do not hang that label around their necks, which is why opinion polls show that they are somewhat surprised at having to shout their Europeanism from the rooftops. There does not appear to be a great tradition of considered Europeanism in Europe. That is not necessarily a good thing, and I welcome with satisfaction the fact that our Europeanism is starting to emerge clearly today from the vast melting pot of concepts, which speak for themselves. Questioning, considering and trying to define it, helps us enormously in understanding ourselves.[16]

In the multicultural and multifaceted world in which we live, the capacity to perceive one's own identity is a prerequisite to peaceful co-existence with other identities. Thinking about Europeanism means asking what set of values, ideals or principles belong in an individual's mind to the notion of Europe, or what is typical of Europe. More than that, it also means starting from the very essence of identity, examining the whole concept critically. To draw the sketches of identity means to define oneself in relation to others and, also, to assess one's own strengths and weaknesses. Jenkins analyses identity construction and demonstrates how it materialises as a result of the interaction between self-identification and external categorisation in various social environments.[17] One might argue, as Václav Havel did, that the idea of conceptualising and defining Europeanism has come too late, that cultural and political integration and introspection should have preceded economic integration in the EU.

Common European values, not the economic benefits, should be at the core. If we adopt the benefits of economic integration as our starting point, we might end up sacrificing the main European values. These are the respect for the individual and their freedoms, their rights and their dignity, the principle of solidarity, equality before the law, the rule of law, protection of minority rights, functioning on the basis of political pluralism and representative democracy, separation of the legislative, executive and judicial branches of power, respect for

---

[16] Václav Havel, Speech at the European Parliament, 16.2.2000, available at <https://www.europarl.europa.eu/sides/getDoc.do?pubRef=-//EP//TEXT+CRE+20000216+ITEM-012+DOC+XML+V0//EN>.

[17] See e.g. R. JENKINS, *Social identity*, 4th ed., 2014 Routledge London, p. 6.

private property and free enterprise, a market economy, and the development of the civil society.[18] The content that these values currently have reflects countless modern European experiences, including the fact that our continent is becoming a main multicultural crossroads.

The key target for the whole EU project is solidarity in a double sense: on the EU Member State level and the EU level. Genuine solidarity between citizens, residents, social groups, communities and regions is the best basis for solidarity which cannot be dispensed on the state level. And in the EU, which needs to function as an instrument of solidarity, the real civil foundations must be even more robust and even more prosperous. Therefore, the viability of the EU depends mainly, perhaps above all, on the spirit in which its citizens accept a European identity.

The ability to accept others – including those of different nationalities and origins – is one of the constituents of the European identity, particularly underlined in recent decades. Europe is to a large extent revolving around migration, and cross-border movements are its natural feature. Racial and cultural diversity, pluralism and openness form a part of the current discussion on European identity, requiring a re-thinking of prejudices and accepting diversity. There is no doubt that migrations were and still are the key to understanding the deep sense of Europe in general, and the European Union in particular.

4. MIGRATION AND CROSS-BORDER FAMILIES

The history of migrations on European soil has been reflected in the history of human relations, especially in families. Both internal and external migrations of increased intensity in the recent times are the reality and fortune of the EU. So are the cross-border families. Such families are already very common and are widely accepted in European societies. Sadly, but naturally, some cross-border couples separate in the end and at this point, their cross-border nature might make it hard for them to deal with the legal consequences thereof.[19]

In this regard, it is very welcome that the EU, promoting the cross-border movement of people through its free movement of persons as one of its fundamental freedoms and other policies and instruments, has also taken steps to assist cross-border couples in case their relationship fails. For this purpose, a considerable number of EU instruments have been adopted. The corpus of European private international family law forms the basis for addressing various challenges faced by cross-border couples. The Twin Regulations

---

[18] See Charter of Fundamental Rights of the European Union, OJ C 326, 26.10.2012, pp. 391–407.
[19] See in particular Chapters 1 and 2 of this volume.

discussed in this volume are important building blocks in setting a clear legal framework for couples whose separation will have to be dealt with before the courts or other competent authorities of EU Member States. Embracing the diversity of national laws, these instruments pave a united EU path not only to the resolution of legally relevant family property relationships but also to the European identity as the identity to which migration and cross-bordering are nothing short of essential.

INDEX

A
authentic instrument   42, 63, 133, 158–187

B
Brussels I bis Regulation   84, 90, 94, 97, 131, 150, 153, 173, 185, 241
Brussels II bis Regulation   5, 7–15, 19–21, 23, 32, 60, 62, 78–80, 86–87, 94, 97, 130, 137, 202, 238, 240

C
choice of court agreement   62, 64, 83–85, 100, 228, 233–240
choice-of-law agreement   62, 65–66, 82, 204, 214, 216–217, 228, 235–236, 239–240

D
de facto   27, 35, 45, 224, 245–268

E
enhanced cooperation   8, 26, 34–36, 42, 58, 66–68, 70, 72–73, 131, 134, 154, 160–161, 174, 217, 222, 225, 228, 265, 271

H
habitual residence   7–11, 13–14, 18, 22, 53, 55, 61, 67–69, 76–77, 79, 82, 85–87, 139, 194–196, 200–201, 213–214, 216–217, 228–229, 231, 235, 237–239, 280–282, 295, 305, 308, 310–311

I
in rem   47, 52–53, 272, 275–276, 285, 287, 289–290

L
lex fori   7, 11, 14, 21–22, 91, 95–96, 114, 117, 140, 185, 197–199, 208, 225–226, 232, 275–276
lis pendens   10, 12, 63, 72, 97, 99, 238

M
Maintenance Regulation   6, 14–17, 21–23, 32, 51, 60, 130, 136, 154, 213, 241

N
nationalities
nationality   7, 8, 10–11, 17, 50, 53, 55, 67–69, 71, 77, 80, 82, 85–88, 91, 145, 169, 194, 211, 214, 230–231, 235, 238–240, 295, 307, 311

O
ordre public (public policy)   31, 114, 130, 141, 146–150, 153, 176, 178, 197, 209, 216, 231, 233, 235, 240–243, 303
overriding mandatory provisions   114–115, 117

P
party autonomy   7, 11, 72, 82, 187, 217, 234, 307

R
renvoi   7, 117
Rome III Regulation   6–9, 11–12, 18, 20–21, 23, 25, 32, 60, 62, 68, 131, 194, 202–203, 233

S
same-sex couple   27–29, 44, 54–58, 60–61, 67, 70, 89, 93, 219–220, 222–226, 229–241, 243–244, 247, 252, 254–256, 259, 263, 265
Succession Regulation   6, 19, 32, 70, 74–78, 90–91, 99–100, 117, 130–131, 136, 143, 154, 159, 161, 163, 165, 171, 176, 237, 290, 293–312

T
temporal scope   61–66
third-country nationals   7, 9, 57, 319

U
universal application   11, 67, 70, 107, 215

Intersentia   323

ABOUT THE EDITORS

Lucia Ruggeri is an author and an editor of numerous publications. She was the coordinator of the EU Project "Personalized Solution in European Family and Succession Law – PSEFS". At the moment, she is the coordinator of the EU Project "E-training on EU Family Property Regimes – EU-FamPro".

Agnė Limantė has a number of publications in the field of private international family law. She is actively engaged in international research projects. Recently, she took part in several EU co-founded projects that were designed to train judges, lawyers and social services on private international family law instruments.

Neža Pogorelčnik Vogrinc has published several papers in national and foreign journals, is an author of the individual chapters of ten books and a sole author of the book "Začasne odredbe v civilnih sodnih postopkih" (Provisional measures in civil court procedures). She is a researcher at the three national and three European projects in the field of civil and European law.